Ethics and Security in Canadian Foreign Policy

Canada and International Relations

Kim Richard Nossal, Brian L. Job, and Mark W. Zacher, General Editors

The Canada and International Relations series explores issues in contemporary world politics and international affairs. The volumes cover a wide range of topics on Canada's external relations, particularly international trade and foreign economic policy.

1. David G. Haglund, ed., *The New Geopolitics of Minerals: Canada and International Resource Trade*
2. Donald McRae and Gordon Munro, eds., *Canadian Oceans Policy: National Strategies and the New Law of the Sea*
3. Theodore H. Cohn, *The International Politics of Agricultural Trade: Canadian-American Relations in a Global Agricultural Context*
4. Russell S. Uhler, ed., *Canada-United States Trade in Forest Products*
5. A. Claire Cutler and Mark W. Zacher, eds., *Canadian Foreign Policy and International Economic Regimes*
6. Andrew F. Cooper, Richard A. Higgott, and Kim Richard Nossal, *Relocating Middle Powers: Australia and Canada in a Changing World Order*
7. Lawrence T. Woods, *Asia-Pacific Diplomacy: Nongovernmental Organizations and International Relations*
8. James Rochlin, *Discovering the Americas: The Evolution of Canadian Foreign Policy towards Latin America*
9. Michael Hart, with Bill Dymond and Colin Robertson, *Decision at Midnight: Inside the Canada-US Free-Trade Negotiations*
10. Amitav Acharya and Richard Stubbs, eds., *New Challenges for ASEAN: Emerging Policy Issues*
11. Donald Barry and Ronald C. Keith, eds., *Regionalism, Multilateralism, and the Politics of Global Trade*
12. Daniel Madar, *Heavy Traffic: Deregulation, Trade, and Transformation in North American Trucking*
13. Elizabeth Riddell-Dixon, *Canada and the Beijing Conference on Women: Governmental Politics and NGO Participation*
14. Nelson Michaud and Kim Richard Nossal, eds., *Diplomatic Departures: The Conservative Era in Canadian Foreign Policy, 1984-93*
15. Rosalind Irwin, ed., *Ethics and Security in Canadian Foreign Policy*

Edited by Rosalind Irwin

Ethics and Security in Canadian Foreign Policy

UBC Press · Vancouver · Toronto

This book is printed on acid-free paper that is 100% ancient forest free (100% post-consumer recycled), processed chlorine free and printed with vegetable based, low VOC inks.

National Library of Canada Cataloguing in Publication Data

Main entry under title:

Ethics and security in Canadian foreign policy

(Canada and international relations, ISSN 0847-0510; 15)
Includes bibliographical references and index.
ISBN 0-7748-0862-4

1. Canada – Foreign relations-1945- – Case studies. 2. Canada – Foreign relations – Moral and ethical aspects. 3. Security, International – Moral and ethical aspects – Canada. 4. International relations – Moral and ethical aspects – Canada. I. Irwin, Rosalind. II. Series.
FC600.E86 2001 327.71 C2001-910771-4
F1034.2.E83 2001

This book has been published with the help of a grant from the Humanities and Social Sciences Federation of Canada, using funds provided by the Social Sciences and Humanities Research Council of Canada.

UBC Press acknowledges the financial support of the Government of Canada through the Book Publishing Industry Development Program (BPIDP) for our publishing activities.
Canadä

We also gratefully acknowledge the support of the Canada Council for the Arts for our publishing program, as well as the support of the British Columbia Arts Council.

Set in Stone by Brenda and Neil West, BN Typographics West
Printed and bound in Canada by Friesens
Copy editor: Joanne Richardson
Proofreader: Lesley Cameron
Indexer: Christine Jacobs

UBC Press
The University of British Columbia
2029 West Mall, Vancouver, BC V6T 1Z2
(604) 822-5959
Fax: (604) 822-6083
E-mail: info@ubcpress.ca
www.ubcpress.ca

Contents

Part 7: Conclusions

Preface

Recent public opinion polls suggest that Canadians support a policy of assertive internationalism in accordance with core Canadian values of democracy, peacekeeping, and human rights. However, foreign policy decision making inevitably involves weighing these values within a changing historical context that has particular constraints and opportunities for action. A growing interest in ethical issues has created a demand for authoritative, informed analysis of the relationship between ethics and security from a Canadian perspective.

While provoked by recent debates and events, the analyses presented here go beyond the headlines to provide an in-depth, incisive, and enduring set of reflections. Contributors to this volume deal with both the abstract notions of value, culture, norms, and ethics, and the concrete questions of policy, law, and enforcement. The authors span the domestic and international contexts of law, norms, diplomacy, and politics. They trace in detail the theoretical and practical issues of ethics and security in Canadian foreign policy, using case studies to illustrate key problems. They assess the challenges and the opportunities presented by new concepts – such as human security, mutual vulnerability, soft power, global cultural scripts, "good governance," and niche diplomacy – for foreign policy decision making. This collection brings together a wide range of perspectives from some of Canada's leading scholars on issues such as Canadian nuclear policy and human rights and democratization. Collectively, they provide a comprehensive and critical consideration of issues of ethics and security from a Canadian perspective in the rapidly changing global environment of the twenty-first century.

Acknowledgments

The editor gratefully acknowledges the financial and organizational support of the York University Centre for International and Security Studies and Director David Dewitt in the preparation of this volume. Thanks go as well to Steve Mataija and Heather Chestnut as well as to all of those who participated in the Centre for International Security Studies' Ethics and Security Workshop, particularly Bernie Frolic, John Saul, Andrew Latham, Paul Gecelovsky, Anne-Marie Traeholt, Gerald Dirks, Pat Sewell, Eric Fawcett, Matina Karvellas, Cheshmak Farhoumand-Sims, Maire O'Brien, Timothy Donais, Nigmendra Narain, Yasmine Shamsie, Mark Neufeld, Claire Turenne Sjolander, and John David Cameron. Thanks to David Leyton-Brown for his inspiration. The editor would also like to thank three anonymous readers for their invaluable assistance. Some research was aided by the library of the Canadian Institute of International Affairs as well as the YCISS Library. Thanks also go to speakers in the YCISS Canadian Defence and International Security Seminar Series, particularly Andrew Cooper, Cranford Pratt, Kim Nossal, and Chris Shelley.

Part 1
Introduction

1
Linking Ethics and Security in Canadian Foreign Policy

Rosalind Irwin

The relationship between "ethics" and "security" is one of the most important problems of international relations. Scholars and practitioners have debated the nature of the linkage between ethics and security since the time of the Peloponnesian War in ancient Greece.[1] The theoretical tradition of realism in international politics has historically treated "security" as "synonymous with the security of the state against external dangers, which was to be achieved by increasing military capabilities."[2] Seen through the lens of the Cold War nuclear competition between the superpowers, realist scholars emphasized the exclusion of ethical from security considerations in foreign policy. Critics argued that this narrow approach to security led to a paradoxical failure: the pursuit of national security was ultimately not able to provide security from many of the threats that appeared on the horizon. These included, for example, resource shortages (such as the 1970s oil crisis), civil war and conflict, threats to human rights, global warming, and destabilization caused by poverty and famine. In addition, globalization appeared to make the notion of a "hard shell" of national sovereignty and national security increasingly problematic in the context of rapid global communication and exchange. These tensions led critics of the traditional approach to articulate more positively the nature of the linkages between ethics and security considerations in international relations, and specifically in foreign policy decision-making processes. Efforts to understand the nature of these relationships have been considerably more notable in, although are not exclusive to, the post-Cold War era.

Just as the meaning of "security" has been a subject of intense recent debate,[3] so the concept of "ethics" has also received more attention in recent years. In the study of international relations, and of foreign policy specifically, scholars and practitioners have taken note of the intrinsic importance of values, norms, and ethics in shaping the processes of decision making. Analysts have argued that decision makers must distinguish between multiple threats, identify different or similar circumstances, interpret information, and rank values that need protection – all of which involves making "ethical" judgments that draw upon explicit or implicit normative sources or codes. Although the study of ethics "resists reduction to a single theory or method,"[4] in general it seeks to analyze these various systems of morals and values, and to investigate the ways in which they affect international relations. What kinds of "values" are represented? How effective are they in decision-making processes?

As globalization has produced more complex interlinkages among states, civil society actors, and individuals, it has challenged the traditional categories (particularly the notions of Westphalian state sovereignty) through which international relations are studied. The tensions between levels of analysis, therefore, pose particular problems for students of ethics. How and in what domains or levels should ethical issues be determined? What are the "sources" of ethics and values and how are they derived? In the "procedural," or "positive," view, ethical codes are developed in clearly established written documents, such as treaties, agreements, protocols, or international declarations. A second, or "comprehensive," view argues that ethics are derived from universal foundational principles, such as the "natural law" of human rights, often seen to be the basis of written codes such as the Universal Declaration of Human Rights. These distinctions have implications for how, in an era of growing interdependence, we define our obligations and duties vis-à-vis those who live beyond our borders.

Other important questions have centred on the scope for ethical decision making in the post-Cold War era. Should "ethics" be approached narrowly or broadly in foreign policy and security policy? While neorealist scholars emphasize the continued importance of the national interest (narrowly defined) as a guiding principle, critics have taken a larger view, arguing that "state interests are defined in the context of internationally held norms and understandings of what is good and appropriate."[5] An expansive agenda provokes cautious consideration of commitment, resources, and effectiveness in decision making. Selectivity, on the other hand, begs the question of the normative criteria by which issues or problems are identified and acted upon.

Debates continue in the post-Cold War era about the derivation of ethics, its scope in international affairs, and its meaning in a world of diverse cultures, languages, values, and religions. While the contributors to this volume do not agree on a common approach to questions of ethics and/or security, their contributions share a common recognition that attention to ethical questions is important to an understanding of Canadian foreign policy issues. In this sense, then, there is a shared recognition of the fact that, as Nardin et al. point out: "to think ethically is to move back and forth between the general and the particular – to draw upon general principles in reaching particular judgments and decisions and, at the same time, to revise those principles in the light of the particular circumstances in which they are used. Ethics involves principles but it also involves interpretation, choice, and action."[6]

Human Security

Recently, the concept of "human security" has gained some currency in Canadian foreign policy, and this shift provides an important problematique for these contributions. Human security suggests that environmental (ecosystem), economic, social, political, and cultural security are all necessary dimensions of security policy. It develops a notion of society interests as independent from states' interests. Following this logic, this redefinition of security "proposes that states move away from the unilateralism that typifies traditional national security policies toward a more collective and co-operative approach."[7]

Human security seeks to expand the security agenda to enable states to address more fully the global problems caused by increasing levels of interdependence. As Canada's former minister of foreign affairs, Lloyd Axworthy, states: "as borders become increasingly porous, and Cold War threats fade, foreign policy practitioners deal increasingly with issues directly affecting the lives of individuals: crime, drugs, terrorism, pollution, human rights abuses, epidemics, and the like."[8] Canadians have traditionally responded to this interdependence with a high level of support for multilateralism and commitment to the values of democracy, peacekeeping, and human rights. These values are in turn rooted in the general philosophical idea that "the most fundamental requirement of any system of political morality, whether domestic or international, is that institutions should respect the equal moral standing, or one might say, the equal moral worth of everyone whom they affect."[9] In this sense, the concept of human security is rooted in the Western tradition of liberal cosmopolitan ethics and, therefore, is not necessarily "new" or unique to the post-Cold War era.

The concept of human security as a universal, interdependent, people-centred system of protection from threat has recently been developed internationally in the United Nations Development Program's 1994 *Human Development Report*[10] and in former UN secretary-general Boutros Boutros-Ghali's *An Agenda for Peace*.[11] The concept dates back as far as the UN Charter and the Universal Declaration of Human Rights,[12] and it has echoes in the Brundtland and Brandt Commission Reports of the 1980s as well as in the Conference on Security and Cooperation agreements in Europe in the 1970s.[13] In Canada, the International Development Research Centre's publication *Beyond Development Cooperation*,[14] the 1994 Special Joint Committee's report on Canada's foreign policy,[15] and the many policy statements of Foreign Minister Axworthy appear to have embraced and promoted this concept as an ethical guide to foreign policy.

However, at the broader level, the world's institutions and structures, including the United Nations and those of its agencies that have espoused human security, continue to reflect the unequal Westphalian divisions of political sovereignty as well as global structural inequalities of power and wealth. As a result, within this context, human security has come to have ambiguous, selective, and even contradictory meanings, and it has been unevenly integrated into foreign policy decision making. As many of the contributors to this volume point out, it is important to be cautious in assessing the impact of this concept in policy terms, in Canada and elsewhere.

Critics of the human security agenda argue that state sovereignty persists as the defining feature (or norm) of international politics following the Cold War and that lack of attention to state structures and interests can result in the neglect of such important causes of insecurity as "failed states."[16] However, it is equally clear that states themselves, with their concentration of resources and power, can represent great threats to human security. This became particularly clear, for example, in the cases of Rwanda and Yugoslavia, where leaders perpetrated or condoned massive systematic violations of human rights.[17] Furthermore, critics argue that an over-reliance on military instruments and the use of force, fuelled by changing technologies and a global media culture oriented towards swift but perhaps "shallow" action, compromises rather than reinforces the principles of human security.

More generally, there are questions about the priorities extended within the human security agenda. The 1994 Human Development Report listed among its major concerns, in addition to the protection of human rights and individual security, the urgency of addressing economic security (security of income and of work); food security (an adequate distribution of food and the necessary purchasing power); protection against threats to public health; and protection against environmental degradation, pollution and disasters. However, in contrast, much of the human security agenda in Canada and elsewhere has downplayed economic and social concerns, focusing instead on the protection of individual security from violence. This limited response to the structural challenges of global distributive problems reveals a conservativeness in policy approaches.

Whether or not "human security" will continue to resonate both in Canada and abroad is an open question. In general, one must agree with Robin Hay that, although many critics do not disparage the notion of human security in principle, they are cautious about its adoption as "a major plank of Canadian foreign and security policy."[18] While offering the promise of integrating ethical concerns into traditional security concerns, human security only partially addresses the tensions between national security and ethics. Addressing these problems involves developing a clearer analysis of what human security represents and the wider questions of ethics and decision making that it entails. What have been the changes (or lack thereof) in the ethics/security nexus given the transition from a Cold War era to a post-Cold War era? What is the meaning, importance, or relevance of the "new" concept of "human security"? Sorting out the variety of interpretations and meanings of human security, as well as the specific impact it has had on decision making, are thus central challenges addressed by the contributors to this volume.

Chapter Overviews

The contributions to this volume reflect upon the broader meaning of the changes described above for Canadian foreign policy in the twenty-first century. They address three sets of themes: (1) the meaning of "ethics" and "security," (2) the question of historical continuity and change (more specifically, the impact of the post-Cold War context), and (3) the implications of these shifts for Canadian foreign policy. Chapters tend to mix the theoretical with the concrete. In general, however, the volume moves from the conceptual issues of ethics and security (dealt with in Parts 1 and 2), through the more pragmatic and practical questions of Canadian foreign policy decision making (dealt with in Parts 3-6), to reflections on the issues raised in the work as a whole (Part 7).

The contributions in Part 2, "Ethics and Security: Conceptual and Analytical Issues within a Changing Gobal Context," focus on the conceptual questions of "ethics" and "security," while taking account of historical and policy factors from a Canadian perspective. Taking the explicitly normative position that "without an explicit ethical basis, any definition of security is meaningless," Jorge Nef begins the discussion with an examination of the historical foundations for reformulating the meaning of ethics and security. Using a core-periphery analysis that resists a state-centric approach, Nef suggests that a broadening foreign policy agenda should include the concept of "mutual vulnerability," whereby "the weakness of the periphery increases the exposure of the centre." Using this framework, Nef analyzes such non-traditional threats as crime and counter-crime, terrorism and counter-terrorism, neoliberal globalization, growing civil wars, and neofascism. He discusses the implications these new threats may have for Canada.

Complementing this normative approach, Peter Penz assesses a range of theoretical levels and perspectives, using the issue of development assistance to illustrate the assumptions and implications of each. Drawing on moral and political philosophy, Penz evaluates the ethical requirements of realism, sovereigntism, and cosmopolitanism regarding relations among states and among people across borders. Opting for a cosmopolitan approach, he argues that it is not a singular ethic but, rather, a framework within which different ethical notions, such as those of maximizing well-being, equality, and self-determination, compete. His own approach involves a radical interpretation of obligations concerning human security. Concerning the issue of setting conditions on the provision of development assistance, Penz uses the non-state-centric cosmopolitan ethic but recognizes the particular implications of having to work within the institutional structure of the state system. The discussion concludes with implications for Canadian development-assistance policy. He accepts a limited form of conditionality in the provision of development assistance rather than wide-ranging human-rights conditionality.

The above chapters demonstrate the different ways in which scholars can approach the conceptual questions of "ethics" and "security" in the study of foreign policy. In the next part, contributors focus more on specific dilemmas faced by decision makers, using case studies to provide insights into the processes, outcomes, and implications of decision making. The case studies address bilateral and multilateral levels, reflecting the increasingly complex linkages between domestic and foreign policy decision making. They also focus on the ethical dilemmas provoked by changes in the post-Cold War era, many of which are emerging from a shift from an East-West to a North-South nexus. While confronted by complex emergencies such as those in Haiti or Africa, decision makers must also cope with more persistent long-term structural inequalities in global order. This growing inequality places issues of develoment assistance into the policy agenda. The themes of ethics and security in Canadian foreign policy are particularly salient when seen against this historical background.

Public support for, and official advocacy of, Canadian international development assistance has long been founded on the belief that Canada has obligations towards those countries that are vastly poorer than it. If any aspect of Canadian foreign policy is likely to reflect ethical values prima facie, then we might expect it to be Canadian foreign aid. Yet very few scholarly studies of Canadian aid policies have suggested that ethical values have been a key determinant of Canadian aid policies.

In Chapter 4, Cranford Pratt looks afresh at the question of the role of ethical values in Canadian aid policies. Although finally deciding that international economic and political interests have again become the dominant determinants of Canadian aid policies, he suggests that, between 1966 and 1976, a confluence of circumstances resulted in public policies on development assistance that seemed to justify the hope that ethical values were having an increasing and decisive impact upon them. Pratt argues that that confluence then dispersed. Although Canadian ethical values have continued to have some impact on Canadian development assistance policies, he suggests that dominant class interests and Canadian international political interests have reasserted their primacy as the determinants of these policies. If this is true about foreign aid policies, he concludes, then how much more likely is it that other components of Canadian foreign policy will be even less responsive to the needs of those living beyond our borders?

Heather Smith continues the discussion by suggesting that, although the human security agenda is broad, Canada's human rights stance has been less "expansive" than "limitationist," and that this has compromised the cosmopolitan, ethical notion of human security. Niche diplomacy, which prioritizes the "economic pillars" of comparative advantage, efficiency, and maximum impact in the national interest rather than broader human security, represents the practices underlying Canadian foreign policy, she argues. Her recommendations and conclusions focus on the necessity of improving credibility in Canadian foreign policy by making "a genuine commitment of aid to meet the basic needs of those beyond our borders."

Terisa Turner and her co-authors examine the exploitation of local women farmers within the context of a "male deal" with the forces of globalization – a deal through which the commodification of nature, commonly held resources, and human labour has expanded. By questioning the moral equations of intervention, structural adjustment policies, and neoliberal free trade, the authors challenge the idea that food security is found in traditional notions of development and suggest that foreign policy should include a concern with sustenance rights. They conclude that "an ethical foreign policy consistent with human rights must be a policy that supports the strategies of rural women for strengthening the sustenance economy."

The contributors to Parts 4 and 5 develop the contentious issues of humanitarian law and intervention, focusing first on the "soft power" instruments of norms and law, and then on the dilemmas of bilateral and multilateral intervention to support human rights and democracy. W. Andy Knight argues that, as a "norm entrepreneur" working together with other "like-minded small or middle powers," Canada has used "soft power" and moral suasion as part of its expanded "human security" agenda to attempt to establish an international criminal court. Pointing to historical changes that have heightened threats to individuals, the international community has been spurred to develop the legal machinery to deal with the perpetrators of genocide, crimes against the peace, war crimes, and crimes against humanity. Knight points out that Canada has, as part of its humane internationalist posture, traditionally cultivated the possibility of contributing to the development of international humanitarian law. And he argues that it should continue to do so if it wishes to remain a significant player on the multilateral scene.

David Black's chapter, in contrast, focuses on the politics of differentiation in human rights norms. Black uses a comparative analysis to examine the ways in which normative differences have influenced Canada's human rights strategies in South Africa and Nigeria. This line of analysis suggests that norms (as distinct from geo-political or economic pressures) play an important role in facilitating or constraining foreign policy. The nature and impact of dominant norms varies over time and between and within subsystemic communities. This suggests a need for a better understanding of how diverse normative contexts affect Canada's ability to support and enforce broader norms of human rights and democracy as well as a more nuanced approach to decision making.

Andrew Latham uses a genealogical approach to shed light on the sources of the ethical standards that sometimes shape foreign and security policy. His analysis focuses on how a global "standard of civilization" came to be applied during the 1997 "Ottawa Process" to ban anti-personnel landmines. Resisting the traditional dichotomy between "ethics" on the one hand and "interest" and "power" on the other, Latham seeks to illuminate the way in which the "national interest" sometimes comes to be understood in terms of the promotion of "ethical" security policies that are constructed at the global level "rather than simply emerging out of a country's domestic cultural or political milieu." His analysis thus points to the global sources of ethical standards and "the politics of stigmatization" that have driven the anti-landmine campaign and the formation of Canadian foreign policy on this issue.

In Part 5, we see that humanitarian intervention, democratization, and the related concepts of peacebuilding and peace enforcement, which have been a recent focus of Canadian foreign policy, are activities that generate particularly difficult ethical dilemmas. Howard Adelman argues that in situations of complex emergencies, such as the refugee crisis in Zaire, the "unwillingness of interveners to act unless there is a crisis" has contributed to the international community's inability to choose among competing values. For Adelman, such ethical decisions are, of necessity, contextual and entail the development of meta-ethical "complementary second order norms": correspondence, coherence, control, consistency, and context. In this sophisticated assessment, ethical choices go beyond the simple state/individual or realist/moralist dichotomies to encompass the need to rank ethical values in a pragmatic way. Adelman concludes that Canadian internationalism should, therefore, become more effective with regard to context analysis and with respect to making the difficult judgments that are concomitant with taking into account competing moral perspectives.

Tom Keating complements Adelman's analysis of the complex normative issues in Zaire with a case study of Canadian experiences in Haiti. Keating, like Adelman, reflects critically on the interventionist climate of the post-Cold War world order, arguing that problems of promoting democracy in Haiti exemplify a fundamental ethical dilemma: how to maintain both an "ethics of responsibility" and an "ethics of commitment." Keating argues that there are inherent limitations imposed on projects of humanitarian intervention and that these include, among others: the intrusion of material interests on humanitarian goals, the costs of long-term commitments, and the tendency to impede the development of indigenous social movements. Consensus, coordination, capabilities, and conviction are all essential prerequisites if Canada is to develop "an effective ethically informed intervention."

In Part 6, we see that nuclear technologies and natural resources present ethical and security dilemmas that cross over political, social, economic, and ecological boundaries. Duane Bratt argues that, rather than acting at "cross-purposes," "security and ethics have worked in tandem to constrain the export of CANDUs." The result, in the post-Cold War era, has been that "the division is now solely between economics and security/ethics." While narrow or material interests often seem to be paramount, it is inevitable that the complex international relationships created by trade in CANDUs give rise to wider concerns. In analyzing CANDU sales to Turkey, Argentina, South Korea, Romania, China, India, and Pakistan, Bratt concludes that the expected rise in ethical considerations will, primarily, be a by-product of economic considerations.

As new technologies, including nuclear technologies, are revolutionizing traditional security dilemmas for decision makers, so resource scarcity problems are pointing to increasingly complex ethical and security challenges. Peter Stoett's study of the turbot dispute examines the interplay of traditional statist politics and evolving international norms in global ecopolitics. He suggests that international conservationist norms of precaution and equality can be reinforced by unilateral state action, even when motivated by "national interest" and domestic concerns. The risks of doing so, however, are high, and include the loss of credibility on future issues of international law. He concludes that, if Canada is to meet the challenges of environmental security, then it will have to overcome short-term thinking and strive for "progressive domestic problem solving," which includes paying attention to habitat preservation.

Concluding Comments

An increasingly interdependent and turbulent global order provokes questions surrounding the sources of ethics and ethical codes, the scope for ethical decision making, and the meaning and implications of "ethical" approaches to security. Such questions will continue to be approached in different ways, at different levels of analysis, and with different assumptions concerning the sources, explanations, and implications of the ethics/security nexus. As suggested above, just as the processes of decision making inevitably provoke questions regarding the role of ethics and values in international relations, so do specific historical examples and real-world case studies provide clues to the meaning and significance of abstract concepts such as "human security." The relationship between ethics and security, the meaning and application of the concept of human security in the context of ethical debates, and the practical questions of what these linkages imply for decision makers are thus intimately connected. While analytical and methodological issues concerning the meaning of ethics and the questions of security are sometimes cast in abstract terms, with few linkages to policy, the themes of this book have been designed to provoke consideration of the ways in which theory and practice are linked; to encourage us, in Nardin's terms, to "think ethically"; and to move back and forth from the general to the particular. This suggests the need to examine both the "ends" and "means" of policy, and to consider both prescriptive and descriptive perspectives. The purpose here is not necessarily to provide definitive answers to these complex questions but, rather, from a Canadian perspective, to promote clear and critical thinking about the meaning of the linkages between "ethics" and "security," both in theory and in practice.

Notes

1 See, in particular, Thucydides' "The Melian Dialogue," in *Classics of International Relations,* ed. John A. Vasquez (Upper Saddle River, NJ: Prentice-Hall, 1996), 9-14.

2 J. Ann Tickner, "Re-visioning Security," in *International Relations Theory Today,* ed. Ken Booth and Steve Smith (University Park, PA: Pennsylvania State University Press, 1995), 176.

3 See, for example, Keith Krause and Michael Williams, eds., *Critical Security Studies: Concepts and Cases* (Minneapolis: University of Minnesota Press, 1997); Barry Buzan, Ole Waever, and Jaap De Wilde, *Security: A New Framework for Analysis* (Boulder, CO: Lynne Rienner, 1989); Ken Booth, "Security and Emancipation," *Review of International Studies* 17, 4 (1991): 313-26; Jessica Tuchman Mathews, "Redefining Security," *Foreign Affairs* 68, 2 (Spring 1989): 162-77.

4 Terry Nardin and David R. Mapel, "Ethical Traditions in International Affairs," in *Traditions of International Ethics,* ed. Terry Nardin and David R. Mapel (New York, Cambridge: Cambridge University Press, 1992), 3.

5 Martha Finnemore, *National Interests in International Society* (New York: Cornell University Press, 1996), 2.

6 Nardin and Mapel, "Ethical Traditions in International Affairs," 5.

7 Mark Charlton, "Is Security Really Being Redefined in the Post-Cold War World?" in *Crosscurrents: International Relations in the Post-Cold War Era,* ed. Mark Charlton (Scarborough: ITP Nelson, 1999), 255.

8 Lloyd Axworthy, "US Urged to Bolster Weak Support for UN, Human Security, and World Criminal Court," *Canadian Speeches* 12, 3 (June 1998): 8-12.

9 Charles R. Beitz, "Recent International Thought," *International Journal* 43, 2 (Spring 1988): 191.

10 United Nations Development Program, in *Human Development Report 1994* (New York: Oxford University Press, 1994).

11 Boutros Boutros-Ghali, *An Agenda for Peace* (New York: United Nations, 1992). This theme has also been recently extended and championed by Boutros-Ghali's successor as UN secretary-general, Kofi Annan.

12 Timothy Donais, "Of Soft Power and Human Security: Canada and the UN Security Council," *Peace Magazine* 15, 2 (March-April 1999): 18-19.
13 Paul Heinbecker, "Human Security," *Behind the Headlines* 56, 2 (December 1998-March 1999): 4-9.
14 Fauzya A. Moore, *Beyond Development Cooperation: Toward a New Era of Global and Human Security: IDRC report on a conference organized by the Society for International Development, 15-16 October 1993* (Ottawa: International Development Research Centre, 1994).
15 "Report of the Special Joint Committee of the Senate and the House of Commons Reviewing Canadian Foreign Policy," in *Canada's Foreign Policy: Principles and Priorities for the Future* (Ottawa: The Committee, 1994).
16 Fen Osler Hampson and Dean F. Oliver, "Pulpit Diplomacy: A Critical Assessment of the Axworthy Doctrine," *International Journal* 53, 3 (Summer, 1998): 379-406; see also Kim Richard Nossal, "Pinchpenny Diplomacy: The Decline of 'Good International Citizenship' in Canadian Foreign Policy," *International Journal* 54, 1 (Winter 1998-99): 88-105.
17 Edward Broadbent, "Rights Must Transcend National Sovereignty and Global Trade," *Canadian Speeches* 9, 2 (May 1995): 36-39.
18 Robin Jeffrey Hay, "Present at the Creation? Human Security and Canadian Foreign Policy in the Twenty-first Century, in *A Big League Player? Canada Among Nations 1999,* ed. Fen Osler Hampson, Michael Hart, and Martin Rudner (Oxford: Oxford University Press, 1999), 224.

Part 2
Ethics and Security: Conceptual and Analytical Issues within a Changing Global Context

2
The Ethics of Mutual Vulnerability: A Developmental Perspective for Foreign Policy

Jorge Nef

A Global Crisis in Search of a Paradigm

This chapter sketches a theoretical framework within which to examine the relationship between ethics and security in foreign policy. Ethics is defined as a guiding set of basic principles, or value-standards, that sets the parameters of behaviour deemed acceptable, appropriate, and/or desirable. Security – a term that will be discussed in greater detail below – entails the probability of the reduction of risk and uncertainty: the abatement of insecurity. Foreign policy refers to a particular type of public policy – that directed towards events and circumstances outside the territorial boundaries of a given national actor. It involves the decisions, non-decisions, actions, and inactions of that single actor regarding other extraterritorial actors and/or the international system as a whole.

This interpretive essay straddles two seemingly contradictory conceptual intersections: the one between domestic and international security, and the one between analytical and normative considerations in foreign policy. A closer and more careful look, however, suggests that internal (or micro) and external (or macro) security are two sides of the same coin. The same can be said of the distinction between normative and analytical foreign policy paradigms. It is my contention that, without an explicit ethical basis, any definition of security is meaningless.

Though this chapter is broadly general and comparative, it aims specifically to provide a conceptual, analytical "grid" for addressing ethical dilemmas in Canadian foreign policy. These dilemmas take place within an uncertain post-Cold War context; are driven by the globalization of technology, ideology, and economics; and are an integral part of an emerging system of "mutual vulnerability." For instance, pronouncements by the Department of Foreign Affairs and International Trade (DFAIT) have identified some human security issues, such as human rights, sustainable development, culture and values, as key elements in the country's international agenda. A basic problem here is not only the compatibility and consistency of these goals, but also their concrete instrumentalization in decisions and actions. Another ostensible dilemma is posed by the impact of globalization on Canadian security, broadly defined. Canada-US relations, the weakness of the Canadian dollar, freer trade, membership in international organizations, the Asian crisis, the large role of foreign investment and ownership, Canada's place in international governance, peacekeeping versus peacemaking – all affect the "domestic" scene. That is, "internal" questions of prosperity, equality, cultural sovereignty and identity, federalism, separatism, and the quality of life of Canadians are closely interconnected with the ongoing dynamics of the world system and Canada's role in it. The fact is that, either by choice or drift, Canada has been involved in these entanglements in multiple, but often unpredicted, confusing, and even disturbing ways. Most significantly, this involvement has occurred without an explicit security paradigm able to account for the post-Cold War environment. In my view, the idea of human security offers a promising point of departure. While the term has become an ostensible label in the current discourse of the Canadian government (as well as in those of Norway and Chile), fundamental questions of equity are not central in the official agenda. In fact, there is a substantial gap between the comprehensive notion of human security discussed here and actual practice. However, an approach that incorporates the ethics of human security and human rights can address the many sources of insecurity facing Canadians and the world. Most important, it can also provide a measuring rod against which actually existing policies and practices can be assessed and evaluated.

For some elite sectors in the G-7 (Group of Seven) nations, the present world order may appear to contain few significant security threats. In the New World Order discourse, the collapse of communism has been readily translated into a "winner-take-all" game: a global victory for liberal capitalism and Western civilization. The Cold War has ended with the collapse of the USSR, while crippling debts have transformed most governments in the periphery into harmless "receiver states."[1] Many "hot spots" have moved towards settlement, auguring potential reductions in military expenditures,[2] refugee flows, local insurgencies, and international terrorism. Optimistically, it has even been suggested that "life for the majority of the world's citizens is getting steadily better in almost every category."[3]

There is, nevertheless, another side to the picture. As Amnesty International's general secretary stated in 1992, "far from international cooperation, we see the world community floundering in the face of human-rights disasters."[4] The disintegration of Eastern Europe has unleashed deep political and ethnic tensions. The predicament of the ex-Soviet Union threatens regional and global stability. Genocidal civil wars, such those in Rwanda, Burundi, Congo, Chechnya, Kosovo, and East Timor, have generated humanitarian crises requiring interventions by the international community. The simultaneous meltdown of the Russian and the Asian economies, particularly the once hailed NICs (Newly Industrialized Countries) and Japan, are equally, if not more, foreboding. In his "premonition of the future," Robert Kaplan envisions "worldwide demographic, environmental, and societal stress, in which criminal anarchy emerges as the real 'strategic' danger."[5] For others, the "potential for multitudes of such disasters in the next decade seems clear, and we are inadequately equipped as a world community to confront them."[6] And regressive trends are not visible only among the Third World nations: declining quality of life and expanding insecurity are also evident in sectors of the population of the First and former Second Worlds.

It seems clear that we live in a time of uncertainty. There may be a dearth of paradigms that will enable us to understand the present crisis, but decision makers still have to respond to events, make day-to-day choices, and formulate polices in an ever more chaotic environment. Ordinary citizens too must cope with the effects of these policies. Unsavoury events, such as the treatment of prisoners in Somalia or the apparent support for former Indonesian dictator Suharto, have tarnished Canada's self-image as a "do-gooder," an honest broker supporting humanitarian causes. There is a need to develop analytical frameworks that will enable us to understand this seemingly random, turbulent, and chaotic period. There is also a need to establish evaluative and operational criteria and mechanisms for policy formulation and conflict management based upon that understanding.

The constructs that decision makers used to take for granted have crumbled. The world stage no longer functions as an exclusive meeting place for individual and sovereign nation-states, representing monolithic "national interests," to discuss their foreign policies.[7] While traditional questions of peace and security, such as war-prevention and containment of "aggressive states" (e.g., punitive actions against Iraq), still hit the front pages, a host of trade and finance issues have now become important. Geopolitics has been overshadowed by geoeconomics, whose prime directives involve protecting finance capital and safeguarding the social sectors that own and manage these resources.

Such conventional academic paradigms as classical realism and complex interdependency seem unable to provide suitable frameworks for understanding the present and gazing into the future. New vogues, such as Francis Fukuyama's "End of History"[8] and Samuel Huntington's "Clash of Civilizations,"[9] do not offer signposts for policy, let alone ethical reference points for decision making, other than doing more of the same. Furthermore, these theses have been formulated from a distinctively American government and/or business standpoint.

New Foreign Policy Priorities, Actors, and Instruments

From the above discussion, it seems that what is needed is an alternative paradigm for Canadian foreign policy. In order to sketch an operational framework along these conceptual lines, I must first spell out a number of the general characteristics of the present world order. A first observation is that systemic *boundaries* are today much less territorial and ideological and much more functional, permeable, and imprecise[10] than the conventional concept of sovereignty would imply. In fact, collective defence[11] is in a state of rapid transition and is converging with collective security. Second, the shape of the international *power structure* has moved from the rigid bipolarism of the Cold War to a diffuse monocentrism. There is one national "pole" (the US) in association with a cluster of developed economies represented in the OECD (Organization for Economic Cooperation and Development) and the G-7. The core ruling elites, which enjoy a significant degree of relational control (or metapower) within the G-7, are closely interrelated in an increasingly unipolar web of interactions, with the US being paramount. This loosely unipolar world system is mutually interconnected, turbulent, and intrinsically unstable. It is also highly stratified, with a transnationalized elite core and numerous differentiated and heterogeneous socio-economic peripheries.

There has been a shift of *priorities,* from military issues to "softer" security issues, such as trade, health, the environment, and human rights. As purposes change, so do the *instrumentalities* of crisis management. The limited ability of reactive instruments (such as peacekeeping) to contain crises has highlighted the need for proactive mechanisms emphasizing crisis-prevention.[12] For example, Canada has considerable resources and expertise in the areas of medical emergencies (including epidemics) and famines. Other issues, such as environmental degradation, refugees, and domestic strife, suggest a similar need for "preventive strategies."

The *actors* within this system are also quite diverse. They include subnational, national, international, and transnational groups (e.g., ethnic and linguistic minorities, insurgents, NGOs [non-governmental organizations], criminal syndicates, businesspeople, individual heads of state, diplomats and functionaries, the UN, regional organizations, and transnational corporations). These structures coexist with a few significant nation-states (the US, the UK, Germany, France, Japan) and semi-peripheries, which include the now-fading Asian NICs, Russia, China, and India.

With the shifting of the *central polarities* from North-South and East-West to a single core-periphery axis of relations, there has occurred systemic restructuring. The victorious Western core, the First World, remains basically as it was – an interdependent and stratified bloc of dominant trading partners. The other two worlds have collapsed into one heterogeneous conglomerate of "newly industrializing," "developing," "poor," and "transitional societies." The core-periphery conflict persists, without its Cold War connotation, but it is not so much between rich and poor nations as it is between social sectors within these nations. It takes place between transnationally integrated and affluent elites (and their related clienteles), and a large and fragmented mass of subordinate sectors at the margins of the modern and integrated global society.[13] These social conflicts can remain latent, become open and manifest, or evolve into more institutionalized, albeit asymmetrical, regimes. At any rate, they exist simultaneously at the global and local levels – what some refer to as the *"glocal"* level.

Mutual Vulnerability: A Framework for Analysis

Mainstream development theory and dependency theory have postulated that development and underdevelopment are opposite ends of a unidirectional and irreversible historical continuum: developed regions are "secure," insecurity being the trademark of the "other world." However, the seemingly secure societies of the "North" are becoming vulnerable to events in the less secure regions of the globe. Even those living in the most affluent and modern societies dwell in a world of mutual vulnerability,[14] an echo of the mutually assured destruction (MAD) of the era of nuclear stalemate.

Mutual vulnerability arises from a radical transformation of world politics, rooted in three groups of circumstances. The first group consists of changes in pervasive and innovative technologies, especially in warfare, transportation, and communications. The second group consists of changes in the ideological and political matrix (i.e., the sharp divide between Marxist-Leninism and liberal capitalism has been replaced by hegemonic neoliberalism). The third, and perhaps most important, group relates to the transformation from *international* trade and finance (among states) to *global* and *transnational* economics.

In this increasingly interconnected system, the hard shell of territorial sovereignty, with its image of invulnerability, is no longer viable; rather, the weakness of the periphery increases the exposure of the centre, making the entire configuration unstable. Interconnectedness means that dysfunctions in the weaker components of the global fabric result in self-reinforcing cycles that have wide implications. Given the nature of these trends, no region of the world can be immune to crises of potentially catastrophic proportions.

Seeing the world through the prism of mutual vulnerability conveys a historical and systemic approach to foreign policy, one with a long-range and holistic point of view rooted both in "historical sociology"[15] and in international political economy.[16] From this perspective, the micro and the macro, the short run and the long run, the parts and the whole, are analytically interrelated. Although the proposed framework focuses on the convergence between international relations and development studies,[17] its overall direction is interdisciplinary, straddling economics, political science, history, and sociology.

Core, Centres, and Peripheries in the World System

The idea of a global system is specifically derived from world system theory,[18] and it entails the notion of a dominant and integrated pattern of global production, distribution, and power with unequal exchanges between a centre and a periphery. The global system goes back to the sixteenth and seventeenth centuries, but its expansion and consolidation have evolved over the last two centuries.[19] Despite the use of geographical and spatial concepts (such as core-periphery), relations within the present system take place between concrete social actors: groups, classes, and individuals. The "core" refers to transnationally integrated socio-economic elite groups. Centre, on the other hand, refers to the developed geographical regions, which contain, as do peripheral regions, their own elite "core" and a non-elite "social periphery." Development and underdevelopment are conditions experienced by people, not disembodied aggregations that define the totality of a territory. The notion of world system highlights the transnational integration of dominant groups as well as the marginalization of the bulk of its inhabitants. In contrast to the often more mechanistic approaches of dependency and complex interdependence[20] theories, the notion of world system looks at the underlying logic that links cores, semi-peripheries, and peripheries, making them part of one single structure and historical process.

Regimes

A world system includes regimes, or mechanisms of governance, with structures of decision making, rules, and influence.[21] Unlike "organizations," which possess differentiated, formally sanctioned norms and authority structures, "regimes" are structures for conflict management among actors for the handling of particular clusters of issues. Such regimes are subsystems of the larger global system. Some are highly institutionalized and enjoy a notable degree of concentricity, while others are loose and lack a recognizable structure. They also vary considerably in terms of their effectiveness in managing the issues that fall within their areas of concern.

Power, Metapower, and Governance

One important empirical task in the analysis of regimes involves ascertaining who really governs, since power structures are not always either formalized or transparent. Power is the very essence of the global system and its constituent regimes.[22] So is powerlessness. But the ability, or inability, to wield power is essentially dynamic and multidimensional. Power is much more than the sum total of the resource capabilities or commitments of an actor or alliance. In the last analysis effective power can only be measured in terms of outcomes, vis-à-vis objectives pursued and resources utilized. Thus, authority, in the Weberian sense of legitimated power,[23] requires minimal amounts of force (or, conversely, "payoffs") to obtain compliance. This is also true of "hegemony" in the Gramscian sense.[24] Authority represents an effective element of regime governance. Here, conflict management by both the government and the governed involves a minimal use of violence and coercion to attain compliance.

An important aspect of regime governance is the distinction between power and metapower.[25] The latter refers to the ability to affect the outcome of decisions, non-decisions, actions, and inactions in a given regime by altering the rules of the game. At any given time, very few actors possess legitimacy, or can articulate hegemonic discourses,[26] or have established control over the sources of uncertainty.[27] More often than not, those who are able to affect the outcomes, both within regimes as well as within the global system, are elites residing within the developed core.

Elements of the System

Conceptually, a system can be seen as being comprised of five major elements: (1) a context, both current and historical, that defines its basic parameters; (2) a culture – ideologies, cognations, feelings, and judgments that give the system value, meaning, and orientation; (3) a structure of actors that compete and coalesce in the pursuit of valued outcomes; (4) processes of cooperation and conflict by which actors attempt to pursue their goals; and (5) outcomes – the intended and unintended consequences of actions, inactions, and processes. For the sake of simplicity, the global system can be seen as a juxtaposition of five major interconnected subsystems: (1) the ecosystem, or environment; (2) the economy; (3) the society, or socio-demographic system; (4) the polity; and (5) the cultural system. Each subsystem is structured around a cluster of relatively homogeneous and recognizable issues, reflecting the specific nature of its constituent elements (context, culture, structure, processes, and effects), and is governed by a particular regime. The dynamics of the system involve the actions and interactions of actors pursuing goals, utilizing resources, and having effects upon a given context.[28]

Changing circumstances within the above context generates feedbacks. Feedback loops do not imply that social systems are inherently self-correcting. In fact, as the historical record indicates, entropy and self-destructive behaviour are always real possibilities. In other words, not all feedbacks are "functional" in the sense of providing instantaneous adjustments and "system maintenance"; rather, self-correction is a function of awareness, learning, perception, and will, not of built-in automaticity. The cultural software of any form of association, from a single household to an extended empire, contains the seeds of greater instability and, at the same time, opportunities for innovative problem solving and creative equilibrium.

Dysfunctions produced at the core end up having destructive impacts not only upon the subordinate actors, but also upon the centre itself. Conversely, cumulative dysfunctions in the periphery are bound to flow "upstream," increasing the instability of the centre and of the entire configuration. More than a "zero-sum game," in which the stakes are limited and where someone's gains are someone else's losses,[29] we are confronted with the possibility of a "negative-score game," in which all players stand to lose (see Table 2.1).

Human Security: The Link between Peace, Security, and Development

Since the end of the Second World War, peace and development have been the teleological axis of international relations. These two goals were inextricably interrelated and defined the overriding "ethical matrix" for foreign policy making and evaluation. For over three decades, global survival meant the prevention of the Third World War and the avoidance of direct military confrontation between the US and the USSR. Perversely, the nuclear balance of terror deterred war. However, superpower confrontation was manifested through political and economic conflict in the Third World. The heavier human and material tolls of Cold War confrontation were borne by the world's poor.

East-West relations between 1945 and 1989 were dominated by "national" (a euphemism for bipolar) security concerns. Fear of the other side provided the justification for doctrines of military security, with their corollaries of external and internal "enemies." The friend-foe syndrome permeated the ethical matrix of choice for both superpowers and their client regimes. North-South interactions, in turn, were predominantly characterized by Western scholars in "development" terms, even though this frequently masked the harder side of civic action and counter-insurgency.[30] Despite frequent references to mutuality and cooperation, this formulation was defined by the logic of international and internal containment, which subordinated the ethics of foreign policy to the struggle between the "Free World" and communism. A perverted example of this was the National Security Doctrine, under whose mantle extreme abuses of human rights were perpetrated with Western assistance throughout the nations of the South.

After the Cold War, security and development issues cannot be viewed simply in zero-sum terms. As mentioned earlier, negative-score games, in which there is not only a "win-lose" situation, but also a real danger of losing altogether, must be incorporated into the analysis. This is also the case with the pursuit of "win-win," or cooperative, strategies. Peace is not just

Table 2.1

The system

Variable	Ecology (life)	Economy (wealth)	Society (support: well-being, affection, respect, rectitude)	Polity (power)	Culture (knowledge, skill)
Context	Natural setting: the biophysical surroundings of social action	Styles of development economic models	Social expectations and traditions	Internal and external conflicts: capabilities/ expectations, elite/ mass, sovereignty/ dependence	Images of the physical and social world and collective experiences
Culture	Ecoculture: place of environment in cosmo-vision	Economic doctrines: ways of understanding the economy	Social doctrines: values, norms, and attitudes: identity and model personality	Ideologies: the function of the state and its relation to the citizen	Philosophy (axiologies, teleologies, and deontologies), moral and ethical codes
Structures	Resource endowment and spatial distribution: relation between environment and resources	Economic units: consumers/producers: labour/capital	Status and roles: social structures, groups, classes, fractions	Brokers and institutions; interest groups, parties, cliques, governments, bureaucracies	Educational structures, formal and informal: schools, universities, learning institutions
Processes	Depletion/regeneration of air, water, land, flora, and fauna	Production and distribution of goods and services	Interactions: cooperation, conflict, mobilization, and demobilization	Conflict-resolution: consensus, repression, rebellion, stalemate	Learning: building of consciousness, cognitions, basic values, procedures, and teleologies
Effects	Sustainability/ entropy	Prosperity/poverty	Equity/inequity	Governance/violence	Enlightenment/ ignorance

the absence of war. It must transcend realpolitik, counter-insurgency, and palliative development, and it must relate to sustainability, well-being, quality of life, and human development. The prime normative consideration of human security has operational and empirical references (e.g., the United Nations indexes of Quality of Life and Human Development).[31]

To develop this, our definition of security is based on the probability of "risk-reduction." It emphasizes the prevention of the causes of insecurity rather than merely the containment of its symptoms. We are primarily concerned with the insecurity of the bulk of the population, especially those subject to greater vulnerability. Risk-reduction at the higher levels of the global system depends upon the achievement of security at the lower levels. Any system is only as strong as its weakest link. In turn, specific and localized security is reciprocally affected by over-all security. Thus, the attainment of sustainable homeostasis in any society will depend upon a significant and continuous reduction of risk and insecurity at all levels. Security, however, cannot consist of the maintenance, at any cost, of a given status quo (or structure of privileges and inequalities). Nor can it be synonymous with repression or protracted stalemate. Paraphrasing the late Brazilian bishop, Dom Hélder Cámara, order cannot be conceived as "stratified disorder." On the contrary, a "security community" possesses a political system capable of managing, and solving, socio-economic conflicts through relatively consensual adjustments. The consensual option offers in absolute terms an opportunity for reducing the overall level of coercion and violence. Its central ethical principles are respect for life and the recognition of human dignity[32] as organizing principles for social action. These are synonymous with human rights.

Dimensions of Human Security

Substantively, the idea of human security implies, at a minimum, a number of interwoven dimensions. For the sake of systematization, we have used the same fivefold classification made earlier: the ecosystem, the economy, the society, the polity, and the culture.[33] These subsystems are connected among themselves by specific "bridges": resources between environment and economy, social forces between economy and society, brokers and alliances between society and polity, and ideology connecting politics with culture. The concrete interplay among and between regimes and their linkages defines the nature of systemic entropy, or homeostasis, at any given point in time and at any level, whether global, regional, national, or local. It also sets the fundamental ethical parameters of foreign policy.

The first dimension is environmental, personal, and physical security. This involves the right of individuals and communities to the preservation of their own lives and health and their right to dwell in a safe and sustainable environment. This security has an intergenerational quality: it provides for a linkage between past and "future" history. The second dimension is economic: accessibility to employment and resources to maintain one's existence, to reduce scarcity, and to permit the improvement of the material quality of community life. The third dimension is social: protection from discrimination based on age, gender, ethnicity, or social status. This implies access to "safety nets," knowledge, and information as well as the ability to associate. The fourth dimension is cultural security: the set of psychological orientations geared to preserving and enhancing a society's ability to control uncertainty and fear. Finally, there is political security: the right to representation, autonomy (freedom), participation, and dissent, combined with the power to make choices with a reasonable probability of effecting change. This security includes, but is not limited to, legal-juridical security: individual and collective access to justice and protection from abuse.

Democracy and Security

Although all these individual and collective dimensions of security are equally central to the realization of human dignity, the political dimension (which relates to the configuration of regimes and governance) holds the key to the safeguarding of physical-environmental, economic, social, and cultural "rights." Politics, understood here in its most conventional sense as the "allocation of values" through "authoritative choices,"[34] constitutes the organizing principle of a community's life.

In this sense, substantive and procedural democracy lie at the core of political security. The latter involves an ongoing process of conflict management (and resolution) among three fundamental and interrelated contradictions. The first is that between economic capabilities and social expectations, the second is that between elites and masses, and the third is that between sovereignty (autonomy) and subordination. Yet the ability of a polity to overcome crises and to provide security for its members depends, more than on its resource-base and autonomy, upon its learned capacity for conflict management; that is, it depends upon governance.

The global political regime is a loose conglomerate of local, regional, and international interactions, bound together by limited rules, practices, and institutions. This regime, which includes the United Nations, regional arrangements, international conventions, jurisprudence, and regulations, gives the system a superficial semblance of order and authority. But this image is deceiving, for structural power rests with a small number of national and transnational actors, primarily the elite core in the OECD countries. The existing mechanisms for global conflict management, such as the UN Security Council and the ever more important "summit diplomacy," have become tools of the foreign offices of a small number of countries – especially the US State Department and transnational business. In other words, the global political order is increasingly subservient to the transnational economic regime.

The International Monetary Fund (IMF), the World Bank, and the World Trade Organization (WTO) are at the centre of the global political regime and configure a de facto, though not always effective, mechanism for global governance.[35] This is where effective policies and regulations governing the world order are to be found. All other kinds of policy making formally rest with the over 170 heterogeneous states that comprise the UN General Assembly. The implementation and enforcement of regulations occurs more readily in the restrictive and elitist realm of business elites than in the formal structures of government and international organizations, which offer some – albeit limited – possibilities for broader interest representation.

The internal structure and operations of states have also been profoundly transformed in recent years. With the advent of receiver states, financial decision making has displaced other forms of "high politics." Ministries of finance, treasury boards, central banks, and the like have become the managers of governability the world over, subordinating other functions, ministries, and agencies to structural adjustment policies of fiscal restraint. Globalized agendas, not national priorities or popular demands, increasingly determine government policies at the national *and* subnational levels.

With the fading away of territorial sovereignty, persistent centrifugal tendencies and primeval identities (ethnic, linguistic, or subregional) are more pronounced, making the political process increasingly fragmented. Subnational conflict is, at the same time, endemic and highly transnationalized. This generates overall systemic instability, experienced by the unequivocal signs of disintegration manifested by many nation-states. Globalization and national disintegration, closely associated with economic restructuring and downsizing, reduce the state's capacity for national integration and conflict management. The result is ungovernability.

Threats to Human Security

Security threats are a direct consequence of dysfunctional regimes, and they affect both the global and the domestic spheres. These spheres are systemically related, so that dysfunctions in one tend to express themselves in other subsystems; that is, mutual vulnerability is constituted by multiple dysfunctions – environmental, economic, social, political, and cultural – that are linked in vicious circuits of multiple causality. Unlike the US and most of the European members of the G-7, Canada is particularly vulnerable to these processes. Historically, it has been a highly penetrated political system, with a heavily transnationalized economy. In recent years, massive deregulation and liberalization have made its currency, capital markets, and trade highly volatile and unstable. Dialectically, these centrifugal proclivities have been enhanced by a weakening of federalism and a crisis of the Canadian state.

The New Insecurity

Today's global order is inherently fragile and asymmetrical. Major security threats, though basically subsystemic, are today much wider, unpredictable, and fractal. The rapid disintegration of other forms of systemic associations, such as the East European bloc, the Non-Aligned Movement, and (for that matter) the Third World, has left a systemic vacuum. It has also limited the brokerage options of "middle powers." This tendency manifests itself in two directions. One is the emergence of strong economic blocs; namely, the European Community (EC), the Asia-Pacific Economic Cooperation (APEC) countries, the North American Free Trade Agreement (NAFTA), and (more recently) MERCOSUR (Mercado Comun del Sur – Common Market of the South). The other is the apparent industrial decline of the US vis-à-vis Europe and Japan. But this polycentrism is deceiving, since US military and economic/financial supremacy has remained formidable. Susan Strange used the term "structural power"[36] to refer to this American paramountcy – and metapower – under a new constellation of global interests that now includes European and Japanese elites.

Power in this New World Order is functional rather than territorial. Underpinning the geographical poles of growth in Asia-Pacific or Europe, or even the semi-peripheries, there is an enormous concentration of force and wealth in the hands of a global ruling class whose economic and organizational commonalties are growing. In fact, transnational integration and national disintegration have gone hand-in-hand.[37] The main consequence of this globalization has been a profound weakening of the sovereignty and the governability of most nation-states. Canada has been profoundly affected. The shrinkage of the public sector in a nation where the state played a central role in constructing civil society has severely weakened national unity and the social and economic security of most Canadians.

Symptoms of Crisis

The contemporary political crisis involves the juxtaposition of two macroprocesses. One is the transformation of the global political order at the end of the Cold War, the other is a profound alteration of the state itself as a mechanism for conflict management and for the making of authoritative choices. Five major dysfunctional manifestations emerge from this. The first is the spread of subnational "low-intensity" conflict and civil strife; the second is the pervasiveness of extreme forms of violence, such as terrorism; the third is the increasingly endemic decline of the rule of law, expressed in soaring rates of crime; the fourth is the breakdown of the nexus between state and civil society brought about by neoliberalism and the receiver states; and last but not least is the rise of authoritarian strains, particularly neofascism. I will briefly discuss each of these dystopic manifestations and its impact on human security.

The Spread of Conflict

In an interconnected world, conflict cannot be easily contained within national boundaries. Involvement and intervention often mean entangling and costly operations, such as those that occurred in Kuwait, Somalia, and Yugoslavia. Peacekeeping, developed for the purpose of preventing the escalation of localized conflicts, has given way to a less focused, less transparent, and more unilateral notion – "peacemaking." As conflicts expand in scope and intensity, they may involve theatres other than the primary arenas of confrontation. Even under the restraint of bipolarism, primarily local confrontations – such as in the Korean and Vietnamese civil wars, the Israeli-Palestinian conflict, civil strife in Central America, and power struggles in Afghanistan – showed a tendency to become internationalized. Without the dangers of unintended head-on superpower collisions, internal conflicts have become the principal sources of violence and population displacement. During the period between 1989 and 1990 there were thirty-three armed conflicts in the world, only one of which was between nation-states. In another example, some two million people fled the former Yugoslavia as refugees or displaced persons.[38] With arms trade expanding and disintegrating armies entering this lucrative game, the acceleration and expansion of internecine conflicts is likely to occur.

Terrorism and Counter-Terrorism

Non-conventional forms of violent struggle, such as low intensity conflicts, drug wars and terrorism,[39] are increasingly fought on the global stage. Though most terrorist activity takes place in the periphery and involves generally unreported acts by states (e.g., Indonesian atrocities in East Timor), core regions are not "off-limits" to such activities. Western societies, once perceived as secure, have been rendered porous by such dramatic events as the destruction of Pan-Am flight 103 over Lockerbie and the bombing of the New York World Trade Center. Terrorism is a tactical expression of many ideological strains. Yet ethnic, religious, linguistic, and other forms of irredentism are the most frequent sources of terrorist activity. The resolution of some of the most enduring national and territorial questions (as in Palestine and Northern Ireland) will likely bring an end to the violent spate begun in the 1970s. But, in a world of disintegrating nation-states, the spectre of nationalist, criminal, radical, vigilante, or government-sponsored terrorism remains an ever-present security threat.

In this systemic sense, a real threat posed by terrorism lies in its "cure." In many instances counter-terrorism means little more than terrorism with a minus sign in front of it. It nurtures secrecy and has a proclivity to circumvent civil liberties and due process, which are the very values that counter-terrorist measures are supposed to protect.[40] In the recent past, many policies designed to fight "subversion" had the effect of multiplying insecurity on both the periphery and in the centre. In the less developed societies, anti-terrorism, often in the form of death squads and vigilantism, means the exacerbation of violence and the development of unabashed state terrorism.[41] A similar danger can be found in the "moral entrepreneurship" of the "war on drugs" and other public safety campaigns that today replace the counter-insurgency and counter-terrorist discourse of the past. These tendencies increase North-South entanglements, erode the ethical foundations of politics, and, in the long run, weaken global and domestic security.

Crime and Counter-Crime

Criminality, violent or otherwise, in the midst of a deepening economic crisis constitutes a related security threat. It manifests itself in two ways. The first is in the erosion of the ethical bonds that link political systems together. Without those, neither governance nor security is possible. There is a media-driven perception of a "crime epidemic" sweeping many regions of the world, from the poverty-ravaged cities of Africa, to the drug-exporting regions of Latin America, to the disintegrating societies of Eastern Europe, to the North American inner cities. It appears to affect the poorest slums as well as the highest offices. Some of its milder expressions involve increased corruption, venality, abuse, theft, and vandalism. Its nastier manifestations include alarming increases in violent crimes in the streets, in schools, in the workplace, and in the home. This violence is desensitized, glorified, and even legitimized by mass culture. Depressed economic conditions make crime a lucrative opportunity for some and the only opportunity for many. Once internalized as a social practice, crime has become part of the culture and a persistent systemic condition. The drug problem is a case in point. Beginning with peasant producers in remote, poor regions, it continues with corrupt officials in the periphery, crime syndicates both in the exporting and importing areas, and functionaries "on the take" at the centre. Ultimately, it proceeds all the way to retailers and First World users. It is essentially a consumer-driven process, operating with the purest market logic. Therefore, its containment requires addressing its social and economic causes, including the roots of addiction.

The measures used to control criminality can also constitute a security threat. Such measures include expanded enforcement and containment, including police controls to protect property and maintain law and order. As with terrorism, there is a dysfunctional dialectic between the problem of crime and its supposed solutions. As military demobilization occurs and public expenditures on social services shrink, internal security allotments soar. In increasingly polarized and fragmented societies, enforcement agencies become politicized. Intervention becomes focused on specific classes or groups labelled as potential "law-breakers" (the poor, minorities, the young, those with non-conventional lifestyles). The growth in security forces, however, does not seem to bring about a reduction of crime. Without denying the need for crime prevention in all societies, this trend constitutes a wide-ranging threat to democracies. It raises questions about public scrutiny, accountability, uncontrolled red tape, and corruption. The above is particularly disturbing given the worldwide resurgence of racist, ethnic irredentist and neofascist movements, which have arisen precisely from the present crisis and influence enforcement functions.[42] Important as they are, policing issues are rarely matters of public debate. The interplay of crime and counter-crime creates a self-fulfilling prophecy: numerous social or political activities become, in one way or another, "criminal." When this happens, the legitimacy of enforcement agencies and of the rule of law is brought into question. Most significantly, it raises broader and fundamental ethical questions regarding human rights.

Neoliberalism

A related global trend is the effort by socio-economic elites and their institutional intellectuals to circumvent established democratic traditions in the name of making politics "governable." The trend towards creating "limited" democracies, able to respond to "market" (i.e., elite) forces, constitutes an attempt to reduce political participation. The 1975 report to the Trilateral Commission, *The Crisis of Democracy,*[43] articulated this view. The neoliberal solution has favoured limiting the role of the state to enforcement and the facilitation of private accumulation, while reducing the scope and salience of political participation. Without the legitimization of welfare policies and popular participation, strong connections develop between neoliberal policies, induced poverty, political alienation, and the potential emergence of police states. Essentially, these trends lead to a re-drafting of the implicit social contract. The "regime" of governance that regulates the pattern of labour relations (and income-distribution) in society is altered.

As a project, neoliberalism is distinctively exclusionary and heavily biased in favour of business elites. Its ethical foundations are rooted in social Darwinism. The so-called "leaner but meaner" state resulting from adjustment and debt-reduction policies has built-in limitations on equitable social policies. Monetarist measures and the drive for "macroeconomic equilibrium" are effectively excluded from public debate. This elitist tendency to facilitate the "governability" of democracies reduces governments' capacity for governance and produces an effective loss of citizenship. From such a restrictive perspective, an inequitable socio-economic order is construed as the only possible choice. In Margaret Thatcher's famous dictum: "there is no alternative." Critics and dissidents end up being labelled "subversives." As John Sheahan comments, the neoliberal policy package is "inconsistent with democracy because an informed majority would reject it. The main reason it cannot win popular support is that it neither assures employment opportunities nor provides any other way to ensure that lower income groups can participate in economic growth."[44] In fact, the economic policies charted under this economic doctrine are better suited to authoritarian political regimes than to Western-style democracy.

The juxtaposition of economic "freedom" with political repression is the essence of the formula known as "authoritarian capitalism." Liberalization without democratization is observable in Latin America, in Asia, and in many of the former socialist republics of Eastern Europe. These new democracies are based upon a peculiar semi-corporatist arrangement – a pact of elites. Their goal is to secure a "healthy economic climate" for private accumulation by means of free trade, privatization, and deregulation policies. This is accomplished via debt service and the execution of the conditions attached to the negotiation of such a service, thus giving rise to "receiver states."

However, receivership status is not circumscribed to the periphery of the "other" world, nor is a large foreign debt crisis one of its intrinsic characteristics. Western elites have been applying a similar political agenda in their own societies, fuelling the kind of globalization that numerous civic groups protested at the 1999 Seattle World Trade Organization Summit. Regressive socio-economic policies have been rationalized on the grounds of keeping down inflation, reducing taxes, and facilitating global capital mobility. Economic "restructuring," as experienced by Canadians since the 1980s under all party labels, is their programmatic expression.

Neofascism

With pronounced declines in living standards affecting the once secure bastions of the middle and blue-collar sectors in the First and the former Second Worlds, socio-political conditions similar to those of post-First World War Europe have been created.[45] The unemployed, alienated youth and an economically threatened middle class constitute a propitious culture for "extremism from the centre." In recent years these trends have become more pronounced. There are full-fledged Nazi organizations in areas of continental Europe that have experienced a large influx of immigrants and refugees.[46] Many of these movements have a significant presence in the electoral arena and have been able to influence national policies. Electoral politics, however, has always been but a minor component in past fascist movements. A careful analysis of their alternative, extra-parliamentary strategies is essential to ascertaining their full impact.

Marked racist and proto-fascist tendencies are also increasingly evident in the Americas, having found homes in fringe organizations with a high capacity to penetrate mainstream movements and public institutions, including political parties, the bureaucracy, the police, and the military. Contemporary fascism is perhaps less nationalistic and more anti-left than its historical counterparts, and it does not question, as did classical fascism, the tenets of economic liberalism. Today's fascism is primarily defined by xenophobia and racism rather than by a coherent socio-political doctrine (e.g., corporatism) or a national project. It appeals to the young and to those displaced by economic dislocations, uncertainty, and the trauma of a loss of community and identity.[47] In this sense, the skinhead phenomenon in Germany, the United Kingdom, and elsewhere[48] deserves particular attention.

Signposts for Policy

These developments are likely to have a long-term impact on human security – an impact that goes well beyond the sphere of the political. Environmental, economic, social, and cultural security are equally at stake as they are at the heart of the ethical dilemmas discussed here. One way of looking at these consequences is to concentrate on human rights. Bearing in mind that the specific content of "human rights" is changing and evolving, the political trends discussed so far point to a deterioration of human dignity on a planetary scale, irrespective of the standards of measurement. Perceptive observers, such as Amnesty International's Pierre Sané, have noticed that, throughout the world, human rights are being rolled back. Frustration and bitterness are fuelled by economic policies that make the rich richer and the poor poorer. Governments with dismal human rights records turn to more inconspicuous "arm's-length" ways of achieving their aims – setting up or supporting death squads and civilian defence forces to do their dirty work. Others, while proclaiming the sanctity of human rights, turn a blind eye while people in the streets are murdered by government, or government-backed, forces. Every year thousands of people are assassinated in Brazil and Colombia – "even children whose only crime is their homelessness."[49]

Wherever people's humanity is denied through ethnic "cleansing," torture chambers, discrimination, and oppressive conditions, the pretended post-Cold War global order is being challenged. So are policy makers and analysts who are supposed to make sense of "the world out there" and make it a good place to live.

Rational and effective foreign policy formulation and implementation requires analytical and operational frameworks that strengthen the decision makers' capacity to understand and anticipate global, regional, and bilateral trends. Such frameworks must also be able to emphasize substantive teleological and ethical considerations over purely reactive and mechanical concerns. These must also offer an integrative approach, linking the micro and macro levels of the policy process. Ethics is more than an aesthetic nicety, a fad, or good public relations for policy legitimation and "political correctness." It is at the core of a sound and accountable foreign policy that links the security of Canadians to global security in a mutually vulnerable world. Most important, an ethical framework must be able to replace the moral bankruptcy of both the pseudo-pragmatism of market-driven logic and the hypocritical double standards of Cold War thinking. In this respect, a global theory centred on human security may offer an explicit and transparent conceptual construct to identify and anticipate the dilemmas faced by policy makers. It may also provide a flexible, multidisciplinary, and strategic approach to policy planning and choices within the rapidly changing Canadian security context.

Notes

1 A "receiver state" is a state whose major role is the management of debt repayment. It is an executor of receivership and structural adjustment conditionalities imposed by the international finance community (i.e., transnational banks, the International Monetary Fund, and the G-7).
2 Ruth Leger Sivard, *World Military and Social Expenditures* (Leesburg: WMSE Publications, 1989).
3 Marcus Gee, "Apocalypse Deferred," *Globe and Mail,* 9 April 1994, D1, D3.
4 Pierre Sané, speech in London, UK, quoted by Kevin Kreneck, "Amnesty's Report Card from Hell," *Globe and Mail,* 10 December 1993, A21.
5 Robert Kaplan, "The Coming Anarchy," *Atlantic Monthly* 273, 2 (1994): 46.
6 Roger Winter, "The Year in Review," *1993 World Refugee Survey* (Washington: US Committee on Refugees, 1993), 2, 3.
7 Richard Mansbach, Yale Ferguson, and Donald Lampert, *The Web of World Politics: Nonstate Actors in the Global System* (Englewood Cliffs: Prentice Hall, 1976), 1-10.
8 Francis Fukuyama, "The End of History?" *National Interest* 16,3 (1989): 2-18.
9 Samuel Huntington, "The Clash of Civilizations?" *Foreign Affairs* 72, 3 (1993): 22-49.
10 Kaplan, "The Coming Anarchy."
11 Defined as a system of alliances against a would-be external aggressor predicated on a solution of continuum between passive strategies (deterrence and defence) and aggressive strategies (compellance and offence).
12 This aspect is emphasized by Howard Adelman's chapter in this volume. For instance, he states that "one of the most important contextual factors is the unwillingness of interveners to act unless there is a crisis."
13 Osvaldo Sunkel, "Transnational Capitalism and National Disintegration in Latin America," *Social and Economic Studies* 22, 1 (1973): 156-71.
14 Ivan Head, *On a Hinge of History: The Mutual Vulnerability of South and North* (Toronto: University of Toronto Press, 1991), 1.
15 Bernhard J. Stern, *Historical Sociology: The Selected Papers of Bernhard J. Stern* (New York: Citadel Press, 1959), 3-14, 15-35.
16 Martin Staniland, *What Is Political Economy? A Study of Social Theory and Underdevelopment* (New Haven: Yale University Press, 1985), 10-25.

17 G.K. Helleiner, "Conventional Foolishness and Overall Ignorance: Current Approaches to Global Transformations and Development," in *The Political Economy of Development and Underdevelopment,* ed. Charles Wilber and Kenneth Jameson (New York: McGraw Hill, 1992), 55-80.

18 See Immanuel Wallerstein, *The Modern World System II* (New York: Academic Books, 1980); Johan Galtung, *The True Worlds: A Transnational Perspective* (New York: Free Press, 1980); Robert Cox, *Production, Power and World Order. Social Forces in the Making of History* (New York: Columbia University Press, 1978), 1-35, 407-15.

19 See Wallerstein, *The Modern World System;* also Alfred Bergesen, ed., *Crisis in the World System* (Beverly Hills, CA: Sage, 1983), 5-7.

20 Robert Keohane and Joseph Nye, *Power and Interdependence: World Politics in Transition* (Boston: Little, Brown, 1977), ix, 19-22.

21 See ibid.; Raymond Hopkins and Donald Puchala, *The Global Political Economy of Food* (Madison: University of Wisconsin Press, 1978), 20.

22 Robert Dahl, *Modern Political Analysis* (Englewood Cliffs: Prentice-Hall, 1970), 14-24. Power is defined as the ability of one actor or cluster of actors to induce compliant behaviour in actors who would not otherwise have behaved in such a way.

23 Max Weber, *The Theory of Economic and Social Organization,* trans. A.M. Henderson and Talcott Parsons (New York: Oxford University Press, 1947), 145-54.

24 See Robert Cox, "Gramsci, Hegemony, and International Relations: An Essay on Method," *Millenium: Journal of International Studies* 12, 2 (1983): 163-64.

25 Thomas Baumgartner, Tom Burns, and Philippe DeVille, "Reproduction and Transformation of Dependency Relationships in the International System: A Dialectical Systems Perspective," in *Proceedings of the Annual North American Meeting of the Society for General Systems Research,* 1977, 129-36.

26 Cox, *Production, Power, and World Order.*

27 Michel Crozier, *The Bureaucratic Phenomenon* (Chicago: University of Chicago Press, 1964), 112, 142.

28 K.J. Holsti, *International Politics: A Framework for Analysis* (Englewood Cliffs: Prentice Hall, 1972), 20-22.

29 Karl Deutsch, *The Analysis of International Relations* (Englewood Cliffs: Prentice Hall, 1968), 114-22.

30 J. Nef and O.P. Dwivedi, "Development Theory and Administration: A Fence Around an Empty Lot?" *Indian Journal of Public Administration* 27, 1 (1981): 42-66.

31 UNDP, *Human Development Report* (New York: Oxford University Press, 1994/95), 22-40.

32 Harold Lasswell, *Politics: Who Gets What, When and How?* (New York: Peter Smith, 1950), 3-25.

33 *Human Development Report* (1994).

34 David Easton, "An Approach to the Analysis of Political Systems," *World Politics* 9, 3 (1957): 384-85.

35 Huntington, "Clash of Civilizations," 47.

36 Susan Strange, "The Future of the American Empire, *Journal of International Affairs* 42, 1 (1988): 1-17.

37 Sunkel, "Transnational Capitalism."

38 UN Department of Economic and Social Development, *Report on the World Social Situation* (1993), xxi.

39 G. Wardlaw, *Political Terrorism* (New York: Cambridge University Press, 1989), 16.

40 J. Schmid and P. Crelisten, *Western Responses to Terrorism* (London: Frank Cass, 1993), 229-31.

41 Noam Chomsky and Edward Herman, *The Political Economy of Human Rights* (Montreal: Black Rose, 1979), 6.

42 V. Golov, "Crime and Safety in the Public Consciousness," *Izvestia,* 23 July 1993, 4.

43 Samuel Huntington, Michel Crozier, and Joji Watanuki, *The Crisis of Democracy Report on the Governability of Democracies to the Trilateral Commission,* Triangle Papers 8 (New York: New York University Press, 1975).

44 John Sheahan, *Patterns of Development in Latin America: Poverty, Repression and Economic Strategy* (Princeton: Princeton University Press, 1987), 234.
45 Liz Fakete, "Guide to the Fascist Labyrinth," *New Statesman and Society* 16, 1277 (1993): 24, 23-26.
46 Geoffrey Roberts, "Right-Wing Radicalism in the New Germany," *Parliamentary Affairs* 45, 3 (1992): 367.
47 Tony Bunyan, "Jeux sans frontières: It's a Lockout," *New Statesman and Society* 6, 277 (1993): 23-26.
48 B'nai B'rith, Anti-Defamation League, "Neo-Nazi Skinheads: A 1990 Status Report," *Terrorism* 13, 3 (1990): 244.
49 Sané, "Amnesty's Report Card."

3
The Ethics of Development Assistance and Human Security: From Realism and Sovereigntism to Cosmopolitanism

Peter Penz

What is a satisfactory ethic for governing international development assistance offered by states like Canada? How does human security fit into an ethical approach to development assistance? What is an ethical approach to aid conditionality? These are the questions addressed in this chapter. Development assistance is one aspect of foreign policy in which ethics has been particularly stressed. By focusing on development assistance rather than on foreign policy as a whole, it is possible to sort out differences in perspective within somewhat less complex analytical terrain. However, the analytical framework developed here should be equally applicable to foreign policy more generally.[1]

In addressing the three questions posed, I provide a number of distinctive orientations. One is that, rather than *describe* or *explain* the ethical dimension in foreign policy, I try to articulate what an ethical approach *requires*. In other words, like Jorge Nef (Chapter 2, this volume), I offer a chapter that is explicitly normative, evaluative, and prescriptive – one that falls into the discipline of political philosophy. Second, I take a theoretical approach to ethics; that is, I focus on *general principles* rather than on particular cases. It is true that the plausibility of such principles depends, in part, on whether they make sense when applied to particular cases, but my task is to articulate the general principles in the first place.[2] Third, I present a range of theoretical perspectives that serves as the basis for an argument for a particular perspective – that of cosmopolitan ethics. In addition, I relate the notion of "human security" to this as well as to the other perspectives. Finally, for illustrative purposes, I focus on particular issues within development assistance, namely, the human-security issue of population displacement due to development projects and the policy issue of conditionality. Thus, while I share with Cranford Pratt (Chapter 4, this volume) a focus on development assistance and ethics, I am more explicitly normative, focusing on contending theoretical positions, and like Turner, Brownhill, and Kaara (Chapter 6, this volume) I use as illustrations inappropriate or harmful assistance rather than insufficient giving.

Realism and State Sovereignty

The first issue in international ethics is whether there is any scope at all for ethics in international relations. Two dominant positions on this question are (1) realism, which, in its strongest forms, argues that there is no scope for ethics in international relations,[3] and (2) the "morality of states,"[4] which argues for the centrality of the principle of state sovereignty. The latter emphasizes liberty at the level of states and requires that the principle of non-interference be respected; thus, I refer to this approach as "sovereigntism."[5]

While realism and sovereigntism have focused primarily on military and state-authority matters (i.e., "security" in the traditional sense), they also have implications for economic development. Neither recognizes any moral obligations regarding socio-economic development in other countries; assisting another state's development efforts is strictly a voluntary matter. Within both perspectives, development assistance can be like the "foreign-aid" policy of the Byzantine Empire 1,000 years ago and that of the Achaemenid Persian Empire 2,500 years ago: it serves state security by building alliances and paying off potential enemies.[6]

Despite this commonality, there is also an important difference between these two positions. Sovereigntism entails the requirement not to subvert another country's development efforts, whereas realism's only aim is to pursue the security of the policy maker's state, which may well involve impeding another country's development. Under sovereigntism development assistance may be extended as a gesture of good will, without an expected payoff; realist norms of conduct would require a payoff. Sovereigntism thus allows for interstate altruism (although it does not require it), while realism does not.

Realism can be readily shown to be in error with respect to international ethics. Its argument has both (1) an explanatory and (2) an ethical form. The explanatory form holds that international relations are anarchic (i.e., that all states are in a perpetual struggle to ensure their own security). As a result, while cooperative and generous actions can serve the interests of the policy maker's state in the long run, any action that is strictly moral (i.e., that goes beyond mere national self-interest) will occur at the expense of security. This is because such moral action can strengthen the power of the receiver state,[7] which could then become a threat in the future. Any strictly moral action could also occur at the expense of building the economic power of the policy maker's own state. The ethical explanation of the realist argument holds that foreign-policy makers have a moral responsibility only to their own citizens. This makes interstate altruism immoral. Upon close examination, both the explanatory and ethical forms of the realist argument are unpersuasive.

First, with respect to the explanatory form of the realist argument, not all conceivable moral actions by one state towards other states will be at the expense of state security. This holds particularly for relatively prosperous states, such as Canada. I am not aware of any case of a state going into a security crisis because of an overly generous development-assistance policy.[8]

Second, with respect to the ethical form of realism, a morality that claims that political leaders have moral responsibilities only to their own citizens[9] is an arbitrarily circumscribed morality. It is much more reasonable to set the geographic boundary to moral concerns using such criteria as cross-border impact vulnerability (i.e., all those who are vulnerable to the actions of policy makers are entitled to moral consideration).[10] States, at least rhetorically, accept that mere might does not make right. State action is characteristically defended on moral grounds, which are seen to transcend state borders, rather than on the grounds of who has the power to carry out such action. This is true even when states behave amorally within the international arena. In fact, this mode of justification "is so prevalent in the world of states as to make that world the paradigmatic example of the homage paid by vice to virtue."[11] With respect to development assistance, this is reflected in the repeated commitment that states have made to the development-assistance target of 0.7 percent of their gross national products (GNPs). Even when widely violated, this is generally justified as a temporary problem of financial stringency and affordability.

This critique of realism does not argue that international affairs are essentially shaped by ethical ideals; rather, it argues that there is *some* scope for ethical considerations and that, therefore, ethical assessments of foreign policies are appropriate.[12]

Sovereigntism and Its Shortcomings

Sovereigntism, unlike realism, offers a clearly moral principle – non-intervention in the affairs of other countries. It arose from the recognition that states form a certain kind of community – one that needs to be regulated by appropriate moral norms. Non-intervention does not mean avoidance of relations with other countries; it merely means avoiding interference that runs counter to that state's internal management of its affairs. However, rejecting realism in favour of sovereigntism advances the moral case for development assistance only to a limited extent. As mentioned above, sovereigntism *requires* merely that other states refrain from subverting any particular state's development. It also *allows* other states to provide development assistance, but this is not a moral obligation.

For three reasons, sovereigntism, with its primary principle of non-intervention, is insufficient as a moral norm for regulating interstate relations. First, it fails to recognize mutual vulnerability between states in any form other than aggression. Countries are now so entangled, due to economic, cultural, and ecological cross-boundary effects, that states are vulnerable to each other in many important ways. As Jorge Nef argues (Chapter 2, this volume), mutual vulnerability has now become pervasive. As a result, it is difficult to sort out particular forms of harm and to deal with them in the manner of tort law.

Second, sovereigntist ethics lacks a principle concerning international cooperation. When global problems such as climate change and widespread economic disruption threaten security, it is not merely a matter of convenience for states to cooperate; their interdependence makes it a moral requirement.[13] Under these conditions, it is crucial to recognize the need for international cooperation and to develop ethical norms for it. Such norms certainly have to go beyond the prohibition of interference. Moreover, morally required cooperation also entails fair sharing of sacrifices and benefits.

Third, sovereigntism is clear about the rules that are to be respected, but it is less clear about what is to happen if they are violated. Normally, violation of sovereignty can be assumed to involve harm, the injustice of which can be rectified by restitution. A norm of compensation for harm is workable in principle if the harm is straightforward and is the exception rather than the rule. However, such harm may be so complex and diffuse that it is too difficult and contentious to establish just restitution. Moreover, throughout history so many violations of political sovereignty (conquests, genocides, expropriations, displacements, subordinations) have occurred (quite apart from more indirect economic harm), that it is difficult to visualize how one would go about undoing all these violations and making restitution for them. These historical violations have come to constitute the present structure of states, their territories, and membership. Furthermore, the people who committed the violations are no longer alive. This is evident, for example, in relations between European settler colonies (including Canada) and Aboriginal populations. But the phenomenon is worldwide. The fact that such historical violations of sovereignty are, in large part, irreversible does not constitute an argument for accepting the current division of land and people as just; instead, these violations constitute at least a prima facie case for minimizing inequalities in the endowments of states and peoples.[14]

Statist Internationalism

An alternative to sovereigntism is an ethic of interstate relations that goes beyond mere non-intervention but that keeps the focus on relations between states. I will refer to it as "statist internationalism." Here two principles are applicable: (1) cooperatively promoting the interests of all states and (2) fair sharing.[15] Within this framework, there are obligations pertaining to cooperation (e.g., in developing and contributing to international financial institutions that rescue states in financial crisis), to self-restraint (e.g., greenhouse gas emissions), and to redistribution (e.g., mandated development assistance). These state obligations are matched by corresponding rights; that is, state rights.[16]

The statist-internationalist approach, however, suffers from difficulties that arise from confining moral considerations to relations between states. First of all, it is not clear what "fair sharing" between states means. If it means equal sharing, then how is that to be applied between an extremely populous state, such as China, and one with a tiny population, such as the island state of Nauru? Surely equal (or some other form of equitable) sharing of material resources makes sense only with reference to people (as opposed to states). Once distributive entitlements and obligations are determined on a per capita basis, we are part way to an interpersonal conception of distributive justice. Moreover, if the case for some form of equal sharing in the present rests on accumulated historical injustices that are now too difficult to disentangle or that cannot be morally rectified through restitution, then certain historical changes in the relations between states and their people become both relevant and problematic. Since there have been shifts in state borders as well as in membership through international migration, historical injustices have to be seen as having affected *people rather than states*. These injustices can still manifest themselves in unjust relations *within* states, such as between Canada's settler population from Europe and its Aboriginal population or between Arabs and Kurds in Iraq.

The state focus of statist internationalism also distorts the articulation of the international general interest, such as in the prevention or containment of global warming or global economic depressions. The interest of states is to maintain themselves. A conception of the international general interest as pertaining merely to the interests of states does not conform to the emerging notion of the general interest of humanity. Again, this requires reference to people rather than to states.

Finally, even the principle of self-determination falls short when it is articulated entirely in statist terms. Within states, there are cultures, communities, and individuals, and each can make plausible, but potentially conflicting, moral claims to self-determination. Communitarianism stresses self-determination by cultures and communities, while libertarianism stresses individual self-determination. Self-determination is warranted at several levels, not just at the level of the state (nor just at the level of the individual). In fact, in line with today's democratic values, state sovereignty needs to be harnessed by the interests and rights of communities and individuals within the state. Without that, state sovereignty, in both its external and internal aspects (i.e., self-determination and supreme authority, respectively), merely serves the interests of rulers.

The Cosmopolitan Approach to Development Assistance

In contrast to this interstate ethic, an alternative global ethic has emerged – cosmopolitanism. It is strikingly reflected in the pervasiveness of appeals to international human rights. It is a non-statist ethic in that it takes moral principles that hold within national societies and applies them to the worldwide human community. Moral rights and obligations hold among the members of the global community, and states are merely instruments for the purposes, rights, and obligations of individuals. Under full-fledged cosmopolitanism, state borders are without moral significance; they do not demarcate moral obligations and entitlements. The citizens of one country have obligations to those of another country, which means that states, as agencies representing their citizens, have extraterritorial obligations not just to other states, but also to the citizens of other states.

This perspective, however, does not yield a singular ethic; rather, it is a framework within which different forms of social ethics can compete. These distinguish themselves by giving more emphasis to one or another of three principles: (1) maximally promoting human well-being worldwide, (2) providing for distributive justice worldwide, or (3) protecting the self-determination and freedom of individuals worldwide. Each of these principles represents the core of an alternative form of cosmopolitanism.[17] The implications of cosmopolitanism for development assistance, therefore, depend on the *form* of cosmopolitanism to which one is referring.

The form of cosmopolitanism represented by the first principle is a utilitarian one: it prescribes the maximization of human well-being and depends heavily on the consequences of development assistance.[18] First, it requires that the improved human well-being brought about by development assistance be sufficiently beneficial to outweigh the costs of providing it. Development assistance that is wasted or that is detrimental (e.g., that leads to massive environmental damage) will clearly fail in terms of this criterion. How beneficial development assistance actually *is* is a matter of considerable controversy.[19] I will not pursue this question here (as do Turner, Brownhill, and Kaara [Chapter 6, this volume]); rather, I will focus on the *criteria* by which we are to assess whether or not development is worthwhile and justifiable.

Cost-benefit analysis is sometimes presented as an operational form of utilitarianism.[20] In that case, as long as there are development projects with net benefits, development assistance should be provided to implement them (assuming they are not precluded by alternative projects with still higher net benefits). However, the cost-benefit-analysis approach requires assigning public funds to development assistance only if the net benefits of such projects are greater than are those of all other possible projects or uses of these funds, including leaving them in the pockets of citizens to spend for their private purposes. This certainly does not seem to be in the spirit of development assistance. While the requirement for assistance to be beneficial clearly makes sense, the cost-benefit criterion misses the basic rationale of development assistance because it neglects all distributive considerations.

There is, however, another interpretation of the utilitarian approach, and this is articulated, for example, by Peter Singer.[21] Rather than make comparisons in terms of the values of individuals expressed through their market choices (the basis of cost-benefit analysis), this interpretation focuses on the contributions of redistribution to overall well-being. It takes the quite plausible (but not undisputed) position that $100 in the hands of a poor person contributes much more to well-being than does $100 in the hands of a rich person. The idea is that transferring $100 from a rich person to a poor person increases overall well-being because the loss in well-being to a rich person is less than is the gain in well-being to a poor person. Once one adopts this interpretation of the total-well-being ethic, one's moral obligations become quite radical. The requirement then is to keep redistributing until either full equality is reached or until the redistribution stops generating more benefits in the hands of the recipients than losses to the donors and to the community as a whole (e.g., by impairing production incentives). The latter constraint will normally apply before anything like full equality is reached. Nevertheless, this means that, assuming development assistance does not get siphoned off through corruption and does not get frittered away by ineffective or even harmful projects, redistribution for development assistance will certainly have to go much beyond 0.7 percent of the GNP. In fact, once assistance to development projects becomes saturated, redistributing directly to individuals might become more effective in advancing human well-being worldwide.

The form of cosmopolitanism represented by the second principle focuses on distributive justice. Based on the previous arguments about statist internationalism, one plausible position is that the current distribution of resources and productive capacities is deeply affected by historical injustices. This requires an egalitarian redistributive regime of some kind. While the rationale for this approach is quite different from that for the approach that focuses on redistribution for the maximization of human well-being, the direction in which it will push policies concerning development assistance is very similar. (One difference, though, is that an egalitarian approach will focus on the poorest of the poor no matter how difficult it is to improve their living conditions, while a total-well-being approach will pay relatively more attention to how costly it is to reduce poverty.)

The form of cosmopolitanism represented by the third principle focuses exclusively on self-determination. The requirement here is for noninterference, the idea being that this will protect the self-determination of both individuals and small communities. However, an exclusive focus on this single (even if rather open-ended) value suffers from the weaknesses already identified in sovereigntism, especially the lack of norms for cooperation. Still, as a constraint on total-well-being and distributive-justice approaches to development assistance, self-determination represents an important value. Individuals and communities need a sphere of control. The constant subordination of self-determination to the public interest and/or distributive justice, whether national or global, will jeopardize something that most humans value. Integrated into a broader ethical framework that focuses on well-being for all and distributive justice, self-determination plays a crucial role.

The approach I propose is pluralistic in that it draws on all three of the principles used to articulate a moral position on development assistance. One could attempt to construct a theory, such as Rawlsian social contract theory, to fix the role that each of these principles is to play. However, to do that prior to their actual application to policy issues is to run the risk of either being so abstract as to offer little guidance or so specific as to invite contention over matters of theory regardless of whether or not they have any bearing on policy. It thus seems preferable to merely establish general theoretical reference points and to focus debate on their application to concrete policy discussions. This strikes me as a more fruitful approach to the theory-practice dialectic than the application of a particular, highly refined theory.

Human Security and Human Rights

So far I have made minimal reference to two concepts that have, in fact, been central to discussions of foreign policy. One is the traditional norm of security, the other is the more recent norm of human rights. I will now bring these into the framework developed so far.

The traditional notion of "security" in international relations does not have the same meaning that it has in everyday conversation. It involves two crucial restrictions: (1) it refers to a particular threat; and (2) it refers to a particular subject to be protected. The threat is military invasion or military support for internal insurgencies; the subject to be protected is the state. Thus, traditional "security" refers to keeping states safe from military aggression. It is true that "national security" is often referred to. But this is usually part of the language that conflates "nation" and "state," so that "nation" really refers to "state" – as in many uses of "international," which are to be understood as "interstate." It is true that this is part of a vision in which the state is the agent and protector of the nation; but whether or not this is really so has, in the past, typically not been raised with reference to "national security." Restrictions on the international-relations use of "security," its focus on military threats, and its statism have all come to be questioned since the end of the Cold War has done away with the mentality of polarization. The first point is that external threats to states are not merely military. States can be threatened (e.g., by economic sanctions; depressions; trade wars; competition; and such ecological cross-border effects as deprivation of crucial surface and underground water supplies, depletion of fish in international rivers or oceans, pollution that affects economic productivity or the health of the population, and cross-border population flows.) (See Nef [Chapter 2, this volume] for a more extensive treatment of such threats.)

More significant, however, is dropping the statist restrictions on "security." It has lately become popular to refer to "human security." This not only reinforces the multiplicity of threats just mentioned (in that people, and certainly particular groups, are even more vulnerable to harm through such cross-border processes than are states), but it also shifts the ethical perspective. Again, realism, with its self-reliance approach to state security, does not involve international moral obligations. Sovereigntism requires merely refraining from harming or threatening other states and from undermining their security. If environmental and economic dimensions of security are brought into the picture, then what constitutes interference becomes very complex. Statist internationalism with respect to security requires not merely refraining from harming other states, but also cooperating in assuring the security of all states. It may require coming to the aid of a state that is being attacked or that is threatened by some other external threat. The introduction of "human security" into foreign policy discourse provides for a further ethical shift, one that potentially involves two steps.

The first step involves shifting from "national security" to "human security." This, in itself, does not create international obligations but, rather, raises the obligations of states to their own citizens. It requires states, first, not to constitute a threat to their own citizens (e.g., through persecution or corrupt policing) and, second, to serve them by protecting them against other threats. The latter has implications for foreign policy. Cross-border common interests, such as protecting the various kinds of international environmental commons and preventing global depressions, requires interstate cooperation for the sake of the interests of each state's own citizens.

What makes the introduction of human security into foreign-policy discourse a truly fundamental shift, however, is the second step: treating the security of *all* human beings as a foreign policy concern. This step moves us clearly into the cosmopolitan realm. It not only creates obligations concerning international assistance, but it also creates obligations concerning intrastate threats to people in other states. Such threats may be directed at citizens by their own state (e.g., persecution) or they may arise due to the negligence or limited capability of the state in question (e.g., famine, pervasive criminal violence, or a dangerously toxic environment). Not only does this create obligations for affluent countries (which are expected to assist states that are committed to advancing social justice and the well-being of their citizens but that are unable to do so), it also creates obligations for states to restrain other states when the latter harm their own citizens. (The issue of harm will be briefly explored below, with reference to the case of population displacement resulting from development policies.) As long as both steps in introducing human security into foreign-policy discussions are accepted, it can be adequately addressed within the framework of cosmopolitan ethics.

This aspect of human security gives rise to the issue of human rights. How one determines human rights depends on one's particular ethical perspective. Consider, for example, the ethical perspectives outlined in this chapter and how they relate to human rights. First, only cosmopolitanism provides a basis for *universal* human rights. Sovereigntism and statist internationalism, on the other hand, generate rights only for states in their relations with each other; and realism (at least in its strong form) provides for no rights at all. These statist perspectives do not rule out *intrastate* human rights, but they do not provide for human rights that require attention in international dealings. Second, a libertarian individualistic self-determination approach to development issues typically emphasizes civil liberties, privacy, private-property rights, and democratic control. Utilitarian and distributive-justice approaches, on the other hand, encompass economic and social rights, equal opportunities, certain basic livelihood protections, and elementary forms of assistance. Given the different ethical perspectives underlying human rights and their various formulations, this chapter will continue by addressing these underlying ethical perspectives rather than human rights as such.

Cosmopolitanism as European Hegemony?

Contemporary cosmopolitanism is, of course, universalist and has its roots in European thinking. This opens it to the charge of being the product of Western ideological hegemony. That is to say, it is open to being criticized for presenting the value system of one region of the world as applicable to the whole world and for imposing this on other regions.[22] In response to this critique of cosmopolitanism, several points need to be made.

First, cosmopolitanism is not a specific morality but, rather, a framework within which contending perspectives compete. It can encompass cosmopolitan forms of utilitarianism, libertarianism, Kantian ontology, egalitarianism, contractarianism, and so on. The balance between self-determination, the public interest, and fair sharing is struck differently by each form. Cosmopolitanism merely requires that, whatever morality is taken to apply within nations, it applies equally to the rest of humanity. Different schools of ethics compete within this framework. Cosmopolitanism can even accommodate what has been referred to as "cosmopolitan localism" – the universal entitlement to local self-determination[23] – although this is probably the most minimal form of cosmopolitanism conceivable.

Second, Western, or North Atlantic, values are not in fact predominantly cosmopolitan. The predominant view is still that distributive justice applies within Canada and not between Canada and, for example, Mozambique. Cosmopolitanism, far from being the predominant value system of the North Atlantic region, is here presented as an appealing ethical framework that is still struggling for acceptance in the "West."

Third, the value systems of other cultures make equally universalist claims. A cosmopolitan framework in itself is, thus, not distinctively "Western." In fact, it can provide a framework within which values rooted in European traditions and those of other cultures (e.g., neo-Confucianism, Gandhian ethics, Islamic schools of thought, etc.) compete for international acceptance. That these perspectives have not been very audible in international dialogue is not the consequence of cosmopolitanism but, rather, of Western parochialism. In other words, a cosmopolitanism that reflects Western hegemony is a skewed and inadequate cosmopolitanism.

Fourth, while any universal value system must be carefully reviewed to determine whether or not it reflects covert domination by a privileged group or part of the world, any local value system must be similarly reviewed for such domination by powerful groups within the local culture. Thus, the mere fact that one finds a universal value system and a local value system at odds with one another does not, in itself, mean that the local value system is to be privileged – just as it does not mean that the universal value system is to be privileged. This requires further analysis and dialogue.

Fifth, cosmopolitanism does not require uniformity. It is true that worldwide values concerning human rights and distributive entitlements need to be articulated in general terms. However, it can then be left to local value systems to give them concrete expression.

Institutional Deficiencies Regarding Cosmopolitanism

A major problem for cosmopolitanism is that the institutional structure that will give it effect does not exist. Ideally, it requires a global democracy with the authority to enforce universal human rights and, in the case of a cosmopolitan morality of fair distribution, redistribution. Both of these involve the global authority's interference in state sovereignty. Global democracy requires states to refrain from certain actions against their citizens and to provide them with certain protections; redistribution either imposes an external tax burden on (the richer) states or, conceivably, circumvents states altogether by directly taxing their citizens or certain of their transactions. (A global tax could take the form of a carbon tax on pollution or on non-renewable energy use, a "Tobin tax" on international financial transactions, a "bit tax" on electronic transactions, or a global income tax.) International redistribution under a global authority also infringes on the sovereignty of receiving states since, in order to satisfy cosmopolitan norms of distributive justice, the distribution of the transferred funds would have to be governed by the global authority rather than the receiving state (even if the latter administers the distribution).

These institutional structures, however, do not exist. Fulfilling cosmopolitan obligations of distribution, therefore, remains a matter of moral behaviour rather than legal process. This gives rise to the problem of participating in development processes that are either fundamentally unjust or that at least involve injustices. On the one hand, a cosmopolitan ethic of distributive justice imposes obligations to transfer resources to the poor; on the other hand, states responding to such obligations often have to work through other states that use such funds according to their own priorities, which may or may not conform to cosmopolitan values. Just as donor states can subvert or entirely neglect their moral obligations by subordinating them to their own business interests (e.g., through tied aid – see Cranford Pratt [Chapter 4, this volume]), so aid-receiving states can ignore international norms regarding development assistance by using it for purposes that are at odds with assisting the disadvantaged. They can, for example, allocate such funds to the enrichment of state leaders, implement projects that displace vulnerable groups, or privilege the consumer interests of the upper classes. For cosmopolitans, each of these cases is straightforward: they simply should not occur because they in no way contribute to cosmopolitan justice.

Development assistance becomes particularly difficult when a receiver state uses it to the advantage of some and to the disadvantage of others (e.g., tubewell projects under a kleptocratic regime that skims off a percentage of the assistance for self-enrichment, rural electrification that improves living conditions for some poor groups but displaces and impoverishes others as dams are built, industrial development that largely ignores the current generation of poor but that may provide employment for the next generation). While such dilemmas are not exclusive to a world lacking cosmopolitan institutions, they are particularly difficult to avoid in this setting.

Development Assistance and Conditionality

One way of dealing with this and similar dilemmas is for donor states to put conditions on receiver states. Is this morally justifiable? I will address this with reference to two kinds of conditions: (1) the avoidance of development-induced harm, illustrated with reference to the specific issue of the displacement of people due to such development projects as the building of large dams for power generation and irrigation;[24] and (2) the observance of universal human rights (which can range from civil rights emphasized by liberals to economic-security rights stressed by socialists) that may not be directly related to the development project or process. Both conditions are potential aspects of human security; the first is quite clearly so.

In addressing conditionality, it is useful to return briefly to the statist perspectives on international ethics. For the sovereigntist, conditionality is not a problem. Even though a sovereigntist is committed to avoiding interference, conditionality is not coercive interference. It involves an offer by a donor state of assistance under certain conditions: a package that the receiver state can accept or reject. It is not forced on the receiver state. It is true that the receiver state may be desperately poor and very badly in need of the assistance and, thus, not in a strong position to bargain about the conditions attached to it. Although taking advantage of the poor state's weakness may be exploitation, it is not coercive interference.[25] Such imbalance in bargaining power is ubiquitous in the economic relations among states and between states and business organizations. Moreover, it may involve taking advantage of the state's weakness in order to promote the interests of its citizens. This would be introducing cosmopolitan considerations in the attenuated form of charity (i.e., evincing concern for citizens in other countries without recognizing such concern as an obligation). Thus sovereigntism does not treat conditionality as problematic because it is simply a feature, optional to the donor state, in the formally non-coercive offer it makes to the receiver state.

On the other hand, under statist internationalism, where there are interstate obligations beyond those of non-intervention, aid conditionality has a very different ethical status. To the extent that development assistance is an obligatory feature of interstate justice (e.g., reparations for past violations of state sovereignty), attaching conditions to it is clearly an intrusion into the sovereignty of the state entitled to such "assistance." Although the receiver state can refuse such assistance, doing so would deny it something to which it is entitled. More fundamentally, it is unjust to encumber entitlements with new conditions: this would be like an individual paying for culpable damages arising from a car collision but making such payment conditional on the claimant treating his children better. Under statist internationalism conditionality of this kind is unjustified.

This review of the prescriptions of sovereigntism and statist internationalism is useful to the cosmopolitan approach to development assistance adopted here because: (1) the latter shares with statist internationalism the requirement to contribute to development; and (2) it shares with sovereigntism the permissibility of applying conditions (within limits). Conditionality, in fact, becomes a requirement for cosmopolitanism. Since state borders are not seen as limits to moral obligations, participants in development have an obligation to ensure that they are not party to injustices. For example, with regard to multilateral development credit, the World Bank's stipulation of conditions concerning the compensation and resettlement of those evicted by the Sardar Sarovar Dam in the Narmada system of dams[26] (which led the government of India to reject further World Bank credit) is morally justified under a cosmopolitan ethic.

Under suitable cosmopolitan institutions, any conditionality attached to development assistance would be centrally determined in a collective forum within which representatives of both donor and receiver populations would participate in decision making. The imposed requirements would take the form of global rules. Justice requires fair representation in the process for determining these rules and the assurance that it is not controlled by particular countries. Given that national self-determination would not be unimportant even under cosmopolitanism, definite jurisdictional limits to central decision making would need to apply. This would mean that states would be the components of a federation within which certain matters (e.g., the prevention of war and the protection of the global ecological commons) would come under the jurisdiction of the global federation, while others would remain within the jurisdiction of individual states.[27]

Development assistance, or, rather, international redistribution, would clearly fall under global jurisdiction. To the extent that such funds would go to states rather than to individuals or local communities, conditions would normally need to be applied to their utilization; however, these conditions would be determined centrally and collectively rather than unilaterally by donors. As far as universal human rights observance is concerned, this, too, would be a global matter and thus enforced at that level (at least ultimately).

The upshot of this very brief review of cosmopolitan values within an imagined suitable institutional structure is that, under ideal conditions, conditionality would be policy-specific rather than a lever for changes in other or broader spheres of policy. In other words, assistance-specific conditionality, such as the prevention of displacement or the requirement of suitable compensation for displacement, would be justifiable, but conditionality linking development assistance to other issues would not. I will refer to the latter as "broad conditionality."

What does this imply for the pursuit of cosmopolitan values within a predominantly sovereigntist institutional structure? Assistance-specific conditionality certainly is necessary. Cosmopolitan distributive justice requires that international redistribution amount to more than mere transfers from rich states to poor states; that is, it must perform certain functions (e.g., alleviating poverty). However, within bilateral state relations, there are still various options, one of which is to take the approach that the donor is the guardian of cosmopolitan values and that, therefore, unilateral conditionality is appropriate. Conversely, one could argue that it is the receiver state that should be viewed as the protector of cosmopolitan values and that, therefore, there should be no external conditions imposed; the receiver state will apply the appropriate conditions by itself. In the absence of a multilaterally determined set of cosmopolitan conditions, the only alternative to these one-sided options is to have the donor and receiver states negotiate appropriate conditions, on the assumption that, prima facie, neither represents cosmopolitan values better than the other.

Beyond the issue of the representation of cosmopolitan values, a cosmopolitan approach leaves considerable latitude to the aid-receiving state, either in the bilateral formulation of the contract or in its implementation. In the first place, self-determination, including national self-determination, is itself one of several cosmopolitan values. In the second place, the receiver state will normally have more knowledge about local needs and the efficacy of development initiatives than will the donor state. In the third place, to the extent that the receiver state is democratic, there will be representational pressures on it to deliver the assistance in a manner suitable to the population.[28] At the same time, the donor state has cosmopolitan obligations to ensure that assistance is not diverted to enrich a state elite, does not serve the better-off sections of society, and is not incompetently delivered.[29] Equally, the receiver state has an obligation to make every effort to keep development assistance from being corrupted by business interests in the donor state. Assistance-specific conditionality, according to a cosmopolitan ethical perspective pursued in a sovereigntist institutional framework, should thus be negotiated, with both sides having an obligation to attend to the efficacy of the conditions in promoting crucial values and, in particular, in alleviating deprivation.

While, with regard to ideal institutions for a cosmopolitan approach, assistance-specific conditionality has been shown to be justifiable, this is not the case with regard to broad conditionality (i.e., pertaining to human rights or, for that matter, structural adjustment). Does this negative conclusion hold when cosmopolitan values are pursued within the context of the sovereign-state system? Certainly, fundamental human rights are central to cosmopolitan values. In the absence of appropriate cosmopolitan institutions, cosmopolitanism has to take its promoters from wherever it can. They may be economically powerful states that are in a position to flex their economic muscles in support of human rights.

There are, however, three major difficulties with this: (1) powerful states can sneak their national interests into an ostensible human rights agenda; (2) there has been a tendency for richer, Western states to interpret human rights in liberal, civil rights terms rather than in economic security terms;[30]

and (3) there is a particular problem in applying human rights conditionality to development assistance. If, for example, a regime victimizes its people as a whole (or certain sections of the population), then withholding development assistance will victimize the poor even more. This is a dilemma that is best resolved in consequentialist terms; that is to say, it is best assessed situation by situation, weighing the impact of such conditionality on the most disadvantaged. It may well be that providing only certain kinds of assistance, but not engaging in other kinds of economic relations, may be the most effective way of promoting cosmopolitan values. A general rule, other than to maximally apply cosmopolitan values, is not evident here. While in the statist institutional context, human rights conditionality cannot be ruled out in quite as categorical a fashion as it can be in the cosmopolitan institutional ideal, it is, nevertheless, unlikely that development assistance is an ethically appropriate policy instrument to which to attach it.

Thus, if the argument for the superiority of cosmopolitanism is persuasive, only assistance-specific conditionality is justifiable. This holds more or less categorically under a global federation, an institutional framework that is ideal for cosmopolitanism. However, while it holds more contingently under the more adverse institutional framework of sovereign states, it is still unlikely that broad conditionality can be justified, especially with respect to development assistance. Regarding assistance-specific conditionality, negotiated rather than unilateral (take-it-or-leave-it) conditionality is appropriate. In particular, it has to be recognized that the donor state is not necessarily a more reliable representative of cosmopolitan values than is the receiver state.

Notes

1 I would like to express my appreciation to Delna Karanjia for bibliographical and library assistance.

2 In contrast, the theory in Jorge Nef's chapter applies to the analysis of the global situation, while its ethics involves the articulation of the *particular* ethical challenges that this analysis raises.

3 There are some who consider themselves realists in that they accept that, to a large extent, international relations involve power struggles and that certain moral aims should be pursued within this frame. However, as far as their ethical position is concerned, these are not strict realists.

4 Charles R. Beitz, *Political Theory and International Relations* (Princeton: Princeton University Press, 1979), 67-123.

5 This use of "sovereigntism" is to be clearly distinguished from the much more specific notion of Quebec sovereigntists, which has now come to be identified with secession. However, the doctrine of sovereignty is, by and large, at odds with any unilateral right to secession, unless constitutionally permitted.

6 Adam Watson, *The Evolution of International Society: A Comparative Historical Analysis* (London: Routledge, 1992), 109-11.

7 My use of the term "receiver state" differs from Nef's in the previous chapter. He used it to refer to financial indebtedness, while I use it to refer to the "receiver" of aid.

8 This is different from a legitimation crisis due to a lack of citizen support for prevailing levels of development assistance – as may have been the case in Canada since the late 1980s. See Cranford Pratt, "Humanitarian Internationalism and Canadian Development Assistance Policies," in *Canadian International Development Assistance Policies: An Appraisal,* ed. C. Pratt (Montreal and Kingston: McGill-Queen's University Press, 1994), 335-36.

9 Jack Donnelly, "Twentieth-Century Realism," in *Traditions of International Ethics,* ed. Terry Nardin and Donald R. Mapel (Cambridge, UK: Cambridge University Press, 1992), 91-93.

10 See e.g. Robert E. Goodin, *Protecting the Vulnerable: a Reanalysis of our Social Responsibilities* (Chicago, IL: University of Chicago Press, 1985).

11 R.J. Vincent, "The Idea of Rights in International Ethics," in *Traditions of International Ethics,* ed. Terry Nardin and Donald R. Mapel (Cambridge, UK: Cambridge University Press, 1992), 258.

12 For a fuller discussion of the significance of the tension between power and ethics, see Penz, "Environmental Justice, Power, and International Relations," in *Surviving Globalism,* ed. T. Schrecker (Basingtone, UK: Macmillan, 1997), 108-22.

13 In the language used in Andrew Latham's chapter, a "global cultural script" is required and has, in fact, established itself.

14 For a more extensive argument along this line, see Peter Penz, "Sovereignty, Distributive Justice, and Federalism: A Cosmopolitan Perspective," in *Globalism and the Obsolescence of the State,* ed. Y. Hudson (Lewiston, NY: Edwin Mellen Press, 1999), 121-46.

15 This perspective is roughly represented by the demands for a New International Economic Order put forward by the countries of the South in the 1970s. For discussions of interstate justice, see Peter Penz, "International Environmental Justice: The Global Environment and Rich-Country Obligations," in *Canadian Issues in Environmental Ethics,* ed. A. Wellington, A. Greenbaum, and W. Cragg (Peterborough, ON: Broadview Press, 1997), 386-400; and "International Economic Justice and Exploitation," in *Global Justice, Global Democracy,* ed. Jay Drydyk and Peter Penz (Halifax, NS: Fernwood Publishing, 1997), 71-88.

16 Compare Vincent, "The Idea of Rights," 256-59. This kind of internationalism should not be confused with international regimes that represent elements of a cosmopolitan ethic to which states have agreed to adhere (e.g., human rights treaties, which go beyond protecting the interests of states).

17 This classification roughly corresponds to three of the perspectives on social justice found in standard political philosophy; namely, utilitarianism, libertarianism, and egalitarianism. Another perspective, that of contractarianism, is an amalgam of these three. Communitarianism can take a variety of forms; I cover it by making occasional references to collective forms of self-determination. For such classifications, and explanations of the perspectives contained within them, see David M. Smith, *Geography and Social Justice* (Oxford, UK: Blackwell, 1994), 52-85; and James P. Sterba, ed., *Justice: Alternative Political Perspectives,* 2nd ed. (Belmont, CA: Wadsworth Publishing, 1992).

18 The impression that a utilitarian ethic requires action in order to be self-serving is entirely erroneous. In fact, utilitarianism is sometimes criticized for requiring too much altruism in that it tells us to count the well-being of anyone else as equal to our own and to promote society's or humanity's total well-being over our own.

19 See Kevin Watkins, *The Oxfam Poverty Report* (Oxford: Oxfam [UK and Ireland], 1995), 188-215; and Robert Cassen and Associates, *Does Aid Work?* (Oxford: Clarendon Press, 1986).

20 See Peter S. Wenz, *Environmental Justice* (Albany, NY: State University of New York Press, 1988), 155-209.

21 Peter Singer, *Practical Ethics,* 2nd ed. (Cambridge, UK: Cambridge University Press, 1993), 218-46.

22 This critique is reflected, for example, in Andrew Latham's (Chapter 9, this volume) discussion of the "global cultural script" that structures international discourse.

23 Philip McMichael, *Development and Social Change: a Global Perspective* (Thousand Oaks, CA: Pine Forge Press, 1996), 234; see also Wolfgang Sachs, "Global Ecology and the Shadow of 'Development,'" in *Global Ecology: A New Arena of Political Conflict,* ed. W. Sachs (London: Zed Books, 1993), 3-21.

24 The discussion will deal relatively briefly with the *international* ethics of development-induced displacement; for a discussion of the basic ethics of this issue, in terms of the values of overall well-being, self-determination, and distributive justice, see Peter Penz, "The Ethics of Development-Induced Displacement," *Refuge* 16, 3 (August 1997): 37-41.

25 The distinction between coercive interference and exploitation is developed at greater length in Peter Penz, "International Economic Justice and Exploitation," in *Global Justice, Global Democracy,* ed. Jay Drydyk and Peter Penz (Halifax, NS: Fernwood Publishing, 1997), 74-75.

26 Bradford Morse and Thomas Berger, *Sardar Sarovar: The Report of the Independent Review* (Ottawa, ON: Resource Futures International, 1992).

27 This discussion is not meant to indicate how a global government would actually operate; it is merely an attempt to articulate how a properly cosmopolitan institutional structure would express cosmopolitan values.

28 This point should not be overplayed: democracy in many states is superficial, often leaving the poor badly represented; moreover, majoritarian democracy is not necessarily distributively just.

29 Partly circumventing receiver states by using non-governmental organizations to deliver development assistance may well be highly efficacious from a cosmopolitan perspective. But it does mean that the donor state and the delivering non-governmental organizations set themselves up as the representatives of cosmopolitan values.

30 To the extent that there is a trade-off between these two kinds of human rights, the economic power relations behind the pressure for human rights could bias their promotion in favour of one rather than the other. To the extent that the relationship between these two sets of rights is mutually supportive, however, this argument has no weight. This position is widely held. See, for example, various Indian contributions in Smitu Kothari and Harsh Sethi, eds., *Human Rights: Challenges for Theory and Action* (New York, NY: New Horizons Press, 1989); and Jack Donnelly, *Universal Human Rights in Theory and Practice* (Ithaca, NY: Cornell University Press, 1989), 163-202.

Part 3
Ethics and Canadian Policies towards Human Rights and Development Assistance

4
Moral Vision and Foreign Policy: The Case of Canadian Development Assistance

Cranford Pratt

In the preceding chapter, Peter Penz challenges the realist and neorealist paradigms that still dominate the study of Canadian foreign and defence policies. He explores three differently based ethical challenges to the assumption central to these paradigms; that is, that international politics is, unavoidably, an amoral arena within which states act to promote their own self-interests. The three alternative foundations for an ethical foreign policy he labels sovereigntism, state internationalism, and cosmopolitanism. Sovereigntism requires that the pursuit of national self-interest be constrained by an ethical obligation to respect the sovereignty of other states. State internationalism recognizes that many highly desirable state objectives can only be pursued jointly with other states. In addition to the obligation of states to refrain from intervening in the affairs of other states, is the obligation to cooperate fairly and equitably in the promotion of objectives that they share with those states. Cosmopolitanism breaks free of the state-centred focus of both these ethical positions to argue that foreign policy must acknowledge the compelling force of obligations that we owe to those who live "beyond our borders."[1]

Penz argues that Canadian development assistance policies should reflect, indeed should be grounded in, cosmopolitan ethics. Within the ranks of those of us who wish Canadian policies to be more solidly grounded in ethics, there is much discussion about what this would in fact imply. Terisa Turner et al. (Chapter 6, this volume) in effect continue the discussion of cosmopolitan ethics by exploring a component that they see as essential to the articulation of ethically founded development assistance policies. They argue, on the basis of a powerful gendered analysis of the class struggle around agriculture development and land tenure in Kenya, that such an analysis must inform any development assistance policy that is genuinely to advance the poor in the societies it putatively seeks to help.

This chapter, along with Heather Smith's (Chapter 5, this volume), takes a different tack. Both chapters ask an essential but awkward empirical question, awkward in its potential to undermine the practical significance of any discussion of what are the most essential components of an ethical foreign policy: *Have the obligations towards those beyond our borders that a cosmopolitan ethics imposes upon Canadians in fact had a significant impact on Canadian foreign policy?* Smith explores whether recent Canadian foreign policy, despite its rhetoric, has been significantly responsive to the ethical obligation to protect and advance the human rights of those beyond our borders, surely an expected and needed component of any foreign policy that claims to be at all responsive to cosmopolitan ethical values.

This chapter asks whether cosmopolitan ethical considerations have played an important role in shaping Canadian foreign aid policy, a second element of Canadian foreign policy that might reasonably be expected to have been influenced by ethical values. This question fits uneasily within the intellectual paradigm that has long dominated the study of international relations at Canadian universities. That paradigm, neo-realism, accords little influence to ethical considerations in the shaping of the foreign policies of modern states; instead, at least in its earlier years, it sees international politics as essentially determined by the interaction of sovereign states, each motivated by the pursuit of national security and the advancement of national interests. Typically within this paradigm, it is assumed not only that states are not motivated by considerations of ethical obligations towards those beyond their borders, but also that it would be foolhardy and destructive of national interests for any state to seek to act ethically within the international realm.

Nevertheless, neo-realism has evolved in sophisticated ways to move it beyond its initial neo-Hobbesian assumption that international peace is best assured when there is a hegemonic superpower able to discipline any other state that might threaten international peace. Neorealist scholars have proven able to accommodate state behaviour that clearly does not issue from a single-minded pursuit of immediate national self-interests. Thus, for example, neorealists now easily acknowledge and, indeed, celebrate the contribution of widely accepted rules and understandings – "regimes" – that are legally unenforceable but that nevertheless greatly influence the behaviour of states and, despite the absence of a hegemonic power, ensure order and stability within a widening range of international policy areas. Similarly, neorealists are able to acknowledge a wide range of international initiatives to alleviate poverty or to promote peace in far distant lands – initiatives that seem, on the surface, to have been at least partially ethically motivated. In each of these examples, however, neorealists suggest that the dominant motivation continues to be national self-interest, but one informed by a sense of what will best ensure the *long-term* security of the state and advance its *long-term* national interests.[2]

There is here a conceptual distinction of central importance. Neorealists are not constrained by their paradigm to argue that states are motivated only in terms of their governments' perceptions of the immediate requirements of security and national interest. They can, for example, argue that there are circumstances in which a government can and should recognize that the long-term security and economic interests of its state require that it act in ways that would appear to contradict its immediate interests. Thus there can be arguments for foreign aid and for the promotion of international regimes that are essentially neorealist rather than ethical. Similarly, it can be argued as a neorealist proposition that the security of a state is best safeguarded not by a powerful military concerned only with the protection of its sovereignty but, rather, by active engagement with other states in projects to advance their common security.

It is certainly an important shift within the realist paradigm to move from a belief that the behaviour of states is best understood as the pursuit of immediate power and wealth advantages in a threatening world of equally selfish states to the view that states dare act upon the long-term advantages that flow from cooperation (and even a measure of generosity). However, this shift is not a response to anything that should be labelled ethical. Ethics intervenes when the motivation is no longer centrally focused on *national* security and *national* interests, however refined their conception and however extended their time frame. A foreign policy acquires an ethical component when it responds significantly to a concern for the welfare and well-being of foreigners for reasons unrelated to national interests and in response to sentiments of human solidarity and to an awakening acceptance of obligations towards those beyond its borders.[3]

That most international relations scholars continue to deny to cosmopolitan ethical values any significant role as an autonomous influence on the international conduct of states has always been more than a little anomalous. Particularly in democratic societies, public interest citizen groups, acting in resolute defiance of neorealist assumptions, are constantly seeking to make the foreign policy of their governments more responsive to ethical values. In no area of Canadian foreign policy is this anomaly more apparent than in regard to foreign aid. From the early 1960s on, a wide range of Canadian non-government organizations (NGOs) have actively advocated that Canadian development assistance should be more generous and more unambiguously focused on helping the world's poorest countries and peoples. Public opinion polls in Canada have long confirmed not only that a substantial majority of Canadians have supported Canadian foreign aid, but also that Canadians have ranked humanitarian reasons far higher than such narrowly national reasons as advancing Canadian trade and political interests as their explanation for this support.[4] A recent well focused and methodologically sophisticated poll confirms that these sentiments still predominate.[5]

These values and this advocacy have had a significant impact on the public discourse in Canada about foreign aid. Ethical values were central to the objectives for Canadian aid which were recommended by each of the three parliamentary committees that have reviewed Canadian aid policies since 1975.[6] As well, in 1975 and 1987, ethical considerations were centrally emphasized in the two major official policy statements of the objectives of Canadian aid policies, which were issued in the twenty-five years following the creation of the Canadian International Development Agency (CIDA) in 1968.[7]

Nevertheless very few scholarly commentators on Canadian aid policies have concluded that humanitarian considerations have in fact played a major role in the shaping of Canadian aid policies;[8] instead, a surprisingly wide range of other influences have received emphatic mention. These include international factors such as the politics of the Cold War, the example and influence of other major donors, the importance attached to Canada's primary alliances, considerations particular to Canada as a middle power, and domestic factors such as bureaucratic politics and the government's particular responsiveness to Canadian trade and investment interests. In contrast, Canadian ethical values are hardly mentioned in this literature.

This chapter revisits this issue. It asks afresh about the influence on Canadian development assistance of Canadian ethical values. For this volume it is a particularly telling question to raise. Prima facie, it seems reasonable to expect that a sensitivity towards the welfare of non-Canadians is unlikely to have an impact on Canadian defence and trade policies. However, such ethical sensitivities might nevertheless be expected to influence those foreign policies that do directly relate to the welfare of non-Canadians, policies such as those towards international human rights, towards international environment issues, and towards global poverty and international inequalities. The consideration here of the extent to which ethical values have influenced Canadian foreign aid is, therefore, likely to be generally indicative of the impact of ethical values within this cluster of foreign policies – policies that are at least nominally humanitarian in their purpose.

A Reappraisal of the Influence of Ethics on Canadian Development Assistance Policies

Ethical values within a dominant class perspective

The severely limited role that much scholarly writing acknowledges for ethical values in the shaping of Canadian foreign aid policies can be illustrated by their role within the theoretical perspective that I have found most illuminating – a dominant class perspective.[9] This perspective begins with the proposition that, within the broad parameters of the liberal public philosophy[10] that was dominant in Canada from 1945 until quite recently, the government has enjoyed significant autonomy in the shaping of Canadian foreign policy. It notes that this did not result in randomly determined policies. The senior decision makers have constituted a highly professional corps with a shared understanding of international politics, a common view that their responsibility is to advance Canadian interests, and, in many instances, a consensus on how Canadian interests can best be promoted. It is reasonable to call this cluster of dominant attitudes and convictions an ideology. That ideology is marked by an acceptance that one of the primary responsibilities of Canadian foreign policy is to ensure the health of the capitalist economic system on which the prosperity of Canadian society depends.

This ideology sets a second crucial factor alongside this influence. The world of Canadian foreign policy decision makers has long been dominated by considerations of sovereignty and national interests. For these officials, the preservation and expansion of Canadian influence and the containment of those states that are seen as potential enemies has been a second "natural" objective of Canadian foreign policy, additional to a particular sensitivity to the long-term interests of capitalism in Canada.[11]

Left at that, this theoretical approach would have been too schematic. Room had also to be found within it for the haphazard and unintegrated responses of government to societal pressures and, in particular, because of the nature of Canadian politics, to the lobbying of business interests. This approach need not totally exclude the influence of ethical values. For example, within its framework, it could be argued that societal values help determine the outside political limits that contain the autonomy of the decision makers. As well, it could be suggested that, as ethical values have provided the rhetoric that the government has used in presenting its aid program to the Canadian public, the government is likely to be susceptible at times to pressures to live up to its rhetoric. There is also room within this perspective for an occasional successful popular initiative that forces the government to act in ways that are counter to its actual wishes. Those working within this perspective, however, would argue that initiatives in which factors such as these have been important are few in number. Were they numerous and important, a dominant class perspective would need to yield place to a pluralist approach in which pressures from society itself are seen to be the key determinants of foreign policy.[12]

The clear implication of this analysis of Canadian policies towards less-developed countries has thus been that. while it is not impossible for ethical values to influence foreign policy decisions, it is unlikely to happen whenever that which is seen as ethically compelling conflicts significantly with either the economic interests of the dominant class in Canada or with important Canadian security or international political interests. The ideology that is dominant within Canadian decision-making circles operates to filter out such "soft" ethical objectives as promoting human rights or helping the world's poorest peoples, leaving security, trade and international political considerations as the dominant determinants of Canadian foreign policy.[13]

This perspective, I believe, remains substantially valid. However, a recent major study of the influence of ethical values on the foreign aid policies of the industrialized states, David Lumsdaine's *Moral Vision in International Politics: The Foreign Aid Regime 1945-89,*[14] provides an alternative, and radically different, framework of analysis. It is, at the least, an excellent foil against which to test currently held views.

Foreign aid as the realization of an emerging moral vision

Lumsdaine's central argument is that the primary determinant of the foreign aid programs that were initiated by most industrialized countries beginning in the 1950s and early 1960s was a new moral vision that had become a powerful component of the political values of their societies. One component of this vision was an acceptance that society has an obligation to care for the welfare of those of its citizens who suffered or were impoverished through no fault of their own. By the 1950s, this ethical obligation already had had a significant impact on public policy, producing in country after country the phenomenon of the welfare state. The second part of this moral vision was an emerging sense of global solidarity, a belief that a more just international order was achievable in the post-1945 era and that it ought to be pursued.

Lumsdaine does not deny that foreign aid to the newly independent states was first developed to keep them out of the Soviet camp and that this continued to be an important part of the motivation behind the foreign aid programs of Western governments. However, he suggests that, without the presence and influence of these ethical convictions – this moral vision – within the political cultures of the industrialized countries, foreign aid programs could not have become a significant part of their foreign policies. They would, indeed, have been politically inconceivable. Lumsdaine thus challenges both the dominant class approach and a wide range of neorealist interpretations of the determinants of the foreign aid policies of these states. He is not alone in this conviction. Jean-Philippe Thérien and Noël Alain have recently demonstrated that there is a close correlation in the industrialized donor states between ethically responsive domestic welfare programs values and generous foreign aid programs.[15]

Lumsdaine recognizes that commercial and geo-political objectives have often greatly influenced foreign aid, especially in its early years. Nevertheless, he argues that ethical considerations gradually displaced economic and geo-political factors as the key determinant of Western aid policies. How else, he asks, can one explain why so much aid has been spent on countries that are of little economic or political significance, or why those countries with the most generous programs (such as the Nordic countries and the Netherlands) are countries with strong domestic social programs but without major economic or geo-political interests in the Third World?

Lumsdaine offers a plausible multiple-cause explanation of how ethical values have actually had the influence that he attributes to them. He notes that when Western governments presented their aid programs to their own publics, for domestic political reasons they typically stressed that this aid was humanitarian in purpose. Aid advocates were then able to use this rhetoric against their governments whenever that aid showed clear signs of becoming more commercial or political in its objectives. He points to the fact that in each of the donor countries there were strong and articulate advocates of generous humanitarian aid programs. They became the voice of their society's conscience, holding its government to the policy commitments implied in its rhetoric. Their efforts were aided by the bureaucracies of the official aid agencies who, in most states, were committed to the putative development and humanitarian objectives of the programs they administered and were their vigorous advocates within their governments. Having good aid programs was, in turn, seen as an appropriate way for states to win both international and domestic approval, thus providing solid neorealist considerations that also favoured respectable aid policies.

Does the richly detailed analysis offered by Lumsdaine illuminate the Canadian experience? Can the history of CIDA be read as a gradual but increasing realization, in policy and practice, of the cosmopolitan component of Canadian ethical values?

Reappraising the influence of ethics on Canadian foreign aid policies

Any reappraisal must begin with the fact that, at its inception, Canadian development assistance was very much a product of Cold War alliance politics.[16] In the late 1950s and early 1960s, only the United States, France, and Britain had significant foreign aid programs. As a major purpose of their aid was to contain any expansion of Soviet influence, these major powers (particularly the United States) pressed their allies to assume part of this burden. Canadian aid thus began, timidly and somewhat begrudgingly, as an obligation arising from our major alliances. It can hardly be seen as having been required by, or even issuing from, the ethical values of Canadian society.

Nevertheless, any adequate explanation of the origins of Canadian development assistance needs to acknowledge that, in the years immediately after the Second World War, there were present in Canada many factors that were identical to, or that closely paralleled, those emphasized by Lumsdaine. The advent of the welfare state, the international idealism generated by the war aims pronounced by the Allied leaders, and the success of the Marshall Plan (which was popularly viewed as a grand humanitarian enterprise) all contributed to an intellectual and ideological climate in Canada that made foreign aid to the newly independent countries seem almost self-evidently a particularly appropriate way to contain communism.

There was then a period of about ten years, from 1966 to 1976, during which Canadian overseas development assistance (ODA) grew quite prodigiously, from US$96.5 million in 1965 to US$880 million in 1975. This aid rose as a percentage of Canada's GNP from 0.2 percent in 1965 to 0.55 percent ten years later.[17] Many of the factors that Lumsdaine identifies were certainly present in Canada during these years and contributed to this transformation of the Canadian aid program. There was in Canada, as in the Scandinavian countries and the Netherlands, widespread and deep-rooted public support for strong social welfare programs at home. Thus there was a fundamental congruity between domestic social values and the values needed to underpin a vigorous aid program. Moreover, the government presented the aid program as a humanitarian enterprise, thus underlining that link. A surge of citizen involvement with the issue of global poverty provided a foundation of strong public support for an expanded aid program. Finally, there was within the federal government an enlarged CIDA bureaucracy that was very much committed to, and actively promoting, the humanitarian objectives of the program.

All of these influences were, in turn, powerfully reinforced by several additional factors that were quite specific to those years. At that time it was comparatively easy to expand the aid program, for the Canadian economy was prosperous and government revenues were rising. More directly relevant, there was a political need in the late 1960s for the government to demonstrate that, despite its caution about criticizing the US war in Vietnam, it was well able to articulate a foreign policy different from that of the United States. Because of the strength of social idealism in Canada at that time, a major foreign aid policy that was genuinely committed to humane internationalist objectives was seen as a particularly appropriate way to demonstrate Canada's independence from the Unites States. Finally, as if confirming and consolidating the humanitarian and developmental focus of Canadian aid, in 1975 the Canadian Cabinet endorsed a five-year strategy for CIDA that articulated ethical considerations to a far more substantial extent than had any earlier policy statement.[18]

All this closely fits Lumsdaine's analysis. However, this conjuncture of circumstances, which worked to the distinct advantage of the aid program, did not last. As a result, Canadian aid policies cannot really be interpreted as illustrating the increasing realization in public policy of a new moral vision that had seized the consciences of the world's rich countries. If simply transcribed to the Canadian case, Lumsdaine's analysis would miss too much. It would severely underplay the central importance of the commitment of the Canadian government to protect and advance the interests of capitalism in Canada. It would also miss the undeniable truth that moral visions not only flower, they also wilt. Lumsdaine made an important contribution by linking the emergence of the international aid regime to the social values that were prominent in most of the industrialized countries in the years between 1945 and the late 1970s. However, from then on, those values have been in marked retreat, leaving development assistance with a less secure foundation within Canadian social and political values.

The liberal internationalism that had been central to Canada's foreign policy yielded to a preoccupation with Canada's relations with the US and with Canada's membership in the Economic Summit. The global economic crisis of the post-Organization of Petroleum Producing Countries (OPEC) era and the long-term structural problems in the Canadian economy to which it drew attention, generated a powerful official preoccupation with Canada's international economic prospects, crowding out any concern for global equity. Those urging that more effective expression be given internationally to Canadian humanitarian values suddenly sounded naive.

Following the appointment of Michel Dupuy as president of CIDA in March 1977, the dominant trend in Canadian development assistance policies quickly became very much the reverse of Lumsdaine's expectations. It is the judgment of most scholarly observers of CIDA that Canadian aid policies since 1977 have been increasingly subverted to serve Canadian trade and foreign policy interests.[19] Humanitarian considerations have not been obliterated, but they have been required increasingly to yield place to self-interested Canadian economic and international political objectives.

Examples of this are many. The 1975-80 CIDA strategy paper, with its clear humane internationalist thrust, quickly ceased to be a major determinant of policy; instead, CIDA was called upon to give far greater emphasis to Canadian trade and foreign policy interests. From the early 1980s on, CIDA became, in the words of its president at that time, "a policy taker not a policy maker."[20] The policies that were made for it emphasized that aid must serve Canadian trade and international political interests. Many developments illustrate this. The portion of CIDA's bilateral program that was reserved for countries in which Canadian exporters had a special interest was recurrently increased, rising from 8 percent in 1972 to 25 percent in 1986. In these same years, CIDA developed major aid programs in countries such as Thailand, Indonesia, and the Philippines in order to provide an entry into these countries, which were important geo-politically and constituted rapidly expanding markets. It introduced a range of programs under which Canadian aid to recipient countries was dependent on the award of contracts to Canadian businesses. It planned to use half of the excess of CIDA's budget – over 0.5 percent of Canada's GNP – for an aid-trade fund that would be centrally concerned with trade promotion. All Canadian food aid, including emergency food aid, remained very narrowly tied to Canadian products, with the value to the recipients of that aid further lessened by the inclusion in the non-emergency aid of less appropriate products that were, however, forming a current surplus in Canada.[21]

The collapse of the Soviet Union in 1989, far from releasing resources (some of which might have augmented the foreign aid budget), provided an additional justification for further cuts to the aid budget. The two central components of the ideology that dominates Canadian foreign policy making – a commitment to advance the interests of capitalism in Canada and a concern to increase Canada's influence in international affairs – operated to ensure that the end of the Cold War brought neither additional resources to foreign aid nor an increase in its focus on humanitarian objectives, both of which Lumsdaine had predicted would occur in donor states after the end of the Cold War. A recent authoritative analysis reports that the ratio of Canada's ODA to its GNP, which was a not-inspiring 0.5 percent in 1984-85, had been cut to 0.27 percent by 1998.[22] Coincidental with this, the government's central preoccupation with improving Canada's competitive position in the international economic system further intensified the erosion of the humane internationalist focus of Canadian aid policies.

The pressures from within government for this erosion came in particular from the Department of External Affairs and International Trade. For several months, beginning in December 1992, the department sought to bring CIDA more closely under its policy direction. To that end it sought Cabinet approval of an International Assistance Policy Update paper.[23] This paper proposed "an over-arching policy framework to provide coherence in objectives, strategies and funding in accordance with foreign policy priorities." It gave major emphasis "to position[ing] the private sector for long-term market penetration" and to the creation of "foreign policy thematic funds ... [that] would permit us to remain in countries of significant importance to Canada." It favoured a quite dramatic shift in the distribution of the resources that CIDA devotes to its bilateral programs, from assistance to the poorest countries to programs that would be closely related to Canadian economic and political interests.[24] Though the pending federal election finally led the prime minister to decide that this paper would not be acted upon, its very existence revealed how distant the Department of External Affairs and International Trade was from an ethically informed view of the objectives of development assistance.

This trend in Canadian aid policies was finally enshrined in public policy by the Liberal government in its 1995 foreign policy statement.[25] This statement significantly diluted the government's formal commitment to devote its aid funds to helping the world's poorest; instead it declared: "International assistance is a vital instrument for the achievement of the three key objectives being pursued by the government. It is an investment in prosperity and employment ... It connects the Canadian economy to some of the fastest growing markets ... [I]t contributes to global security ... [and] is one of the clearest expressions of Canadian values."[26] Thus, even in regard to foreign aid, emphasis was first given to trade and security considerations.[27]

Despite this erosion of the humane internationalism of Canada's aid policies since 1977, the humanitarian component within Canada's aid program has not been obliterated. Humane internationalism retained a resilience that is not easily explained in dominant class terms. As already noted, the important 1987 parliamentary committee that reviewed Canadian aid policies called for a renewal of CIDA's primary commitment to humanitarian objectives. There were still, within CIDA, many who are striving to preserve as much as possible of CIDA's earlier commitment to reach and help the poorest. Even after the lessening of the emphasis on poverty alleviation in the mandate given to CIDA in *Canada in the World,* and coincident with the severe cuts to the aid budget, CIDA, under the leadership of President Hugette Labelle and Vice-President John Robinson, manoeuvred to retain a significant focus on assistance to the world's poorest. As a result, much Canadian aid still goes to very poor countries that are of little economic or geo-political interest to Canada. Meeting the basic needs of the poorest was reaffirmed as a centrally important objective of CIDA policies,[28] and, more important still, in 1996 CIDA issued a policy statement that sought to establish poverty reduction as the common integrating theme of all CIDA programs.[29] All this was strongly endorsed by the NGO community. In 1996, the Canadian Council for International Cooperation (CCIC), still speaking out for older humane internationalist values, launched a major national public education program, "In Common," which advocated that poverty eradication must become a top priority of Canadian domestic and foreign policies.[30]

Nevertheless in the summer of 1999, CCIC was forced to conclude that "overall trends in funding suggest that poverty reduction remains a relatively low priority."[31] It pointed out that:

- the current allocation for sustainable basic human needs is 19.4% of total Canadian ODA, far short of the target of 30% recommended by CCIC
- between the years 1990/91 and 1995/96 CIDA spending on agriculture food and nutrition fell by 49% and by 80% in Africa
- aid to sub-Saharan Africa declined in nominal dollars by 29.1% between 1992/93 and 1997/98

- Canadian aid to the forty-eight Least Developed countries which had earlier approached the UN target of 0.15% of GNP, fell to a low of 0.07% in 1997-98
- Canadian aid to such UN institutions as UNDP and UNICEF whose programs concentrate on assistance to the poorest, fell by 29.4% between 1992/93 and 1997/98.

The judgment offered here is that ethical considerations continue to have a lessening impact on Canadian foreign aid policy, though they still retain a capacity to influence. Both aspects of this judgment are illustrated by two important recent inputs into foreign policy decision making that were specifically political in origin. The first of these were the efforts of Lloyd Axworthy, as minister of foreign affairs, to make "human security" central to his many expositions of the objectives of Canadian foreign policy.[32] He projected into the international arena the proposition that the advancement of the personal security of the individual, rather than protection of national sovereignty, ought to become a central guiding principle in international relations. Axworthy's advocacy of human security cannot be viewed as a subterfuge for a special advocacy of international action on issues of special importance to Canadian security or commercial interests. His leadership in the successful international campaign to ban anti-personnel landmines, his championing of international agreements to eliminate child labour, and his efforts to halt the proliferation of military small arms all reflected genuine ethical commitment.

However, for those favouring an ethically responsive foreign aid policy, Axworthy's championing of human security nevertheless merits only two cheers. He repeatedly failed to include effective action to lessen global human poverty and to increase global equity as essential components of a foreign policy that takes seriously the promotion of global human security as one of its central objectives. Axworthy's human security was, in effect, liberal internationalism especially tailored for a Liberal government that was overwhelmingly preoccupied with fiscal restraint, trade promotion, and Canada's international economic competitiveness in an open international economic order. His failure to address global poverty and severe international inequities quite probably reflected a political judgment that the initiatives he was taking were the most that his colleagues would accept. Such an assessment does justice to Axworthy's integrity and political shrewdness, but, by implication, it also reinforces the view argued here that the Canadian government has, in recent years, given less weight to ethical considerations in its determination of Canada's foreign aid policy.

The second recent input into Canadian foreign aid policy making – which might, at first, be seen as a heightened responsiveness to international ethical obligations but which, in fact, illustrates how constrained is any such effort on the part of a minister of international cooperation – has been the particular policy input of Maria Minna, who was appointed minister of international cooperation in August 1999. She brought to CIDA a concern for the welfare of the poor that had long been central to her approach to domestic social and economic issues. She worked hard to ensure that CIDA would give far greater emphasis to the social development component of its programs. These efforts culminated in the publication, in September 2000, of a CIDA policy statement concerning its social development programs.[33]

Anticipating the early announcement of a federal election in November 2000, Minister Minna had rushed this announcement of new social development priorities (SDP) and attempted, within it, to commit whoever might become the minister of international cooperation after the pending election, to major increases in CIDA spending in the social development policy areas she favoured. There is little indication that they represent a consensus within CIDA. As well, many key elements within the framework paper are identified as issues that are still to be settled. These include the identification of CIDA programs that will be cut in order that the proposed expansions can go forward as well as the countries, far fewer than those now receiving Canadian bilateral aid, that are to be the recipients of the substantial increases in social development assistance.

This framework paper very much reflects Minna's ethical commitments. It identifies four policy areas to which it assigns the highest priority – basic education, health and nutrition, HIV/AIDS, and child protection. In addition, it set out a schedule of expenditures for each of these, which, if followed, would raise the total annual spending on them from $222 million in 2000 to $585 million in 2005. The SDP framework paper thus constituted a major ministerial effort to give greater ethical content to Canadian aid policies.

However, several aspects of this SDP framework paper must be noted, as these, like Axworthy's human security initiative, call for a cautious assessment. Minister Minna and CIDA have failed to place these policies within a holistic poverty reduction strategy.[34] They have not integrated them within a wide range of other measures that are equally relevant to poverty reduction and equally essential to a comprehensive poverty-focused development strategy. These additional measures would include programs to increase the access of the poor to land and employment, to meet other of their basic human needs, to improve their productivity, to empower them socially and politically, and to lessen environmental insecurity. It is clear from an earlier exchange of letters between the minister and the CCIC that Minna had wanted to achieve a holistic strategy on poverty reduction. Addressing her desire to increase CIDA spending on basic education, health and nutrition, HIV/AIDS, and child protection, she wrote:

> I see the strengthened programming in these four areas as but the first step in reinvigorating CIDA's effectiveness in delivering its core mandate, poverty reduction. I am pleased to see you underline the importance of using a poverty eradication "lens" to guide our actions, and agree that it is the analytical framework that can prevent strengthening in one area from undermining supportive action in others ... For effective long-term development policy to work, we must use holistic, participatory methods.[35]

Minna, however, has not been able to ensure that the Social Development Priorities paper was followed by the production of a long-term strategy for Canadian development assistance that would recommit CIDA to a primary emphasis on helping the poorest peoples and countries to augment their welfare, increase their productivity, and enhance their social and political empowerment. Instead, more powerful determinants of Canadian aid policies reasserted themselves. A new president of CIDA was appointed, Mr. Len Good, who initiated a major and sustained effort to re-order CIDA's major programs so that they would reflect and assist important Canadian foreign policy interests, including, in particular, securing the cooperation and participation of developing countries in international negotiations and agreements relating to international trade and the global environment.

It is fundamentally unlikely that any Canadian government will move markedly to a poverty-focused strategy for foreign aid – one that would be more fully responsive to cosmopolitan values. The underlying social values of such an aid strategy would be clearly out of harmony with both the dominant ideology in senior foreign policy making circles and with Canada's declining acceptance of public obligations towards its own poor. In the decade between 1966 and 1976, the shift in the Canadian public philosophy that underlay the development of the welfare state greatly facilitated the development of an aid program that was both much more substantial and significantly more responsive to the needs of the poorest peoples and countries. Today, with dominant Canadian values in marked retreat from the values of that era, it is much less likely that any Canadian government will, on ethical grounds, increase significantly the resources it devotes to foreign aid and ensure that such assistance is used more effectively to aid the poorest peoples and countries.

References to ethical values clearly must still figure in any adequate explanation of what is happening to Canada's aid program. However, these references are more likely to refer to determined rearguard efforts by their champions both inside and outside government to retain a significant humanitarian component within the aid program than to any increasing influence of these values on Canadian aid policy.

Conclusions

This reappraisal of the determinants of Canadian foreign aid policies suggests that the emergence of a greater responsiveness to the needs of Canadians who are in severe poverty greatly facilitated the emergence of greater foreign policy responsiveness to the challenge of global poverty. This was, in turn, an important determinant of the major growth in the foreign aid program between 1966 and 1975, and of its increasing focus on aiding and helping the poorest peoples and countries. As well, the continuing strength of the commitment to these values within CIDA and, more widely, within the NGO community, helps to explain the surprising resilience until very recently of CIDA's efforts to ensure that the reduction of poverty remain the integrating feature of its programs.

However, it is just not possible to claim that Canadian development assistance illustrates the gradual embodiment, in public policy, of a moral vision. From 1976 on, the government's central preoccupation with advancing Canadian international economic and political interests has consistently diluted the putative humanitarian focus of Canadian aid, reversing the earlier ten-year trend that had suggested an increasing government responsiveness to humane internationalist values. In the years since then, this retreat has been significantly reinforced by a diminution in the responsiveness of Canadian governments to the needs of those who live in severe poverty in Canada itself and, pari passu, with the needs of those who live in poverty beyond our borders.

Thus it must be concluded that ethical values, though still an influence to be acknowledged in any assessment of the determinants of Canadian aid policies, have had neither a sustained nor an increasing impact on Canadian development assistance policies over the last two decades. If this is true in regard to aid policies, then it is reasonable to expect that it is also true in regard to other areas of Canadian foreign policy.

Acknowledgment

Research for this chapter was made possible by a grant from the Social Sciences and Humanities Research Council, and this is gratefully acknowledged.

Notes

1 I borrow this expression from one of the most influential essays of recent decades on the reach and force of cosmopolitan obligations, Stanley Hoffmann's *Duties beyond Borders: On the Limits and Possibilities of Ethical International Politics* (Syracuse: Syracuse University Press, 1981).

2 Two important Canadian examples of this employment of security arguments for proposals that might alternatively have been advocated for ethical reasons are *Canada 21: Canada and Common Security in the 21st Century* (Toronto: Centre for International Studies, University of Toronto, 1994); and International Development Research Policy Task Force, Maurice Strong, Chairman, *Connecting with the World: Priorities for Canadian Internationalism in the 21st Century* (Ottawa: IDRC, 1996).

3 This is not to suggest that what is ethically required of a state is not often also in its long-term interests. Indeed, it is within a fine tradition in ethical philosophy to argue that ethically correct behaviour will prove, in the long run, to be more genuinely self-fulfilling than more hedonistically motivated conduct.
4 These polls are summarized in Réal Lavergne, "Determinants of Canadian Aid Policies," in *Western Middle Powers and Global Poverty: the Determinants of the Aid Policies of Canada, Denmark, The Netherlands, Norway and Sweden,* ed. Olav Stokke (Uppsala: Scandinavian Institute of African Studies, 1989), 36-40; and in my "Humane Internationalism and Canadian Development Assistance Policies," in *Canadian International Development Assistance Policies: An Appraisal,* ed. Cranford Pratt (Montreal and Kingston: McGill-Queens University Press 1994/96), 334-38.
5 Angus Reid Group, *Canadians Support for Development Assistance: Final Report* (Ottawa: CIDA, September 1997), 22.
6 The Parliamentary Task Force on North-South Relations, *Report to the House Of Commons on the Relations Between Developed and Developing Countries* (Hull: Supply and Services, 1980); *For Whose Benefit? Report of the Standing Committee on External Affairs and International Trade on Canada's Official Development Assistance Policies and Programs* (Ottawa: Supply and Services, 1987); and the Special Joint Committee Reviewing Canadian Foreign Policy, *Canada's Foreign Policy: Principles and Priorities for the Future* (Ottawa: Parliamentary Publications Directorate, 1994).
7 *Strategy for International Development Cooperation, 1975-1980* (Ottawa: CIDA, 1975); *Sharing Our Future: Canada's International Development Assistance* (Ottawa: Supply and Services, 1987).
8 This is true of Keith Spicer, *The Samaritan State: External Aid in Canadian Foreign Policy* (Toronto: University of Toronto Press, 1966); Leonard Dudley and Claude Monmarquette, *The Supply of Canadian Foreign Aid: Explanation and Evaluation* (Ottawa: Economic Council of Canada, 1978); Linda Freeman, "Canada's Interest in Development Assistance: The Political Economy of Canada's Foreign Aid Programme," presented to the annual meeting of the Canadian Political Science Association, Montreal 1980; Robert Carty and Virginia Smith, *Perpetuating Poverty: The Political Economy of Canadian Foreign Aid* (Toronto: Between the Lines, 1981); Monique Dupuis, *Crise mondiale et aide internationale: stratégie et développement Tiers-Monde,* (Montreal: Edition Nouvelle Optique, 1984); Kim Nossal, "Mixed Motives Revisited: Canadian Interest in Development Assistance," *Canadian Journal of Political Science* 21, 1 (1988): 35-56; Patricia Appavoo, "The Small State as Donor: Canadian and Swedish Development Assistance Policies Compared 1960-1976," (PhD thesis, University of Toronto, 1989); Cranford Pratt, "Canada: An Eroding and Limited Internationalism," in *Internationalism Under Strain: The North-South Policies of Canada, the Netherlands, Norway and Sweden,* ed. Cranford Pratt (Toronto: University of Toronto Press, 1989); Martin Rudner, "Canada's Official Development Strategy: Process, Goals and Priorities," *Canadian Journal of Development Studies* 12, 1 (1991): 9-37; Mark W. Charlton, *The Making of Canadian Food Aid Policy* (Montreal and Kingston: McGill-Queens University Press, 1992); Cranford Pratt, *Canadian International Development Assistance Policies: An Appraisal* (Toronto, University of Toronto Press, 1994, 1996); and David Morrison, *Aid and Ebb Tide: A History of CIDA and Canadian Development Assistance* (Waterloo: Wilfrid Laurier University Press, 1998). The major exceptions are Réal Lavergne, "Determinants of Canadian Aid Policies," in Stokke, *Global Poverty,* 9-33; and Noël Alain and Jean-Philippe Thérien, "Welfare Institutions and Foreign Aid: Domestic Foundations of Canadian Foreign Policy," *Canadian Journal of Political Science* 37, 3 (1994): 529-58.
9 For a fuller exposition of this theoretical perspective, see Pratt, "Canada: An Eroding ... Internationalism." The label, a dominant class perspective, draws attention to that feature that separates this approach from the predominant statist emphasis in much of the literature. The most influential statist reading of Canadian aid policies is Nossal's "Mixed Motives Revisited ." The two approaches are authoritatively contrasted in Morrison, *Aid and Ebb Tide,* 430-42; and in David Black and Heather Smith, "Notable Exceptions: New and Arrested Developments in Canadian Foreign Policy Literature," *Canadian Journal of*

Political Science 36 (1993): 745-74. See also my "Competing Perspectives on Canadian Development Assistance," *International Journal* 51, 2 (1996): 235-58.

10 Ronald Manzer has given the term "public philosophy" to the dominant set of values that shape a country's outlook on public affairs. See Ronald Manzer, *Public Policies and Political Development in Canada* (Toronto: University of Toronto Press, 1985).

11 Mark Neufeld has advanced the subtlety and coherence of this dominant class perspective by incorporating into it the neo-Gramscian idea of capitalist hegemony, thus linking the dominant class factor and the international political factor. See Mark Neufeld, "Hegemony and Foreign Policy Analysis: The Case of Canada as a Middle Power," *Studies in Political Economy* 48 (1995): 7-29.

12 A similar argument could also be developed in regard to the ability of a statist perspective on the determinants of foreign policy to accommodate ethical influences. Indeed, Kim Nossal did just that in his influential "Analyzing the Domestic Sources of Canadian Foreign Policy," *International Journal* 39, 1 (Winter 1983-84): 1-22. Such a perspective permits a limited role for a society's ethical values in terms not dissimilar to those suggested above in the context of a dominant class perspective; however, as with the dominant class perspective, if that role were seen as significant, the perspective would slip into a pluralist approach.

13 A similar reading of the ideology dominant within the Department of External Affairs and International Trade is provided in Victoria Berry and Allan McChesney, "Human Rights and Foreign Policy-Making," in Robert Matthews and Cranford Pratt (eds.), *Human Rights in Canadian Foreign Policy* (Montreal and Kingston: McGill-Queens University Press, 1988), 59-78.

14 David Halloran Lumsdaine, *Moral Vision in International Politics: the Foreign Aid Regime 1949-1989* (Princeton: Princeton University Press, 1993).

15 Noël Alain and Jean-Philippe Thérien, "From Domestic to International Justice: The Welfare State and Foreign Aid," *International Organization* 43, 2 (1995): 523-53.

16 The early years of Canadian aid are fully discussed in Morrison, *Aid and Ebb Tide;* Appavoo, "The Small State"; and Spicer, *The Samaritan State.*

17 These figures are drawn from *Development Assistance: Efforts and Policies of the Members of the Development Assistance Committee* 1969 Review (Paris: OECD, 1970), 298 and 309; and *Development Cooperation: Efforts and Policies of the Members of the Development Assistance Committee, 1978 Review* (Paris: OECD, 1979), 191.

18 Canadian International Development Agency, *Strategy for International Development Cooperation 1975-1980* (Ottawa: CIDA, 1975).

19 See, for example, Rudner, "Canada's Official Development Strategy"; Pratt "Canada: An Eroding ... Internationalism"; the contributions of Morrison, Gillies, Burdette, and Pratt in Pratt, *Canadian International Development Assistance;* and Morrison, *Aid and Ebb Tide.*

20 As quoted in Phillip Rawkins, "An Institutional Analysis of CIDA," in Pratt, *Canadian International Development Assistance Policies,* 162.

21 This reading of Canadian aid policies in the years 1977 to 1989 summarizes the analysis in Pratt, "Canada: An Eroding ... Internationalism."

22 Brian Tomlinson, *A Call to End Global Poverty: Renewing Canadian Aid Policy and Practice – A Policy Background Paper* (Ottawa: Canadian Council for International Cooperation, March 1999), 57.

23 As part of the interdepartmental infighting at the time, this important paper was leaked to the NGO community in January 1993. The quotations below are from copies of that paper that were made available to the author by the Canadian Council for International Cooperation and the North-South Institute.

24 This paper is more fully discussed in Pratt, "Humane Internationalism," 359-61.

25 *Canada in the World: A Government Statement* (Ottawa: Department of Foreign Affairs and International Trade, 1995).

26 Ibid., 40.

27 For fuller elaboration of the evidence for this reading of the development of Canadian aid policies under Liberal rule, see my "Development Assistance and Canadian Foreign Policy:

Where We Now Are," *Canadian Foreign Policy* 2,3 (1994-95): 77-85; and "DFAIT's Takeover Bid of CIDA: The Institutional Future of the Canadian International Development Agency," *Canadian Foreign Policy* 5, 2 (1998): 1-14.

28 *CIDA's Policy on Meeting Basic Human Needs* (Hull: CIDA, 1997).

29 *CIDA's Policy on Poverty Reduction* (Hull: CIDA, 1996).

30 For details of the arguments offered from the NGO community, and for evidence of their quality, see *What We Can Do: A 10-Point Agenda for Global Action against Poverty* (Ottawa: CCIC, 1997); and Brian Tomlinson, *A Call to End Global Poverty: Renewing Canadian Aid Policy and Practice* (Ottawa: CCIC, 1999).

31 CCIC, *Strategies for Renewing Canadian Aid: Key Messages*. Available at <www.fly.web.net/ccic>.

32 Axworthy's advocacy of human security as a central focus of Canadian foreign policy has been subjected to extensive critical scholarly dissection, the most sustained and accomplished of which is Fen Osler Hampson and Dean Oliver's "Pulpit Diplomacy: A Critical Assessment of the Axworthy Doctrine" *International Journal* 54, 3 (Summer 1999): 379-406. My own contribution to this discourse is my "Competing Rationales for Canadian Development Assistance," *International Journal* 54, 2 (Spring 1999): 306-23. For examples of Lloyd Axworthy's spirited advocacy, see his "Canada and Human Security: The Need for Leadership," *International Journal* 52, 2 (Spring, 1997): 183-96; and "Notes for an Address by the Honorable Lloyd Axworthy, Minister of Foreign Affairs, to the 51st General Assembly of the United Nations" (available at <www.dfait.maici-gc.ca>).

33 *CIDA's Social Development Priorities: A Framework for Action*. Available at <www.dfait-maici.gc.ca>.

34 This point was forcefully put by CCIC in its comments on the framework paper. See Policy Team, Canadian Council for International Cooperation, *CIDA's Social Development Priorities: A Framework for Action – A CCIC Summary and Analysis* (September 2000), 9. Available at <www.fly.web.net/ccic>.

35 From a letter from Minister Minna to the CCIC, dated 7 July 2000. See CCIC, *Minister Minna's Social Agenda for CIDA: An Exchange of Letters* (July 2000), 4. Available at <www.fly.web.net/ccic>.

5
Niche Diplomacy in Canadian Human Rights Policy: Ethics or Economics?

Heather A. Smith

> The human security agenda is an effort to construct a global society in which the safety of people is an international priority and a motivating force for international action; where international humanitarian standards and the rule of law are advanced and woven into a coherent web protecting the individual; where those who violate these standards are held fully accountable.
>
> – Lloyd Axworthy

The words above come from a statement made by Minister of Foreign Affairs Lloyd Axworthy in June 1999.[1] From this pronouncement, and many others, one would conclude that human security is at the centre of Canadian foreign policy (CFP). Human security, new to the CFP lexicon, leads us to consider the interrelated threats, ranging from environmental degradation, gross human rights violations, and poverty, that affect humans and not just states. Human security, if it was actually ever put into practice in any substantive way, has the potential to give expression to a more humane cosmopolitan internationalism. The term "cosmopolitan" is meant to denote an ethical foreign policy – one that accepts our moral obligations and duties to others. It also recognizes the interconnectedness of global issues, thus militating against focusing on one pillar to the detriment of another. It demands that decision makers think broadly and recognize the linkages between issues rather than dissect the whole for the sake of the parts.

Minister Axworthy has recently claimed that human security is now more than a theoretical construct: it is now practice. In the case of Canadian human rights practices this claim is hard to substantiate. Human security remains an aspiration. CFP is not driven by the global cosmopolitan humane internationalism that Axworthy espouses and that this author supports; rather, CFP has been, and continues to be, driven by a narrow variant of internationalism that, while recognizing some level of interconnectedness, dilutes ethical obligations and tends to assign greater status to the liberal economic pillar of human security.[2] This is especially obvious in the case of human rights.

The privileging of the economic pillar is reflected in the theory and practice of niche diplomacy. Niche diplomacy can best be understood as a strategy for achieving particular policy ends. But strategy is not isolated from guiding principles. Driven by neoliberal and realist principles, niche diplomacy clashes with the cosmopolitan aspirations of human security. In the end, it is a niche diplomatic strategy that is realized in Canadian human rights policies that sacrifice human dignity to the pursuit of economic competitiveness.

The pronouncements of the minister of foreign affairs, Lloyd Axworthy, particularly during the period between 1996 and 1997, gave clear expression to the concept of niche diplomacy as articulated by Andrew Cooper and Evan Potter.[3] While the minister had stated that he prefers the term "selective foreign policy,"[4] he nonetheless identified Canadian niches in several issue areas, including human rights, peacebuilding, and international communications.[5] Axworthy's more recent statements have a softer tone, possibly suggesting a move away from the neoliberal and realist logic of niche diplomacy. This does not represent, however, a fundamental shift away from niche diplomacy in practice; and such efforts to bolster the image of a Canada that is driven by humane internationalism must be greeted with scepticism.

This chapter begins with an overview of the concept of niche diplomacy. This idea merits careful consideration because it comes with a political and economic agenda that legitimizes the narrowing of CFP and, thus, undermines the credibility of foreign policy initiatives in areas such as human rights. I then turn to an assessment of niche diplomacy as articulated by foreign policy decision makers. It will be seen that, while the idea of niches and its attendant concepts are especially obvious in statements made between 1996 and 1997, the influence of niche diplomacy can also be identified in more recent statements. The third substantive section of the chapter considers the relationship between human rights policy and niche diplomacy, arguing that the assumptions of niche diplomacy, rather than human security, inform Canadian human rights policy. The final section reflects on the implications of this chapter for human security and human rights policy.

Niche Diplomacy Described

Niche diplomacy is premised on the view that, in an era of fiscal restraint, Canada must make some hard choices if its foreign policy is to remain credible. Cooper argues that we are faced with a commitment-credibility gap and that it is in our national interest to adopt a discrete, rather than a diffuse, approach to Canadian foreign policy.[6] Potter, too, points to the need to ensure that our policy choices are made with a "clear and identifiable Canadian interest"[7] in mind. We must rationalize, be selective, and draw on areas of Canada's comparative advantage. Foreign policy must be effective, and we must select areas where we have "maximum impact."[8]

These authors make several prescriptions for the implementation of niche diplomacy. First, areas of specialization must be identified. The suggestions from both authors tend to focus on non-traditional areas of foreign policy that have received substantial support from Axworthy. Specific issue areas include women's rights, children's rights, comprehensive security, reform of financial institutions, protection of natural resources, and peacebuilding. Potter emphasizes the importance of soft power, which comes from knowledge and ideas rather than from the use of force, and he links soft power to information technologies and the "energizing of the cultural pillar of the foreign policy agenda."[9] Potter also focuses on international communications and international migration as areas worthy of niche selection.

The devolution of foreign policy responsibility to non-governmental organizations (NGOs), academics, philanthropic organizations, and business groups, is also suggested. Additional components of this strategy, identified by Potter, include making use of individuals in important portfolios in various international organizations, downsizing diplomatic missions and withdrawing from business promotion in Western Europe and the United States.[10]

Both authors concede that these prescriptions will face obstacles, but they also argue that a complex international agenda demands that we practise niche diplomacy. By making the necessary choices and targeting resources, we will close the commitment-credibility gap, thus ensuring that Canada continues to play a leading role in the world. But we are cautioned by Cooper that, if we are to continue to play this leading role, then "Canada must make its priorities clear and effectively marshall its talents and resources by devolving responsibilities to other countries and societal actors."[11] Potter concludes by stating that selective diplomatic initiatives "maximize Canada's inherent advantages, are cognizant of growing financial constraints in the public sector, recognize the utility of non-governmental actors, and still allow Ottawa to maintain a high profile on the international stage."[12]

Niche diplomacy is premised on a notion of diplomatic comparative advantage, which, in the context of neoliberalism, advises "states to specialise in goods and services they can produce most cheaply."[13] Comparative advantage is situated in the broader neoliberal discourse where, according to Scott Burchill, "Western governments became more concerned with efficiency and productivity and less concerned with welfare and social justice."[14] In niche diplomacy, neoliberal assumptions are merged with realist premises. The influence of realism is especially evident, as I have argued elsewhere, in the use of terms such as "maximum impact," which "bring to mind the words of Hans Morgenthau who, in his classic *Politics among Nations,* advocates a rational foreign policy that 'minimizes risks and maximizes benefits.'"[15] The combination of realism and neoliberal assumptions are at the heart of the niche diplomatic strategy, both in theory and in practice.

Niche Diplomacy in Practice

The end of the Cold War arguably marked the beginning of a new era for CFP: an era characterized by the assertive promotion of human security. Certainly, the language of human security is new; however, one would be hard pressed to conclude that Canadian practices in the area of human rights have fundamentally altered. In the past we justified action or inaction on human rights on the grounds of either strategic or economic interests. Now, economic interests have come to the forefront. Canadian human rights policy was and continues to be inconsistent and self-interested. This continuity is explained by the fact that the logic driving niche diplomacy is not new.

Many of the terms adopted by the Chrétien government are new, but the spirit of niche diplomacy is not.[16] Cranford Pratt, for example, has identified a narrowing of Canadian foreign policy during the 1970s and into the early 1980s. He observes the development of what he calls the "new official consensus." This consensus is characterized by, among other things, remnants of Pearsonian internationalism, the prioritization of corporate interests, the near exclusion of ethical considerations, and an emphasis on quick economic gain.[17] Mark Neufeld extends Pratt's analysis to the Mulroney era and into the early years of the Chrétien government, characterizing Canadian foreign policy as being defined by limitationist internationalism.[18] Thus, niche diplomacy sits comfortably within this discourse, which predates and easily accommodates its use. This suggests that niche diplomacy, rather than heralding a new era in foreign policy making, is instead a continuation of pre-existing ideas.

This continuation is carried forward in more recent government policy. Rioux and Hay show us that the self-interested economic emphasis of CFP can be seen in the Liberal Red Book and the 1995 government foreign policy statement, *Canada in the World.*[19] *Canada in the World* defines the three primary objectives of CFP: (1) the promotion of prosperity and employment, (2) the promotion of global peace as the key to protecting our security, and (3) the projection of Canadian values and culture.[20] Consistent with the logic of comparative advantage, it is also stated that, in a time of fiscal restraint: "more effective and less costly will have to be the watchwords guiding our approach to international relations ... We will not do everything we have done in the past, nor shall we do things as we have done before."[21]

In practice, and like Pratt's characterization of the new official consensus (which is accepted here), niche diplomacy does not appear to have been used to suggest the end of some vision of internationalism; rather, human security, which has a strong streak of internationalism, recognizes a set of non-traditional threats, such as poverty, human rights abuses, terrorism, and environmental degradation.[22] Focusing on human rights, one can identify priority issues such as children's rights, particularly child labour.[23] Niches are then identified within particular areas. Canada's niche, or area of specialization, within the context of human rights is defined as "working from within."[24] A similar pattern can be identified within the area of peacebuilding.[25] Niches, then, are few and far between. Priority areas have been selected.

In keeping with the general economic orientation of the government, we can find expressions of niche diplomacy in the statements of a number of ministers. Art Eggleton, former minister for international trade, articulated the spirit of niche diplomacy in a 1996 speech to the Pacific Basin Economic Council when he declared that we "need to *focus* our energy and resources and not try to be all things to all people."[26] References to Canada's areas of comparative advantage can also be identified. In a May 1996 speech, Raymond Chan, secretary of state (Asia-Pacific), identified the following as areas of competitive advantage: agriculture, transportation, and telecommunications.[27] Maximum impact, an objective stressed by Potter, has also been used by Axworthy with respect to Canadian cultural relations with the Asia Pacific, Europe, and the Americas.[28] In a March 1999 speech to human rights non-governmental organizations (NGOs), Axworthy emphasized that "the aim is to maximize Canada's effective influence by choosing the levers that, we hope, will produce the best results."[29]

The use of soft power and the importance of coalition building – both areas suggested by Potter and Cooper – have also been repeatedly alluded to by Canadian decision makers. Soft power, in terms of telecommunications, was seen as a way to "present Canada, and Canadian values such as respect for human rights, to the outside world."[30] Promoting Canadian values is equated with advancing Canadian interests.[31] Soft power, as related to norm promotion, agenda setting, and consensus building, is viewed as an important tool for Canadian diplomacy. Coalition building with NGOs is a theme stressed in speeches on peacebuilding[32] and human rights.[33] Building coalitions with "like-minded" states is another integral part of Canadian diplomacy. This combination of soft power and coalition building with various other actors epitomizes the Canadian vision of new diplomacy, where effective outcomes are reached by means of "great ideas and pooled resources."[34]

What this analysis shows, in combination with the preceding section, is that there are parallels between the statements of Cooper and Potter and those of various federal ministers. The government has gone so far as to identify a number of niches. We must acknowledge, however, some divergences between scholars and practitioners with regard to the place of human security. In contrast to scholars' suggestions, practitioners, particularly Axworthy, have given human security the status of a guiding principle. Recent statements by Axworthy have toned down the economic rhetoric and placed even greater emphasis on soft power, leadership, and human security. In place of the language of niches we find the less market-oriented term "priorities," but the intent of niche diplomacy continues to underpin CFP. This includes targeting specific issue areas, acting in a fiscally sound manner, and functioning as a leader. The minister has stated clearly that, "with limited resources and unlimited wishes, establishing priorities in foreign policy becomes a critical, if complex, task."[35] This consistency is explained by the fact that a liberal economic philosophy that emphasizes economic competitiveness, the enhancement of trading opportunities, and fiscal responsibility has driven, and continues to drive, CFP.

Niche diplomacy sits easily within the dominant liberal discourse and resembles Pratt's elite analysis. Remnants of Pearsonian internationalism remain within government rhetoric. On the surface, Canada is a rare idealist state. However, this norm promotion, epitomized by the use of soft power, lacks substance and is undermined by the liberal economic strategy that implements the norms. Efficiency, effectiveness, and maximum impact place a priority on economic gain or, at the very least, minimum cost to Canada and Canadian corporations. Soft power is cheap to use, a point made by several scholars.[36] Promoting ideas, or norm entrepreneurship, as identified by Andy Knight (Chapter 7, this volume), is admirable, but it is also considerably less expensive and less onerous for the Canadian economy than is increasing aid budgets or imposing sanctions on human rights abusers.

Human Rights and Niche Diplomacy

Here I argue that CFP is functioning under the logic of niche diplomacy; that this is representative of a liberal and realist logic; and that this, in turn, negatively affects human rights goals. If Canadian human rights policy was informed by niche diplomacy, then we would expect the following: human rights policy would be in our national interest, it would achieve maximum impact, and it would support Canadian claims of leadership.

Based on government statements, one would first expect that the niche of "working from within" to achieve human rights goals is somehow distinct. Second, we would expect that human rights is a foundation stone of Canadian foreign policy[37] and that it is integral to Canada's leadership on human security. According to the former minister of foreign affairs, "Canada has both the capacity and credibility to play a leadership role in support of human security in the developing world."[38] One might also expect, given this "new" vision of CFP, that Canada's approach would be different from that taken in the past, thereby countering the arguments that Canadian human rights policy is largely symbolic and is diluted by, for example, economic interests.[39] What we find is that niche diplomatic assumptions inform human rights policy and that it is these assumptions, not the government's claims for the primacy of human security, that drive CFP.

The Chrétien government has been active in the area of human rights. Under the aegis of human rights, the areas of children's rights (particularly child labour, indigenous rights, and women's rights) have been targeted. Child labour, for example, was the focus of a parliamentary committee report.[40] Efforts to combat child labour have been supported by the Child Labour Fund, which was established in 1997 with the aim of supporting the efforts of the business community to develop and promote voluntary guidelines for child labour.[41] The government has also tried to combat the sexual exploitation of children by putting forward legislation – Bill C-27 – that makes Canadians engaging in the child sex trade abroad liable for prosecution at home. Promotion of the International Criminal Court, discussed by Knight (Chapter 7, this volume), is further testimony to Canada's activity in the human rights arena.

Recognizing that these issues tend also to be development issues, human rights initiatives have been coupled with the delivery of aid to countries around the world. One can find evidence of considerable activity in the development field, which, arguably, supports the promotion of human rights. For example, in 1997 the Canadian International Development Agency (CIDA) was involved in several projects to support judicial reform in China as well as a whole series of environmental projects.[42] The connection between human rights and development is in keeping with the assumptions of human security articulated by the minister of foreign affairs, who has argued that "human security recognizes the complexity of the human environment and accepts that the forces influencing human security are interrelated and mutually reinforcing."[43] Therefore, to say that the government has been inactive would be false. However, we must also be cognizant of the fact that CIDA budgets have been drastically slashed in the last decade[44] and that Canada continues to support states with egregious human rights records. Indonesia is one example of such a state, and it is discussed below.

Axworthy has described Canadian human rights policy as principled pragmatism. We are seeking effective influence. The Canadian position is one that does not make "a crude choice between trade or human rights."[45] What we want is responsible trade because, while "trade on its own does not promote democratization or greater respect for human rights ... it does open doors."[46] The Department of Foreign Affairs and International Trade contends that this is the best approach because we "don't have the economic leverage or international clout to force change."[47] In the area of human rights, Canada may not have the economic leverage to act unilaterally and thus force change, but how is it that Canada is willing to "punch above its weight"[48] and build coalitions of the like-minded on some issues and yet not on others? There are choices involved here. The choice in terms of human rights is to "work from within."

In many instances, it is the aim of the Canadian government to "work from within" the states in question. With reference to China, Christine Stewart stated in March 1997 that we need to build a "constructive bilateral dialogue on the basis of mutual respect. And we will urge all governments to engage in similarly constructive dialogues."[49] The imposition of sanctions is not the favoured strategy, although there are obvious cases, such as Nigeria and Burma, where sanctions have been used by the Chrétien government. The case of Nigeria, discussed by David Black (Chapter 8, this volume), provides us with an instance in which Canada took an outspoken position on human rights abuses. What is interesting to note, as Black does, is that there are few economic ties between Canada and Nigeria. Canada appears to take less aggressive positions when the economic relations between it and the states in question are more significant. Moreover, these states are also, typically, high on the list of Canadian aid recipients.

Indonesia is one good example of this. Terry Keenleyside has chronicled how Canada maintained aid with Indonesia after its invasion of East Timor.[50] A 1997 CIDA document on Canada and East Timor outlines Canadian initiatives while at the same time referring to human rights abuses in East Timor as alleged.[51] This document further indicates that "Canada continues to monitor developments in East Timor closely, and supports efforts to reach a negotiated solution that is acceptable to all interested parties and to the international community."[52] While Canada has been monitoring the situation, aid to Indonesia has risen. In 1994-95 Indonesia stood fifth among aid recipients, up from eighth in 1980-81.[53] Trade, too, has increased. The East Timor Alert Network reports that two-way trade with Indonesia in 1996 stood at six billion dollars, in spite of the continued repression of pro-democracy movements in that state.[54] Canada did indeed speak out against the "cruel suppression of the independence agreement in East Timor"[55] after the international media shone the spotlight on the egregious activities of pro-Indonesian militias in September of 1999. Additional aid of $1.5 million was also announced for East Timor,[56] and the minister halted all new military export permits to Indonesia. Unfortunately, four outstanding military export permits[57] were not cancelled. Thus, in an ironic twist, the Canadian government and Canadian companies are supporting with hard power the same Indonesian government that Axworthy was condemning through the use of soft power.

The situation with China is similar. Since 1970, when Canada established diplomatic relations with China, the Canadian relationship with that state has been dominated by commercial interests, coupled with strategic interests during the Cold War era. The events of June 1989 at Tiananmen Square led Canada to institute a series of sanctions that were largely symbolic.[58] Since the election of the Liberal government in 1993, the emphasis has been on commercial interests. The Team Canada mission to China in 1995 is indicative of that interest. In 1980-81 China was not among the top ten recipients of aid, while in 1994-95 it stood in first place.[59] In 1994 Canadian domestic exports were higher to China than they were to Germany.[60] In 1996 Raymond Chan described exports to China as rising at "unprecedented levels," having reached a record level of $3.39 billion in 1995.[61] More recently, International Trade Minister Sergio Marchi witnessed the signing of "46 commercial agreements worth $720.8 billion during the Canada-China Forum."[62]

Axworthy has argued that we should not dichotomize between rights and trade, that the issue is more complex then is "suggested in calls for blanket conditionality on trade," and that we need to practise responsible trade.[63] As complex as the issue may be, it nonetheless raises the obvious question: what constitutes responsible trade? Is the promotion of trade with China, which includes the construction of two Canadian CANDU nuclear reactors (see Duane Bratt, Chapter 12, this volume), responsible trade? Is exempting this sale from the provisions of the Canadian Environmental Assessment Act responsible trade? Similar questions can be raised about trade with Indonesia. Is the maintenance of export permits to Indonesia after the violence in East Timor really responsible trade? One must ask: responsible to whom? How is human security promoted by allowing Canadian companies to support the military in Indonesia?

In order to explain Canadian behaviour on human rights we need to return to the basic premises of niche diplomacy, as outlined in the beginning of this section. The first dimension of niche diplomacy was national interest. Does Canadian human rights policy promote our national interest? We are told that our activities must be in Canada's national interest, and it should be an identifiable interest. The obvious question is, whose interest? And how do we measure interest? Interest, in the niche diplomacy literature, is defined primarily in economic terms. The federal government has called for a foreign policy that promotes Canadian prosperity and employment. The strategies of "working from within" and "responsible trade" grant us the necessary flexibility to pursue our economic ends. Our human rights policies do not interfere with our trade and are supported by the liberal assumption that economic development, as promoted by working from within, will lead to democratic and peaceful states. Canadian economic interests are placed above the individual security of the East Timorese when we allow our companies to support the Indonesian military – a practice that hardly lends itself to peace and stability. Placing Canada first reflects the fusion of neoliberal and realist tenets that privilege national economic interests.

"Maximum impact" is another slippery concept. Potter's work implies that maximum impact translates into the "biggest bang for the buck." This makes one wonder: maximum impact for whom? Martin Rudner has argued that aid policy (and one may speculate that this applies equally to human rights policy) has become "results oriented" and that the reference clientele has become "Canadian politicians, aid managers and stakeholders"[64] as opposed to developing countries. He further notes that our aid policy is epitomized by "self-righteousness and self-interest."[65] This same self-interest infuses our human rights policy as we seek justification for continuing relationships with many states that have poor human rights records. After all, how does one compare the potential of over $700 million worth of business with China alone to the paltry sum of $62 million spent in 1997 on projects focused on human rights and democratic development?[66] Maximum impact, like national interest, is defined in economic terms. Our greatest gain does not come from delivering aid or promoting human rights: it comes from trade and investment.

Effectiveness is equally hard to measure in this context. China and Indonesia have opened their doors to trade, and programs are in place in these states that could be seen as meeting the aim of "working from within." So we may observe some degree of effectiveness, at least in terms of meeting our objectives. In terms of the protection of human rights, claims of effectiveness are more difficult to support. Canada, for example, prides itself on its support of the Indonesian National Commission on Human Rights. Canadian support for such initiatives is not unimportant, but we must recognize that the effectiveness of the institutions we support abroad is sometimes questionable. The 1997 United Nations analysis of Indonesia's human rights record notes that the Indonesian "National Commission on Human Rights ... lacked the powers and resources to be fully operational and independent, and that there was no consistency in the cases taken up."[67]

Finally, Potter and Cooper argue that a niche diplomatic strategy would close the commitment-credibility gap and facilitate Canadian leadership. Unlike with the other dimensions discussed here, we should hesitate before applying the term "leadership" to Canadian human rights initiatives. Given that leadership is an element common to niche diplomacy and government pronouncements, this element will be discussed later in this section.

Based on government statements, we would expect that the niche strategy of "working from within" is distinct from the activities of other states and from past Canadian behaviour. However, our policy initiatives in the area of human rights are neither distinct from other states nor from past initiatives. Regarding the claims of being distinct from other states, it serves to note that Canada's human rights policy towards China, for example, closely parallels that of the United States, suggesting that Canada does not want to be out of step with its largest trading partner. President Clinton was criticized for his administration's policy of constructive engagement with China. A Human Rights Watch editorial observes that the American administration has justified its policy by arguing that "China is too important to be isolated" and that the "US-China relationship is too important to be held hostage to human rights."[68] Canada is also unwilling to isolate China. So the question is, how is "working from within" distinctive?

The case of East Timor, for example, shows fairly consistent support for the Indonesian government by successive Canadian governments. The Chrétien government has pursued a "business as usual" approach. This lack of distinction, from other states and from the past, has implications for foreign policy, broadly speaking, that will be addressed in the concluding section of this chapter.

The second theme identified in the government statements is that human rights is a foundation stone of CFP. To what extent is this the case? As noted earlier, there is considerable activity in the area of human rights. Our support for various international conventions on humans rights of all types is stated publicly and often. Human rights is an issue area of high rhetorical importance to the government, and it has been active. This is to be applauded. And yet, one must question the integral place assigned to human rights, especially given the notion that it constitutes a "foundation stone" of CFP. The government claims that it is promoting constructive dialogue and engaging in responsible trade. These strategies, we are told, will foster change. But when does diplomacy become complicity? Can we accept the rhetoric of human rights as a foundation stone when we consistently engage with states that practise torture, arbitrary detention, and public executions?[69] Are we only willing to circumscribe our trading relations with states (e.g., Nigeria) where the trade is minimal?

If human rights is not a foundation stone of CFP, then what does this tell us about claims of leadership in the area of human security? Human rights is a key component of human security. In a November 1998 statement the minister defined the relationship between human rights and human security as follows: "the protection of the human being and the advancement of human dignity is what human security is about and is what provides the foundation for our evolving human security policy."[70] Is Canada a leader in this area? The answer is simple: Canada may be a leader in the promotion of human security, but it is not a leader in the practice of human security.

Minister Axworthy has promoted human security at every opportunity, but what happens to the integrity of human security when we observe cases like Indonesia or China, where Canadian economic interests take precedence over human dignity? Is human security "issue-specific"? Is it state-specific? Do some states deserve it while others do not? The cases of China and Indonesia do not reinforce an image of a holistic approach to human security, where human rights are a foundation and are on par with the other components of human security. The assumption of interconnectedness between the components of human security is challenged when we conclude that Canadian human rights policy seems consistent with past behaviour, where "human rights are much more emphasized in Canadian foreign policy when the policy consequences re-enforce rather than work counter to cold war or commercial considerations."[71] The Cold War is over, but commercial interests remain: and they dominate. This makes claims of leadership in the practice of human security suspect, and it widens rather than closes the commitment-credibility gap. The widening of this gap results in Canada adopting a position akin to the old saying: "do as I say, not as I do." This is, indeed, a problem.

Some Concluding Reflections

Canadian humans rights policy is complex and at times confusing. It is definitely marked by what Black refers to as "consistent inconsistency" (Chapter 8, this volume). Perhaps consistency in an absolute sense is a harsh standard. The problem is that the standards for human rights promotion appear to vary according to the power of the state involved. Quiet diplomacy or constructive dialogue are adopted when Canadian economic interests seem to be at stake. Sanctions seem to be imposed when there is little perceived economic loss for Canada. Assertive public pronouncements seem to be made when an international spotlight has been thrust upon an issue and Canada is eager to maintain some image of a "good international citizen."

This kind of behaviour undermines Canadian credibility in the human rights arena. If human rights is a priority of the Canadian government, as is suggested by Andy Knight (Chapter 7, this volume), then surely Canada would endeavour to narrow the commitment-credibility gap. Canada has recently had the audacity to chastize states in the United Nations for not supporting the grand vision of human security. Such moralizing is shallow and nothing short of hypocritical when we are selectively applying to ourselves the standards that we promote internationally. Perhaps, as Denis Stairs suggests, Canada should be more modest and forego moralizing, "otherwise expectations at home and abroad alike get out of hand, fatalism and battle-fatigue set in, and citizen cynicism ... further ensues and further deepens."[72]

The commitment-credibility gap emerges, in part, because the rhetoric of human security is undermined by the strategy of niche diplomacy. The holistic cosmopolitan vision of human security, which implies ethical obligations and duties to those beyond one's borders, clashes with the inward-looking and self-interested assumptions that are central to a niche diplomatic strategy. This suggests that practitioners must be aware that "the tactics and strategies of diplomats and soldiers are derivative of philosophies (whether they recognize it or not) which have ethical foundations."[73] Can we say that the minister is aware that, in adopting the language of niches, he adopted a concept that is rife with market assumptions?

The adoption of human security rhetoric relates to the claim to distinction, an element central to a Canadian human rights agenda. Such claims are made, in part, to foster a sense of difference. It is, fundamentally, an identity issue. If we are not somehow different, and perhaps better, in our support of human rights around the world, then can we actually claim to be part of the "moral minority" – that select group of states that call for the "creation of a just and more equitable world order"?[74] Similarly, if we are not distinct, then how do we make claims of leadership? We must look carefully at the image we project.

The issue of distinction relates to a central theme in this text: what values do Canadians represent and how effectively are those values represented in CFP? On the surface – that is to say, in the statements of the minister – Canada represents an image of a kind, caring, and nurturing country, committed to the promotion of a new global ethic. According to Hampson and Oliver, the Canadian public is proud of Canada's international activities and the ideas that are promoted abroad.[75] Human security appears to promote an image that impresses the Canadian public: it sells well with the electorate. But, as argued in this chapter, those values do not translate into Canadian human rights policy specifically or into CFP generally. Stripping away the myth that Canada is part of a moral minority, we find that the values expressed in the speeches of the minister of foreign affairs are not implemented; rather, practice supports the argument made here that Canada is placing its emphasis on economic interests and that, as a result, human rights are addressed according to the economic clout or market potential of the state in question.

Niche diplomacy counsels us to make choices. This is not ill-advised. The concern here is not whether or not we must make choices but, rather, the choices we make and the circumstances we accept as determinants of those choices. The minister has justified Canadian human rights policy based on the premise that we have limited influence in this arena. In accepting these power assumptions he automatically accepts the limitations imposed upon middle powers. Yet he did not accept those limitations when he proposed the landmines treaty. We can accept that there are different dimensions to leadership, but are some of the limitations in the area of human rights self-imposed? As Denis Stairs asks: what happens if we give over to circumstance?[76]

There is at least one choice that, if made, will bolster Canada's image at home and abroad and actually provide for the security of individuals beyond Canada's borders. The commitment to poverty reduction promoted by the Canadian International Development Agency, and identified by Cranford Pratt (Chapter 4, this volume), needs to be enhanced and maintained as part of an overall increase in the commitment of official development assistance (ODA). The minister has noted that development and human security are intertwined, and indeed they are. To address basic needs in a genuine and sustained fashion would enhance the credibility of Canada's claims regarding human security and would, in a small way, counter critics, such as Kim Nossal, who have observed in CFP "a meanness of spirit."[77] A renewed commitment to ODA would signal some recognition of obligations and duties beyond Canada's borders, thus deflecting some of the criticisms raised by Nossal and in this chapter.

Greater financial commitment to ODA would also benefit Canada internationally. As it stands, Canada claims to work with coalitions of the "like-minded." These coalitions frequently include states such as Sweden, Norway, and the Netherlands. In 1998, as a percentage of gross domestic product Canada's ODA was 0.29 percent while the other three states were, respectively, 0.72 percent, 0.91 percent and 0.8 percent.[78] Given these statistics, it would appear that coalitions of the like-minded are not coalitions of the like-acting. Canada's image would be bolstered with like-minded states if we "put our money where our mouth is."

Finally, a genuine commitment of aid to meet the basic needs of those beyond our borders would ultimately go further in the provision of human security than would ill-conceived trade deals that, while beneficial to Canadian companies, ultimately result in further harm and enhanced insecurity for those beyond our borders. The year 1999 marked an outstanding year for exports,[79] and there is much talk of a budget surplus. Does this invalidate the arguments for the need to be fiscally responsible? It might be argued that we must continue to act in a fiscally sound manner, and while this may be true, perhaps we can consider our commitment to others and share a little of the wealth.

This chapter speaks to us of continuity and change. The international system has changed. The bipolar structures and Cold War tensions have dissipated. The world is becoming more interconnected via technology, and we are becoming increasingly more aware of the interconnectedness between peoples. War continues to affect individuals on a daily basis, as does hunger and the violation of fundamental human rights. The Canadian government has offered us a new vision of security – a vision that is different from the past and hopeful for a better future. Human security fits with the realities of the lives of many, as it is recognized that security has many dimensions. One would expect that this new vision would result in a different kind of CFP. However, in the realm of human rights, Canada continues to find reasons to legitimize inaction. In the past, human rights were sacrificed in the name of geo-strategic and economic necessity. Now, economic necessity and Canadian competitiveness rule the day. Thus there is a continuity in Canadian human rights policy, as we continue to place Canadian interest first. Perhaps it is naive to assume that we can modify our human rights policies, but modify them we must if we wish to claim that Canadian foreign policy is driven by a humane human security and not by a diplomatic strategy that emphasizes comparative advantage, efficiency, and maximum impact. People cannot be reduced to dollars and cents, and foreign policy cannot be reduced to market-based analyses.

Acknowledgments
The author would like to acknowledge the research contribution of Cameron Ortis to this project and would like to thank Claire Turenne Sjolander for comments on an earlier draft. Selections of this chapter have been published previously in Heather A. Smith, "Caution Warranted: Niche Diplomacy Assessed," *Canadian Foreign Policy* 6, 3 (Spring 1999): 57-72.

Notes

1 Department of Foreign Affairs and International Trade, *Statement,* Notes for an Address by the Honourable Lloyd Axworthy, Minister of Foreign Affairs, to the G-8 Foreign Ministers Meeting, 9 June 1999, 1. Available at <http://198.103.104.95/human-rights/statement-e.asp>.

2 For an extended discussion of these points, see: Cranford Pratt, "Humane Internationalism: Its Significance and Its Variants," in *Internationalism Under Strain: The North-South Policies of Canada, the Netherlands, Norway and Sweden,* ed. Cranford Pratt (Toronto: University of Toronto Press, 1989), 13-22.

3 Andrew F. Cooper, "In Search of Niches: Saying 'Yes' and Saying 'No' in Canada's International Relations," *Canadian Foreign Policy* 3, 3 (1995): 1-13; Evan H. Potter, "Niche Diplomacy as Canadian Foreign Policy," *International Journal* 52, 1 (1996-97): 25-38.

4 "An Interview with the Minister of Foreign Affairs, Hon. Lloyd Axworthy," *Canadian Foreign Policy* 4, 3 (1997): 1.

5 Department of Foreign Affairs and International Trade, *Statement,* Notes for an Address by the Honourable Lloyd Axworthy, Minister of Foreign Affairs, at the Consultations with Non-Governmental Organizations in Preparation for the 53rd Session of the United Nations Commission on Human Rights, 5 February 1997; *Statement,* Notes for an Address by the Honourable Lloyd Axworthy, Minister of Foreign Affairs, at York University, "Building Peace to Last: Establishing a Canadian Peacebuilding Initiative," 30 October 1996; *Statement,* Notes for an Address by the Honourable Lloyd Axworthy, Minister of Foreign Affairs, to a Meeting of the National Forum on Foreign Policy "Canadian Foreign Policy in a Changing World," 13 December 1996.

6 Cooper, "In Search of Niches," 1.

7 Potter, "Niche Diplomacy as Canadian Foreign Policy," 25.

8 Ibid.
9 Ibid., 26.
10 Ibid., 30-35.
11 Cooper, "In Search of Niches," 13.
12 Potter, "Niche Diplomacy as Canadian Foreign Policy," 37.
13 Scott Burchill, "Liberal Internationalism," in *Theories of International Relations,* ed. Scott Burchill and Andrew Linklater (New York: St. Martin's Press, 1995), 55.
14 Ibid.
15 Heather A. Smith, "Caution Warranted: Niche Diplomacy Assessed" *Canadian Foreign Policy* 6, 3 (Spring 1999): 59.
16 For example, the language of effectiveness resonated through the foreign policy planning of the Trudeau government. See Ivan Head and Pierre Trudeau, *The Canadian Way: Shaping Canada's Foreign Policy, 1968-1984* (Toronto: McClelland and Stewart, 1995), 13-14.
17 Cranford Pratt, "Dominant Class Theory and Canadian Foreign Policy: The Case of Counter-Consensus" *International Journal* 39, 1 (1983-84): 122-26.
18 Mark Neufeld, "Hegemony and Foreign Policy Analysis: The Case of Canada as a Middle Power," *Studies in Political Economy* 48 (1995): 7-29.
19 Jean-François Rioux and Robin Hay, "Canadian Foreign Policy: From Internationalism to Isolationism?" *International Journal* 54, 3 (Winter 1998-99): 66-67.
20 Government of Canada, *Canada in the World* (Ottawa: Supply and Services Canada, 1995) 10-11.
21 Ibid., 9.
22 Human security is raised in almost every speech given by Axworthy. See also Lloyd Axworthy, "Between Globalization and Multipolarity: The Case for a Global, Humane Canadian Foreign Policy," *Etudes Internationales* 28, 1 (1997): 105-21 (available at <www.dfait-maeci.gc.ca/english/foreignp/humane.htm>); and "Canada and Human Security: The Need for Leadership," *International Journal* 52, 2 (Spring 1997), 183-96 (available at <www.dfait-maeci.gc.ca/english/foreignp/sechume.htm>).
23 See, for example, the following Department of Foreign Affairs and International Trade (DFAIT) statements: *Statement,* Notes for an Address by the Honourable Lloyd Axworthy, Minister of Foreign Affairs, at the World Congress against the Sexual Exploitation of Children, 27 August 1996; *Statement,* Notes for an Address by the Honourable Christine Stewart, Secretary of State (Latin America and Africa) at the Amsterdam Child Labour Conference, 26 February 1997; *Statement,* Notes for an Address by the Honourable Lloyd Axworthy, Minister of Foreign Affairs Before the Standing Committee on Foreign Affairs and International Trade on Child Labour, 23 April 1997.
24 Department of Foreign Affairs and International Trade, *Statement,* Notes for an Address by the Honourable David Kilgour, Secretary of State (Latin America and Africa) at the October Meeting of the Diplomatic Press Attaché Network, National Press Club, "Canadian Foreign Policy in an Ever-Shrinking World," 15 October 1997; *Statement,* Notes for an Address by the Honourable Lloyd Axworthy, Minster of Foreign Affairs, at McGill University, "Human Rights and Canadian Foreign Policy," 16 October 1997.
25 Department of Foreign Affairs and International Trade, *Statement,* 30 October 1996.
26 Department of Foreign Affairs and International Trade, *Statement,* Notes for an Address by the Honourable Art Eggleton, Minister for International Trade on the Occasion of the Pacific Basin Economic Council Luncheon, 1 November 1996, 3.
27 Department of Foreign Affairs and International Trade, *Statement,* Notes for an Address by the Honourable Raymond Chan, Secretary of State (Asia-Pacific) to the Canadian Business Forum, 14 May 1996, 2.
28 Department of Foreign Affairs and International Trade, *Statement,* Notes for an Address by the Honourable Lloyd Axworthy, Minister of Foreign Affairs, at the Harbourfront Centre on the Launch of Canada's Year of Asia Pacific Cultural Program, 8 February 1997, 5.
29 Department of Foreign Affairs and International Trade, *Statement,* Notes for an Address by the Honourable Lloyd Axworthy, Minister of Foreign Affairs, to the Opening of the Human Rights NGO Consultations, 4 March 1999, 5. Available at <http://198.103.104.95/human-rights/statement-e.asp>.

30 Department of Foreign Affairs and International Trade, *Statement,* 5 February 1997, 10.

31 Department of Foreign Affairs and International Trade, *Statement,* Notes for an Address by the Honourable Lloyd Axworthy, Minister of Foreign Affairs, "Foreign Policy in the Information Age," 6 December 1996, 2.

32 See Department of Foreign Affairs and International Trade, *Statement,* 30 October 1996.

33 See Department of Foreign Affairs and International Trade, *Statement,* 5 February 1997.

34 Department of Foreign Affairs and International Trade, *Statement,* Message from the Honourable Lloyd Axworthy, Minister of Foreign Affairs, to the Hague Appeal for Peace, 13 May 1999, 2. Available at <http://198.103.104.95/human-rights/statement-e.asp>.

35 Department of Foreign Affairs and International Trade, *Statement,* 4 March 1999, 2. Available at <http://198.103.104.95/human-rights/statement-e.asp>.

36 See, for example, Fen Osler Hampson and Dean F. Oliver, "Pulpit Diplomacy: A Critical Assessment of the Axworthy Doctrine," *International Journal* 53, 3 (1998): 379-406; and Kim Richard Nossal, "Pinchpenny Diplomacy: The Decline of 'Good International Citizenship' in Canadian Foreign Policy," *International Journal* 54, 1 (Winter 1998-99): 88–105.

37 Department of Foreign Affairs and International Trade, *Statement,* Notes for an Address by the Honourable Lloyd Axworthy. Minster of Foreign Affairs to the 52nd Session of The United Nations General Assembly, 25 September 1997.

38 Axworthy, "Canada and Human Security," 6.

39 See, for example, Kim Richard Nossal, "Cabin'd, Cribb'd, Confin'd?: Canada's Interests in Human Rights," in *Human Rights in Canadian Foreign Policy,* ed. Robert O. Matthews and Cranford Pratt (Kingston: McGill-Queen's University Press, 1988), 46-58; Paul Gecelovsky and T.A. Keenleyside, "Canada's International Human Rights Policy in Practice: Tiananmen Square," *International Journal* 50 (1995); Robert O. Matthews and Cranford Pratt, "Conclusion: Questions and Prospects," in *Human Rights in Canadian Foreign Policy,* ed. Robert O. Matthews and Cranford Pratt (Montreal and Kingston: McGill-Queen's University Press, 1988), 285-311.

40 See Canada, House of Commons, Standing Committee on Foreign Affairs and International Trade, Subcommittee on Sustainable Human Development, *Ending Child Labour Exploitation: A Canadian Agenda on Global Challenges,* 35th Parl., 2d Sess., issue no. 10 (Ottawa: Queen's Printer, 1997).

41 Department of Foreign Affairs and International Trade, *Statement,* 23 April 1997, 5.

42 Canadian International Development Agency, *News Release,* "Canada Signs Two Cooperation Agreements with China" (available at <http://w3.acdi-cida.gc.ca/cida_ind.nsf>); and "List of Bilateral Projects in China" (available at <http://w3.acdi-cida.gc.ca/cida_ind.nsf/>).

43 Axworthy, "Canada and Human Security." Available at <www.dfait-maeci.gc.ca/english/foreignp/sechume.htm>.

44 See Tim Draimin and Brian Tomlinson, "Is There a Future for Canadian Aid in the Twenty-First Century?" in *Leadership and Dialogue: Canada among Nations, 1998,* ed. Fen Osler Hampson and Maureen Appel Molot (Toronto: Oxford University Press, 1998), 144-46.

45 Department of Foreign Affairs and International Trade, *Statement,* 16 October 1997, 8.

46 Ibid.

47 Ibid.

48 Lloyd Axworthy and Sarah Taylor, "A Ban for All Seasons: The Landmines Convention and Its Implications for Canadian Diplomacy," *International Journal* 52, 2 (Spring 1998): 203.

49 Department of Foreign Affairs and International Trade, *Statement,* Notes for an Address by the Honourable Christine Stewart, Secretary of State (Latin America and Africa) before the United Nations Commission on Human Rights, 19 March 1997, 2.

50 T.A. Keenleyside, "Development Assistance," in *Human Rights in Canadian Foreign Policy,* ed. Robert O. Matthews and Cranford Pratt (Montreal and Kingston: McGill-Queen's University Press, 1988), 187-208.

51 Canadian International Development Agency, "CIDA in East Timor." Available at <http://w3.acdi-cida.gc.ca/cida_ind.nsf> (1997).

52 Ibid., 3.

53 OECD, "Major Recipients of Individual DAC Members' Aid: Canada." Available at <www.oecd.org/dac/htm/dacstats.htm> (1997).
54 East Timor Alert Network, "Canadian Trade with Indonesia" Information/Action Kit, 1996.
55 Department of Foreign Affairs and International Trade, *Statement*, Notes for an Address by the Honourable Lloyd Axworthy, Minister of Foreign Affairs, to the 54th Session of the United Nations General Assembly, 23 September 1999, 2. Available at <http://198.103.104.95/human-rights/statement-e.asp>.
56 Canadian International Development Agency, News Release, "Maria Minna Announces $1.5 Million in New Aid for East Timor," 25 October 1999.
57 East Timor Alert Network, "Canada Called on to Stop All Military Sales to Indonesia and to Fund War Crimes Inquiry for East Timor." Available at <www.etan.ca/etannews_99nov17.html>.
58 See the discussion in Gecelovsky and Keenleyside, "Canada's International Human Rights Policy in Practice," and Jeremy T Paltiel, "Negotiating Human Rights with China," in *Democracy and Foreign Policy: Canada Among Nations, 1995,* ed. Maxwell A. Cameron and Maureen Appel Molot (Ottawa: Carleton University Press, 1995), 165-86.
59 OECD, "Major Recipients of Individual DAC Members' Aid: Canada." Available at <www.oecd.org/dac/htm/dacstats.htm> (1997).
60 Industry Canada, *Strategies: Trade Data Online*. Available at <http://strategis.ic.gc.ca> (1997).
61 Department of Foreign Affairs and International Trade, *Statement,* 14 May 1996, 1.
62 Department of Foreign Affairs and International Trade, *News Release,* "Canadian Business Deals in Beijing Strengthen Canada-China Business Relationship," 20 November 1998, 1.
63 Department of Foreign Affairs and International Trade, *Statement,* 5 February 1997, 5-6.
64 Martin Rudner, "Canada in the World: Development Assistance in Canada's New Foreign Policy Framework," *Canadian Journal of Development* 27, 2 (1996): 216.
65 Ibid., 217.
66 This number comes from Department of Foreign Affairs and International Trade, *Statement,* Notes for an Address by the Honourable Lloyd Axworthy to the International Conference on Universal Rights and Human Values, "A Blueprint for Peace, Justice and Freedom," 3.
67 Human Rights Internet and DFAIT, *For the Record: The UN Human Rights System,* 5. Available at <www.hri.ca/fortherecord1997/vol3/indonesia.htm>.
68 Kenneth Roth, "Clinton Administration's Policy on Constructive Engagement with China Rings Hollow," *Editorials,* Human Rights Watch (1997), 2. Available at <www.hrw.org/campaigns/chinaed.html>.
69 See *For the Record: The UN Human Rights System,* for a discussion of China and Indonesia. Available at <www.hri.ca/fortherecord1997/index.htm>.
70 Department of Foreign Affairs and International Trade, *Statement,* 27 November 1998, 2.
71 Cranford Pratt, "The Limited Place of Human Rights in Canadian Foreign Policy," in *Human Rights, Development and Foreign Policy: Canadian Perspectives,* ed. Irving Brecher (Halifax: IRPP, 1989), 174.
72 Denis Stairs, "Canada and the Security Problem: Implications as the Millennium Turns," *International Journal* 54, 3 (Summer 1999): 402.
73 Ken Booth, "Human Wrongs and International Relations," *International Affairs* 71, 1 (1995): 110.
74 Hampson and Oliver, "Pulpit Diplomacy," 381.
75 Ibid., 379.
76 Denis Stairs, "Will and Circumstance and the Postwar Study of Canada's Foreign Policy," *International Journal* 50, 1 (Winter 1994-95): 39.
77 Nossal, "Pinchpenny Diplomacy," 89.
78 Organization of Economic Cooperation and Development, "Aid at a Glance." Available at <www.oecd.org/dac/htm/dacount1.htm>.
79 Department of Foreign Affairs and International Trade, *News Release, Canada's 1999 Exports at Record Levels,* 18 February 2000.

6
Gender, Food Security, and Foreign Policy Toward Africa: Women Farmers in Kenya and the Right to Sustenance

Terisa E. Turner,
Leigh S. Brownhill, and Wahu M. Kaara

Particular configurations of gender relations underpin a vast agenda of foreign policy issues including women's rights as human rights, housing and subsistence as human rights; refugee and political asylum eligibility; ecological preservation and rehabilitation; foreign aid; military and peacekeeping interventions; food security; strengthening the capacities of civil society organizations; democratization; and most important, the macro policies of neoliberalism including structural adjustment and free trade. These last policies have been fundamental to Canada's development and aid initiatives over the past twenty years. Moreover, globalization from above (for example, corporate expansion) and globalization from below (for example, coordination amongst social movements) mean that the realities of a single locale permeate other societies across the globe with ever-growing rapidity. This acceleration will increasingly define the changing global security environment, coming to include what Jorge Nef underlines in this volume as the "mutual vulnerability" of core and periphery societies under pressure from "non-traditional" security threats such as neoliberal globalization, civil war, and neofascism.

The transition to a post-Cold War reality accelerated capitalist expansion. The world no longer is broken into two camps; capital has a free hand and has aimed its expansion at the further commodification, or packaging for the world market, of nature, commonly-held resources, and human labour. As this process gained momentum in the early 1990s and began to inform foreign policy in Africa, it met with an already mobilized force of women farmers in Kenya who had, since 1986, increasingly resisted commodity agricultural production. Their resistance involved rebuilding food-based sustenance production and trade with concomitant efforts to equalize power relations between women and men and between citizens and the state, all integral to the democracy movement of the late 1980s and early 1990s. The post-Cold War era signified in East Africa the start of hot wars between peasants eager to expand sustenance and the corporate-backed states pursuing the neoliberal imperative to further commodify nature, resources, and labour.

In this chapter, we define ethical foreign policy as that which prioritizes life over profits and promotes movement towards universal access to goods necessary to life, as opposed to privatization and exclusion of most people from these life goods.[1] Long-term security can be engendered through the adoption of such an ethic in foreign policy. This is especially so in an era of globalization in which "human security" is becoming more relevant than "national security." How, then, do gender relations shape the contexts within which these foreign policy issues are treated? What methods of inquiry will produce gender analysis of a quality and immediacy such that can directly inform foreign policy debates? The following case study addresses these questions by seeking to achieve three objectives. First, it outlines a research method called "gendered class analysis." Second, it applies the method to examine an effort by African women farmers to resist neoliberal "development" policies. Third, it links some of the insights from the Kenyan case to debates on ethics, security and foreign policy.

Canadian foreign policy is increasingly challenged to take into account the ethical and human rights claims articulated by local and foreign interests within a rapidly changing global security context. This chapter argues that central to humane ethical claims are gender relations as they are embedded in particular histories and organizations of production. A detailed examination of gender relations in rural Kenya is presented to illustrate the centrality of gender to foreign policy. More specifically, it is argued that foreign development and aid policies that promote the sustenance of life rather than money accumulation are policies consistent with national, global, and human security. The case study thus supports Peter Penz's advocacy of a global, cosmopolitan ethic for governing international development assistance (Chapter 3, this volume). The analysis supports Cranford Pratt's case, for "humane internationalist" development assistance policies by seeking to link policy "target groups" with those within the Canadian International and Development Agency (CIDA) and the non-governmental organization (NGO) communities who are engaging in "determined rearguard efforts" to reach and help the poorest (Chapter 4, this volume). These are mainly rural women and their children who, to the extent that they succeed in supplanting anti-humane neoliberal "aid" policies, are the allies of Canadians who seek to reinvigorate foreign policy with humane internationalist social values.

This chapter traces the struggles in Kenya of one group of landless women to resist neoliberal development and assert control over agricultural production between 1986 and 2000. The women of Maragua have refused to produce coffee, an export cash crop, and instead are producing bananas and selling them independently. The study uses a "gendered class analysis" to consider how, at the household, national, and international levels, women farmers resist exploitation. The success of women in sustainable, sustenance[2] agriculture is linked to their success in establishing control over their own labour power, in the face of efforts by husbands, the state, and private firms to retain control. This study has a number of implications for Canadian foreign policy both directly and indirectly: (a) it shows that food security is sought by the poor through their own efforts and not through ceding responsibility to the government; (b) it critiques structural adjustment programs which emphasize export or other cash crops that are the focus of rural women's rejection; and (c) it suggests that foreign military and food aid intervention such as that considered by Canada in Fall 1996 in the case of Rwanda could well be part of a larger pattern of repressing autonomous sustenance agriculture engaged in by women who are asserting control over production resources including their own time, skill, knowledges, land, and inputs.

This account of how women in rural Kenya supplant structural adjustment directives to produce export crops with their own economic planning for sustenance production has implications for two dimensions of Canada's foreign policy: development assistance and military intervention for peacemaking or peacekeeping. One implication is that development assistance supports rural Africans' efforts to overcome poverty to the extent that it promotes land rights for producers, especially women, who then typically prioritize food security and the strengthening of community solidarity. Food security is a precondition for civil peace and global security. Structural adjustment programs have undermined this security and other social services formerly supplied by the state.[3] The other side of this coin is that development assistance shaped by Canadian or international commercial and speculative interests is fiercely resisted by "target groups" such as women agriculturalists who refuse to produce the cash and export crops that benefit commercial interests. Resistance to land privatization is equally trenchant. So fierce is this resistance that often only military force can overcome it.

In Kenya, Rwanda, and probably throughout the developing world, violence is being visited on rural people committed to life-sustaining production.[4] This violence is highly organized. Evidence has surfaced implicating foreign government and corporate arms suppliers with backing from the World Bank.[5] Allegations have been laid against the French government for continuing to deliver weapons to Hutu authorities in Rwanda after they had begun the massacre of opponents and the Tutsi minority.[6] Despite the involvement of these international actors, the media typically construct these struggles, especially in Africa, as series of ethnic clashes, rooted in atavistic tribal conflicts and even witchcraft.[7] The violence is geared in part at clearing from their land those (mainly women) agriculturalists who refuse to produce the cash crops that serve the commercial interests informing donor governments' foreign aid policies. It presents opportunities for intervention by armed forces from the national and international arenas. While this military intervention is labelled peacemaking and peacekeeping, it may be, in practice, the violent enforcement of development "aid" policies so fiercely resisted especially by women farmers. The governments involved in "peacekeeping" promote the neoliberal policies of export commodity production and privatization which the poor seek to supplant. For example, in February 2000, the Canadian government announced that "no sanction would be taken against Talisman Energy for its activities in Sudan, in spite of the link established by a government-appointed mission between the oil extraction in which Talisman is involved, and the deadly war currently under way."[8] Similarly, the Canadian mining corporation, Tiomin, is carrying out explorations for titanium on the Kenya coast[9] while others explore for diamonds in the Democratic Republic of Congo and in Sierra Leone amidst continuing violence in the immediate areas.

As economic warfare escalates into mass killing, "humanitarian aid" is organized by peacekeepers for refugees in flight from what is now commonly represented as "ethnic cleansing." Men in the Kenyan "clashes" between 1991 and 1998 were the first targets of the killers. Many men in Rwanda fled to the forests and mountains to try to defend themselves. Women were the majority of those struggling to survive in the refugee camps. At Marafa, a Somali refugee camp in Kenya, weekly marriage markets were held in which men, mainly Muslim Kenyans, came to the camp to "buy" a wife. In 1997, chiefs at another refugee camp in western Kenyan which accommodated Kenyan refugees from the "ethnic clashes" of the mid 1990s, were allegedly offering women as maids and wives to men in the surrounding communities for the price of their subsistence.

In practice, relief "aid" floods the markets on which local producers depend, thus eliminating their economic base. Cranford Pratt has shown (Chapter 4, this volume) that Canadian food aid, including emergency food aid, is "very narrowly tied to Canadian products, with the value to the recipients of that aid lessened by the inclusion in the non-emergency aid of less appropriate products that were, however, in current surplus in Canada." Furthermore, food aid enriches corrupt government and private-sector middlemen allied with the very commercial interests served by the foreign aid and development policies that provoke local resistance.

These largely unseen connections are exposed by the Kenyan case study's focus on gendered class relations. An implication of this study for Canada's foreign policy with respect to peacekeeping is that, in order for it to embody a humane ethic, it must support rather than undermine the sustenance economy that women farmers defend. We suggest that the militarization of

East and Central Africa can be understood, in part, as a response to indigenous struggles to reorganize production relations, as are illustrated by the Maragua banana growers in Kenya's Murang'a District.

This chapter concludes that Canadian foreign policy considerations might usefully give greater emphasis to understanding and supporting the initiatives of the predominantly women agriculturalists in Africa. Such an understanding might lead Canadian foreign policy to be less inclined to support food aid (unless very carefully orchestrated), as well as "peacekeeping" or other kinds of military intervention. It might lead to the rejection of an approach to development assistance which centralizes structural adjustment policies, because these undermine the sustenance economy which rural women are championing in the face of neoliberal export orientations. We concur with Heather Smith (Chapter 5, this volume) that Canadian foreign policy, with its emphasis on "niches," is incompatible with humane internationalist goals.

The first section considers some theoretical aspects of gendered class analysis while the second section traces the shift from coffee to banana production in Maragua. The conclusion notes two lessons from the case study, identifies possible future developments, and links the Kenyan analysis to debates on ethics and security in Canadian foreign policy.

1. Theorizing Gendered Class Struggle

In theorizing rural women's struggles we draw on Turner and Benjamin's argument that "individuals and groups who directly produce the majority of the goods and services needed for the production of their own labour power and the labour power of others, have a direct interest in preventing capitalist commodification of communal relationships, natural environments, and public space." Furthermore, "those individuals and groups whose relationship with capital is primarily defined by the work of producing labour power have a unique social power to appropriate and abolish the technical/structural divisions of the working class in the struggle against capitalist enclosure."[10] This unique social power resides both in the potential to strategically refuse to produce labour power and in the control that certain labour power producers exercise by virtue of their involvement with non-commodified communal relationships, natural environments, and public space.

A "gendered class analysis" encourages us to consider how the dynamic between exploited women and men changes with pressure from government and corporate interests. This analysis highlights the reciprocal nature of interactions between classes comprised of people of specific ethnicities and genders. It also underlines how capitalists themselves seek to strengthen bonds with categories of exploited men who are instrumentalized to control their wives' labour, redirecting it to activities that will generate more profit for capital. This "male deal" between husbands and capitalists, in turn, contributes to impelling transformative activities by exploited women.[11] Finally, a gendered class analysis is distinctive in that it encompasses the breakup of the cross-class male deal and the forging of what we call "gendered class alliances," cross-gender cooperation amongst the exploited, against class antagonists. In this study the gendered class alliance consists of some female farmers, with the support of some of their menfolk, who challenge the cross-class male deal. Social reconstruction involves the process of alliance building between exploited women and men and the challenges that gendered class alliances pose to male dealers. This analysis is aimed at creating new, humane, and ethical social relations. These in turn hold out the promise of improved local and international security.

The project of social reconstruction involves the emergence of a new local and global society. The process of struggle through which this transformation emerges involves organizations of the recomposing, neoliberal world system. These struggles draw from what McMurtry calls the "civil commons" defined as "society's organized and community-funded capacity of [generating] universally accessible resources to provide for the life preservation and growth of society's members and their environmental life-host," or "what people ensure together as a society to protect and further life, as distinct from money aggregates."[12] The project of social reconstruction involves the replacement of exploitative "neoliberalized" social relations with gendered class relations which are egalitarian and consensual at all levels from the household to the international market.

2. From Coffee to Bananas: Maragua Peasant Women Replace Export Crops with Local Food Crops[13]

In her study "Gender and Command Over Property," Bina Agarwal came to the conclusion that dispossessed women need independent rights in land.[14] This is our starting point. How have women cultivators organized to gain rights in land? Are there lessons to be learned and applied elsewhere? We worked closely with women in Maragua, Kenya throughout the 1990s and learned about their efforts to reclaim and reshape customary rights to land that had been appropriated by colonization and male deals.[15] Their struggle provides insight into the gendered character of the process of reclaiming land and social relations for subsistence.

"Every woman belongs to at least one woman's group," Alexiah Kamene told us, as if it were the most obvious fact of life. Kamene is a widow who lives in Maragua and grows bananas and vegetables on her one-acre (0.4 hectare) farm. She works part-time for a hotelier as a domestic servant and seasonally hires herself out with a group of other women to weed or harvest in the gardens of farmers with larger holdings. "Banana money is better than coffee money. Men do still take the money from women. Single women manage better. You will find that banana traders are mainly divorced or widowed women."

Kamene described the situation in Maragua as she sees it. It is not a utopia for landless women. But it is better than it was fifteen years ago when dutiful and unwaged women picked coffee that fetched incomes for their husbands, state officials, and international merchants. Beginning in 1986, Maragua farming women have taken steps towards a new organization of society in which they, as producers, manage resources, outputs, and incomes.

Maragua is a rural farming community in the area surrounding Mount Kenya, about eighty kilometres north west of Nairobi, Kenya's capital. Some 100,000 people live there.[16] Husbands own most of the small, one-to-five-acre (0.4-to-two-hectare) farms in Maragua. Technically and legally, their wives are landless. In practice, peasant women in central Kenya have customarily had the right to work on their husbands' farms and control the use of foodstuffs they themselves produced. Since the 1960s, coffee production has slowly intruded into women's food gardens. This has been a source of conflict within families. Women cultivators have historically belonged to collective work groups that applied themselves to large tasks on each other's food plots. However, these groups never worked on men's cash crop plots because the income from cash crops did not cater to women's needs. Wives worked individually, with children or with casual labourers, on husbands' cash crop plots, but did not control the yield. When women's food plots shrunk, the time they had to work collectively with other women also diminished.

At independence the government lifted colonial restrictions on coffee growing by Africans. In the 1960s and the first half of the 1970s, coffee production on small holdings provided farmers with substantial incomes, and provided the state with more foreign exchange than any other commodity. In the last half of the 1970s coffee began to lose its attraction to producers. State corruption swallowed sales income with the result that producers were not paid fairly or promptly. Between 1980 and 1990 real international prices for Africa's coffee exports fell by 70 percent.[17]

By 1986 Kenyan farmers had faced ten years of declining income from coffee. Increasing numbers of women coffee cultivators received nothing from the coffee payments that the government remitted to male landowners. Oral testimony and direct experience confirm that more and more women threatened to stop caring for their husbands' coffee. Some men responded by declaring that if their wives would not work, they would chase the women away from the farms.[18] Government chiefs intervened to mediate between embattled wives and husbands. The chiefs sought to preserve both the marriages and the coffee production, and thereby, to safeguard the profits upon which government revenues depended and upon which debt repayment and continued good relations with the International Monetary Fund (IMF) and the Paris Club of donors were premised.

By 1986 the contradiction between female coffee workers and male coffee farm owners contributed to a situation of declining overall production.[19] In response to lower coffee export earnings the World Bank and IMF provided funds to increase coffee production. The government raised coffee payments to encourage husbands to defend the industry by forcing recalcitrant wives back to work in coffee. The IMF introduced "user fees" in health and education, which created a greater need amongst producers for cash. This need constituted a coercive incentive to resume the production of cash crops. In effect, the IMF mounted formidable obstacles to women's efforts to refuse coffee production, first by introducing incentives in the form of conditional loans to the state and second, by requiring the state to pay higher coffee prices to men.

Despite the harsher discipline faced by women in their households, many of those who refused to produce coffee resolved to stay with their husbands and preserve their marriages. But the women planted beans between the coffee trees, contrary to restrictions against intercropping with coffee. They thus provided their families with food and began the tedious process of renourishing the chemically damaged soil. But this was not enough. Their husbands and state officials stood in the way of women's needs to produce food and secure cash income. Finally, the women took decisive action. In Maragua and elsewhere in Kenya, women uprooted coffee trees and used them for firewood.[20] The penalty for damaging a coffee tree was imprisonment for seven years. By late 1986 most women farmers in Maragua had planted bananas and vegetables for home consumption and local trade instead of coffee for export. This pattern was repeated with varying intensity throughout Kenya and the East and Central African regions as a whole.

By and large, in Maragua in 1986, the typical working man secured his food supplies by participating in his wife's rejection of coffee. Husbands recognized that their wives' resistance contributed funds and organizational coherence which allowed men to hold onto their land in the midst of expanding and accelerating large-scale enclosures. Not only did Maragua women cultivators plant food. They also reinstated producer control over land. And they re-established and strengthened their collective women's work groups, which form the basis for many activities such as savings and credit "merry-go-rounds."[21]

In 1996 the IMF loaned 12 billion Kenyan shillings (US$218 million) to the government. In October 1996, Kenyan president Moi launched an agriculture policy paper aimed at "enabling the sector to run as a fully commercial enterprise,"[22] with emphasis on export crops. Though Maragua farmers escaped the exploitation of the coffee market, the alternative they built exists within the framework of an increasingly privatized and commodified society. The state and multinational corporations continue to regulate working women's labour by giving credit to (male) title deed holders to encourage horticulture. Foreign and local capitalists entice landowning men in Maragua into labour-intensive and chemical-dependent export production. Husbands of women who have rejected coffee may view horticulture as a means to reassert command over women's labour. Such is the temptation of the male deal. Meanwhile, the state upholds laws which favour men. Into the new millennium, the Constitution of Kenya allows discrimination based on sex. This legal framework works in favour of the corporate agenda in that it limits women's subsistence choices.

Through reviving self-organized and autonomous customary work groups, the women have begun to reconstruct subsistence society, for instance through rebuilding a regional trade system.

In sum, the women's dramatic attack on the coffee trees broke and restructured long-standing social relationships at three levels: local, national, and international. First, the Maragua insurgents shifted effective control over resources from their husbands into their own hands. Second, they broke their relationships of debt peonage and subjection to the state coffee apparatus and established an alternative self-regulated banana trade. In doing so, they contributed to forcing the single-party state to legalize opposition parties.[23] Third, the Maragua women extracted themselves from state-mediated relationships with foreign suppliers of agro-chemical inputs and a global coffee market that enriched commercial traders at the expense of producers.

Conclusion

In the past fifteen years, many farming women of Maragua have attempted to gain control over land for food production. They have confronted the state, corporations, and often, their own husbands. The relations of production imposed upon producers by capital and the state have organized dispossessed women to resist. They began by refusing the discipline meted out by husbands who sought high returns on the crops women produced. While the IMF and World Bank are stepping up pressure to privatize state assets, including coffee milling and marketing bodies, women producers are creating an alternative to corporate takeover – one grounded in a resuscitated civil commons.

There are many lessons that might be taken from the experience of women cultivators in Maragua, one of which is that the organization of global and local markets strengthens women to break exploitative relationships with men and then to join with other women to pursue common class objectives that are shared by people of different ethnicities. This study suggests that exploited men's abdication of domination over women workers and wives not only extends the scope of workers' initiatives to control resources but also breaks hierarchical relationships that subordinate women and men producers.

A second lesson involves the movement of women cultivators into direct confrontation with international firms. Our analysis confirms the insight that neoliberal strategists predicate their structural adjustment programs on the effectiveness of husbands' discipline over wives' labour. Those women who reject exploitative relations of production appear to do so through a transformative process that starts by satisfying the needs of the dispossessed. They focus attention on a crucial source of ethnic antagonisms: competition amongst factions of the exploited for resources which are increasingly privatized, especially by international firms. In repudiating export crops, rural women enhance food supplies for the dispossessed who are, thus, less divided. In repudiating gendered exploitation, women cultivators in Maragua offer an alternative to neoliberalism.

Following upon Agarwal's research on women's need for independent land rights, we have analyzed how some Kenyan women have collectivized their struggle to control land and pursue a livelihood. These women took command of their own labour and other resources by spurning often violent discipline by husbands, defying state policies, and resisting their own incorporation into global markets, on corporations' terms.

As the Maragua case suggests, the pivotal struggle in East and Central Africa today is one of commodification versus sustenance. In resisting export crop agriculture women are expanding the terrain for a much more sustainable, ecologically sound, sustenance agriculture. Women are at the forefront of the many forms of resistance to structural adjustment. They are joined by those men who decline to be overseers of their wives' production on behalf of the state and capital.

Structural adjustment's insistence on more cash crop production for export, combined with untrammelled private appropriation of the commons and public property under the rubric of neoliberal privatization, has thrown small-scale farmers (who are overwhelmingly women) up against an array of opponents. These may disguise the complex gendered class struggles as "tribalism," while inviting militarization and debilitating "aid" from interests that are fully committed to rapid structural adjustment and the poverty it imposes.[24] The original challenge posed in the mid-1980s by women cultivators, such as those in Maragua, to exploitation mediated by their husbands has evolved into a confrontation with the forces of globalizing corporations fifteen years later.

In the future, two patterns are likely to unfold. First, women can be expected to coordinate their actions regionally and internationally to a much greater extent and with the involvement of allied men. An avenue through which this is happening is the international Jubilee 2000 debt cancellation campaign. Second, the militarization of the region by international interests can be expected to increase. The United States initiative to establish and train an African intervention and peacekeeping military capability is one expression of this heightened militarization. Another is the involvement of mercenaries plus several countries' armed forces in the on-going strife in the Democratic Republic of the Congo, Algeria, Sierra Leone, and Mozambique. Maragua women's struggles for sustainable agriculture stand as evidence of the real reasons for what Minister of Foreign Affair Lloyd Axworthy has called "humanitarian military intervention."[25] They call for a response of solidarity from people elsewhere to oppose the military reconquest of Africa and to stand with the women farmers and their allies as they resist neoliberal enclosures by fighting to replace export crops with food production.

Finally, we conclude by identifying some links between the Kenyan gendered class analysis and debates on the ethics of Canadian foreign policy within a changing global security context. This study's results have at least three implications for Canadian foreign policy.

First, the Kenyan case shows that food security is sought by the poor through their own efforts and not through ceding responsibility to the government. In Kenya there is zero confidence in the efficacy of the government's food relief programs. More broadly, virtually all food imports are effected within a set of relationships that ensures profiteering for the politically well-placed, potential ruin for local producers, and more hardship for the poor. In 1998 for instance, scandal attended the importation of duty-free sugar, which was done with the specific support of the World Bank office in Nairobi. The result was the definitive sacrifice of the local sugar industry to structural adjustment.[26]

Rural Kenyan women insist on obtaining access to land and on maintaining control over land that they have obtained. This drive to secure land is evident in the growing incidence of squatting, forest cultivation, "urban gardening," land invasions, sabotage of those farmers deemed by community members to be using land illegitimately, and reappropriation of property enclosed by "land grabs" under the protective cover of the structural adjustment ideology that champions privatization. These initiatives are increasingly coordinated through, for example, the 3,000-strong Muungano Wana Vijiji (Kiswahili for Organization of Villagers), which mounts legal challenges to back direct action to defend small producers' land claims and to prevent the demolition of markets and homes by the state. The primary reason that women and men seize and defend land is for food production.

The reality that women rely on themselves to establish food security must be set against the official policies of the World Bank, the UK program for Overseas Development Assistance, and other governmental agencies that define food security as the ability of a government to allocate sufficient foreign exchange to pay for adequate food imports.[27] The Kenyan case study shows that the World Bank conception of food security in fact contradicts indigenous, grassroots definitions of food security. Our analysis shows that some Kenyan women refuse to produce export crops for foreign exchange generation, knowing, from bitter experience, that food for their families will not be organized through government action (directly, through NGOs, or via the private sector). Given this contradiction, the World Bank is implicated, along with the Canadian and other member governments of the United Nations, in forcing upon rural Africans policies consistent with the official notion of food security.

Second, the Kenyan analysis stands as a critique of structural adjustment programs, particularly with respect to their emphasis on export or other cash crops rejected by rural women. Despite widespread recognition of the unworkability of the agricultural export orientation (coffee, tea, cut flowers, French beans), in the late 1990s, officials of the World Bank in Kenya regularly reiterated in the national media the imperative character of such policies. Nevertheless, throughout the region (e.g., in pockets of the highly fertile Rift Valley, the former "White Highlands" of colonial Kenya), farmers with two or three acres continue to repudiate export crops (such as pyrethrum) and replace them with food and other sustenance production.

In East Africa and the Great Lakes Region, since the early 1990s, so-called "ethnic clashes" have driven agriculturalists off their flourishing small holdings and into poverty-stricken desperation, frequently in refugee camps or squatter communities. Some of Kenya's most prosperous and productive small-holders, the largely female-headed households of the Molo communities in the Rift Valley, were terrorized by government-organized massacres in the early 1990s. Vacated lands were then seized and resold. The highly successful sustenance economy was virtually destroyed and the stage has been set for profit taking by large-scale agro-industrial ventures owned by government favourites and foreign firms.

Furthermore a "market" has been created for "relief," with all that it entails for the further destruction of the livelihood of the small rural producer. The Kenyan government continues to be funded by World Bank, IMF, and Paris Club loans, and it continues to implement the neoliberal policies required by these governmental organizations. The foreign policies of these governments are consequently directly implicated in massive human rights abuses, including massacres both small and large.

Third, the Kenyan case study suggests that foreign military and food aid intervention such as that considered by Canada in the fall of 1996 in the case of Rwanda, could well be part of a larger strategy of repressing autonomous sustenance agriculture by women who are asserting control over production resources including their own time, skill, knowledges, land, and inputs. The much-criticized reductionism that represents internal violence in African societies as being "caused by tribalism" should no longer be allowed to veil the fundamental gendered class dynamics that, under the impetus of neoliberal market forces, have repeatedly given rise to ethnocide.

African rural women's direct action for food security is taking place in the face of neoliberal trade policies that militate against sustenance production. Their resistance to programs imposed by Western governments is a major force in the civil wars or "ethnic conflicts," into which Canadian military involvement in Africa is drawn. The contention here is that substantial circumstantial evidence exists suggesting a causal connection linking:

(a) women's insistence on taking direct responsibility for food security
(b) women farmers' refusal to produce according to the policy dictates of structural adjustment, effecting a prolonged strike
(c) women farmers' replacement of commodities with products for the sustenance of their families and local and regional trade on their own account
(d) declines in government revenue from the sale of imported agrochemical inputs to coffee farmers and from the trade of coffee on the international market, leaving the government and its foreign lenders with reduced sums of foreign exchange
(e) narrow attempts by the government, international financial institutions and NGOs to diversify into horticultural commodities (French beans, strawberries, flowers) and genetically modified bananas, in order to bring ex-coffee farmers' land back under foreign exchange-earning commodity production
(f) peasants' lack of faith in government-sponsored and -managed commodities programs and subsequent rejection of new horticultural initiatives, with continued commitment to sustenance production and trade
(g) violent repression of sustenance producers by the state and state-organized paramilitaries (misrepresented as "ethnic clashes," whether in Kenya, Rwanda, or elsewhere in Africa); and
(h) finally, the prospect of "humanitarian military interventions" from abroad which, as Jean Daudelin of the North South Institute in Ottawa says, "invariably favour one side over the other(s) ... while not necessarily leading to a peaceful and durable political outcome ... offer[ing] no guarantee that the countries in which they take place will improve politically or economically, or even that the humanitarian situation will not deteriorate further once the intervention ends."[28]

These links are strong enough and serious enough to at least put on the agenda for further debate the hypothesis that an ethical foreign policy consistent with human rights must be a policy supportive of rural women's own strategies for strengthening the sustenance economy.

This chapter has delineated a case meant to provoke debate about the effects of existing policies on rural women in Africa and the "fit" between existing policies and the goals and purposes of humane internationalism and human security. A dramatic about-face is required in the "trade *uber alles*" that guides Canada's foreign policy if further disintegration of human security, in Africa and on a global scale, is to be avoided. A starting point for changes to Canadian foreign policy would be a full range of studies and supportive activities focused on rural women's direct responsibility for food security, and the related maintenance of peace in their communities and regions.

Acknowledgment
This study is based on oral histories, interviews, and secondary material collected between 1994 and 1998 by the authors as part of a small international network of researchers called First Woman (East and Southern African Women's Oral Histories and Indigenous Knowledge Network). We are informed by Sandra Harding's work on standpoint theories which "show how to move from *including* others' lives and thoughts in research and scholarly projects to *starting from* their lives to ask research questions." (Sandra Harding and Janet G. Townsend, *Women's Voices from the Rainforest*, [London: Routledge, (1991-95), 133]). Portions of the work have been previously published as "Social Reconstruction in Rural Africa: A Gendered Class Analysis of Women's Resistance to Export Crop Production in Kenya." in *Canadian Journal of Development Studies* 18, 2 (1997): 213-38.

Notes

1 John McMurtry, *The Cancer Stage of Capitalism* (London: Pluto, 1998).

2 The concepts of "sustenance" and "sustenance agriculture" are based on the concepts of "subsistence" and the "subsistence perspective" elaborated by Maria Mies and Vandana Shiva in *Ecofeminism* (London: Zed and Halifax: Fernwood, 1993), 55-69, 297-323. The concepts of sustenance versus commodified economies are consistent with John McMurtry's broader conceptions of the "life sequence of value" in which means of life are transformed into more life, on the one hand; and on the other, the "money sequence of value" in which money is transformed into more money through the production of commodities, means of destruction or mere speculation. See McMurtry, *The Cancer Stage of Capitalism*.

3 Meredeth Turshen and Clotilde Twagiramariya, eds., *What Women Do in Wartime: Gender and Conflict in Africa* (London: Zed, 1998).

4 L. Sophia (Leigh S. Brownhill and Terisa E. Turner), "Algeria and Kenya: Similar Story," *Mtetezi*, Newsletter of the Release of Political Prisoners (RPP) Pressure Group, Nairobi, 1, 9: 10.

5 Michel Chossudovsky, *The Globalization of Poverty* (London: Zed and Third World Network, 1998).

6 "France accused of aiding Hutus," *Globe and Mail* (reprinted from *The Guardian)*, Toronto, 13 January 1998.

7 Reuters, *Daily Nation* (Nairobi) (7 December 1996), 8; Meredeth Turshen and Clotilde Twagiramariya, eds., *What Women Do*, 4.

8 Jean Daudelin, "Kosovo, Claymore Mines and Talisman: Is Reality Catching Up With Canada's Rhetoric?" (Ottawa: North South Institute, March 2000). Available at <www.nsi-ins.ca/ensi/news_views/oped11.html>.

9 Farmers have begun to make international links in their efforts to resist Tiomin. "The

farmers quote studies by reputable international environment NGOs on the firm's activities in other countries. They are also demanding an independent environmental impact assessment report. They are basing this demand on NGO reports that mining companies only fouled the environment in Third World countries." See Kauli Mwatela, "Titanium firm told to pay more," *Daily Nation* (Nairobi), 11 March 2000. Available at <www.nationaudio.com/News/DailyNation/Today>. In 2001, the court issued a temporary injunction to halt Tiomin's prospecting and mining, but farmers seek a permanent injunction.

10 Terisa E. Turner and Craig S. Benjamin, "Not in Our Nature: The Male Deal and Corporate Solutions to the Debt-Nature Crisis," *Review: A Journal of the Fernand Braudel Center* 28, 2 (Spring 1995): 211.

11 Carol L. Dauda, "Yan Tatsine and the Male Deal: Islam, Gender and Class Struggle in Northern Nigeria" (MA thesis, University of Guelph, 1992); Turner and Benjamin, "Not in Our Nature."

12 John McMurtry, *Unequal Freedoms: The Global Market as an Ethical System* (Toronto/Connecticut: Garamond/Kumarian, 1998), 24.

13 A more detailed account is available in Leigh S. Brownhill, Wahu M. Kaara, and Terisa E. Turner, "Gender Relations and Sustainable Agriculture: Rural Women's Resistance to Structural Adjustment in Kenya," *Canadian Woman Studies/Les Cahiers de la Femme* 17, 2 (Spring 1997): 40-44. Available at <www.yorku.ca/org/cwscf/home.html>.

14 Bina Agarwal, "Gender and Command over Property: A Critical Gap in Economic Analysis and Policy in South Asia," *World Development* 22, 10 (1994): 1459-61.

15 All interviews are cited as "First Woman," followed by the date.

16 Republic of Kenya, *Murang'a District Development Plan, 1994-1996, Rural Planning Department: Office of the Vice President and Ministry of Planning and National Development* 1993 (1): 12.

17 World Bank, *Adjustment in Africa: Reforms, Results and the Road Ahead* (Washington DC: World Bank, 13 March 1994).

18 First Woman, 2 January 1997.

19 Catherine Mgendi, "Sector Records Negative Growth Rates," *Daily Nation* (Nairobi), 13 December 1996: 4; Catherine Mgendi, "Reasons for Decline in Agricultural Production," *Daily Nation* (Nairobi), 3 October 1996, I.

20 In April 2001, hundreds of Kenyan farmers continued to be involved in the uprooting and abandoning of coffee trees. Farmers in the Nyamira District "ousted" officials in local coffee cooperative societies and "replaced [them] with interim committees. The farmers, drawn from 18 factories, cite low payment, mismanagement of their societies and delayed payment [as an explanation] for their action. Some farmers who have not uprooted their trees have resorted to selling their coffee to middlemen who sell it to a neighbouring country, where prices are said to be high. Last year's earnings was Sh78.5 million, a drop from the previous year's Sh109.7 million." Nation Correspondent, "Frustrated Coffee Farmers Uproot Their Trees," *Daily Nation* (Nairobi), 13 April 2001.

21 The merry-go-rounds are called "esusu" in Ghana, "susu" in Trinidad and Tobago. In the merry-go-rounds, every week each woman in the group contributes a small sum of money into a "pot," and every week, a different member receives the pot. She typically uses her share to pay school fees or to buy household utensils or a goat.

22 Catherine Mgendi, "Government Plans Fundamental Reforms for Agriculture," *Daily Nation* (Nairobi), 3 October 1996, 1-2.

23 In the town of Sagana, near Maragua town, small business women refused to deliver coffee to government buyers and simultaneously demanded that the KANU regime repeal section 2(A) of the Kenya Constitution which outlawed opposition political parties. When the coffee industry collapsed, the Paris Club of donors, in 1991, ordered Kenya's President Moi to legalize multi-party democracy. He complied in 1992. First Woman, 7 October 1996.

24 Peter Abwao, "Food Crisis: Kenya Needs Urgent Overhaul," *Kenya Times* (Nairobi), 16 July 1996, 16.

25 Daudelin, "Kosovo, Claymore Mines and Talisman."

26 Sugar and coffee farmers do not sit idle once the markets for their crops fail. Many plant other crops and strengthen local markets. Likewise in the rice industry, where in early 2001 it was reported that "200,000 bags of rice in Mwea [Irrigation Scheme] cannot be

sold due to a glut in the market caused by imports. Mwea rice farmers have not sold their produce for the year 2000/2001 crop ... The farmers took over control of the scheme by force and started delivering their crop to the [cooperative] society. During the take-over, two people were shot dead by police and scores injured ... The scheme is facing an acute water shortage ... [as river waters] have been diverted to other uses." Nation Correspondent, "Farmers Lose as Rice Imports Clog Market," *Daily Nation* (Nairobi), 3 April 2001.

27 V. Jamal, "African crisis, Food Security and Structural Adjustment," *International Labour Review* 127, 6 (1988): 649-812; Hans Singer, personal communication, 3 March 1997.

28 Daudelin, "Kosovo, Claymore Mines and Talisman."

Part 4
International Humanitarian Law and Norms

7
Soft Power, Moral Suasion, and Establishing the International Criminal Court: Canadian Contributions

W. Andy Knight

This chapter examines, through the use of a case study on the evolution of the International Criminal Court (ICC), ways in which the Canadian government has tried to add ethical content to its foreign policy. It combines an exploration of concepts such as "human security" and "soft power" with a historical analysis of how the ICC idea emerged and evolved and an explanation of Canada's role in that process.

After seventy years of debate and deliberation concerning the need for a permanent criminal court at the international level, 147 member states of the United Nations (UN) system signed into force, on 17 July 1998, the Rome Statute of the International Criminal Court. What began in 1989 as a "soft power" initiative by the government of a Caribbean micro-state, Trinidad and Tobago, to kick-start negotiations on the wording of a draft statute for an international criminal court, finally gained momentum in the spring of 1996 and led to the consolidation of the ICC final draft statute.[1] It took only thirty days to finalize the treaty that would serve as the ICC's legal foundation, but it may take several years before the international community has a clear indication of what this court will be able to achieve and how effective it will become. Simply signing a treaty at a diplomatic conference does not make international law; treaties have to be ratified by states, and they can only bind consenting states.

Of the seven states that objected to the final draft statute, the US promises to pose the greatest challenge to the court's jurisdiction. Efforts by that government to ensure that the actions of its citizens, particularly US military personnel and political leadership, will remain outside of the jurisdiction of this court, could result in the stillbirth of this judicial body. Without the political and monetary backing of the only remaining superpower, the future of this organization may be in some doubt. However, there is an outside chance that the steadfast support of the ICC by a number of like-minded small and middle-sized states could sustain the idea behind it just long enough for moral suasion to assist in the entrenchment of international criminal law and, therefore, that adherence to the principles of this law will, over time, overcome neorealist pessimism. As we have seen in the case of the Ottawa landmines negotiations, powerful countries like the US can find themselves "sidelined by history"[2] and by the exercise of "soft power."

The purpose of this chapter is to provide the reader with a succinct historical account of the development of the concept of a permanent mechanism to deal with international criminals; an empirical and interpretive examination of the role Canada played throughout the preparatory phase and the actual conference of plenipotentiaries that ushered in the ICC; and some critical reflections on "soft power" and "moral suasion" in the conduct of Canadian foreign policy and on the development of a normative framework to underpin such policy. First, however, in light of the themes of this volume, it is necessary to make the connection between ethics and security with respect to Canada's attempt to find a niche for itself within the diplomatic community at this particular historical juncture.

Ethics and Security in Canadian Foreign Policy: The Normative Context

Within Canada there is a growing interest in the ethical, normative, and moral aspects of foreign policy. This comes at a time when Canada's security environment is changing, and its government is faced with making hard choices between pragmatism and moralism. Caught between those two choices, it appears that the Canadian government has decided to adopt a foreign policy that blends utilitarian objectives with selective moralistic pursuits. The message being sent is that Canadian foreign policy cannot be "all things to all people." Yet there are certain causes that Canadians hold dear and that ought to be pursued with moral zeal at the international level.[3]

Examples of this more narrow and selective "niche" diplomacy can be found in Canada's recent foreign policy rhetoric and conduct, which attempts to link what is being termed as a human security agenda with soft power activity. In this regard, it is instructive to follow the public record statements of Canadian foreign affairs minister Lloyd Axworthy. In a 1998 interview with the *Ottawa Citizen,* Axworthy gave some insight into Canada's new "niche" diplomacy and put some flesh on the conceptual bones of "human security" and "soft power." The minister began by acknowledging the extent to which the security context for Canada and the world had changed since the end of the Cold War. In his words, "the nature of war has changed dramatically from the conventional conflicts between states and governments to internal ones. Many of the weapons being applied have reached a volume where the victims are women, children, civilians, innocent people. The old rules, the old Geneva Convention, simply don't give them any protection anymore." Then he went on to give examples of the changing security context and, in so doing, provided the rationale for the selectivity in Canadian post-Cold War foreign policy.[4]

The key issue for Axworthy is how to frame a foreign policy so that the specific ethical concerns of Canadians can be addressed internationally. The most logical frame seems to begin with what is being considered as a transformation in the "meaning of security" from state security to human security, and with the centrality of humanitarian issues both to Canadians and to Canadian political culture. From this flows the normative context within which the minister would like to see Canadian foreign policy conducted. That context, according to Axworthy, requires the establishment of "a new body of international law of a humanitarian kind."[5]

Examples of some of the humanitarian concerns for Canadian foreign policy include addressing problems associated with anti-personnel landmines and the proliferation of small arms. Not only do these two issues demonstrate the extent to which Canada's post-Cold War perception of the international security context has changed, they also point out the need for all governments to develop an ethical and moral basis within policy making. Anti-personnel landmines are weapons that, even after they have fulfilled their military purposes, can inflict great harm on ordinary citizens. Small arms have reached an epidemic level, particularly in Third World countries, and have tended to destabilize societies, increasing their level of insecurity. The situation becomes even more morally repugnant when those small arms get into the hands of children. The child soldier has become a major problem for the international community, for even after wars are over children who were recruited to fight may take these weapons with them and become a threat to their own societies.

For Axworthy, the solution to the above problems lies in the solidification of international humanitarian and criminal law. Early on the minister backed the notion of establishing a draft code of crimes and a permanent ICC to try such international criminals. To quote from his above interview:

> The reason why I think the international court has become so crucial, is that the new body of humanitarian law ... needs some way of holding not only presidents and prime ministers and ministers accountable, but to hold individuals accountable. Once you do that, it begins to provide its own deterrent to behaviour, whether it's abusing children or recruiting children or propagating hate or committing acts of genocide. All of a sudden you realize that sometime, somewhere, you're going to be held accountable.[6]

This is the normative context within which the "new" Canadian foreign policy is being made. Obviously, the post-Cold War security context opens up a window of opportunity for Canada to reframe its foreign policy goals.[7] Having lost much of its shine, Canadian foreign policy is being repackaged in a selective way. This country has long considered itself a state that abides by core principles of international law. Axworthy seemed to make this a major point of departure for Canada's niche diplomacy and foreign policy conduct.

Soft Power and Norm Entrepreneurship

While the above setting explains Canada's pursuit of international humanitarian law and a new set of international standards and practices in support of that law, it was the genocidal massacre of more than half a million people in Rwanda and the senseless ethnic cleansing in Bosnia that sparked, within Canada, renewed interest in the establishment of a supranational judicial mechanism to deal with states and individuals suspected of genocide, war crimes, and crimes against humanity. In addition, the impunity enjoyed by most architects and perpetrators of some of the worst massacres and atrocities of this century (e.g., Pol Pot and the Khmer Rouge in Cambodia, Idi Amin in Uganda, Saddam Hussein in Iraq, Pinochet in Chile, Radovan Karadzic in Bosnia, Slobodan Milosevic in Serbia/Kosovo, and the Hutus in Rwanda) further underlay the drive by Canadian diplomats within the UN to assist in the establishment of the ICC.

However, it is one thing to have laudable goals in foreign policy and another to find the appropriate means to achieve them. Consistent with the model of diplomacy employed during the Ottawa Process – the campaign to ban anti-personnel landmines – Canada joined with a bloc of like-minded small and medium-sized states and became a leading force for the establishment of the ICC. Canada became the chair of this group of states and was influential in guiding the multilateral process and negotiations around the creation of this court.[8] It is during this process that Canada demonstrated what, these days, is being labelled "soft power."[9]

Soft power is not easily defined, and the hard/soft power dichotomy may be too simplistic to be analytically useful. However, it is instructive to return to Canada's foreign minister for some indication of what this term has come to mean in the minds of Canadian foreign policy makers. Axworthy likes to refer to soft power as a case of "punching above one's weight." In Canada's case, according to the minister, what it really means is "the power to influence the behaviour of others" through the use of "ideas, values, persuasion, skill, and technique."[10] Soft power is, therefore, used in contrast to "hard power"; that is, the use of military might and economic clout to get others to do what, otherwise, they would not do.

One example used by the minister was Kofi Annan's negotiations with

Saddam Hussein to end the crisis over weapons inspections in Iraq. In that case, the UN secretary-general used his own moral authority and skills of persuasion to accomplish what the threat of American military might was unable to do. At the same time, it is important to remember that military might was nevertheless present, in the background, and may also have provided needed backing for the soft power initiative. This leads one logically to question whether soft power can be effective on its own or whether it needs material support from hard power elements in order to be successful. In any event, Axworthy's example might not have been the best one, given the final turn of events in Iraq.

A more productive approach may be to consider how some states, with little or no demonstrative material capability to speak of, can use norms to galvanize support for pet issues. In this sense norms are typically portrayed as either constituting, regulating, or enabling actors in their environment. The more robust a norm the more influential it will be on interests, on individual actor behaviour, or on the collective practices and outcomes of a number of like-minded actors. From this perspective, norms do not necessarily determine outcomes, but they can create permissive conditions for foreign policy action.[11] Norms, therefore, can structure realms of possibilities and create "options" that may not have been self-evident in their absence.[12]

Martha Finnemore and Kathryn Sikkink advance a theory of the "norm lifecycle" as a means of trying to understand and explain the origins and emergence of international norms and the process through which they influence state and non-state behaviour. They are also concerned with the question of whether or not (and under what circumstances) norms matter.

Norm emergence, the first stage in this three-stage process, is facilitated by norm entrepreneurs, who attempt to persuade and convince other actors to embrace a particular or "new" norm. The second stage is seen as an attempt to socialize other actors into becoming norm followers. Finally, in the third stage, norms are internalized through institutionalization. At this stage, norms may gain the status of being taken for granted, particularly if they are perceived as "robust."

However, the completion of the lifecycle is not an inevitable process, since many emerging norms fail to gain broad support among other actors or fail to become institutionalized.[13] Thus norm entrepreneurs are essential to the process of norm building and making norms robust.

Norm Entrepreneurs

Although little theoretical work has focused on the origins of norms or on the process of "norm building," those who have paid attention to norm evolution stress the importance of agency with regard to the latter. Here is where the concept of moral entrepreneurs/norm entrepreneurs comes in. Norms, such as those associated with human security, do not simply appear out of thin air. They are actively built by agents who have a strong notion of appropriate behaviour in their community. These entrepreneurs call attention to, create, and frame issues in a way that makes them desirable. Thus, they are critical in developing consensus on what may generally be considered appropriate, right, or good policy.

New norms, or old norms framed in a novel way, can shape new interests and enable new or different patterns of behaviour, even if they do not guarantee the consistency of such patterns. These norms, whether new or remodelled, do not emerge in a vacuum. They have to compete with other emerging or extant norms and values. Hence, efforts to promote new norms take place within the existing framework of "appropriateness," a framework usually circumscribed by pre-existing or established norms. If a new, emerging, or remodelled norm can be portrayed as corresponding with the existing logic of appropriateness, then it is much more likely to gain influence than it would be if it challenged the existing logic.

The human security concept, advocated by Minister Axworthy and others, is based on the principle that, while the security of states is essential, the safety, protection, and well-being of the world's people should take priority in a country's foreign policy.[14] The norms that flow from this position obviously challenge the state-centric view of security, but they are generally framed within the logic of an extension of national security. Under the existing "logic of appropriateness," therefore, notions of human security and a shared understanding of human dignity seem to have influenced norm entrepreneurs such as Canada and its like-minded counterparts to try to eliminate some of the obstacles that lie in the path of the establishment and consolidation of humanitarian and criminal law at the international level.

Overcoming Deficiencies in International Criminal Law

One of the glaring deficiencies in international law has been the absence of a satisfactory means for adopting, applying, and enforcing legal norms.[15] Whereas in a country like Canada courts can rely upon federal or provincial legislative bodies to adopt and adapt laws, and upon police forces to apply and enforce such laws, the international community must rely upon the UN (a voluntarist institution) to develop international criminal law through the accumulation of a body of precedents and customs and ad hoc multinational treaties that are not binding on non-signatories.

Although there are conventions dealing with a broad range of international crimes,[16] the absence of a permanent mechanism for prosecuting individuals guilty of these crimes effectively weakens these legal instruments. As Christopher Joyner points out, the reality is that, "despite development over the past seventy years of relatively sophisticated, universalistic, sanctions-equipped international organizations – namely, the League of Nations and the UN – the world community still relies primarily upon the principle of self-help to enforce international legal sanctions."[17] The International Court of Justice (ICJ) does not have compulsory jurisdiction to deal with these issues and is, in any case, an underutilized judicial institution.[18] In any event, we are all too aware of how states tend to attach crippling reservations to their acceptance of ICJ rulings.

The Canadian government has always been aware of the deficiencies in international law making and enforcement and has, since 1945, sought to strengthen the norms that form the foundation of such law. Canadian representatives, for instance, have worked diligently with other like-minded states (especially the Nordic countries, the Netherlands, Australia, New Zealand, and some Caribbean nations) within the UN system to explore ways of strengthening the rule of law within the international system. They have drawn upon the UN Charter – a relatively dynamic document that lays out general principles upon which to base international laws – to establish bodies through which specific international legal concerns can be addressed and international laws developed. Clearly, the collective actions of states within the UN – a body that has become increasingly universal since its founding – has resulted over the years in the progressive development of international law.[19] In addition, Canada is one of a few countries to have war crimes legislation linked to the international genocide treaty.[20]

The main deficiency to be overcome in the establishment and institutionalization of international criminal law has been the absence of a permanent body to enforce such law. For Canada, getting agreement on the establishment of this permanent body was considered to be not only necessary, but also possibly the most significant improvement to the UN's ability to maintain peace and security since the advent of peacekeeping.[21]

Stepping Stones Leading to the Establishment of an International Criminal Court

The steps leading to the creation of an international court to address international war crimes and crimes against humanity can be traced back to 1474, when Peter Von Hagenbush was tried by an international tribunal of the Holy Roman Empire for war crimes committed in Breisach, Germany. Since that time, there have been several attempts to deal with war criminals through international institutions. For instance, in 1810, the Congress of Aix-la-Chapelle exiled Napoleon Bonaparte to the island of Elba for waging an unjust war. And the Hague Peace Conferences in 1899 and 1907 drafted conventions that raised the notion of developing binding customs based on the laws of humanity and the dictates of public conscience. However, those "laws of humanity" were not as yet clearly delineated, nor were they articulated in any international legal document. The atrocities of the First World War again raised the level of consciousness of humanity with regard to the need for a clear link between state aggression and international crime. There was a general sense at the time that those who were responsible for offences against the established laws and customs of war and against the natural law principle of humaneness should be liable for criminal prosecution.

This sentiment was expressed in the aftermath of the First World War at the 1919 Paris Peace Conference, where an international criminal tribunal was proposed. However, this institutional mechanism did not materialize. The Treaty of Versailles did provide a mechanism for the trial of war criminals.[22] But the deficiencies of international law at the time perhaps explain the failure of the proposed five-country special tribunal to bring Kaiser Wilhelm and other war criminals to trial.[23] The absence of political will on the part of the big powers (i.e., the victors) to establish an independent international criminal court to deal with such atrocities was all too present during the brief existence of the League of Nations. Japan's aggression against Manchuria in 1931 did not appear sufficient to goad the powers that could do something about it into judicial action. However, in 1934 France called for the codification of international criminal law and the creation of an international criminal court to punish terrorists such as those responsible for the assassinations of King Alexander of Yugoslavia and the French foreign minister. This led, in 1936, to the drafting of the Convention for the Prevention and Punishment of Terrorism and the Convention for a Criminal Court at the international level.[24] Yet only India saw fit to ratify the Convention for the Criminal Court, and neither convention was ever brought into effect.

It was only after the world was shocked by the atrocities of Hitler's "total war" and genocidal activity, and the excesses of Italy and Japan during the Second World War, that the allied powers and nations affected sprang into action. In January 1942, those nations most affected by Hitler's actions convened in St. James Palace (London) and declared that those in Germany who were guilty of crimes against humanity would surely face punishment through a mechanism of organized justice. Once similar declarations were made by the Allied Powers, a team of international legal experts began the task of drafting a new convention to create an international criminal court. Germany's defeat made it easier to pursue the prosecution of those who perpetrated heinous crimes against the Jews and others prior to and during the Second World War. The Charter for an International Military Tribunal was drafted and signed into international law and was unanimously approved and affirmed by the UN's first General Assembly. It, in essence, expressed the custom that assumed that the initiation of a war of aggression was the paramount international crime.

The London Charter of 1945 created the Nuremberg and Tokyo Tribunals. By the end of the Second World War, the victorious Allied Powers insisted on prosecuting those Germans and Japanese responsible for genocide in Europe and Asia during the war years. The London Charter became the first institutional framework within which international crimes – such as crimes against peace, war crimes, and crimes against humanity – could be prosecuted. The 1945 tribunals provided the first arguments for a more permanent international court, although they were hampered by the precedents set out in the inter-war years. Since "crimes against humanity" had already been defined, the drafters of the London Charter were forced to apply that definition to the conduct of the German government against German citizens. This made it difficult to prosecute those responsible for the crimes against German Jews before the Second World War.

Both the Nuremberg and Tokyo Tribunals were important steps in the attempt to curb atrocious international crimes through using the rule of law. However, three major criticisms were levied against these efforts. First, the retroactive application of the law offended the principle of no crime without law, especially with respect to crimes against peace and humanity. Second, victor's justice resulted in the apprehension and trial of losers of the war, while none of the offending victors was subjected to the same fate. And third, the many procedural problems, the absence of appeal provisions, and the imposition of the death penalty in certain cases all caused some observers to caution against using these tribunals as models for future tribunals.[25]

Some of the UN's early actions included passing a resolution condemning genocide as an international crime, establishing committees responsible for drafting a code of crimes, and establishing rules for a future international criminal court. Indeed, the International Law Commission (ILC) was established by the UN General Assembly on 21 November 1947[26] and assigned the task of codifying principles formulated by the International Military Tribunal during the war crimes trials at Nuremberg.[27] However, the advent of the Cold War and resultant stalemate in the UN Security Council, due to tensions between the US and the Soviet Union, made it next to impossible for the council to accomplish its goals. Thus, UN delegations haggled for decades over the need for an international criminal court when no consensus could be reached either on what would constitute a code of crimes or on the definition of aggression, genocide, war crimes, and crimes against humanity. In the meantime, as Benjamin Ferencz reminds us, "acts of genocide, aggression, war crimes and crimes against humanity were committed in many parts of the world with impunity."[28]

The case for a permanent international criminal court could be made even more strongly to anyone who observed the British War Crimes Trials of suspected war criminals in Italy between 1945 and 1947. There were forty such trials conducted in Italy during that period against individuals suspected of committing crimes against primarily British and Commonwealth Prisoners of War (POWs) during the Second World War. Jane L. Garwood-Carter, one of the few scholars who has researched these trials, notes that the purported war crimes were originally reported to the UN War Crimes Commission (UNWCC) but quickly lost any association with that body because the British never filed reports to the UNWCC after the trials were completed.[29]

The ad hoc nature of these trials, the cursory nature of the records kept by the British ad hoc courts in Italy, the reluctance of the Italian government to turn over some suspects for trial, the fact that some of the suspected war criminals escaped justice or got away with light sentences, and the poor preparation of some of the prosecutors and investigators are all testament to the need for the institutionalization of an international criminal court system. Even when convictions were laid, the British government was placed in a situation in which it had to negotiate an informal agreement with the Italian government that would allow the Italians to hold convicted war criminals in Italian prisons.

In 1954, the ILC finalized a *Draft Code of Offences against the Peace and Security of Mankind* at its sixth session and submitted it to the UN General Assembly. But it was not until 1974, when the Cold War had begun to thaw, that agreement was reached on the definition of aggression.[30] This definition, albeit still containing some ambiguities, cleared the path for further progress on the drafting of a code of international crimes and on the groundwork needed for the establishment of an international criminal court. The ILC continued to work on an elaboration of the *Draft Code of Offences* at the behest of the UN General Assembly.[31] Nevertheless, this progress was in drips and drabs until 1991, when Yugoslavia erupted into internecine violence that pit Serbs, Muslims, and Croats against each other. The practice of ethnic cleansing brought back memories of Hitler's genocidal activity. Nazi-style concentration camps, murders, torture, mass rapes, forced starvation, and forced displacement from homes were all part of the brutal actions occurring in the former Yugoslavia, and they outraged the international public.[32]

These acts, and their potential "spill-over" effect, forced the UN Security Council to consider actions to maintain the peace, using Chapter 7 of the UN Charter. Peacekeeping troops were sent in to separate warring factions, and innovations, such as preventive deployment, were tried as means of limiting the spread of violence. The ILC provisionally adopted and submitted to the UN General Assembly the *Draft Articles on the Code of Crimes*[33] – another major step in the development of international criminal law.

The new atrocities in Yugoslavia provided the catalyst for a return to the concept of establishing permanent international legal machinery for dealing with the perpetrators of genocide, crimes against the peace, war crimes, and crimes against humanity.[34] At the forty-seventh session of the UN General Assembly, member states (including Canada) requested that the ILC give priority to establishing an international criminal jurisdiction and to the draft statute that would be utilized by a permanent international criminal court.[35] In 1993, the UN Security Council and the UN General Assembly approved statutes drafted by the secretariat for an ad hoc international criminal tribunal – the first such criminal court since the Nuremberg and Tokyo Tribunals. Similarly, when the mass killing and genocidal crimes in Rwanda were reported, the council and assembly responded in 1994 by creating another ad hoc tribunal.[36]

These two ad hoc bodies – the International Criminal Tribunal for Yugoslavia (ICTY)[37] and the International Criminal Tribunal for the Prosecution of Persons Responsible for Genocide and Other Serious Violations of International Humanitarian Law in the Territory of Rwanda (ICTR)[38] – were given limited jurisdiction to try crimes in specified territories during a fixed time. Canada's Louise Arbour, as chief prosecutor, headed up both tribunals.[39] Despite administrative limitations, staffing problems, limited finances, and poor enforcement capabilities, the creation of these two judicial organs became an important step in solidifying international criminal law and in moving towards the establishment of a permanent international criminal court. These two tribunals, in addition to showing that a sound mechanism for criminal prosecution could be employed for other circumstances, also spurred on debate about a more permanent tribunal.[40]

The Conference of Plenipotentiaries for a Permanent ICC

On 27 November 1995, the sixth committee, at its fiftieth session, entertained the notion of establishing a preparatory committee (PrepCom) that would be open to all UN member states, members of specialized agencies, and/or members of the International Atomic Energy Agency (IAEA). This PrepCom would be assigned the combined tasks of considering issues arising out of the draft statute mentioned above and of negotiating the final text of the statute for the proposed permanent ICC.[41] Space limitation does not permit a detailed account of the important work of the PrepCom leading up to the convening of a Conference of Plenipotentiaries for the establishment of a Permanent International Criminal Court.[42] But it is important to note that the committee's final report was submitted to the United Nations secretary-general at the beginning of the UN General Assembly's fifty-first session.[43] At that fifty-first session, there was an agenda item entitled "Establishment of an International Criminal Court." This item allowed for a full discussion of the PrepCom's report as well as of the call to convene an international conference of plenipotentiaries to finalize and adopt a convention on the establishment of a permanent court.[44] The main rationale used for creating a single, permanent international criminal court was to obviate the need for ad hoc tribunals for particular crimes,[45] the implication being that a permanent international judicial structure and process would likely ensure stability and consistency in international criminal jurisdiction.

But what would such a body look like? According to the report, the court was envisaged as a multilateral, treaty-established, independent judicial organ that could remain permanently in session if its caseload so required. It would have a particular administrative structure and specific jurisdiction. The administrative structure would consist of a main court presided over by eighteen judges, each elected to nine-year non-renewable terms by an absolute majority of states party to the statute of the court. The court would have four main organs: a presidency, the chambers, a procuracy, and a registry. Then there would be two chambers – a six-member appeals chamber and a five-member trial chamber. A special five-judge chamber of the court would consider the application of the laws of pardon, parole, or commutation of the state in which an accused international criminal happened to be held. Decisions of the trial chamber could be reversed in the appeals chamber (with a quorum of six and with a majority vote). The procuracy would be an independent investigative arm of the court, headed by a prosecutor, assisted by one or more deputies and supported by a qualified staff. The registry would consist of a registrar chosen via secret ballot (for a renewable five-year term) by an absolute majority of the judges. Support staff would be appointed, as necessary, to facilitate the work of the registrar.

That the court was intended to complement national criminal justice systems, and not to replace them, is evident from the discussions that came out of the Ad Hoc Committee and the ILC. The ILC (on which Canada served) made it clear from the outset that the proposed court would not replace national courts and that states had a vital interest in remaining responsible for prosecuting violations of their respective laws. However, a number of sticky issues arose from these discussions. There would be a need for a clearer definition of the principle of complementarity between the court and national criminal justice systems. There needed to be a clearer determination of who would be responsible for deciding when national courts were inadequate. Several troubling questions were raised as to whether national courts should have priority over the international court, and concern was expressed over the possibility that the primacy of national jurisdictions might, in some cases, lead to the shielding of criminals.

The court's jurisdiction would apply either when a state had custody of an accused person (either because such a state had jurisdiction over the crime or because it had received an extradition request relating to it) or when the crime was committed on its territory. The draft statute also made provision for jurisdiction over crimes referred to the court by the Security Council, acting under Chapter 7 of the UN Charter.[46] Participants on the PrepCom (including the Canadian delegation) generally supported giving the court competence over a "hard core" of crimes such as genocide, war crimes, and crimes against humanity.[47] Agreement was also widespread that the legal principles of *nullum crimen sine lege* (no crime without law) and *nulla poena sine lege* (no penalty without law) should be followed. Thus, in the draft statute, the ILC and the PrepCom took care to precisely define the crimes likely to be dealt with by the court rather than to simply enumerate them. Several state representatives suggested that definitions from the Nuremberg Tribunal Charter and the statutes of the ad hoc international tribunals for the former Yugoslavia and for Rwanda be incorporated into the final *Draft Code of Crimes against the Peace and Security of Mankind.*

The sixty-article draft statute, prepared by the ILC, detailed the establishment of the court, its relationship to the UN, its composition and administrative elements, its jurisdiction and applicable law, the procedures for investigation and commencement of prosecution, the trial process, the appeal and review process, what would be expected by way of international cooperation and judicial assistance, and enforcement methods.[48] It was felt that the court could only operate effectively if it was brought into close relationship with the UN, primarily for administrative reasons but also because part of its jurisdiction is very much consequential upon decisions made by the UN Security Council. Thus, provision was made for the court to enter into a relationship with the world body either by becoming a part of the organic structure of the organization or through a treaty.

The International Law Commission and the Draft Code of Crimes

The forty-seventh session of the ILC, held in Geneva between 2 May and 21 July 1995, produced the thirteenth report on the *Draft Code of Crimes against the Peace and Security of Mankind.*[49] The draft statute created two categories of crimes: (1) those under general international law (such as genocide, aggression, serious violations of the laws and customs applicable in armed conflict, and crimes against humanity) and (2) those covered by treaty provisions. The former can be considered "core crimes," while the latter (i.e., those exceptionally serious crimes that are of international concern) are annexed to the statute under the heading "Crimes pursuant to Treaties," which include the 1949 Geneva Conventions and the conventions on hijacking of aircraft, apartheid, "internationally protected persons," hostage taking, torture, safety of maritime navigation, and illicit traffic in narcotic drugs.

In keeping with the spirit of the twelfth report on the *Draft Code of Crimes against the Peace and Security of Mankind,*[50] the ILC's special rapporteur proposed a strategy aimed at winnowing down the list of crimes to be included in the draft code to offences whose characterization as crimes against the peace and security of humanity would be difficult to challenge (i.e., the least contentious ones). While it was difficult for participants on the ILC to agree on what to include on the list of least contentious core crimes, a compromise position was reached – a position that was highly coloured by the post-Cold War environment. For instance, while military-strategic threats are obviously still considered very important to the consideration of security and peace, other threats must also be considered – including those to human security. It is also worth pointing out the extent to which the post-Cold War era altered the calculus with respect to the issue of considering not just the traditional interstate threats to international peace and security, but also the more non-traditional intrastate ones as well. This is a clear recognition of the erosion of national boundaries when it comes to the consideration of what constitutes threats to humanity.

In any event, more out of expediency than anything else, the number of offences in the new draft code was reduced from twelve to six: aggression, genocide, crimes against humanity, war crimes, international terrorism, and illicit traffic in narcotic drugs. These were considered "core crimes" during the discussions of the Conference of Plenipotentiaries held in June 1998 in Italy.

Canada's Contribution to the Work of the ILC and the Establishment of the ICC

On 18 July 1998, Canada's foreign minister signed the statute that established the framework for the first permanent ICC. For several years now Canada's government and several Canadian NGOs have been at the forefront in the effort to establish an ICC that would be permanent, independent, and effective. So, it is not surprising that the ICC agreement bears a strong Canadian imprint.

Canada was joined in this quest by like-minded states from around the world (such as Argentina, Australia, South Korea, South Africa, Germany, the United Kingdom, the Nordic countries, and Trinidad and Tobago). This group of states was chaired by the Canadians. Its aim was to ensure that this court would not become subordinate to the control of a few powerful states. In essence, the goal was to place morality and ethics in a prominent position at the international level and, in so doing, to subdue realpolitik tendencies to denigrate the emerging international norms that support the establishment of the ICC. In the end, the Rome treaty was passed by a final vote of 120 to 7, with 21 abstentions.

A large part of the Canadian strategy in the above effort was to play a major role in all of the preliminary discussions and bodies dealing with the establishment of the ICC. This is why, from the very beginning, the Canadian government supported the work of the ILC. Norm entrepreneurs like Canada, Belgium, Denmark, Finland, the Netherlands, Norway, Sweden, and the United Kingdom have had a profound impact on the process leading to the codification of international law, particularly international criminal law and, more specifically, the draft statute for a permanent international criminal court.[51] Although it has generally been accused of focusing more on the "petit-point needlework" of international law than on the grander, more imaginative, task of reshaping the broad outlines of that law,[52] nevertheless the ILC has made significant accomplishments in the area of positive law (e.g., note its assistance in drafting conventions and statutes related to the Law of the Sea; diplomatic relations; the problems of statelessness, nationality, and state succession; international liability for injurious consequences arising out of acts not prohibited by international law, and international criminal activity).[53]

Canada's most recent contribution to the ILC was framed within the context of the need for a new international security agenda. Realizing that most of the conflicts since the end of the Cold War were civil ones and that most of the victims of those conflicts were civilians, Canada pressed for the creation of a humanitarian law that would be more likely to address this problem. The most exigent quandary of international relations seemed to be the insecurity of individuals rather than the insecurity of states per se. Thus human security was pushed higher up on the agenda of Canada's foreign policy decision makers. Canada also realized that extant international institutions were not equipped to deal adequately with this problem.[54]

Since Canada saw the new security and justice demands as requiring either new or reformed institutions, it emphasized developing a novel international legal institution that would help deter some of the most serious violators of international humanitarian law and that would have sufficient "teeth" to protect the vulnerable and innocent and punish those who commit "core crimes."[55] Canada led a coalition of about sixty-five like-minded states (from Europe, Asia, and the Third World) in the creation of a court that would have the power to reach out to any part of the globe in order to bring to justice those individuals charged with committing genocide, war crimes, aggression, and crimes against humanity.[56] It pushed for a court that would have inherent jurisdiction over these core crimes and that would not be paralyzed either by norms of sovereignty or by realpolitik. Canadian representatives stressed the need for an independent, highly professional prosecutor for the court – someone who would be in a position to initiate proceedings against state or individual actors involved in the above international crimes. Canada also argued that the court should be sensitive to the issue of gender and required that both the statute and the day-to-day operations of the court integrate a gender perspective. Thus rape, sexual slavery, and other forms of sexual violence were recognized in the draft statute for the creation of a permanent ICC.

Canada contributed leadership on the ILC and at the Rome conference. Philippe Kirsch, a Canadian lawyer and veteran diplomat, was supposed to lead the Canadian delegation to Rome for the ICC negotiations but ended up playing a major role as chair of the Conference of Plenipotentiaries because the initially selected chair, Adriaan Bos, had fallen ill.[57] Some commentators have said that Kirsch "played the role of Solomon during the talks."[58] He certainly was qualified for this job, having served with the Canadian permanent mission to the UN in the past and having chaired numerous international commissions and conferences. Although he was unable to persuade the Americans to sign the Rome treaty, he was able to play up the fact that the US was among the first to support the idea of a permanent court and to keep all states representatives' eyes on the ball.

One should not belittle the notion of moral authority in such cases. Moral authority can be a powerful weapon in the hands of those states whose foreign policy opts for the use of soft power. As seen both in the landmines negotiations and the ICC talks, it is becoming clear that issues of morality do matter in international relations. In the face of tremendous opposition, coming particularly from the world's most powerful nation, Canada and other like-minded states were able to overcome US pressure to water down the Rome treaty. American delegates at the conference tried to make the case that, because the US is the sole superpower, it is somehow an "indispensable nation" and may find it necessary, from time to time, to violate international law in order to uphold it. In other words, these delegates wanted to ensure that the US would not be accountable to this new body of humanitarian and international criminal law.

This position was seen as indefensible and absurd by some commentators, who noted that the immorality of the American argument may, in fact, have actually undermined whatever claim the US had made with respect to world leadership, to being the "global policeman." In a sense, it has tended to put Americans in the position of being tacit advocates of illegality and vigilantism. Such a position has done serious damage to Washington's credibility, particularly since the notion of complementarity is built into the Rome treaty: "the Court will take action only when national legal systems are unable or unwilling to genuinely investigate or prosecute."[59] As it stood, the main opponents to the US position on this matter were its principal allies – Canada, Germany, and the UK.[60] In the end, Canada's "misty minded idealism," principled stand, and soft power won the day in Rome.[61] However, time will tell if it has won the war against the global policeman principle advocated by Washington. The Rome treaty will require sixty state signatories for ratification, and it may still need US military might for enforcement. Thus, the currency of soft power may, ultimately, turn out to be highly dependent upon hard power.

As far as the Canadian government was concerned, the ICJ in the Hague could not be the judicial body to deal with this new classification of international crimes. The ICJ's jurisdiction is limited, primarily, to arbitrating disputes between governments. An ICC would complement the ICJ by investigating and trying individuals and non-state actors accused of genocide, war crimes, and crimes against humanity. For Canada, an ICC would be the living embodiment of fundamental principles of international criminal law. Such a court would be able to hold individuals and groups responsible should they plan, order, or commit gross crimes under international law. It would be able to prosecute such crimes whether the perpetrators were leaders or subordinates, whether they were civilians or members of the military, paramilitary, or police force.

Canada, therefore, saw the creation of an international criminal court as being: crucial to the new norms of justice and global security, necessary for international justice, and a complement to national criminal justice systems. It supports the view that this court should deal only with exceptionally serious international crimes – those that national criminal justice systems either cannot or will not address.[62] Additionally, Canadians involved in the pre-Rome discussions on the draft treaty considered this to be part of the progressive strengthening of international law. Such progressive evolution is in keeping with Canada's foreign policy, which has as one of its planks the encouragement of respect for the rule of law. Therefore, the discourse on the ICC served Canada's goal of drawing more attention to international humanitarian law and of supporting the creation and utilization of multilateral instruments to address problems that cannot be handled effectively or efficiently by the instruments of national government.

This was especially relevant in the immediate post-Cold War period, which coincided with an increase in war-torn societies. As Axworthy once put it: "A key element of healing war-torn societies is restoring the rule of law and ending impunity." In his opinion, this was one of the crucial reasons why, in 1998, the timing was right for the establishment of a permanent, independent, and effective ICC having inherent jurisdiction over core crimes. In Axworthy's opinion, without the presence of an impartial court to "uncover truth and administer justice in the aftermath of war, nations will find themselves plunged into continued cycles of violence."[63]

This explains, in part, why Canada pushed both inside and outside the UN for the establishment of a permanent ICC[64] as well as why it championed the case for a powerful, independent prosecutor to head this body. Canada also contributed to a fund that enabled the least developed countries to participate in the work of the Preparatory Committee on the Establishment of an ICC.[65] In effect, one can argue that this demonstrated this country's commitment to egalitarianism.[66]

Canadian Niche Diplomacy and Soft Power

Realizing that its resources are limited, the Canadian government has chosen what Heather Smith (Chapter 5, this volume) (following Evan Potter and Andrew Cooper), has called "niche diplomacy"; that is, selectivity regarding the issues and areas of foreign policy to be tackled. Human rights and human security are two of those niche issues that the Canadian government has chosen, at least rhetorically, to make a priority for its foreign policy. Under those broad areas one can also add democratization and humanitarian relief. Thus it should not come as a surprise that Canada became actively involved in galvanizing support for the concept of a permanent ICC.

Based on our knowledge of Canada's contribution to the creation of the ICC, this particular form of niche diplomacy does not square with Smith's view. Canada's commitment to a permanent ICC is directly connected to a longstanding position on the nature of the international security environment and Canada's place within it. It is a position that has been necessarily modified by post-Cold War events that, in effect, changed the international security environment. Canada's commitment to the idea of a permanent ICC is also associated with a moral position that has emanated from several successive, high-profile Canadian diplomats over the past fifty-four years or so. Certainly there is a sense of selectivity in the decision to place this issue centrally on the Canadian foreign policy agenda. However, the selection was made because it gave Canada an opportunity to play what it considered to be an important role in designing an emerging international institution – a role with which the Canadian state is quite comfortable.

At the heart of contemporary Canadian foreign policy is the notion of human security. Human security is premised on the need to enhance and promote human rights, to strengthen humanitarian law, to prevent conflicts, and to foster democracy and good governance. A human security approach to foreign policy will be different from a military security approach. Unlike in the Cold War era, post-Cold War security concerns have forced Canadian foreign policy to tackle such transborder global problems as drug trafficking; terrorism; human rights abuse; child labour; and the trafficking, sale, and abuse of women. Due to the globalization of these issues, Canadians are directly affected by them. The pursuit of human security, in Canada's case, is propelled by soft power – the ability to affect and influence other actors' (both state and non-state) behaviour through the use of convincing information, argumentation, and rhetorical skill; through the adoption of certain values and norms; through non-coercive persuasion; and through promoting forms of non-intrusive intervention and other similar techniques. Furthermore, there is a sense that soft power requires collective action, international cooperation (not just between states but also with non-state actors), covenants, rules, and norms in order to be effective.

In response to a critical article written by Kim Nossal – "Foreign Policy for Wimps" – Lloyd Axworthy chastised the academic for holding to a narrow-minded Morgenthauian conception of "hardline power." The Canadian foreign minister then went on to explain what soft power means within the Canadian context: "The reason I use this phrase in my speeches is that it exemplifies the Canadian talent for drawing upon our skills in negotiating, building coalitions and presenting diplomatic initiatives; in other words, for influencing the behaviour of other nations not through military intimidation but through a variety of diplomatic and political tools."[67]

However, Nossal's point that Canada has chosen soft power foreign policy in order to provide foreign policy on the cheap is an argument that has some resonance within the epistemic community in Canada as well as within the transnational NGO community.[68] This position, while well stated, has not been corroborated by any empirical evidence. In fact, it may be too early to make the charge that soft power foreign policy, as pursued by the current Canadian government, is either "on the cheap" or "wimpy." Soft power involves Canada's ability to draw on its diplomats' skills in negotiating, in building consensus and coalitions, and in presenting diplomatic initiatives (with moral ends) that have a broad base of support across a representative number of states and non-state actors within the international community. Canada's work within the ILC and during the ICC negotiations in Italy are examples of Canada's soft power in action. But there are other examples as well.

Witness Canada's role in brokering a global treaty to ban anti-personnel landmines, or its role in developing a hemispheric strategy for addressing the drug trafficking problem, or its initiation of a system of protection for children, or its efforts within international fora to combat terrorism, or its defiance of America's attempt to force certain extra-territorial laws (such as the Helms-Burton legislation) on other states. Such efforts were undertaken by utilizing soft power techniques. They involve building and institutionalizing norms, remodelling international norms to make them more robust, and reshaping or creating international institutions. None of these activities is "cheap." They may not require as much material capital as hard power strategies and techniques, but they certainly use up a lot of human capital. Perhaps rethinking the way in which we measure power and shifting away from the standard positivistic methodologies generally utilized in neorealist scholarship may be a constructive start in the renewed analysis of foreign policy.

Conclusion

One of the major post-Cold War challenges for the Canadian government is to find a niche for itself within the international community. This is not an easy task, given what Neufeld describes as essentially a recasting of the "middlepowermanship" role with which Canada has been familiar.[69] It was made even more difficult with the stain on the country's peacekeeping reputation after the Somalia affair,[70] the obvious failure of its well-touted persuasive abilities in the recent attempt to galvanize support against the human rights abuses of the Nigerian regime (see Black, Chapter 8, this volume), and the Liberal government's reduced commitment to UN peacekeeping and foreign aid. At a time when the Pearsonian legacy has all but faded away and Canada's diplomatic influence appears to be waning, this country's foreign policy makers are attempting a slow climb back up the ladder of diplomatic respectability. They are doing so by initiating and/or supporting a number of major efforts aimed at strengthening the UN system and solidifying international law.

Among these efforts are: the Canadian study that proposed ways of developing and enhancing a rapid reaction capability for the UN system;[71] the Ottawa Process, which resulted in the drafting of a treaty to ban antipersonnel landmines; the assertive position taken against the undemocratic Nigerian government's violation of human rights principles; and the leadership role that Canada played in Italy at the Conference of Plenipotentiaries, which established the ICC.

If, as David Black argues (Chapter 8, this volume), the Nigerian case showed the limitation of middle power leadership, then, to a large degree, the ICC case demonstrates that small and medium-sized powers can overcome limitations and find ways around obstacles. However, it is important to note that when the policy being pursued by Canada is supported by well developed international norms, or by an international norm that is gaining in strength, then the chances of that policy's success are greater than they would be if the norm were weak or non-existent. If this is, in fact, the case, then it will be important, in future examinations of Canadian foreign policy, for scholars to develop a more sophisticated understanding of the normative context within which such policy is made.

Norms have both regulative and constitutive effects. In the latter case, they can play a role in specifying "what actions will cause relevant others to recognize a particular identity. In the former instance, norms specify particular standards of 'proper behaviour.'"[72] Understanding the roles that norms play may be very important for explanations of why decision makers choose to support one policy over another. It is possible that the interest of a state actor might be defined within the context of internationally held norms and understandings of what is considered, at a particular time and in a particular space, as proper, appropriate, or good.[73] It is clear from the ICC case that Canada used robust norms in its attempt to persuade others of the importance of establishing a permanent international criminal court. Substantiation of this hypothesis would lead one to suggest that norms are more than simply constitutive and regulative, they are also enabling.[74]

Unlike in the Nigerian case, Canada did not take a hard line in the negotiations around the establishment of the ICC; instead, the Canadian delegation, in both the PrepCom meetings and the Plenipotentiaries Conference, positioned itself as a consensus builder. Unlike in the Nigerian case, during the negotiations that led to the establishment of the ICC, Canada was never out of step with the majority of actors involved in the multilateral bargaining. Foreign policy successes for Canada seem to have this element. As Black notes with respect to the fight against the apartheid regime in South Africa, Canada was "very much in line with the overwhelming Commonwealth majority."

Another factor that can be taken into consideration in trying to explain Canada's strong leadership role in the establishment of the ICC is the activism of the foreign minister. Lloyd Axworthy is well regarded as one Cabinet minister who wholeheartedly supports a humane internationalist foreign policy for Canada, even if such policy may go against the position of American officials. US concerns about the court have been taken seriously by the Canadian government. However, it is clear from Canada's actions and rhetoric, both during the preliminary process leading up to the June 1998 Conference of Plenipotentiaries and the actual conference itself, that there are times when Canadian foreign policy has taken the high moral road even at the expense of going against American interests. Thus, the argument that the Canadian foreign policy position merely supports the hegemonic line may not always be substantiated. The ICC case provides an example of this. In this particular case, Canada demonstrated that respect for international law should supercede any allegiance it has with its powerful neighbour to the south. But Canada was not alone, and this is significant. It had the backing of major states like Great Britain and Germany, who also refused to back US attempts to exempt itself from the treaty.

Canada stands a good chance of regaining its lost prestige on the international stage if it can continue to champion such high-minded ethical and moral causes and issues. The leadership "norm entrepreneurial" role that Canada played in the establishment of a permanent ICC certainly contributes to the perception, if not the reality, of this country being back in the multilateral game as a significant (if not key) player during this turbulent post-Cold War period. However, it is clear that the tension between Canada's expanded human security agenda and its preoccupation with limitationist "niche diplomacy" needs to be resolved if the goal of a more ethical foreign policy is to be achieved.

Acknowledgment

Research for this paper was funded through a grant from Québec Fonds pour la formation de chercheurs et l'aide à la recherche (FCAR) to conduct research on "subsidiarity and Multilateral Security" as well as through the University of Alberta, Faculty of Arts Support for the Advancement of Scholarship Research Fund. The author wishes to thank Sean McMahon for his research assistance and Antonio Franceschet and two external reviewers for their comments on an earlier draft.

Notes

1 For more details, see United Nations Preparatory Committee on the Establishment of an International Criminal Court, *Report of the Preparatory Committee on the Establishment of an International Criminal Court* (New York: United Nations, 1996).

2 Joe Stork, "In focus: International Criminal Court," *Foreign Policy in Focus: Internet Gateway to Foreign Policy* 3, 4 (April 1998): 5. Available at <www.foreignpolicy-infocus.org/briefs/vol3/v3n4icc.html>.

3 See Don Munton and Tom Keating, "Internationalism and the Canadian Public," *Canadian Journal of Political Science* (forthcoming 2001).

4 "We're Doing Things Nobody Else Can Do: Canada Can Use Its 'Soft Power' to Change the World, Axworthy Says," *Ottawa Citizen,* 5 April 1998, A7.

5 Ibid., A7.

6 Ibid., A7.

7 Note, however, that the moral context of Canadian foreign policy has a fairly long tradition.

8 Lois Wilson, "Canada Has a Key Role in Creating Permanent World Criminal Court," *Toronto Star,* 6 April 1998, A13.

9 It should be noted that the term "soft power" was first coined by American political scientist Joseph Nye in reference to a specific aspect of US foreign policy that did not involve the "big stick" approach.

10 "We're Doing Things Nobody Else Can Do," *Ottawa Citizen,* 5 April 1998, A7.

11 See Price and Tannenwald, "Norms and Deterrence," in *The Culture of National Security: Norms and Identity in World Politics,* ed. Peter J. Katzenstein (New York: Columbia University Press, 1996), 148.

12 Martha Finnemore, "Constructing Norms of Humanitarian Intervention," in Katzenstein, *Culture of National Security.*

13 See Martha Finnemore and Kathryn Sikkink, "Norm Dynamics and Political Change," *International Organizations* 52, 4 (1998): 895.

14 Lloyd Axworthy, "Human Security and Global Governance: Putting People First," *Global Governance* 7, 1 (January/March 2001): 19-23.

15 A. LeRoy Bennett, *International Organizations: Principles and Issues,* 6th ed. (New Jersey: Prentice Hall, 1995), 180.

16 For example, crimes against humanity, aggression, terrorism, war crimes, narcotics trafficking, apartheid, counterfeiting, the slave trade, torture, genocide, piracy, hostage taking, and crimes against diplomats.

17 Christopher Joyner, "The Reality and Relevance of International Law in the Post-Cold War Era," in *The Global Agenda: Issues and Perspectives,* 4th edition, ed. Charles W. Kegley, Jr. and Eugene R. Wittkopf (New York: McGraw-Hill, 1995), 220.

18 W. Andy Knight, "Legal Issues," in *A Global Agenda: Issues before the 51st General Assembly of the United Nations,* ed. John Tessitore and Susan Woolfson (New York: Roman and Littlefield, 1996), 261.
19 See Rosalyn Higgins, *The Development of International Law through the Political Organs of the United Nations* (New York: Oxford University Press, 1963), 2.
20 Although it should be noted that Canada is yet to convict a single war criminal, even though several live and have lived in this country.
21 Lois Wilson, "Canada Has Key Role in Creating Permanent World Criminal Court," *Toronto Star,* 6 April 1998, A13.
22 Article 227 of the Treaty of Versailles called for the arraignment of the German emperor on charges of violating international morality and the sanctity of treaties. See L.C. Green, "Is there an International Criminal Law?" *Alberta Law Review* 21 (1983): 251-54.
23 Note also that efforts to prosecute Turkish authorities for the slaughter of a large number of Armenians came to naught.
24 For the latter, see the League of Nations, *Convention for the Creation of an International Criminal Court,* League of Nations Document C/547/M384 1937 V (1937).
25 Daniel C. Prefontaine, QC, "The Proposed International Criminal Court: An Unfinished Dream," *Advocate* 54, 4 (July 1996): 523.
26 The ILC is the UN's principal instrument for making the necessary recommendations with respect to the development of international law. From the late 1940s until recently, the bulk of this legal activity has been in the realm of studies, discussions, drafting, codification, revision, adoption of conventions by state representative, and ratifications to bring new conventions into force. Some have described the approach of the ILC as "sober, cautious, conservative, and technical, and very, very slow-moving." See Edward McWhinney, *United Nations Law Making: Cultural and Ideological Relativism and International Law Making for an Era of Transition* (New York: Holmes and Meier, 1984), 98.
27 See William H. Forman, Jr., "The United Nations' Proposed International Criminal Court and War Crimes," paper presented at the Eighth Annual Meeting of the Academic Council on the United Nations System, New York, 20 June 1995. Also note that the UNGA directed the ILC to (1) formulate principles of international law recognized in the charter of the Nuremberg Tribunal and the judgment of that body and (2) prepare a draft Code of Offences against the Peace and Security of Mankind. See UNGA resolution 177(2), 21 November 1947.
28 Benjamin B. Ferencz, "A Plea of Humanity to Law: Need for an International Criminal Court," unpublished paper, 1998, 6.
29 Jane L. Garwood-Carter, "The British War Crimes Trials of Suspected Italian War Criminals, 1945-1947," unpublished paper, 1 September 1998, 3.
30 On this issue, see UNGA resolution 3314 (29), UN General Assembly Official Record, supplement no. 31, UN Document A/9631 (1974).
31 See UNGA resolution 36/106, 10 December 1981.
32 See Theodore Meron, "The Case for War Crimes Trials in Yugoslavia," *Foreign Affairs* 72, 3 (Summer 1993): 122-35.
33 See John Rolph, "Perfecting an International Code of Crimes: Establishing Realistic and Viable Mechanisms for Effective Enforcement of International Law," *Federal Bar News and Journal* 39, 9 (October 1992): 528; and General Assembly Official Records of the Forty-Sixth Session, supplement no. 10 A/46/10, para. 173.
34 For a normative position on this issue, see Payam Akhavan, "Punishing War Crimes in the Former Yugoslavia: A Critical Juncture for the New World Order," *Human Rights Quarterly* 15, 2 (1993): 262-89.
35 UNGA resolution 47/33, 25 November 1992.
36 Knight, "Legal Issues," 279-83.
37 See UN Security Council resolutions 808, 22 February 1993; and 827, 25 May 1993.
38 See UN Security Council resolution 955, 8 November 1994.
39 Note that she replaced Judge Goldstone of South Africa, who was the initial chief prosecutor.
40 Kitty McKinsey, "Canada Pushes for War Crimes Justice," *Ottawa Citizen,* 14 June 1998, A12.

41 See UNGA document A/C.6/50/L.14, 27 November 1995; and General Assembly resolution 50/46, 11 December 1995.
42 For details see the Report of the Preparatory Committee on the Establishment of an International Criminal Court, UN document A/Conf/183/2, add. 1 and add. 2.
43 UN Department of Public Information, General Assembly Press Release L/2760, 22 March 1996.
44 Note that the total cost for conference servicing requirements of the preparatory committee was estimated at US$676,400. This is based on interview with a senior UN official.
45 UNGA document A/50/22.
46 Department of Public Information, General Assembly Press Release, L/2760, 22 March 1996.
47 Note that, initially, some doubt was expressed over the inclusion of aggression on the list of "core crimes" because, under the charter, it is the Security Council's mandate to determine the commission of an act of aggression. However, in any event, it has become clear that the more focused the list of "core crimes" for the international court, the better the chance be for an increase in the number of states likely to accede to the statute treaty during the Conference of Plenipotentiaries.
48 See UNGA document A/49/10.
49 UN document A/CN.4/466.
50 See UN document A/CN.4/460 and corr. 1.
51 At times, the like-mindedness of some of these countries is expressed in declaratory form, such as the Lycoen Declaration signed between Norway and Canada in June 1998. See Mike Trickey, "Canada, Norway Change Their Ways," *Ottawa Citizen,* 28 June 1998, A18.
52 Edward McWhinney, *United Nations Law Making: Cultural Ideological Relativism and International Law Making for an Era of Transition* (New York: Holmes and Meier, 1984), 98.
53 For more information on these, see UN documents A/CN.4/480, A/CN.4/479, and A/AC.249/1997/L5.
54 A strong proponent of UN reform, the Canadian government has been troubled by the inadequate funding of this organization, the US withholding of financial contributions to the regular budget, and the seeming inability of the UN bureaucracy to adjust itself sufficiently to meet the needs of the next century.
55 Christina Spencer, "Make Child Soldiers War Crime: Axworthy," *Ottawa Citizen,* 5 April 1998, A2.
56 Mike Trickey, "International Court Moves Closer to Reality," *Ottawa Citizen,* 18 July 1998, A7.
57 Canada, Ministry of Foreign Affairs and International Trade, "Notes for an Address by the Honourable Lloyd Axworthy Minister of Foreign Affairs, Canada," *Speeches/Statements,* 15 June 1998, 1-3.
58 Christina Spencer, "Can We Tell the US We'll See It in Court?" *Ottawa Citizen,* 12 August 1998, A13.
59 "Interview with Philippe Kirsch," *Canada: World View,* 1 (1998): 3.
60 For further comments, both pro and con, on this issue, see George Jonas, "ICC Creates Ethical Confusion," *Ottawa Citizen,* 24 July 1998, A13; and "Absent Superpower," *Ottawa Citizen,* 22 July 1998, A11.
61 Spencer, "Can We Tell the US," B5.
62 See Prefontaine, "Proposed International Criminal Court," 523.
63 Allan Thompson, "Axworthy Pushes for International Court," *Toronto Star,* 31 March 1998, A6.
64 For instance, the Canadian government used the forum of Commonwealth meetings to push for "the creation of a permanent, international court to try war criminals." See Helen Branswell, "Commonwealth Members Hit Up on Land Mines, International Court," *Montreal Gazette,* 28 October 1997, B1.
65 See the Report of the Preparatory Committee on the Establishment of an International Criminal Court, A/Conf/183/2, add. 1 and add. 2.
66 However, the amount of the contribution – $125,000 – allowed for only a limited number of developing countries to participate in the proceedings.
67 Lloyd Axworthy, "Why 'Soft Power' Is the Right Policy for Canada," *Ottawa Citizen,* 25 April 1998, B6.

68 I am using the term "epistemic community" in the sense defined by Haas; that is, as a "network of professionals with recognized expertise and competence in a particular domain and an authoritative claim to policy-relevant knowledge within that domain or issue-area." See Haas, "Introduction: Epistemic Communities and International Policy Coordination," *International Organization* 46 (1992): 1-2.

69 Mark Neufeld, "Hegemony and Foreign Policy Analysis: The Case of Canada as a Middle Power," *Studies in Political Economy* 48 (1995): 7-29.

70 For further reading on the Somalia affair, see Peter Debarats, *Somalia Cover-up: A Commissioner's Journal* (Toronto: McClelland and Stewart, 1997); David Pagliese and Tim Bronskill, "Top Brass Under Fire," *Montreal Gazette,* 3 July 1997, A1; Robert Bragg, "Hello Ottawa, Is Anyone Listening? Inquiries Launched and Then Ignored," *Montreal Gazette,* 8 July 1997, B3.

71 Report of the Government of Canada, *Towards a Rapid Reaction Capability for the United Nations* (Ottawa: DFAIT, September 1995).

72 Peter J. Katzenstein, "Introduction: Alternative Perspectives on National Security," in *The Culture of National Security: Norms and Identity in World Politics,* ed. Peter J. Katzenstein (New York: Columbia University Press, 1996), 5.

73 On this point see Martha Finnemore, *National Interests in International Society* (Ithaca and London: Cornell University Press, 1996).

74 W. Andy Knight and Annika Björkdahl, "Towards a Global Culture of Prevention: the Evolution and Influence of Norms," paper presented at the International Studies Association Annual Convention, 19 February 1999, 10.

8
Echoes of Apartheid? Canada, Nigeria, and the Politics of Norms

David Black

When Prime Minister Jean Chrétien visited Nigerian president Olusegun Obasanjo in November 1999, he and his government were greeted with extraordinary warmth and appreciation. Obasanjo, inaugurated in May as Nigeria's first elected civilian leader in more than fifteen years, told Chrétien at a press conference that in his country's "darkest hours," "you stood against tyranny, against oppression, against undemocratic and inhuman action in Nigeria. When you did, you were almost alone."[1]

In the face of such an expression of gratitude, it may seem ungenerous to emphasize some of the more cautionary lessons to be drawn from Canada's engagement with the Nigerian issue, particularly in the "dark hours" of the 1995-97 period. Yet prior to June 1998, the results of Canada's activism on this issue looked much less hopeful and Nigeria's future much more dismal than the cautiously optimistic situation that prevails at the start of the new millennium. In that month, Nigeria's "transition without end" entered a decisive new stage as a result of two unanticipated events that serve as a telling reminder of the enduring role of fortune in world politics. The death of autocratic general Sani Abacha in June 1998 thwarted plans to manage his own transition from military dictator to elected civilian president – an outcome that would have profoundly challenged Canada and the international community. The tragic death shortly thereafter of Mashood Abiola, the putative victor in the June 1993 presidential elections subsequently jailed by Abacha on charges of treason, had the ironic "benefit" of enabling the military to relaunch its deeply flawed transition, ultimately resulting in the restoration of elected civilian rule under Obasanjo's leadership. It is the very fortuitousness of these events, and the positive light in which they cast Canadian policy, that makes it so important to reconsider some of the troubles that policy encountered in the period between the 1995 Auckland Commonwealth Heads of Government Meeting (CHOGM), during which the Nigerian regime was plunged into unprecedented isolation, and the 1997 Edinburgh CHOGM, when a fragile Commonwealth consensus was achieved, albeit with considerable uncertainty about its ability to hold. It is on this earlier phase that this chapter is focused.

Stung by the execution of Ken Saro-Wiwa and eight other Ogoni activists in November 1995, Canadian foreign policy makers tried to play a leadership role in promoting a forceful international approach to the support of democracy, human rights, and the rule of law in Nigeria.[2] In doing so, they were mindful of, and arguably inspired by, a somewhat stylized and mythologized understanding of Canada's earlier role in the international struggle against apartheid.[3] Yet in contrast to that earlier struggle, and in contrast to Canada's traditional role in multilateral organizations, Canadian representatives became increasingly lonely in their hard-line stand, particularly within the Commonwealth. In the six months prior to the October 1997 Edinburgh CHOGM the gap between Canada and other Commonwealth states was bridged and a degree of consensus regained. However, the basis upon which it was achieved fell considerably short of the forceful actions Canadian representatives had earlier advocated as well as of the organization's 1995 threat to expel the Nigerian regime. Canadian policy makers were also thwarted in their efforts to maintain a dialogue with the "rogue" regime of General Abacha.[4] Why were Canadian efforts so frustrated, both multilaterally and bilaterally?

In seeking to at least partially answer this question, this chapter takes as its point of departure a comparison between the Canadian policy response to Abacha's Nigeria and the response of Prime Minister Brian Mulroney's Progressive Conservative government to apartheid South Africa in the mid- to late-1980s. This is not meant to imply that the Nigerian case replicates that of South Africa; rather, to paraphrase Richard Leaver, it is to show that the two cases relate to each other "like the image that individuals obtain of themselves from a distorting sideshow mirror; the features and details are warped out of all proportion, but the overall picture is none the less recognisable."[5] The comparison is illuminating, however, for two reasons. First, at least initially, both the Canadian and Commonwealth responses to Nigeria were clearly formulated with the South African experience in mind. Second, the points of contrast between the two cases help to clarify and sharpen an understanding of why the Nigerian situation evolved as it did after late 1995 as well as why Canadian policy was frustrated at key turns. Two related sets of conclusions flow from this analysis. The first concerns the importance of norms in both facilitating and constraining decisive international action. In this regard, this chapter serves as a useful counterpoint to Andy Knight's (Chapter 7, this volume) relatively optimistic analysis of the role of norms and "norm entrepreneurship," illustrating how an apparent normative consensus can mask both important variations in the strength with which such norms are held and subsystemic differences in their interpretation. Flowing from this is the second set of conclusions concerning the limitations of "middle power" leadership.

To reach these conclusions, I first describe the principal features of the

Canadian (and Commonwealth) policy response to the Nigerian crisis in the 1995-97 (Auckland to Edinburgh) period. In doing so, I highlight the similarities with Canada's response to the crisis of apartheid in the 1980s. Second, I consider both the similar role played by the two crises within the context of Canadian foreign policy and some key reasons why the two situations unfolded so differently. I then focus on the different normative bases for action in the two cases, emphasizing the relative ambiguity and weakness of the democratic and human rights norms upon which punitive action against Nigeria was premised. Finally, I identify some lessons from this case concerning both Canadian foreign policy and the role of norms in world politics.

In terms of the ethics and security focus of this book, this case facilitates an investigation of the nexus between human rights, democratization, and security. For many Canadians in the post-Cold War/post-communist era, the ethical dimension of foreign policy is most clearly manifested in this country's contribution to the promotion of international human rights and democratization. Moreover, these concepts are now widely assumed to be fundamental to the prospects for security at individual, national, and international levels. This assumption is particularly central to the notion of "human security" championed by Foreign Minister Lloyd Axworthy.[6] There can be no more fundamental security threats to individual human beings than those of, for example, arbitrary arrest, detention, torture, and extra-judicial execution. Even if one does not fully embrace the expansive logic and implications of human security, however, the promotion of human rights and democracy can still be regarded as highly germane to more traditional concepts of security insofar as they are vital to the formation of relatively just and stable political orders. In their absence, political order is likely to remain fragile, at least over the medium to long term.

In practice, however, the relationship between human rights, democracy, and security is not so straightforward.[7] More to the point of this chapter, Canada's ability to advance human rights and democracy – and hence to promote human security – is often sharply limited. This does not mean that the effort should not be made; however, highly sophisticated diplomacy is required if such effort is to be influential. Conceptually, Canadians need to be sensitive to the varied interpretations and emphases given to the values associated with human security across different subsystemic contexts. "Consensus" positions based on such values may be much less secure than they at first appear. Practically, Canadian policy makers and practitioners (both state and non-state) need to recognize the need for careful and patient coalition building, and the need to establish Canadian bona fides through sustained engagement with, and resource commitments to, any given issue area.

Canadian Policy Responses: Nigeria and South Africa Compared

Nigeria Courts Pariahdom

How did Nigeria's Abacha regime became such a focus of international opprobrium?[8] Summarizing briefly, the process began when the previous military regime of Ibrahim Babangida annulled democratic presidential elections – the culmination of a prolonged transition process – in June 1993. Joseph argues that this stunning act, in the face of the freest and fairest elections in Nigerian history, reflected "panic within government circles and among some of its constituencies that, despite all the roadblocks and 'organized confusion,' the Nigerian people were going to elect a president (Mashood Abiola) who could not be relied on, once in office, to do the bidding of the outgoing regime."[9] Beneath this panic lay a deeply politicized military that was unwilling to surrender effective political control as well as the intense rivalries among ethnic and regional elites – rivalries that have bedeviled Nigerian politics since independence (Abiola was a Yoruba from the southwest; both Babangida and Abacha were northerners aligned with that region's political-economic elite). The Babangida regime's autocratic determination to retain control sparked unprecedented popular opposition, followed by a short-lived interim civilian government. In November 1993 Abacha seized control, restoring the military's unrivalled political domination.

There followed a period marked by the ruthless repression of domestic opposition and the cooptation of compliant civilian politicians. Within the army itself, Abacha and his inner circle replaced much of the senior leadership with loyal, anti-intellectual officers.[10] Basic freedoms of speech and association were routinely violated, and, through arbitrary arrests and detentions, numerous opponents of the regime were incarcerated. The best known were Mashood Abiola and the once and current president, Olusegun Obasanjo. Many of these people remained in prison, and extensive human rights violations continued until after Abacha's death.

Meanwhile, on 1 October 1995, a new three-year transition plan was announced. This plan essentially recapitulated the elaborate exercise conducted under Babangida. It was ostensibly designed to result in an electoral transition to civilian rule on 1 October 1998. Yet the process quickly fell behind schedule and showed every sign of being stage-managed to ensure the military government's continued control. At the time of Abacha's death, all five officially sanctioned political parties had nominated him as their presidential candidate.

From 1993 onwards, international criticism persisted and a few symbolic punitive measures were adopted, while some human rights and diasporic groups agitated for substantial sanctions. But the trigger for a sharp escalation in international pressure was the 10 November 1995 execution of Ken

Saro-Wiwa and his Movement for the Survival of the Ogoni People (MOSOP) comrades, following their conviction on charges of murder in a trial widely condemned as a travesty of justice.[11] The executions, conducted just as Commonwealth heads of government were meeting for their biannual summit in Auckland (10-13 November), were an act of breathtaking arrogance on the part of the regime. Commonwealth leaders, mindful of their organization's previous stand against apartheid South Africa and its putative role as a force for international human rights and democracy, as enunciated in their 1991 Harare Declaration,[12] could not let such a provocation pass without a vigorous response. South African president Nelson Mandela, in particular, is said to have reacted with visceral anger, feeling betrayed by the Abacha regime's flaunting of his country's "softly-softly" quiet diplomacy. He and British prime minister John Major reportedly led the move to suspend Nigeria.[13] But Canadian prime minister Jean Chrétien was also primed for tough action, having been the only Commonwealth leader to call specifically for a stay of execution in his opening statement to the conference and to emphasize that carrying out the sentences would fly in the face of the spirit of the Harare Declaration.[14] This juncture, then, launched a new phase in the Nigerian crisis and sharply raised the pressure for tough sanctions in various parts of the world. As Toronto's *Globe and Mail* editorialized: "With this callous step ... Nigeria has declared itself an outlaw state. It should be treated as such. Clearly, only the sternest measures – up to and including suspension or expulsion from the Commonwealth – will persuade Nigeria's tyrants to change their ways. The Commonwealth should not hesitate to take them. And Canada should lead the way."[15]

Canada Responds

The Canadian government's inclination towards a tough line had been foreshadowed by measures adopted in the 1993-95 period. During this time, it had taken the largely symbolic steps of eliminating high-level visits, discontinuing military training assistance, and implementing an arms embargo. Also, in a move calculated to hit the ruling elite "where it hurts," it had denied visas to three Nigerian generals designated as managers of the Nigerian team for the Victoria Commonwealth Games in August 1994.[16]

After November 1995 Canada attempted to respond, in Lloyd Axworthy's words, "through an appropriate blend of pressure, dialogue and assistance."[17] Canadian policy operated at multilateral, bilateral, and transsocietal levels. *Multilaterally,* and most important, the Canadian government focused its efforts through the Commonwealth. Indeed, as with South Africa during the 1980s, it is highly unlikely that it would have taken such an active interest in the Nigerian crisis had it not been for the Commonwealth connection. Canada was a key supporter of the Commonwealth's decision to suspend Nigeria, and it became one of eight members of the Commonwealth

Ministerial Action Group (CMAG) created to "deal with serious or persistent violations of the principles contained in [the Harare] Declaration."[18] CMAG's warrant was to monitor and recommend actions related to the three countries judged to be in serious breach of Harare Declaration principles – the military regimes of Gambia, Nigeria, and Sierra Leone – though its principal focus was clearly Nigeria. Among the committee's first steps was to be a mission to Nigeria to pursue a dialogue with its government. This plan clearly implied the implementation of tougher measures should the dialogue fail. Within CMAG, Canada quickly established its hard-line reputation, maintaining this orientation through the group's eight subsequent meetings.

Within weeks of the drama at Auckland, however, there were already indications that much of the rest of the international community, especially in Africa, was inclining towards a softer line. At the summit of the Francophonie in early December 1995, Prime Minister Chrétien failed in his efforts to obtain a tough statement on Nigeria, with the organization agreeing only to "appeal to the Nigerian authorities to work for the establishment of the rule of law and democracy."[19] West African member states were particularly wary of a stronger position. Within CMAG, Canada was at times sharply out of step with the majority of the committee, particularly through 1996; and although the gap was closed in time for the Edinburgh CHOGM, the committee's final report continued to put off the stronger measures that had earlier been threatened, including expulsion and more concrete sanctions.

The United Nations was the other major focus of Canadian multilateral diplomacy on Nigeria. Canada co-sponsored a resolution in the General Assembly in December 1995 on the human rights situation in Nigeria – a position that received strong general support, though relatively less from African states than from others. This resolution was followed by a UN fact-finding mission in the spring of 1996, which made a series of recommendations (excluding sanctions) to which the regime responded, according to then secretary of state for Latin America and Africa Christine Stewart, in a manner "crafted to give more the appearance than the reality of movement."[20] It is significant, however, that the Nigerian government agreed to receive a mission from the UN while continuing to stall the proposed Commonwealth mission. Abuja took great umbrage at what it regarded as the latter's "selective, discriminatory, and grossly unfair" action in suspending it.[21] In November 1996, Canada again co-sponsored a General Assembly resolution on the human rights situation in Nigeria, which was adopted with a further erosion of support from African countries in particular.[22]

At the UN Commission on Human Rights in Geneva, Canadian representatives also played a key role in negotiating a resolution expressing "deep concern" about rights abuses in Nigeria. This resolution was adopted by consensus in April 1996 and gave two rapporteurs the task of investigating arbitrary executions and the independence of the judiciary, respectively. This was a compromise that was reached when the commission membership was unable to agree to the stronger step of appointing a permanent UN investigator into Nigeria's human rights practices.[23] When the Nigerian government effectively obstructed the efforts of the two rapporteurs to conduct their fact-finding mission, the quest for consensus was abandoned. In April 1997, Canada co-sponsored another resolution on the human rights situation in Nigeria, this one calling for the appointment of a special country rapporteur. It was adopted by a narrow majority of the commission's fifty-three member states.[24]

Bilaterally, Canada gradually added to the relatively minor sanctions implemented prior to 1995. Cumulatively, it: selectively denied visas to members of the governing regime, restricted sports contacts, imposed an arms embargo, removed military attachés and ended military training, downgraded diplomatic missions and cultural links, ceased providing bilateral aid and government export credits, and suspended a double-taxation agreement and negotiations on an investment-protection agreement.[25] While the measures it adopted roughly paralleled those taken by the US and a number of countries in the European Union, Canada was the first Commonwealth member state to adopt the full package of measures recommended (but then held in abeyance) by CMAG in April 1996. On the other hand, the government did not pursue the recommendation of the Canadian House of Commons Standing Committee on Foreign Affairs and International Trade to "take a strong leadership role in coordinating an enforceable oil embargo against Nigeria."[26] This was partly due to the growing resistance of key Nigerian oil importers elsewhere and partly because three of four traditional Canadian importers decided for their own reasons to switch suppliers, while the fourth announced a substantial reduction in its Nigerian imports. In general, and in common with many (if not most) Canadian sanctions attempts, Canada's small and declining trade links with Nigeria[27] were therefore double-edged. On the one hand, they made it easier to impose sanctions; on the other hand, they limited Canadian credibility and leverage in lobbying for new trade restrictions against Nigeria among more substantial trading partners.

While championing the need for pressure, Canadian foreign policy makers also regularly professed their desire to maintain dialogue and to provide transitional assistance to the Nigerian regime. As events unfolded, however, Nigerian leaders clearly acted to forestall dialogue with Canada, first by closing their High Commission in Ottawa in September 1996 and then by failing to cooperate with Canadian efforts to make alternative visa arrangements for travel to Nigeria. Later, Abuja's denial of visas to two RCMP officers who were to accompany Secretary of State Stewart on the long-delayed CMAG mission to Nigeria on 18-19 November 1996 was interpreted as a diplomatic slight in Ottawa, and it resulted in the Canadian delegation's withdrawal from the mission.[28] In March 1997, the Canadian government took the highly unusual step of "temporarily suspending" the operations of its mission in Lagos (i.e., closing it) on the grounds that "Canadian officials at the High Commission have not been given the security assurances we are guaranteed in the Geneva Convention."[29] In so doing, it finally acknowledged the impossibility of any significant dialogue under existing circumstances.

Finally, *trans-societally*, Canadian government ministers asserted that "we must not forget the people of Nigeria." The government provided limited support for the efforts of Canadian and Nigerian non-governmental organizations (NGOs) to promote positive political change through a C$2.2 million "Democratic Development Fund" deployed over two years. Although it was difficult for NGOs (both internal and external) to operate in Nigeria, the Fund was clearly a relatively token contribution.[30] The Department of Foreign Affairs and International Trade (DFAIT) also used its visits program to bring Nigerian opposition figures to Canada with the aim of raising popular awareness of developments there, further antagonizing the Abacha regime in the process.[31] Finally, DFAIT supported the efforts of Canadian businesses with interests in Nigeria to develop a voluntary code of business ethics for companies operating in that country. Overall, government support for trans-societal efforts to promote change was a relatively minor element of its overall policy; nevertheless, it was a burr in the saddle of the Nigerian regime.

Echoes of Apartheid?

The parallels between the policy actions directed towards Nigeria after 1993 and those aimed at apartheid South Africa during the 1980s are striking.[32] Most obviously, the Commonwealth's CMAG strategy closely paralleled an amalgam of its Eminent Persons Group (EPG) and Committee of Foreign Ministers on Southern Africa (CFMSA) structures and strategies. Like the EPG, ironically co-chaired by Olusegun Obasanjo, CMAG aimed to initiate a process of dialogue with the Nigerian government but was positioned to recommend stronger sanctions if the dialogue were to fail.[33] Like the CFMSA, it sought "to provide high level impetus and guidance"[34] to the Commonwealth's efforts. It was the EPG and CFMSA that largely carried forward the Commonwealth's, and Canada's, (partial) sanctions effort against South Africa. Finally, and belatedly, CMAG emulated the CFMSA practice of inviting submissions and presentations from opposition groups to inform its decision making. Canadian representatives apparently began lobbying for presentations from Nigerian and international NGOs in September 1996, and officials argue that the groups that finally appeared before CMAG in July 1997 were important in winning the argument for the maintenance of pressure (however limited) on Nigeria.[35] Of course, the UN also had a long history of increasingly vociferous activism in relation to South Africa, which had an influence on Canadian and Commonwealth policies.[36]

Bilaterally, Canadian officials always claimed to seek a "balance" between pressure and dialogue with apartheid South Africa, striving to bring the regime "to its senses, not its knees" in the government's stock phrase of the late 1980s. Towards this end, diplomatic relations were always maintained despite some domestic and international pressure to sever them. As noted above, a comparable line was taken in relation to Nigeria, with Canada attempting to maintain a watching brief through its High Commission in Nigeria, despite persistent provocations and Nigeria's closure of its mission in Ottawa. The March 1997 suspension of operations by the Canadian High Commission therefore marked an extraordinary break with past practice and with DFAIT's strong preference.

Trans-societally, the Democratic Development Fund earmarked principally for Nigeria was reminiscent of the "positive measures" adopted in support of domestic victims and opponents of the apartheid regime – even if the cumulative value of such measures was much smaller in Nigeria than in South Africa.[37] Finally, the drafting of a voluntary code of business ethics for firms operating in Nigeria echoed the codes of conduct implemented by Canada and other Western countries in relation to South Africa: both were half-hearted and controversial.[38]

Yet the political dynamic of the Nigerian case, and Canada's role therein, evolved very differently from the South African "model." Above all, whereas with regard to Nigeria, Canada (along with New Zealand) found itself increasingly isolated in its hard-line sanctions advocacy within CMAG, with regard to South Africa its support for sanctions was very much in line with the overwhelming Commonwealth majority. Indeed, from 1987 onwards, Canadian policy makers were often accused, by both domestic critics and other CFMSA members (most notably those from Africa),[39] of "backsliding" on their sanctions position. The general point is that, notwithstanding the popular view in this country that Canada took the lead in bringing pressure to bear on South Africa,[40] Canada's "leadership" was part of a much wider coalition of forces. The Mulroney government moved in the company of, and/or under pressure from, governments in various parts of the South; other Western "middle powers" such as Australia, the Nordics, and the Netherlands; and various non-governmental groups linked to the international anti-apartheid movement. It was principally ahead of the political executives of its G-7 partners and a few other Western states. By contrast, Canada steadily lost diplomatic ground in its advocacy of sanctions against Nigeria, especially among those African and

Southern states that spearheaded the campaign against apartheid in international organizations like the Commonwealth and the UN. In the end, Canadian officials were pleased merely to keep the prospect of sanctions alive at the Edinburgh CHOGM.

Significant policy repercussions followed from this basic difference. For example, whereas Canadian policy makers developed quite generous programs of assistance for opposition groups in South Africa during the latter half of the 1980s, partly to demonstrate their continued commitment to the anti-apartheid cause in the face of their critics, comparable political pressure was lacking on the Nigerian issue. This helps to explain why the resources allocated to the Democratic Development Fund for Nigeria were so much more limited. The obvious question is: why did Canada's policy approach to Nigeria – so similar on the surface to its South African policy – receive such a different reception from most African states in particular and many Southern states in general?

Explaining the Differences

There are a number of key factors that help to explain Canada's position on Nigeria and the differences between it and Canada's position on South Africa.[41] Governmental and parliamentary enthusiasm for a strong stand against Abacha's Nigeria reflected, in part, related political-cultural and idiosyncratic considerations. As Cranford Pratt has argued, there has long been a "humane internationalist" strand in Canadian political culture, most strongly manifested on North-South and human rights issues.[42] As Pratt and others have demonstrated, however, the popular perception that Canada can and should use its influence to serve the cause of global justice has been honoured as much in the breach as in the practice. There have always been significant limitations and contradictions in Canada's humane internationalism. As a result, high profile "moral crusades"[43] have held a position of prominence in the collective Canadian imagination as markers of the continued vigour of the ethical dimension of Canadian foreign policy in the face of considerable evidence to the contrary. The pattern of such crusades underscores Heather Smith's point (Chapter 5, this volume) that there is nothing particularly new about "niche diplomacy," especially in the area of international human rights. There is, in other words, a pattern of consistent inconsistency on such issues, with cases like South Africa and Nigeria gaining disproportionate salience in the study and discourse of Canadian foreign policy. In this sense, the two issues have played similar discursive and legitimizing roles, while a good many champions of Canadian internationalism were inclined to overlook or minimize their differences, thereby inviting distorted analyses and expectations within the Nigerian context. Moreover there was – and in many respects continues to be – a widespread assumption that norms of human rights and democracy have grown in popularity and force in the post-Cold War era, as reflected in such developments as the signing of the treaty for an international criminal court (see Andy Knight, Chapter 7, this volume). This assumption reinforced the expectation in this country that egregious rights violators, like the Abacha regime, should be dealt with forcefully.

In the face of such expectations, the early years of the Chrétien government were distressing ones for advocates of humane internationalism. The apparent dominance of trade promotion over all other foreign policy priorities was very discomfiting to many Canadians, especially when it resulted in the eager courting of repressive regimes such as China's and Indonesia's.[44] Thus, when the opportunity arose to reassert the humane dimension of Canadian self-identity on the Nigerian issue, with little material cost, it was embraced not only by some leading Cabinet ministers and parliamentarians, but also by many in Canada's attentive public. It was explicitly seen as an opportunity to recapture the mythologized moral leadership role that the country was supposed to have played on the South African issue, as reflected in a *Globe and Mail* editorial:

> Jean Chrétien, and former foreign affairs minister André Ouellet, were deaf to arguments that Canada could make a difference. From China to Burma, they saw no percentage in speaking out; indeed, they argued that megaphone diplomacy would hurt trade and cost jobs at home. They abandoned the moral high ground that this country had occupied under the Progressive Conservatives, in leading opposition to apartheid in South Africa. The silence on human rights was shameful, the cost to our reputation enormous ...
>
> ... the generals in Lagos will not cower before Canada, but that was never the intention. The purpose of imposing sanctions is to lead by example, which was once second nature to this country on issues of conscience. It is to show that morality has returned to Canada's foreign policy, where it belongs.[45]

The fact that leadership on issues of conscience has always been more intermittent and selective than this editorial suggests has done little to detract from the resilience of the image it projects.

Strongly reinforcing the enthusiasm for activism in this case was a change in foreign policy leadership, with Lloyd Axworthy replacing Ouellet as foreign minister. Axworthy, along with then secretary of state for Latin America and Africa Christine Stewart, was one of the strongest proponents of humane internationalism in the Liberal government. Together, they seized upon the Nigerian issue to signal a change in emphasis in Canadian foreign policy towards a more "ethical" set of priorities.[46]

In explaining why dialogue failed, and why, at least for a time, Canada was increasingly isolated within CMAG, the Nigerian regime's aggressive diplomatic counter-attack should not be discounted. It seems that Canadian policy makers were caught off guard by the vigour and guile of Nigerian officials.[47] Clearly, the Nigerian regime was deeply and loudly offended by the Commonwealth and Canadian positions in the days and months following the executions of the Ogoni Nine. But it is also likely that, just as a hard-line stand on Nigeria offered Canadian policy makers a relatively low-cost opportunity to assert their continued concern for international human rights, so an uncompromising response against Canada by the Nigerians offered the latter a low-cost means of signalling their unwillingness to bend before international – particularly Western – pressure. It was left to representatives of countries such as Malaysia to play the traditional Canadian role of "bridge builder" within the CMAG context.[48]

However, the single most important difference between the Nigerian and South African contexts was the position taken by African (particularly West African) countries and organizations. This, in turn, profoundly affected the receptiveness of the Commonwealth to Canada's position. Whereas on South Africa, African Commonwealth member states and their "Third World" collaborators were strong sanctions advocates and sharp spurs to a stronger Canadian position, on Nigeria, they became advocates of a conciliatory approach, with Abuja's West African neighbours (notably CMAG member Ghana) being the least inclined towards sanctions pressure. This was the precise inverse, rhetorically at least, of the situation in South Africa. How is this difference to be accounted for?

There are a number of relevant factors. First, by the 1980s the domestic societal forces arrayed against the Nigerian regime were considerably weaker and more fractious than were their South African counterparts. They were also a long way from effectively internationalizing their struggle, as the African National Congress (ANC) did over some three decades of international diplomacy. To put this difference into perspective, it is important to recall the fractiousness that beset the South African opposition for many years and the lengthy, tireless efforts of ANC representatives and others in making their case abroad. Yet it remains uncertain whether, given the sharply politicized regional/ethnic divisions within Nigerian society, a strong pan-Nigerian opposition *could* emerge. Regardless, both the impetus for international pressure against the military regime and the organizational vehicles for support to domestic democrats were weaker in the Nigerian than in the South African case, at least as it had evolved by the 1980s.

Vital material and security interests were also in play of course. Among Western countries, for example, Britain's Tory governments remained consistent in their opposition to stronger sanctions across the two cases, albeit less vocally so with Nigeria than with South Africa. Underlying this position was the continued strength of British economic interests in both countries. (The election of a Labour Party government in the months prior to the Edinburgh CHOGM significantly altered the dynamics within CMAG, however, and contributed to the restoration of a measure of consensus.[49]) Similarly, a number of West African countries, including Ghana, depend on Nigeria for relatively inexpensive oil supplies. Others on this economically fragile continent were doubtless susceptible to oil-financed inducements from the Abacha regime (as were certain African-American leaders).[50] Finally, in security terms, there was some fear in West Africa that further isolation and decline could push Nigeria towards anarchy and/or a new civil war, with dire consequences for the whole region. Moreover, the Nigerian military was playing a central role in responses to regional conflicts, notably in Liberia and Sierra Leone.

Yet similar arguments were made about the probable costs and consequences of isolation, economic decline, and civil conflict in South Africa for its regional neighbours, who were no less dependent in relative terms than were Nigeria's West African neighbours. Nevertheless, key southern African countries led their continental counterparts in campaigning internationally for the isolation of South Africa. Various commentators noted the apparent irrationality, in economic and security terms, of the Frontline States' sanctions advocacy and the material costs and risks that they and other African countries bore in supporting liberation struggles in southern Africa.[51] Obviously, then, normative as well as material forces were at work. It is to these normative considerations that this paper finally turns.

The Comparative Politics of Norms

In her book *Norms in International Relations,* Audie Klotz defines norms as "shared (thus social) understandings of standards for behaviour."[52] Klotz argues that both materialist and realist approaches have failed to take account of the autonomous role played by socially constituted norms of behaviour in world politics. Evolving norms have the power to (re)define interests, empower actors, and legitimate both the means and ends of international behaviour.[53] Klotz illustrates her argument by demonstrating how the growing prevalence of a norm of racial equality, rooted in the Western liberal philosophical tenet of individual equality, underpinned the mounting isolation of South Africa in international society and served to justify punitive sanctions against it. Materially weak international actors, such as the ANC and various African states and organizations, gained normative legitimacy and power as the acceptance of this norm grew. Conversely, the South African state came under increasing and eventually irresistible pressure at home and abroad as the legitimacy of its racially discriminatory order was successfully challenged.

Significantly, however, Klotz argues further that the nature and impact of dominant norms will vary not only over time, but also between different subsystemic communities. Thus, for example, the constitutive basis and identity of the Organization for Economic Cooperation and Development (OECD) differs from that of the Organization of African Unity (OAU) or the Association of Southeast Asian Nations (ASEAN). Moreover, the normative basis for action, or inaction, on a "global issue" like South Africa or Nigeria will vary across subsystemic communities. This can lead to misunderstandings concerning the meaning and implications of particular international campaigns, and it can seriously complicate the process of obtaining a broadly based consensus for action on any particular issue.

As Klotz demonstrates, the normative basis for opposition to apartheid varied significantly between the OAU and other international organizations, like the Commonwealth and the UN,[54] and consequently among different countries, such as Canada, India, and Zimbabwe. Canada and its Commonwealth collaborators came to share an interest in dismantling apartheid, and they came to accept the legitimacy of substantial sanctions pressure as a way of bringing this about; but the normative basis upon which this shared understanding of ends and means rested differed. For Canadian policy makers, the struggle against apartheid came to be understood as part of a wider process of advancing "universal" human rights and democracy, of which apartheid South Africa was a particularly egregious and destabilizing violator.[55] As the process of change in South Africa moved towards its tortured but ultimately successful conclusion, its success implied that the same broad standards of behaviour should be applied elsewhere. This conclusion was strongly reinforced by the fall of communist and many other authoritarian regimes in the late 1980s and early 1990s. It is no surprise, then, that in the early 1990s, the Mulroney government moved to embrace a much more expansive and interventionist approach to humanitarian issues and human rights violators, including violators of democratic norms. For example, Mulroney himself sparked controversy at the 1991 Harare CHOGM by suggesting that Canada would henceforth be much more active in linking foreign aid to human rights and democracy in recipient countries.[56]

For African and most other Southern states, by contrast, the core norm necessitating action against South Africa (and other White minority-ruled regimes in southern Africa) was anti-racism, rooted in the process and principle of decolonization.[57] These states provided the impetus for single-issue UN human rights conventions outlawing racial discrimination (the Convention on the Elimination of All Forms of Racial Discrimination, which entered into force in 1969) and apartheid (the Convention on the Suppression and Punishment of the Crime of Apartheid, in force since 1976). It was these documents that enshrined the normative basis for action against apartheid and minority rule, as understood by the UN's "Third World" majority. Significantly too, the Commonwealth's 1991 Harare

Declaration, which entrenched the organization's commitment to democracy and human rights and provided the normative basis for its suspension of Nigeria, singled out racism for particularly strong language.[58] The point is that, for most African and other Southern countries, the logic of imposing sanctions against South Africa rested on the assumption that institutionalized racial discrimination was sufficient grounds to override the principle of national sovereignty. It did *not* imply that violations of broader norms of human rights and democracy were similarly sanctionable.

Thus, Canada and most of its CMAG counterparts came to the Nigerian crisis with different normative baggage. For Canadian policy makers Nigeria's annulment of the 1993 presidential elections, compounded by a pattern of systematic human rights violations culminating in the executions of 10 November 1995, constituted a clear violation of the principles freely agreed to in the Harare Declaration. On this they and their Commonwealth partners were agreed. But for the Canadians, Nigerian behaviour also provided firm normative grounds for strong punitive sanctions. The (Southern) majority of Commonwealth states, by contrast, were much less inclined to contemplate further sanctions beyond the initial step of suspending Nigeria. While there has been much talk in the post-Cold War context of the growing prevalence of norms of human rights and democracy,[59] the degree of consensus on what precisely these norms embody, and what kinds of international action they legitimate, remains limited. Indeed, in many parts of the South, particularly much of Africa and Asia, there has been considerable resistance to and resentment of the imposition of Western conceptions of human rights and democracy. For example, Malaysia – a key CMAG member – has been outspoken in rejecting Western human rights conditionalities and defending the norm of sovereignty within the Asian context. It was unlikely, then, to support a Commonwealth campaign to implement sanctions overriding Nigeria's sovereignty on grounds that it would reject within its own regional context. Thus, the normative basis for building a Commonwealth-wide sanctions campaign against Nigeria – on the grounds that it was in violation of Harare Declaration commitments to democracy, the rule of law, and fundamental human rights – was fundamentally weak and soon began to erode.

For African state representatives on CMAG, and within the wider UN context, there was in addition a countervailing norm of African solidarity. It is well known that the OAU and various regional groupings in Africa have often been troubled by rivalries and resentments. Yet there have always been certain principles and causes that have bound them together, notwithstanding some deviations from those principles in practice.[60] For many years, the most obvious of these was shared opposition to minority-ruled regimes in southern Africa, and support for liberation movements and sanctions aimed at their removal, rooted in the "constitutive commitment to racial equality."[61] But, in addition, there has been a strong tradition of solidarity in the face of open (as opposed to covert) external attacks. As Maxi van Aardt puts it: "Within the pan-Africanist paradigm, an unwritten law, as it were, has developed over the years creating the tradition that African states do not turn on each other in international fora, such as the UN, but close ranks when attacks are made against one or more of them."[62]

Like most norms, moreover, this one applies with greater decisiveness within some contexts than within others, depending on material and historical considerations. In the case of Nigeria – for many years Africa's would-be "great power," the OAU's principal financial supporter, and a stalwart of the anti-apartheid struggle – the solidarity card could be played with particularly telling effect.

It was this solidarity norm that South Africa, still inexperienced in the ways of African diplomacy, ran afoul of with Nelson Mandela's vigorous attacks on the Abacha regime and the advocacy of international sanctions. South Africa further infringed this norm by being the only country from Africa or the "developing world" to recall its high commissioner/ambassador from Nigeria in protest over the executions of the Ogoni Nine.[63] It soon found that even its own Southern African Development Community (SADC) neighbours (including CMAG chair Zimbabwe) were unwilling to act in concert with its hard line, let alone states and organizations elsewhere in Africa. The suggestion that South Africa was acting as a cover for American and other Western interests on this issue was particularly damaging in light of the solidarity norm. Mandela's government soon retreated from its strong stand, striking a more conciliatory, middle-of-the-road stance within CMAG and beyond it (though not without controversy at home).[64] At the Edinburgh Summit, it withdrew from CMAG, to be replaced by its much smaller neighbour Botswana.

For Canada, the effective loss of such an important ally was a telling blow. Post-apartheid South Africa's policy makers had described human rights and democracy as "pillars" of their foreign policy.[65] Together, Canadian and South African representatives in CMAG had the potential to wield substantial influence; with South Africa's retreat, however, Canada's impact on the group was further diminished. The Nigerian issue had exposed the relative weakness of the democratic and human rights norms upon which Canadian policy relied.

This is not to imply that Canadian foreign policy has been consistent on the democratic and human rights norms embodied in the Harare Declaration. Indeed, as suggested above, one of the reasons why Canadian politicians and the attentive public seized so eagerly on the Nigerian issue was precisely because it offered a conspicuous opportunity to regain the moral high ground on these issues after the discomfort associated with the Chrétien government's apparently amoral approach to foreign relations during its early years in office. Yet the very inconsistency of Canadian human rights practice further weakened the credibility of its stand on Nigeria. It left it open to the charge that Canadian policy rested on a normative double standard – one for marginal, notably African, countries, and another for "emerging markets." Such a perception was liable, in its own small way, to reinforce the tendency towards solidarity among African states both inside and outside the Commonwealth.

Conclusion: Implications for Canadian Foreign Policy

The case of Nigeria, and the comparison with apartheid South Africa, underscores the importance of incorporating a sophisticated understanding of normative contexts into both scholarly and policy analyses – a point made by Andrew Knight (Chapter 7, this volume). Such contexts must be understood to be historically contingent and to vary across distinct subsystemic communities. More specifically, this case study highlights the relative weakness of norms of "universal" human rights, democracy, and the rule of law, upon which Canadian policy towards both South Africa and Nigeria was premised, as a foundation for a wider international consensus on punitive action. The compatible but distinct norm of non-racialism – the principal basis for African and Third World opposition to apartheid – was much more widely accepted and robust. It remains to be seen whether some aspects of the broader norms of human rights and democracy will eventually form a sufficient basis for consistent punitive action on a system-wide (as opposed to subsystemic[66]) basis. Interestingly, the very fact that Nigeria is now led by an elected civilian president who has been outspoken in support of such norms stands to reinforce their salience in Africa.

For Canadian policy makers and students of foreign policy, the foregoing analysis suggests a number of more or less familiar lessons. First, there is a need for great care, and more modesty, in interpreting the lessons of our own foreign policy history. There has been a strong tendency to exaggerate the importance of Canadian leadership on the South African issue, especially within the Commonwealth context. In the dominant historical narrative, Canadian politicians and publics have glossed over the degree to which Canada's South African policy moved in concert with a wide range of collaborators. As a result, there seem to have been exaggerated expectations concerning the willingness of other Commonwealth members to follow Canada's moral leadership on what was widely seen in this country as a very similar kind of issue. The frustration that Canadian foreign policy makers sometimes expressed concerning the CMAG process can be at least partly explained by the influence of this mythologized version of the past.[67]

Second, the Nigerian case serves as a useful reminder of the limits of middle power influence, even in relatively hospitable settings such as the Commonwealth. There is a need to carefully coordinate policy with other key players, including national and international officials and non-governmental representatives. For example, more effective and anticipatory strategic coordination with South African policy makers could have significantly reinforced the influence of each. Flexible and strategic coalition building of this type remains essential to the success of any middle power attempt at influence.

Developments leading up to the Edinburgh CHOGM served to underscore this lesson. Many Nigerian and international human rights activists expressed understandable frustration at the Commonwealth's lack of substantial new action against the Abacha regime at this meeting.[68] Nevertheless, the leaders' decision to maintain Nigeria's suspension, and to authorize CMAG to expel Nigeria and to consider a set of substantial new sanctions if the country remained in "serious violation of the Harare principles after 1 October 1998,"[69] represented a stronger position than could have been anticipated six months previously. While a number of factors account for this shift back towards the Canadian position, two in particular underscore the importance of strategic coordination with both state and non-state actors: (1) the new cooperative relationship with the recently elected British government and its foreign secretary, Robin Cook, and (2) the interventions of Nigerian and international human rights NGOs at the July CMAG meeting in support of continued pressure on the Abacha regime.

Third, and closely related to the above, is the need for particular sensitivity to the normative as well as material dynamics surrounding a particular issue. This general injunction applies with particular force to governments, such as Canada's, with relatively few and diminishing material levers to pull, but with a certain amount of "reputational capital" and, therefore, the ability to act, as Knight (Chapter 7, this volume) would have it, as "norm entrepreneurs." If the foregoing analysis is broadly correct, then it seems likely that Canadian policy makers failed both to fully appreciate the wider normative lessons of the South African case and to take sufficient cognizance of the different dynamics at play in the Nigerian case.

Does this then imply that the Canadian government's principled stand against Abacha's Nigeria was a policy failure? Particularly in light of the fortuitous demise of General Abacha and the subsequent restoration of civilian rule, the answer is clearly no. From a narrow political perspective, the government's stand was good domestic politics, and Canada's role in keeping the prospect of further sanctions alive, especially within the Commonwealth context, probably helped to prompt the reforms undertaken by Abacha's successor, General Abubakar.[70] It has also made a friend out of

President Obasanjo, as the opening quote suggests. Moreover, the principles involved are important ones, worth some effort and risk to promote internationally.

Nevertheless, the issue could have been handled with greater finesse and effectiveness, in part by incorporating a keener normative analysis into policy thinking. Moreover, an effective human rights-based stand on this or any other issue needs to be buttressed by a greater degree of consistency than has been manifested in the Chrétien government's foreign policy to date. While rigid consistency is obviously both impossible and unwise, the credibility of any particular normative stand must be buttressed by a broad and reliable commitment to the principles in question. While there are some indications that such an approach was emerging under former foreign minister Axworthy, past practice suggests that it is wise to view such indications with caution, as Heather Smith argues (Chapter 5, this volume).

Notes

1 Anne McIlroy, "Chretien Greeted as a Friend by Nigerians," *Globe and Mail,* 10 November 1999. It should be noted that Obasanjo was previously a general in the Nigerian military and a military ruler of the country. In this capacity, he presided over Nigeria's previous transition from military to civilian rule in 1979.

2 Letter from Foreign Minister Lloyd Axworthy, circa late 1996/early 1997, setting out the government's position on the Nigerian situation.

3 See also Evan Potter, "Nigeria and the Commonwealth: Explaining Canada's Hard-line Approach to Sanctions, 1995-96," *The Round Table* 342 (1997): 219-20.

4 See Richard Joseph, "Nigeria: Inside the Dismal Tunnel," *Current History* 95, 601 (May 1996): 194.

5 Richard Leaver, "Sanctions, South Africa and Australian Policy," Peace Research Centre, Australian National University, Working Paper no. 37 (1988): 37-38.

6 See, for example, Heather Smith, "Niche Diplomacy in Canadian Human Rights Policy: Ethics or Economics?" Chapter 5, this volume; and Lloyd Axworthy, "Canada and Human Security: The Need for Leadership," *International Journal* 52, 2 (1997): 183-96.

7 See D. Black, "Democratization and Security in Africa: An Elusive Relationship," *Canadian Foreign Policy* 4, 2 (1996): 1-18.

8 For fuller accounts see, for example, Joseph, "Nigeria"; Julius O. Ihonvbere, "Are Things Falling Apart? The Military and the Crisis of Democratisation in Nigeria," *Journal of Modern African Studies* 34, 2 (1996): 193-225; and Jeffrey Herbst, "Is Nigeria a Viable State?" *Washington Quarterly* 19, 2 (1996): 151-72.

9 Joseph, "Nigeria," 198.

10 "Sacking the Sultan," *Africa Confidential* 37, 9 (1996): 3.

11 See Investor Responsibility Research Centre (IRRC), "International Business and Human Rights in Nigeria," Social Services Background Report J, 1 (1996): 8-9; and Joshua Hammer, "Nigeria Crude," *Harper's Magazine* 292, 1753 (1996): 58-70. On the importance of a "particularly awesome violation of human rights" in putting a norm-violating state on the international agenda, see Thomas Risse and Kathryn Sikkink, "The Socialization of International Human Rights Norms into Domestic Practices: Introduction," in *The Power of Human Rights,* ed. Thomas Risse, Stephen Ropp, and Kathryn Sikkink (Cambridge: Cambridge University Press, 1999), 22.

12 "Harare Commonwealth Declaration," reproduced in *The Round Table* 321 (1992): 102-04.

13 See Derek Ingram, "Auckland Notebook," *The Round Table* 337 (1996): 1; and Philip van Niekerk, "Mandela's Softly-Softly Betrayal," *Weekly Mail and Guardian,* 17-23 November 1995.

14 Potter, "Nigeria and the Commonwealth," 210.
15 "Nigeria's Crime," *Globe and Mail,* 11 November 1995.
16 See Potter, "Nigeria and the Commonwealth," 207-08; interview with DFAIT official, 18 February 1997.
17 Letter from Foreign Minister Lloyd Axworthy in response to inquiries concerning Nigeria, circa late 1996/early 1997.
18 From "The Millbrook [New Zealand] Commonwealth Action Programme on the Harare Commonwealth Declaration," item 4 (reproduced in *The Round Table* 337 [1996]: 125).
19 Cited in IRRC, "African Leaders Divided on Nigeria Sanctions," *Social Issues Reporter,* December 1995, 3. See also John Stackhouse, "Summit Dilutes Rights Position," *Globe and Mail,* 4 December 1995.
20 "Nigeria: The Challenge to Public and Private Policy," Notes for a Statement by the Honourable Christine Stewart, Secretary of State (Latin America and Africa), to the Canadian Business Forum on Nigeria, 5 November 1996, 4.
21 "Speech by the Nigerian Foreign Minister, Chief Tom Ikimi," Auckland, New Zealand, 13 November 1995, para. 15. Reproduced in *The Round Table* 337 (1996): 134.
22 See Potter, "Nigeria and the Commonwealth," 212. No West African country voted against Nigeria.
23 See Stewart, "Nigeria: The Challenge," 4; and "Commonwealth Urges Sanctions on Nigeria," *Globe and Mail,* 24 April 1996.
24 Economic and Social Council, E/CN.4/1997/L.40, (7 April 1997). The vote was split between Western, Latin American, and Eastern European countries, which supported the resolution, and most African and Asian countries, which abstained or were opposed. There were some important anomalies, however: both South Africa and Uganda voted in favour of the resolution.
25 Department of Foreign Affairs and International Trade (DFAIT), "Nigeria" (Fact Sheet), 2.
26 Minutes of Proceedings of the Standing Committee on Foreign Affairs and International Trade, issue 30, meeting no. 88, 14 December 1995.
27 Canadas trade figures with Nigeria were much lower than were its trade figures with South Africa, even at the latter's lowest point. See DFAIT, "Nigeria," 2; and Potter, "Nigeria and the Commonwealth," 214-15.
28 Communication with DFAIT official, May 1997. See also "Canadian Delegates Denied Visas for Commonwealth Ministerial Action Group Mission to Nigeria," DFAIT News Release no. 212, 18 November 1996; and author's interview with DFAIT official, 20 February 1997.
29 Statement by Lloyd Axworthy, quoted in Hugh Winsor, "Canada Recalls Diplomats from Nigeria," *Globe and Mail,* 13 March 1997.
30 The two-year, C$2.2 million Fund, supporting work in Sierra Leone and the Gambia as well as Nigeria (population roughly 100 million), can, for example, be compared with the more than C$10 million allocated to "victims and opponents of apartheid" in South Africa (population approximately forty million) in 1988-89. See Department of External Affairs, "Canadian Action on South Africa," February 1990.
31 See Potter, "Nigeria and the Commonwealth," 211; and Winsor, "Canada Recalls Diplomats."
32 As Potter notes, many of the Canadian officials who were mobilized to work on the Nigerian issue had been involved with the South African file in the 1980s. See Potter, "Nigeria and the Commonwealth," 218.
33 See Commonwealth Group of Eminent Persons, *Mission to South Africa* (Harmondsworth: Penguin, 1986).
34 See *Report of the Commonwealth Secretary-General, 1989* (London: Commonwealth Secretariat, 1989), 43.
35 Interviews with DFAIT officials, 7 November 1997.
36 See Audie Klotz, *Norms in International Relations: The Struggle against Apartheid* (Ithaca: Cornell University Press, 1995), chap. 3, "The United Nations," 39-54.
37 See note 30 above; see also Linda Freeman, *The Ambiguous Champion, Canada and South Africa in the Trudeau and Mulroney Years* (Toronto: University of Toronto Press, 1997), 277-82.

38 See Mzamo P. Mangaliso, "MNC Disinvestment in South Africa: Codes of Corporate Conduct," in *How Sanctions Work: Lessons From South Africa,* ed. Neta Crawford and Audie Klotz (New York: St. Martin's, 1999), 145-58.
39 See Linda Freeman, *The Ambiguous Champion,* esp. 190-233; and Renate Pratt, *In Good Faith: Canadian Churches against Apartheid* (Waterloo: Wilfrid Laurier University Press, 1997), 263-336.
40 See, for example, Barbara McDougall, "Why Keep the Commonwealth?" *Globe and Mail,* 14 November 1997, A23.
41 See also Potter, "Nigeria and the Commonwealth," 219-20.
42 Humane internationalism is defined as "an acceptance by the citizens of industrialized states that they have ethical obligations towards those beyond their borders and that these impose obligations upon their governments." See Cranford Pratt, "Humane Internationalism: Its Significance and Variants," in *Internationalism Under Strain,* ed. Cranford Pratt (Toronto: University of Toronto Press, 1989), 13. See also Pratt, "Canada: A Limited and Eroding Internationalism," in Pratt, ed. *Internationalism under Strain.*
43 For example, Diefenbaker's role in South Africa's withdrawal from the Commonwealth in the early 1960s; Pierre Trudeau's "peace initiative" in the early 1980s; the Mulroney government's activism on South Africa, also in the 1980s; and, most recently, Lloyd Axworthy's pursuit of a global ban on landmines. See also Cranford Pratt, "The Limited Place of Human Rights in Canadian Foreign Policy," in *Human Rights, Development and Foreign Policy: Canadian Perspectives,* ed. Irving Brecher (Halifax: The Institute for Research on Public Policy, 1989), 172-73.
44 See, for example, Claire Turenne Sjolander, "International Trade as Foreign Policy: Brother Can you Spare a Dime?" in *How Ottawa Spends,* ed. Gene Swimmer (Ottawa: Carleton University Press, 1997).
45 "Punishing Nigeria," *Globe and Mail,* 28 June 1996.
46 See Potter, "Nigeria and the Commonwealth," 217-18.
47 As reflected in interviews with DFAIT officers who readily acknowledged both the "pride" and "cleverness" of Nigerian officials, 18 and 20 February 1997.
48 See Potter, "Nigeria and the Commonwealth," 221.
49 See extract from the transcript of a press conference given by the foreign secretary, Mr Robin Cook, London, 12 May 1997, "Nigeria" (Ottawa: British High Commission), mimeo.
50 See Glenn Frankel, "Oil Buys Excuses for Nigeria," *Weekly Mail and Guardian,* 24 December 1996-9 January 1997.
51 See, for example, Lloyd John Chingambo and Stephen Chan, "Sanctions and South Africa: Strategies, Strangleholds and Self-Consciousness," *Paradigms* 2, 2 (Winter 1988-89): 112-32.
52 Klotz, *Norms in International Relations,* 14.
53 See also Martha Finnemore, *National Interests and International Society* (Ithaca: Cornell University Press, 1996).
54 Klotz, *Norms in International Relations,* 76.
55 Interview with DFAIT officer, 7 November 1997.
56 See Tom Keating and Nichola Gammer, "The 'New Look' in Canada's Foreign Policy," *International Journal* 48, 4 (1993): 720-48; and Freeman, *The Ambiguous Champion,* 252-53.
57 Klotz, *Norms in International Relations,* 73-90.
58 "We recognize racial prejudice and intolerance as a dangerous sickness and a threat to healthy development, and racial discrimination as an unmitigated evil." Harare Commonwealth Declaration, point 4; reproduced in *The Round Table* 321 (1992): 102. This precise language was first adopted in the 1971 Declaration of Commonwealth Principles.
59 See, for example, Boutros Boutros-Ghali, "Democracy: A Newly Recognized Imperative," *Global Governance* 1 (1995): 3-11.
60 See Christopher Clapham, *Africa and the International System* (Cambridge: Cambridge University Press, 1996), esp. chap. 5, 106-33.
61 Klotz, *Norms in International Relations,* 74-80.

62 Maxi van Aardt, "A Foreign Policy to Die For: South Africa's Response to the Nigerian Crisis," *Africa Insight* 26, 2 (1996): 115.
63 Ibid.
64 See Larry Swatuk, "South African Foreign Policy and Nigeria: No Room for Adventure," paper presented to the International Studies Association Annual Meeting, Toronto, 18-22 March 1997; and van Aardt, "A Foreign Policy to Die For."
65 Department of Foreign Affairs (South Africa), "South African Foreign Policy Discussion Document," 1996, 13 (South African Department of Foreign Affairs), mimeo.
66 For example, within the European Union or Organization of American States.
67 See, for example, "Axworthy Lashes Out at Nigeria 'Appeasers,'" *Globe and Mail,* 26 September 1996, A16
68 See, for example, "Lack of Action on Nigeria Draws Criticism," *Globe and Mail,* 20 October 1997, A12
69 "Commonwealth Heads of Government Meeting, Edinburgh, October 1997: The Edinburgh Communiqué," item 16 (London, UK: Information and Public Affairs Division, Commonwealth Secretariat), mimeo.
70 See "Axworthy Welcomes Nigerian Announcement to Restore Democracy," DFAIT News Release no. 177, 20 July 1998.

9

Theorizing the Landmine Campaign: Ethics, Global Cultural Scripts, and the Laws of War

Andrew A. Latham

Since the end of the Cold War, members of the international community have devoted considerable energy to negotiating a global prohibition regime for anti-personnel landmines (APMs). Beginning in the early 1990s, these weapons became the focus of a vigorous global campaign conducted by a "coalition of the willing," which was comprised of Canada, several "like-minded" states, and more than 1,000 non-governmental organizations (NGOs) from over fifty countries. Initially, this campaign was focused on securing a comprehensive ban on the production, stockpiling, trade, and use of APMs at the 1995 Review Conference of the Convention on Conventional Weapons (CCW).[1] Following the failure to achieve a ban in that forum, however, landmine negotiations quickly shifted to two new sites: the UN Conference on Disarmament (UNCD) and an autonomous negotiating forum called the "Ottawa Process." While the UNCD negotiations promptly stalled, by late 1997 the Ottawa Process had resulted in an international agreement, now signed by more than 130 governments, that formally proscribes APMs as legitimate weapons of war.

The conventional wisdom, of course, has portrayed the landmine campaign in general and the Canadian-led Ottawa Process in particular as an inspiring example of how the so-called "new multilateralism" can produce ethical international agreements that promote "human" rather than "national" security. According to this view, the landmine ban was the result of the vigorous mobilizing efforts of certain "moral entrepreneurs" who campaigned to "expose" the "intrinsic inhumanity" of APMs and to heighten awareness of a catastrophic global "landmine crisis." Drawing on international humanitarian law, advocates of a ban were then able to demonstrate to an increasingly concerned global public that APMs were intrinsically inhumane and that they should therefore be banned on ethical grounds. Once this had been accomplished, various grassroots non-governmental organizations formed around the issue and were subsequently able to lobby many national governments to support a ban. Ultimately, or so the argument runs, these lobbying efforts (facilitated and amplified by the new electronic media environment) resulted in a number of politico-diplomatic initiatives to regulate APMs and APM use: efforts that eventually culminated in the successful conclusion of a comprehensive ban in the form of the Ottawa Treaty, which was signed in 1997.

While superficially compelling, however, this account is ultimately problematic for at least four reasons. First, given the incontrovertible cruelty of all instruments of warfare, such an argument cannot by itself provide a sufficient explanation for why some weapons (in this case APMs) are invested with a heightened degree of moral opprobrium while others are considered mundane, or "conventional." Simply stated, there is nothing intrinsic to APMs or other "inhumane weapons" that renders them (or their use) any more or less "humane" than any other weapon. All weapons are cruel and destructive, and in actual battlefield conditions most of them can be used indiscriminately and in ways that cause needless human suffering.

Second, such arguments ultimately shed little light on why inhumane weapons have come to be the focus of global attention *in the 1990s.* Weapons such as anti-personnel landmines have been in widespread use throughout most of the twentieth century and during almost all of that time were considered unexceptional (and even militarily indispensable) instruments of warfare. They were certainly not the focus of Western non-proliferation, arms control and disarmament activities, nor was there any widely shared perception that there was something which might be called a "landmine crisis," despite the fact that such weapons had been used more or less indiscriminately (and with manifestly "inhumane" consequences) for decades.

Third, arguments focusing on NGO mobilization ignore or under-value the crucially important *independent* leadership role played by certain states in advancing the cause of a global APM prohibition regime. Historically, it is *not* the case (as is often simply assumed) that many of the key states involved in the campaign to ban landmines were persuaded to take the lead as a result of NGO lobbying; rather, the reverse appears to be the case: many states became responsive to pro-ban NGOs only after they had already decided to adopt a pro-ban posture. Finally, given the themes of this volume, the conventional wisdom is also problematic in that it ultimately tells us very little about the nature of the ethics/foreign policy/human security nexus. It says little, for example, about the way in which the "national interest" – that ultimate wellspring of foreign policy – sometimes comes to be understood in terms of the promotion of "ethical" security policies. Nor, ultimately, does it shed much light on the sources of the ethical norms, standards, or imperatives that sometimes shape foreign and security policy.

If we are interested in understanding the link between ethics and (Canadian) foreign policy, then what is required is an analysis of the landmine campaign that moves us beyond the shibboleths of the pro-ban community towards a deeper understanding of the way in which "ethical" foreign policy discourses can develop out of a haphazard and historically contingent combination of geo-political transformation, global cultural change, national identity politics, and the lobbying efforts of moral entrepreneurs. In particular, if we are to grasp effectively the connection between ethics and security policy we need to avoid the temptation to simply explain "*why* particular decisions resulting in specific courses of action were made" and pay closer attention to understanding "*how* meanings are produced and attached to various social subjects and objects, thus constituting particular interpretive dispositions that create certain possibilities and preclude others."[2] Only by asking these "how-possible" questions can we hope to move beyond the superficial and self-congratulatory politico-diplomatic histories that have become such a defining feature of the extant landmine literature in order to get at the real politics of the ethics/foreign policy nexus.

In light of these considerations, this chapter proceeds in three sections. The first describes how the various fora within which the laws of war have been negotiated have historically constituted key sites for the performative enactment of global cultural scripts that specify how "civilized" members of the international community should act. The primary argument made in this section is that the true significance of the laws of war is that the diplomatic processes through which they are negotiated provide an opportunity for the performative construction, representation, and reaffirmation of state (and collective state) identities. An important secondary argument is that, at important historical junctures, these identities have been powerfully shaped by what Gerrit Gong has called the "standard of civilization" – that is, a set of global cultural norms that specify the qualifications for gaining the status and privilege of being considered a "civilized nation."[3]

Building on this, the second section of the chapter traces the genealogy of the landmine ban, arguing that the enactment of the new global cultural script that evolved in the aftermath of the Cold War is a crucially important aspect of the process through which APMs have come to be proscribed in the 1990s. Somewhat more specifically, the point made here is that the landmine crisis, campaign, and resulting ban are primarily artefacts of a new (i.e., post-Cold War) global cultural script – one that involves an exhumed set of narratives, self-representations, and norms dealing with "civilized" standards of international conduct.

The chapter concludes with a discussion of the way in which studying the genealogy of the landmine ban can illuminate the complex relationship between ethics and foreign policy. The first conclusion in this regard is that the specific rearticulation of ethics and security that has come to be known as "human security" is less an altruistic or idealistic departure from the familiar discourses and practices of international security policy than it is a reworking of these discourses and practices in light of global cultural change (specifically, the emergence of a new "standard of civilization") and the dynamics of national identity politics in Canada. A second conclusion is that, ironically perhaps, the nostrums and shibboleths of "human security" are intimately bound up with the production and reproduction of global relations of power – relations of power that themselves need to be interrogated for their (questionable) ethical content. Ultimately, this suggests the need for greater caution when thinking about human security as an ethical foreign policy objective.

Global Cultural Scripts, State Action, and the Laws of War

The conventional view is that the laws of war have evolved over time as increasingly civilized societies have sought to "restrain" the conduct of warfare for ethical and humanitarian reasons. According to this perspective, the social purpose of the laws of war is primarily ethical: to reduce "needless human suffering" in times of war by defining the limits of the legitimate use of force. This has been achieved, or so the argument runs, by counter-balancing the demands of "kriegsraison" (the logic of war or military necessity) with two ethical or humanitarian principles. The first of these is the doctrine of "proportionality," which holds that weapons should not be used in a manner that is unnecessarily injurious to combatants; the second is the principle of "discrimination," which proscribes deliberate attacks on non-combatants. The conventional account also – if only implicitly – represents the history of the laws of war as a story of the progressive taming and humanizing of war through the ongoing negotiation and application of a legal-ethical framework based on "reason," "natural justice," and universal standards of humanity. By extension, the landmine ban is viewed as the natural culmination of this historical process; that is, as the latest stage in the long historical march from savagery to civilization marked by the progressive extension of the rule of law to the social institution of war.

Despite these claims, however, and as even the most cursory review of the history of war indicates, the laws of armed conflict have not in fact tamed, humanized, or otherwise meaningfully restrained the conduct of organized political violence.[4] Indeed, quite the contrary appears to be true: "the development of a more elaborate legal regime has proceeded apace with the increasing savagery and destructiveness of modern war."[5] This is so for at least three reasons. First, efforts to negotiate weapons bans have typically sought restrictions on a very narrow range of enumerated weapons, leaving all sorts of other armaments unregulated and thus open to abuse. Simply stated, while it is true that at different times certain weapons have been subject to legal proscription, at any given point in history these banned technologies have accounted for only a tiny percentage of the overall destructive potential available to combatants.[6]

Second, the laws of war have been written in such a way as to privilege *military necessity* (or even *utility*) over moral principle. As a result, the noble humanitarian sentiments often expressed by those responsible for negotiating the laws of war are only partially and imperfectly reflected in the actual corpus of positive international humanitarian law (IHL) (which permits and legitimizes any conduct consistent with military interests).[7]

Finally, even in those cases where weapons and/or practices have been "successfully" regulated by international law, under actual battlefield conditions these legal restraints are quite often simply ignored by soldiers faced with the exigencies of combat and suffering the brutalization of war. During the Second World War, the Korean War, and the Vietnam War, for example, aerial bombing was carried out on a massive scale by the United States in complete disregard for the humanitarian principles of discrimination and proportionality. For all these reasons, it is impossible to conclude that the contemporary laws of war have exercised a substantial civilizing or humanizing effect on the modern battlefield. Indeed, as a number of observers have concluded, while individual treaties may have banned specific technologies or regulated specific military practices, all the evidence suggest that the battlefield has become decidedly more (rather than less) brutal and murderous since the Hague laws were negotiated at the end of the last century.

Given the failure of the laws of armed conflict to achieve (even minimally) their putative purpose (reducing needless human suffering), one is moved to inquire precisely why it is that states periodically devote considerable time and effort to negotiating and promulgating these laws. Rejecting the conventional wisdom, and drawing on the insights of critical legal theory,[8] this chapter attempts to address this question by focusing not on the (negligible) battlefield effects of the laws of war but, rather, on the politico-diplomatic process through which these laws are negotiated and framed. Somewhat more specifically, the argument being made here is that the real significance of the laws of war lies in the fact that the diplomatic fora within which they are negotiated constitute important sites for the enactment of the global cultural scripts entailed in the dominant geo-political discourses of an era. Thus, I will argue, during the nineteenth century the prevailing geo-political script delineated appropriate forms of conduct for "members of the family of nations," requiring "civilized" states to performatively constitute themselves as such in two ways: first, by abjuring *sati,* polygamy, and slavery; and, second, by adhering to the accepted rules of diplomacy and international law.[9] International negotiations related to the laws of war constituted a particularly important stage upon which states enacted this script. Similarly, in the contemporary era, an analogous discourse is operative, although today the global cultural scripts entailed in this discourse specify appropriate forms of conduct for responsible members of "the West," or "the international community," rather than for the "family of civilized nations." And, as at the end of the nineteenth century, negotiations regarding the laws of war have once again become an important site for the enactment of the dominant script of the era.

Underpinning this inherently *dramaturgical* understanding of the laws of war is a theory of state action that departs in significant ways from the prevailing neo-utilitarian orthodoxy. Both neorealist and neoliberal theories, of course, explain state action in terms of an essentially rationalist ontology that views global politics in terms of the interaction of a variety of concrete political actors (typically states, but sometimes non-state actors like NGOs), each of which has "objective" and "self-evident" interests that it purposefully pursues through the more or less utility-maximizing selection of means and methods. On this view, self-interested states purposefully pursue policies that are intended to maximize their (objective and self-evident) interests, while minimizing the risks posed by (equally objective and self-evident) threats to those interests. A state's "foreign policy" is thus understood to be the external expression of this logic; that is, it is the utilitarian pursuit of its "objective" interests in the international arena. The argument made here, however, is that state action, rather than reflecting the instrumental pursuit of objective interests by a rational actor, is, in fact, a form of *social practice*. This means that, while the "national interest" is clearly an important explanatory variable in accounts of state action, contrary to realist claims these interests are neither "objective" nor "self-evident"; rather, they are the product of inherently social *interpretive* processes – processes that produce specific and meaningful understandings of what constitutes the national interest and threats to the national interest.[10] This means that, while state action continues to be guided by the regulative ideal of the national interest, these interests have to be understood, not as more or less obvious correlates or derivatives of the concrete structural "realities" of the international system, but, rather, as products of the "ubiquitous and unavoidable process of representation through which meaning is created."[11]

To the extent that this is true, understanding state action requires understanding the processes of representation and interpretation through which the national interest is constructed and produced. In this chapter, I argue that such an understanding requires a recognition that the representational process is inherently *storied* and that the constitutive representations that govern social life are profoundly narrative in form. Somewhat more specifically, I argue that the meanings that structure social action are produced through the pervasive and inescapable practice of knowing the world and one's place in it through the construction of *ontological narratives*. These narratives are the stories that actors construct out of available cultural and linguistic resources to create meaning out of the confusion and disorder of lived experience. Simply stated, then, ontological narratives are *constitutive* stories; that is, they actually produce (rather than simply attempt to reflect) social facts. They do this by generating the specific forms of knowledge, consciousness, "common sense," practice, and identity that allow people to understand – and thus act in – the world.

At the level of *global* politics, such narratives take the form of *geo-political discourses*, which can be thought of as meaning-generating (and so constitutive and regulative) stories regarding the social field called "international relations."[12] As Gearóid Ó Tuathail puts it, such discourses can usefully be conceptualized as forms of "discursive practice by which intellectuals of statecraft 'spatialize' international politics in such a way as to represent a 'world' characterized by particular types of places, peoples and dramas."[13] Like all ontological narratives, they are constitutive; that is, at the level of practice and social consciousness, they organize the world into a meaningful place by populating it with actors, by investing those actors with identities and (derivative) interests, and by scripting the defining dramas of global political life. Thus, rather than simply providing a more or less accurate reflection or map of the "objective" realities of a particular world order, geo-political discourses are in fact profoundly productive of that order.

It is possible to specify two different types of geo-political discourse operating on two distinct levels of analysis. On the one hand, geo-political narratives clearly operate on the *national* level. In this sense, geo-political discourses can be thought of as ontological narratives that emerge out of local history and culture and that give rise to widely shared understandings of "identity" and the "national interest" within a particular country. These representations are particular to each state and largely account for the "unique" aspects of its foreign policy. On the other hand, however, here is a growing body of literature that suggests that the most important geo-political discourses (i.e., those that actually create and animate the units that comprise the international system) are primarily those that are *global* rather than national or indigenous in nature. Somewhat more specifically, this literature – which comprises both *neo-institutionalism* (sociology) and *constructivism* (international relations) – makes two (related) arguments.[14] First, both neo-institutionalists and constructivists argue that the basic *forms and motives* of the state are intersubjectively produced through institutionalized meaning systems created through interstate interaction. On this view, states have the basic structural form and defining purposes they do not as a result of "rational" responses to objective material demands or systemic realities, nor even because of their alleged functional advantages over other forms of political organization when it comes to providing security and extracting revenue, but, rather, because people warranted to act on behalf of "imagined communities" reflexively enact the "institutional script" of statehood that is entailed in the dominant geo-political discourse of the modern era.

Beyond this basic point, and Alexander Wendt's "systemic constructivism" notwithstanding,[15] these global meaning systems do much more than simply constitute states as legitimate political actors and specify a minimal portfolio of derived interests. Geo-political discourses also exercise a powerful influence on the definition of *specific* national interests in *specific* politico-diplomatic contexts, primarily by providing scripts that specify not just the basic attributes of stateness (sovereignty, self-interestedness, etc.), but also how particular *types* of states ("civilized," "Western," "responsible," etc.) should act within specific dramatic/institutional contexts. The neo-institutionalist literature in particular is replete with studies of the way in which the global cultural environment has shaped the behaviour of states in policy areas such as socio-economic development, individual citizenship rights, the administration of justice, environmental management, and foreign relations.[16] The common thread running through all of these analyses is that global cultural rules "define appropriate institutions, goals, data systems, organization charts, ministry structures and policies" for members of the international community.[17] They also share the view that these global cultural models necessarily entail scripts that are then enacted by state officials, for, as argued above, not to do so would violate their basic sense of who they are at that particular time and place. Finally, constructivist analyses in particular emphasize the *normative* dimension of global cultural rules, arguing that such rules necessarily legitimize certain practices and policies while proscribing and stigmatizing others. In other words, as both David Black (Chapter 8, this volume) and Andy Knight (Chapter 7, this volume) argue, the socially constituted norms and scripts that are entailed in geo-political discourses not only define state interests, but they also establish the ethical or moral context within which a state's foreign policy is conducted and judged. It is to this (evolving) moral context, its impact on scripts of "civilized" international conduct, and the enactment of these scripts during several rounds of landmine negotiations that this chapter now turns.

Towards a Genealogy of the Landmine Ban

As the preceding discussion begins to indicate, the enactment of global cultural scripts within the context of diplomatic negotiations relating to the laws of war is a crucially important aspect of the process through which APMs have come to be stigmatized and proscribed in the 1990s. In what follows, I attempt to illuminate some of the more significant aspects of this process, demonstrating how both the campaign and the resulting ban were artefacts of a post-Cold War global cultural script that not only made key states receptive to claims that APMs had to be banned on humanitarian grounds, but that also actually provided a script of civilized international conduct that many states (and especially Canada) subsequently enacted within the context of the CCW and Ottawa Process negotiations. Needless to say, it is beyond the scope of this chapter to develop a comprehensive account of the historical evolution of the landmine campaign/ban. Nor is that my objective; rather, in the remainder of this section my somewhat more modest goal is to identify and briefly describe a number of key moments in the historical process through which APMs came to be stigmatized and proscribed in the late twentieth century. Where appropriate, particular attention will be paid to the way in which the evolution of the landmine ban was conditioned by the operation of a global cultural script that defined the (changing) nature of civilized conduct on the global stage.

The first significant moment, or episode, in the history of the landmine campaign is actually a moment in its *pre-history,* for, before APMs could come to be placed unambiguously within the category of "inhumane weapon," such a category first had to be constituted as a meaningful element of a broader international moral discourse. Although a variety of contingencies played a role in the historical evolution of the category of "inhumane weapons," the crystallization and development of a moral discourse of "civilized warfare" since the nineteenth century owes much to the historical and mutually constitutive relationship between the "laws of war" on the one hand and the politico-cultural identities of "Christendom," "Europe," and (most recently) "the West" on the other. Against the conventional wisdom that the category of inhumane weapons corresponds directly to a genre of armament "naturally" set apart from more "conventional" forms of weaponry by virtue of certain objective properties, the argument made here is that the definition and codification of the category of inhumane weapons is largely a by-product of European efforts to performatively affirm (to themselves at least) their collective belief that Europe was the very embodiment of certain standards of civilized international conduct. As scholars such as Gerrit Gong and Mark Salter have convincingly demonstrated, by the end of the nineteenth century European political elites had come to view the world as being comprised of "civilized," "barbarian," and "savage" societies, with Europe occupying the position of being both the apotheosis and the arbiter of the community of civilized nations. Once this self-representation had taken hold, European state officials began to enact the entailed cultural script within a variety of politico-diplomatic settings, in the process establishing norms of civilized international conduct within a variety of substantial issue areas.

The Hague Conferences of 1899 and 1907 were particularly important in this respect because, collectively, they provided one of the most important occasions for the performative affirmation of European self-representations as the arbiter and apotheosis of civilized international conduct. The resulting definition of civilized conduct in war (a definition that "outlawed" the *indiscriminate* and *disproportionate* use of force – at least within the family of civilized nations) is crucially important to understanding the long-term evolution of the landmine ban. This is because the codification of a standard of civilized warfare gave rise to the derivative discourse of "inhumane weapons" – a discourse that would become recessive during the Cold War but that would be exhumed in the early 1990s and that would ultimately come to establish and define the discursive and political terrain upon which the recent campaign to stigmatize and ban APMs has been conducted.

The second key moment in the evolution of the landmine ban was the series of negotiations that ultimately resulted in the 1980 Convention on Conventional Weapons (CCW) – and especially Protocol II, the so-called "landmine protocol." Negotiated in the aftermath of the Vietnam War, this agreement established that certain categories of weapons (i.e., certain types of APMs and incendiary weapons) were excessively injurious or had indiscriminate effects and that, therefore, they should be regulated through international treaty. But the CCW was never invested with the kind of political energy necessary to make it an effective instrument of international humanitarian law. It was riddled with loopholes: it unambiguously privileged military necessity over humanitarian principles; it was signed by only a few states (and ratified by even fewer); and it is generally judged to have had little direct effect on the conduct of armed conflict.[18] The reason for this is relatively simple: during the Cold War, the key members of the international community were no longer interested in enacting the script of "civilized" international conduct that had resonated so powerfully during what Agnew and Corbridge have labelled "the era of civilizational geopolitics."[19]

As argued above, by the late nineteenth century the Western discourse of civilized warfare had reached its apotheosis as it converged with a culturally inflected European standard of civilization. At this point, negotiations of the laws of war (especially the Hague Conferences of 1899 and 1907) became one of the key sites for the performative construction of a self-consciously styled and European-centred family of civilized nations. As a result, during this period Western diplomats invested considerable energy in codifying the standards of civilized warfare and in specifying what constituted an inhumane weapon or uncivilized conduct in war, for it was through this process of civilizing that most uncivilized of all social institutions (i.e., war) that they demonstrated to themselves and each other that they were, in fact, members of a civilized community of nations. For most of the twentieth century, however, this discourse of civilized warfare has been "recessive," operating only at the margins of global politics. The reasons for this are complex, and are at least partly attributable to the shock of two total wars that severely strained Western faith in civilized standards of warfare.

Perhaps more important, however, the muting of the discourse of civilized warfare was also a function of the emergence of a new global cultural script following the Second World War. During the Cold War, of course, the West, as an imagined community of states, was not constituted through a discourse of civilizational solidarity; rather, during this period, Western self-images were constructed and articulated through a narrative that focused on the West's difference from and superiority to communist states in general and the Soviet Union in particular. In other words, the West came to view itself during this period as being defined in terms of a global struggle with an antithetical adversary. The language used to describe the West shifted from one based on the standard of civilization to one based on liberal democracy, capitalism, and anti-communism. Within this context, discussions of civilized warfare or inhumane weapons failed to resonate as they had at the end of the nineteenth century. This was for the simple reason that they were not bound up with the core self-representations of the dominant members of international society. The inevitable result of this was that little energy was invested performatively constituting the West through negotiations about the laws of war. This was compounded by the narrative of the "totality" of the struggle with the Soviet Union, which encouraged Western policy makers to emphasize kriegsraison and the *utility* of military technologies (such as napalm) and practices (such as carpet bombing in Vietnam) rather than their putative *inhumanity*.

The third key moment in the evolution of the landmine ban is the series of negotiations leading up to the 1995 CCW Review Conference and the subsequent signing of the Ottawa Treaty. It is commonly assumed that the emergence of the landmine issue and the eventual negotiation of a comprehensive ban in the 1990s were simply functions of changing "objective conditions," such as a vast increase in the number of APMs used or more indiscriminate patterns of use. However, the failure to negotiate a ban (or even effective restraints) on APMs in the aftermath of the Vietnam War suggests that this rationalist explanation is inadequate, for, if widespread and "inhumane" use of APMs in the 1960s and 1970s (not to mention the period from the Second World War through the Korean War) did not result in the emergence of a coalition of states and NGOs capable of successfully negotiating a ban in the 1970s, then it is difficult to see how the widespread and inhumane use of these weapons in the 1980s could produce such a coalition in the 1990s.

A closer examination of the history of the landmine ban suggests that it was, in fact, not simply a rational (or even unproblematically ethical) response to an objective humanitarian problem but, rather, first and foremost an artefact of the new geo-political discourse and global cultural script that evolved in the aftermath of the Cold War. As argued above, following the Second World War the script of civilized international conduct that had underpinned European efforts to negotiate legal restraints on war in the late nineteenth century became less and less important to the performative constitution of the West as an "imagined community" of states. With the demise of the Soviet Union and the end of the Cold War, however, this script began to re-emerge as an important (indeed central) element of Western identity. The reasons for this are complex, and cannot be fully articulated here. Suffice it to say, however, that, as the Cold War nostrums that had long made the world meaningful to Western practitioners of statecraft became increasingly anachronistic in the late 1980s, a new geo-political discourse began to evolve – one that redefined the West as a bastion and champion of civilized international conduct.

At the risk of oversimplification, this new discourse – catalyzed by the Gulf War and assembled out of existing cultural and linguistic resources – mapped the post-Cold War world in the following terms. First, it spatialized global politics by representing the world as being comprised of "the West" (defined as the apotheosis and arbiter of civilized international conduct), a much broader but still Western-led "international community" (including a number of other states meeting certain basic standards of civilized international conduct), and a number of so-called "rogue states" (by definition the antithesis of the West and beyond the pale of civilized international conduct). Second, the post-Cold War geo-political narrative scripted the overall defining drama at the heart of global politics in terms of a heroic struggle on the part of the West to enlarge the sphere of neoliberal, democratic states. Third, this new discourse specified that the principal source of danger, threat, and insecurity in the international system was to be found in rogue states, which were represented both as posing a "clear and present" danger to the West and as failing to meet generally accepted standards of civilized international conduct. As a result of all this, in the aftermath of the Cold War, Western self-representations (and thus interests) underwent a subtle yet profound change. With the demise of the Soviet Union, the old self-image of the West as a collection of democratic, peaceful, and capitalist states opposed to a totalitarian, expansionist, and communist East gave way to a new discursive construction of the West as the world's principal bastion, arbiter, and champion of a new standard of civilization engaged in a global struggle against "rogue states," terrorists, and other actors beyond the pale of civilized international conduct. In turn, this provided a script for Western policy makers and diplomats to enact upon the global stage.

Significantly, as a result of the structural, or "rule-making," power enjoyed by the United States and other Western powers, this new geopolitical discourse also became institutionalized (if somewhat imperfectly) at the global level. Thus, the net effect of these developments was to establish a new *global* cultural script specifying appropriate forms of conduct for responsible members of the international community. Of course, this script was not invented out of whole cloth; rather, it was put together by its (primarily Western) authors through the re-combination, re-valuation, and re-presentation of existing culturally derived narrative resources and their reassembly into new scripts, roles, and forms of identity. As a result, it included a number of partly reworked elements of the standard of civilization that had been operative at the end of the nineteenth century, including, significantly, an exhumed script of civilized warfare that required responsible members of the international community to eschew weapons and tactics that were "indiscriminate" and "disproportionate."

It was at precisely the point when this new global cultural script was beginning to coalesce that a new series of IHL negotiations (the 1995 CCW Review Conference and Ottawa process negotiations) were initiated. Needless to say, it is beyond the scope of this chapter to recount in detail the course of these negotiations. Nor is it crucially important to my argument to do so; rather, the point I wish to make is that, once initiated, these negotiations became key sites for the performance of a narratively derived script of civilized international conduct. And, just as at the end of the nineteenth century, in the early and mid-1990s state officials and diplomats once again began devoting considerable attention to performatively demonstrating to themselves and others that they were in compliance with the prevailing standards of civilized international conduct. This was especially true of Western diplomats and foreign-policy makers, who, having located themselves within the dominant post-Cold War discourse, increasingly came to view the West as both the prime example and most vigorous champion of this new standard of civilization. But it was also true of non-Western states who sought to performatively affirm to themselves and others that they were responsible members of the international community. While not denying the obvious cruelty of landmines or impugning the important work of the International Campaign to Ban Landmines in attempting to bring this to the attention of the global public, it is clear that this inherently dramaturgical dynamic played a crucial (even decisive) role in the long series of negotiations that ultimately produced the Ottawa

Treaty. Simply stated, the evolution of a new narratively derived global cultural script in the aftermath of the Cold War was crucially important in that it established the discursive terrain upon which states, NGOs, and other norm entrepreneurs were subsequently able to campaign for a ban on APMs. In the absence of this script, it seems unlikely that key states would have been any more responsive to calls to ban landmines (or would have exercised any more leadership in this regard) than they were during the first CCW negotiations.

Concluding Remarks

What, then, does studying the genealogy of the landmine ban tell us about the complex relationship between ethics and international security? To begin with, by illuminating the way in which the "national interest" sometimes comes to be understood in terms of the promotion of "ethical" security policies, it sheds some light on the mechanism linking ethics and state action. As the landmine case demonstrates, the decision on the part of key states to pursue, first, tighter regulation of APMs and, later, a comprehensive ban was neither interest-based (in the narrow, neo-utilitarian sense of the word) nor unproblematically "ethical," "altruistic," or idealistic; rather, the decision of Canada and other key states active on the landmine issue appears first and foremost to be an enactment of a global cultural script specifying how civilized states should act within particular politico-diplomatic contexts. Simply put, these states, once they had come to recognize themselves in the new post-Cold War geo-political narrative, necessarily (if reflexively) enacted the "institutional script" entailed by that narrative; that is, they performed the role appropriate to their narratively derived sense of identity. This means that, contrary to the assumptions of neo-utilitarian theories, state officials pursued the landmine ban not because they were motivated by "objective" humanitarian interests, or even because they were responding to the pressures of a vigorous civil society, but "because not to do so would fundamentally violate their sense of being at that particular time and place."[20] It also suggests that "ethical" foreign policies such as those related to landmines need to be understood not as simple expression of some objective national interest – nor even as the products of aggressive lobbying by "progressive" social forces – but, rather, as enactments of a global cultural script that specifies the nature of "civilized" international conduct. Finally, it suggests an analytical focus, not on the dubious ethical or civilizing effects of the laws of war on the battlefield but, rather, on the politics embodied in the diplomatic practices through which the laws of war are negotiated and on the various geo-political narratives through which the entailed global cultural scripts are created.

Viewed from this perspective, the specific rearticulation of ethics and security that has come to be known as "human security" also reveals itself to be, in part at least, a manifestation of post-Cold War geo-political discourse. According to Canada's former minister of foreign affairs:

> Human security is much more than the absence of military threat. It includes security against economic privation, an acceptable quality of life and a guarantee of fundamental human rights. This concept of human security recognizes the complexity of the human environment and accepts that the forces influencing human security are interrelated and mutually reinforcing. At a minimum, human security requires that basic needs are met, but it also acknowledges that sustained economic development, human rights and fundamental freedoms, the rule of law, good governance, sustainable development and social equity are as important to global peace as arms control and disarmament.[21]

In short, human security is represented as a radical reconceptualization of security in the post-Cold War era – a reconceptualization necessitated both by the end of the Cold War and a democratization of Canadian foreign/security policy. On closer inspection, however, the concept of human security takes on a less radical appearance. To start, and despite the claims of its more strident proponents, Canada's human security agenda is still largely derivative of Canada's longstanding national interest in a stable global order; it is not simply an ethical agenda to be pursued in its own right. But human security clearly differs from the traditional "statist" security discourse that has prevailed through most of the modern era. The reason for this is that, for states like Canada, the rhetoric of security is now powerfully informed by the discourses and global cultural scripts associated with the standard of civilization entailed in the newly ascendant post-Cold War geo-political discourse. Indeed, the rhetoric and logic of the human security/soft power discourse is in some ways the ultimate expression of this new standard of civilization, for it allows countries such as Canada to performatively affirm to themselves and others that, because even their security policies are shaped by ethical norms beyond vulgar self-interest, they are clearly more civilized than are other states.[22] Perhaps not too surprisingly, the language of human security and soft power has a particular appeal to middle powers such as Canada and the Nordic countries, whose self-representations have long hinged on being more "progressive," "humane," and "enlightened" than either the great powers or the countries of the developing world. It is this, I would suggest, and not simply the efforts of a morally virtuous foreign minister or progressive social forces that largely accounts for the vigour with which Canada has pursued a global ban on landmines since the mid-1990s.

In addition to shedding light on the relationship between ethics and the national interest, such a genealogy says something about the sources of the ethical norms, standards, or imperatives that sometimes shape foreign and security policy. Conventional explanations of state action tend to assume that the sources of "ethical" foreign policies are largely internal to the state; that is, that they are expressions of a nation's political culture or products of a democratic political process that is open to the input of "progressive" social forces. This is especially true in the landmine case, where most accounts emphasize the role of civil society in pressing states such as Canada to adopt an increasingly vigorous pro-ban position. This genealogy, however, draws our attention to a different level of analysis: the global. It does this by demonstrating how a powerfully resonating global standard of civilization has historically shaped prevailing notions of what constitutes ethical conduct within the international arena. During the nineteenth century, this standard specified ethical standards that required members of the family of civilized nations to abjure *sati,* polygamy, and slavery and to adhere generally to European diplomatic and legal norms (including those pertaining to the conduct of war). Similarly, in the contemporary era, an analogous standard is operative, although today it is more likely to specify ethical norms that oblige members of the West or the international community to respect human rights, to adopt market-oriented economic structures, and to abide by liberal-democratic norms. Significantly, as the contrast between the reaction to NATO's bombing campaign in Kosovo and the Russian campaign in Chechnya clearly demonstrates, civilized states are still ethically obligated to subscribe to historically derived standards of civilized warfare (proportionality and discrimination). The point is that these ethical norms are established at the global level rather than simply emerging out of a country's domestic cultural or political milieu.

This is crucially important to explaining the evolution of Canadian landmine policy. As Andy Knight correctly argues (Chapter 7, this volume), Canada and other states did indeed act as "norm entrepreneurs," promoting, within various multilateral fora, both a ban on landmines and a more effective international criminal court. This raises the question, however, of how and why Canadian foreign policy officials came to define Canada's national interest in terms of promoting these norms. This genealogy suggests that the process was intimately connected to the emergence of a new hegemonic geo-political discourse in the aftermath of the Cold War – a discourse that entailed new identities (and therefore new interests) and that specified new standards of civilized international conduct. Once this new discourse had been articulated, and once Canadian foreign policy makers had located themselves within it, Canadian foreign policy interests had already largely been determined. All that was left was for these officials to enact the appropriate script. Once the landmine issue was placed on the agenda, subsequent international negotiations provided Canadian diplomats with numerous opportunities to do precisely that.

It would be absurd, of course, to argue that global geo-political discourses and their entailed scripts and norms of ethical conduct are exclusively or exhaustively definitive of the institutional scripts enacted by state officials, for, as John Agnew argues, "the identities and interests of states (and other actors) are formed in interaction with one another and in the nexus between global and local social practices."[23] In fact, as argued above, it is possible to specify two different types of geo-political discourse. At one level, there are geo-political narratives that operate on a national scale. These comprise widely shared representations of identity and interest that drive the "unique" aspects of a state's foreign policy. In the landmine case, for example, a complete explanation of why Canada assumed such a high-profile leadership role or why the US ultimately acted as a spoiler during the Ottawa Treaty negotiations would necessarily require a full analysis of these two countries' national geo-political narratives and the impact of these on the definition of their respective national interests and foreign policy preferences. The key argument advanced in this chapter, however, is that while it is necessary to recognize the constitutive role of *national* scripts and cultural narratives, it is even more important to pay careful attention to the world-systemic, or global, meaning systems that determine standards of ethical conduct within the international arena.

Finally, a genealogy such as this highlights the way in which the post-Cold War world order has been partly reconstituted around a thinly veiled (and alarmingly Orientalist) civilizational discourse that places the West in the position of arbiter and champion of ethical conduct in international relations. In addition to being an ethical issue in and of itself, this is important because it draws our attention to the way in which ethical discourses can be bound up with producing and reproducing relations of power at the global level. Simply put, the argument here is that "the politics of stigmatization" that has driven the anti-landmine campaign has ultimately anathematized not just APMs, but also those social actors that have challenged the now prevailing view that landmines are inherently inhumane. Thus, as with *sati* in British India and female genital mutilation today, efforts to ban the "obvious" evil of landmines are necessarily bound up with the production and reproduction of global power relations.

This is not to argue that *sati*, female genital mutilation, and landmines are not in some sense "evil" and worthy of being stigmatized and proscribed. It is, however, to suggest that, in all three cases, ethical campaigns and policies designed to rid the world of these evils have necessarily been implicated in broader discourses and cultural narratives that produce and naturalize social and political hierarchies. The British campaign to ban *sati,* for example, was bound up with British efforts to represent Indian men as uncivilized brutes and Indian women as in need of being rescued from them (presumably by the civilized British).[24] In turn, and despite the fact that *sati* was never as widespread a cultural practice as the British made out, these representations provided part of the justification and legitimation of British rule in India. This genealogy suggests that a similar logic is at work with respect to the stigmatization of landmines: the end might be worthwhile, but the framing of APMs as being inhumane ultimately rests on the prior existence and operation of a (dangerous) geo-political discourse that represents the world as being divided into the West (the apotheosis, arbiter, and champion of civilized international conduct), the Rest (the vast majority of countries), and the so-called "Rogue states" (the antithesis of the West). It also suggests that, in order to grasp fully the ethics of the antilandmine campaign, it is necessary to uncover and expose the relations of power that have been both productive of, and sustained by, efforts to stigmatize landmines.

Notes

1 The official title is: The Convention on Prohibitions on the Use of Certain Conventional Weapons which may be deemed to be Excessively Injurious or have Indiscriminate Effect. It is typically shortened to: The Convention on Conventional Weapons (CCW). The CCW was signed in 1980.

2 Roxanne Lynn Doty, "Foreign Policy as Social Construction: A Post-Positivist Analysis of US Counterinsurgency Policy in the Philippines," *International Studies Quarterly* 37, 3 (1993): 298.

3 On the evolution of the notion of a "standard of civilization," see Gerrit W. Gong, *The Standard of Civilization in International Society* (Oxford: Clarendon Press, 1984).

4 This is not to argue that there have never been restraints on the conduct of war; clearly, these have always existed. It is, rather, to point out that military, political, economic, and even cultural factors are more important than international law in creating and giving practical effect to these restraints.

5 Chris af Jochnick and Roger Normand, "The Legitimation of Violence: A Critical Analysis of the Gulf War," *Harvard International Law Review* 35, 1 (Spring 1994): 387-416.

6 Thus, for example, while the use of poison gas was proscribed by international treaty in 1925, in the intervening years precious little has been done in the way of banning napalm (surely equally horrific in its effects), small-calibre munitions (needlessly injurious by any standard), or, indeed, any of a whole host of equally murderous and brutal weapons.

7 Jochnick and Normand, "The Legitimation of Violence," 68.

8 For a good introduction to this literature, see Jochnick and Normand, "The Legitimation of Violence," 49-95.

9 See Gong, *The Standard of Civilization,* passim.

10 Jutta Weldes, "Constructing National Interests," *European Journal of International Relations* 2, 3 (1996): 280.

11 Ibid., 283.

12 As Somers and Gibson argue, "a relational setting is a pattern of relationships among institutions, public narratives and social practices." See Margaret R. Somers and Gloria D. Gibson, "Reclaiming the Epistemological 'Other': Narrative and the Social Construction of Identity," in *Social Theory and the Politics of Identity,* ed. Craig Calhoun (Oxford: Blackwell, 1994), 70.

13 Gearóid Ó Tuathail and John Agnew, "Geopolitics and Discourse: Practical Geopolitical Reasoning in American Foreign Policy," *Political Geography* 11 (1992): 192. Agnew and Corbridge define geo-political discourses as the "rule and conceptual resources that political élites use in particular historical contexts to 'spatialize' the international political economy into places, peoples and disputes." See John Agnew and Stuart Corbridge, *Mastering Space: Hegemony, Territory and International Political Economy* (New York: Routledge, 1995), 48.

14 One of the best examples of sociological neo-institutionalism is John W. Meyer, John Boli, George M. Thomas, and Francisco Ramirez, "World Society and the Nation-State," *American Journal of Sociology* 103, 1 (July 1997): 144-81. A partial list of key constructivist works in the IR tradition would include Alexander Wendt, "Anarchy Is What States Make of It: The Social Construction of Power Politics," *International Organization* 46, 2 (1992): 391-426; Emmanuel Adler, "Seizing the Middle Ground: Constructivism in World Politics," *European Journal of International Relations* 46, 1 (1992): 101-45; John Gerard Ruggie, "What Makes the World Hang Together: Neo-Utilitarianism and the Social Constructivist Challenge," *International Organization* 52, 4 (Autumn 1998): 855-85; Audie Klotz, *Norms in International Relations* (New York: Cornell University Press, 1995); and Martha Finnemore, *National Interests in International Society* (New York: Columbia University Press, 1996).

15 This term is used by Price and Reus-Smit to distinguish Wendt's narrow constructivism from a more "holistic" variant that pays greater attention to the constitutive role of local and global meaning systems. See Richard Price and Christian Reus-Smit, "Dangerous Liaisons: Critical International Theory and Constructivism," *European Journal of International Relations* 4, 3 (September 1998): 259-94.

16 For an elaboration of this argument, see Meyer et al., "World Society and the Nation-State."

17 Meyer et al., "World Society and the Nation-State," 158.

18 See Louise Doswald-Beck and Peter Herby, "Land Mines: A Critical Examination of Existing Legal Instruments." Available at <www.icrc.ch/icrcnews> (1 May 1995).

19 John Agnew and Stuart Corbridge, *Mastering Space,* 52-56.

20 Ibid., 67.

21 Lloyd Axworthy, "Canada and Human Security: The Need for Leadership," *International Journal* 5, 2 (Spring 1997): 184.

22 I am indebted to Ivor Neumann for this observation.

23 John Agnew, *Geopolitics: Re-Visioning World Politics* (London: Routledge, 1998), 55.

24 See, for example, Jyosanta G. Singh, *Colonial Narratives/Cultural Dialogues: "Discoveries" of India in the Language of Colonialism* (London: Routledge, 1996).

Part 5
Humanitarian Intervention and Democratization

10 Humanitarian Intervention in Zaire: A Case Study of Humanitarian Realism

Howard Adelman

Canada has taken a lead in assisting refugees,[1] in peacekeeping, and in many other humanitarian endeavours within the international arena. This leadership has been particularly significant with regard to responding to complex emergencies.[2] Intended to help construct a better world, Canada's humanitarian initiatives have been part of a new Canadian foreign policy thrust under the conceptual rubric of "human security" that places a focus on the security of people rather than states.[3] These initiatives have focused on the elimination of landmines, attempting to control the export of small arms to regions of violence, the demobilization of child soldiers[4] and, most recently, seeking to define international norms to govern humanitarian intervention.[5] These initiatives appear in stark contrast to international initiatives primarily governed by the self-interest of the intervening state and determined by realism rather than morality.[6] At the same time, Canadian initiatives are not simply the product of abstract principled idealism but are, rather, intended to be practical and efficacious. Such pragmatic idealism, or humanitarian realism, contrasts with realist-based behaviour, with morally dictated behaviour, and also with ignorant behaviour in which neither morals nor rational calculation of interests are involved.

Case studies of Canadian initiatives are useful in understanding how various ethical norms influence humanitarian actions and how conflicting norms are reconciled or mediated. We do not choose between an amoral realism and an abstract principled idealism. We really choose among competing norms in light of the perceived circumstances and the anticipated consequences of each alternative. By examining Canadian case studies, I reveal the norms that influenced particular initiatives as well as the role and impact of each norm. I then consider what role each norm *should have played* in a complex emergency and its concomitant international response. Finally, I suggest which of the competing norms are relevant and should form part of responses to future international crises. Thus, this chapter addresses the connection between ethics and self-interest, including security concerns, in the formation and critique of Canadian foreign policy.

Lessons learned, for Canada or more generally, can vary on a case-by-case basis. For example, Raimo Väyrynen's introductory chapter, "How Much Force in Humanitarian Intervention,"[7] uses Yugoslavia as a benchmark. The Yugoslavian case is complicated by many more political, military, and economic considerations than is the Zaire case and so is difficult to use as a benchmark for examining international ethics. In Zaire,[8] however, two distinct alternatives were considered: (1) addressing the issue of the militants who controlled the camps and (2) restricting activities to support humanitarian operations that might involve providing protection for the delivery and distribution of humanitarian relief supplies as well as protecting the refugees themselves, whether in the camps or in flight. Other, more extreme options were available but were not considered (i.e., taking no action or imposing a regime on the area through the use of overwhelming military force). In the former Yugoslavia, there were many more options, although the capacity of the West to implement most of them was questionable. Yugoslavia was a minefield for modern ethical and political theory. With regard to Zaire, however, no matter how difficult the choices, the theoretical political issues were fewer, the options clearer, and the problem of assessing the ethical issues far less complicated.[9]

Background

Crises and the responses to them are context-dependent. Therefore, in addition to linking ethics with issues of self-interest within the context of the development of Canadian foreign policy, I will place the case within a temporal and geographical context. What can and should be done in Asia or Europe is different than what can or should be done in Africa. Further, since the end of the Cold War, the context for dealing with issues of conflict in Africa has shifted dramatically. The response is no longer determined primarily as a by-product of East-West rivalry.

A civil war had been fought in Rwanda from 1990 to 1994. A genocide took place; at least 500,000 Tutsi were slaughtered.[10] When the war ended with the victory of the Tutsi-led rebel army, the Rwanda Patriotic Front (RPF), both the Hutu population and the perpetrators of the genocide feared reprisals from the rebel army. Hundreds of thousands of Hutu refugees fled to Zaire along with the military and militias who had been implicated in the genocide; namely, the ex-FAR (Forces Armées de Rwanda) and the interahamwe (Rwandese militia under the Habyarimana regime). With the *génocidaires* among the fleeing masses, the refugee camps in Zaire were soon controlled by militants and used as bases to launch attacks into Rwanda, to attack prisons to free those accused of genocide, and to kill potential witnesses who were to appear at the genocide trials in Arusha and Kigali. Thus, the Rwandan civil war continued to be fought from bases in the refugee camps of Zaire. When the attacks began to fail and Mobutu was dying, the militants became concerned that they would be ejected from Zaire. In an attempt to secure a place in Zaire, they allied themselves with local ethnic groups and attacked local Tutsi. When local Zairian Tutsi became the targets, a new civil war began in Zaire.

Three hundred thousand local Tutsi were killed or driven out in the Masisi region in North Kivu. However, when the militants attacked the local Tutsi in South Kivu, the Banyamulenga (the local Zairian Tutsi) repulsed the attacks and, in turn, attacked the Hutu refugee camps led by Kabila's Alliance of the Democratic Forces for the Liberation of Congo (ADFL). Backed by Rwanda, this force eventually attacked the refugee camps from which ethnic cleansing had been launched in the north. The camps were quickly evacuated by hundreds of thousands of fleeing refugees. Over 640,000 Hutu, freed from the intimidating presence of the genocidal militants, crossed the border back into Rwanda. The civil war moved west away from the Rwandan border.

Before the Hutu militants were defeated and the refugee camps released from their control, there had been many calls for the use of coercive force, under UN auspices, to disarm the militants. In 1994, not long after the camps were established, the United Nations High Commission for Refugees (UNHCR) began requesting intervention in order to disarm the militants.[11] The debate resumed in March 1996, when the camps were used to attack the local Tutsi population. When the militants in the camps attacked the local Banyamulenge population in South Kivu and prompted a rebellion, the rebels defeated the Hutu militants and their local allies. As a result, the Hutu refugees were cut off from the humanitarian agencies servicing the camps. Concern for removing the militants shifted to concern for protecting humanitarian workers and ensuring that water, food, shelter, and health services reached the refugees. The discussion of options escalated in the fall, when the camps themselves were attacked and Hutu refugees began to flee.

Many Africans viewed the proposed Fall 1996 intervention that focused only on humanitarian aid as interference in a civil war that would drastically affect the rebels' ability to prosecute the war. But humanitarian intervention was defended as essential to fulfilling the obligation of agencies to provide aid to the refugees. Opponents pointed to the lack of concern for the very same refugees when they were being intimidated by the militants. Defenders countered that the lives of the refugees were not threatened then as they were now. After all the camps had been evacuated and alleged atrocities against the refugees were reported, the position of the defenders was viewed as fully justified. In November 1996, Canada launched a peacekeeping mission to create a protected corridor for delivering humanitarian relief (food, water, health services, etc.) to the Hutu refugees in Zaire.[12]

This particular case needs to be placed within a larger context. The primacy of humanitarian over political approaches to foreign policy is a common characteristic of attempts to deal with intrastate conflicts in the 1990s. This is the result of several factors that were prevalent after the Cold War. A realist paradigm dominated the Cold War era. But when the communist threat disappeared as either an inspiring idea or a real military threat, humanitarian principles emerged from the shadows. Further, the CNN effect – the profound influence of massive media coverage on foreign policy – played an ever-increasing role. The portrayal of humanitarian disasters on television stimulated the public into demanding that the government do something, even if the issue did not affect the self-interest of the state. Two attitudes towards war had developed. The left-leaning public was wary of coercive military action that could initiate a world-destroying nuclear war; the right-leaning public and the military believed that a war must be won quickly, with massive use of force, to avoid losing public and, subsequently, political support and thus leaving the army to suffer a humiliating defeat. The combination of both attitudes resulted in a low- or no-risk attitude to military intervention. There was a demand for military humanitarianism but at no military risk. As with the Gulf War, even when self-interest was at stake and intervention could be defended on humanitarian and legal grounds, massive force was employed under the principle of no or little risk. However, the Gulf War misled policy makers and thinkers. They became convinced that a new principle of morally dictated humanitarian-impelled international action had emerged to replace the dominant realist paradigm. The realist paradigm was not incorporated into the new dominant ethos but, rather, was viewed as contrary to it. Realists, in turn, caricatured these principles as unrealistic bleeding-heart moralism.

The Principles of Intervention

Though the case of Zaire is relatively more straightforward than is the case of former Yugoslavia, common principles seem to emerge from both. These refer to the treatment of the victims of conflict, relations with local states and prime actors in the conflict, and the conduct of interveners from the international community. This list of principles does not purport to be exhaustive.

1. Repatriation of Refugees: Repatriation to the home country was viewed as the best solution for refugees. No consideration seemed to be given to the possibility of resettlement abroad or the permanent settlement of the refugees in Zaire.
2. Voluntary Repatriation: Voluntary repatriation for refugees was promoted as a dominant principle despite overwhelming evidence that refugees were not free to return to their homes, even if they wanted to, because of intimidation by extremists.[13]
3. Physical Protection for Refugees and the Internally Displaced: The

international community considered itself legally and morally obligated to provide physical and legal protection for refugees. In reality, there was some success in providing physical protection but little headway in protecting the rights of refugees subject to control and manipulation by extremists.

4 Humanitarian Aid and Assistance: Providing humanitarian assistance to the refugees was not only a moral imperative, but also the dominant governing principle for most NGOs and international agencies. For many it eliminated the consideration of other ethical imperatives.

5 Refugees and Refugee Warriors: International Refugee Law as well as the Organization for African Unity (OAU) Convention[14] stipulate that refugee camps must not be used as bases to attack others. This principle was recognized but not enforced by the international community.

6 Respect for Sovereignty: As is characteristic of classical peacekeeping, consent of the parties was a governing principle of any peace operation. However, the consent of the Zairian government was nominal. The Zairian government was ignored when it came to obtaining permission to establish the entry point for the peacekeepers or the advance military mission. That military mission communicated directly with the rebels without the permission of the Zairian government.

7 Political Impartiality: The intervention was intended to be neutral. Canada was chosen to lead the mission partly to provide an image of impartiality and downplay the differences and leanings of major powers, specifically France and the United States. Yet a number of African states regarded the type of intervention and its purpose as biased. The Rwandan government viewed the intervention as a way of preserving the status quo for the refugee warriors, as inhibiting the prosecution of the civil war, and as favouring the other side.[15]

8 Financing Humanitarian Aid versus Humanitarian Intervention using Peacekeepers: Major powers, particularly the United States, were wary of the financial burden of peacekeeping, particularly if peacekeepers could become embroiled in a civil war. Failure to deal with underlying political issues may be more costly in the long run, especially when a new conflict is merely postponed; however, there seemed to be greater readiness to absorb the high cost of humanitarian aid and reconstruction after the conflict than the cost of military intervention to prevent the conflict.

9 Low Risk Military Humanitarian Intervention: A low-risk, or even no-risk, approach to international peacekeeping seemed to be the governing norm. However, at the very least, international intervention is a moral obligation in cases of genocide.[16] The conflict between these two imperatives resulted in impotence.[17]

(a) When refugee men in a UNHCR camp in the former Yugoslavia were slaughtered when the camp was overrun by the enemy, the UN was unwilling to take effective action.

(b) When the militants in the Zairian camps attacked the local Banyamulenge population in Masisi in the spring of 1996 as a continuation of the genocide, no humanitarian intervention was contemplated, despite that fact that the military capacity of the militants was limited (certainly, at least, in comparison to Yugoslavia).

Thus, the feature characteristic of the Zaire case (a feature shared by the Yugoslav case) was the governing principle adopted: delivery of humanitarian aid was more important than a political or military solution. Military forces were required to ensure the delivery of that aid, regardless of the merits or demerits of the contending sides. The international community maintained the right to the limited use of force for self-defence and humanitarian purposes. However, the potential for even a limited degree of military action served as a deterrent to military intervention. At the same time, pressure for such an intervention increased merely to ensure the continued provision of humanitarian aid to the refugees. Ironically, to ensure that the military would not be used (and, if it were, that casualties would be limited), when the intervention was sanctioned, it was authorized under UN Chapter 7 (rather than Chapter 6, passive peacekeeping), which permitted the active use of force. This allowed a very activist militant approach to those undermining the humanitarian effort while, at the same time, deterring any such effort being used against them.

10 Coherence among the Interveners: It was asserted, as is commonplace, that intervention should not take place unless the intervening parties were governed by agreed-upon goals and governing norms. But the decision to intervene was a by-product of the conflict between the United States and France. France supported the Mobutu regime and, therefore, at least indirectly, the extremists in the camps. The United States supported Rwanda and, indirectly, the rebels. The Americans, following PDD 25,[18] were reluctant to become involved[19] and were inclined to leave the resolution of the problem to local states, in particular Rwanda and Uganda. For a short period in October 1996, the Americans deviated from this pattern, but they quickly returned to their post-Somalian norm of strictly limiting American involvement in humanitarian interventions. At the other extreme, France was willing, if not eager, to send troops to Zaire to protect the refugees, inhibit the advance of the rebels, and thereby, protect Mobutu. Although each country approached the problem from opposite standpoints, and although each had a unique logistical capacity to airlift troops and equipment, both were opposed to becoming involved in disarming

the extremists in the camps. The United States emerged as a reluctant supporter of humanitarian intervention. Western intervention proposals stood in total opposition to the regional African states who had volunteered to send troops to separate the militants from the rest of the refugees but wanted an international sanction as well as financial and logistical support for such an initiative.

Counting, Classifying, and Accounting

The number of refugees became a central ethical *and* political issue in Zaire. There were three ethical issues related to the number of refugees: accuracy, association, and accountability. The most basic of factual issues becomes an ethical issue when we consider the issue of accuracy. How many refugees were there? The issue of association is demonstrated by the question, "How many genuine refugees were there?" More specifically, "How many genuine Rwandan Hutu refugees were there in the camps as distinct from Burundian refugees or militants?" The issue of accountability focuses on the responsibility of agencies and states when they disseminate inaccurate and misleading figures. In other words, who was to blame for the confusion about the numbers?

The variations in numbers had significant political effects. If there were 1,200,000 refugees and only 640,000 returned, then 560,000 refugees fled west.[20] Since most did not reappear, they were allegedly slaughtered. This made the treatment of these refugees almost equivalent to the genocide in Rwanda. If the genocide in Rwanda obligated international intervention, then so did the disaster in Zaire. In light of the failures in Rwanda, the plight of the refugees, and the concern to prevent or at least mitigate the possibility of another genocide, the international community was obliged to intervene in Zaire to save the lives of the refugees.[21] The American military was accused of trying to "air brush" the refugees out of history.[22]

These central issues were rooted in what became known as the *bataille des chiffres*. What are the facts? How many refugees were there in Zaire in the first place? Purportedly, 1,200,000 refugees had fled to Zaire.[23] A joint mission (UNHCR, World Food Program [WFP], United States Assistance for International Development [USAID], and the European Community Humanitarian Organization [ECHO]) estimated that there were 1,106,000 people in camps in Zaire before the upheaval of Fall 1996, when large numbers of refugees returned to Rwanda.[24] Note that the figure refers to people, not refugees.[25] Of these, 140,000 were Burundians.[26] Assuming the joint mission figures were correct, this meant that a total of 966,000 Rwandese refugees and refugee warriors were in Zaire.[27]

I emphasize, this figure includes refugee warriors. Of over 1.5 million Hutu Rwandese who fled Rwanda between April and July 1994, 10 percent to 15 percent "were alleged to have participated directly in [the] mass killing" in Rwanda. The extremist militant group included the hard-line political leadership at all levels. Almost all of them fled to Zaire. Thus, of 966,000 Hutu Rwandans, 97,000 to 140,000 were genocidal killers. If families are included, then the numbers easily double.[28]

The estimate of the number of militants or refugee warriors could be approached in several other ways.[29] A report to the UN secretary-general in 1994[30] divided the non-refugee Rwandan population in eastern Zaire into three groups:

1 former leaders, principally consisting of fifty families lodged in villas at Bukavu
2 an estimated 16,000 military personnel of the ex-FAR (with families, the population of this group numbered 80,000)
3 the militants in the militia, possibly 50,000 but probably closer to 35,000 and, in any case, difficult to enumerate because they lived amongst the refugees (including family members, since far fewer of them than of the ex-FAR were accompanied by families, their numbers perhaps totalled around 100,000).

This meant that at least 180,000 refugee warriors and their family members were in the camps. Deducting the militants and their families from the realistic figure of 966,000 Hutu Rwandan refugees in the camps leaves approximately 786,000 genuine refugees in the camps, assuming that the original UNHCR figures were accurate. The calculation is as follows:

Total Hutu refugee and refugee warrior population in camps			966,000
Less refugee warriors and families that fled west			– 180,000
Balance (of genuine refugees in camp)			786,000
Less returnees	1st	15,000	
	2nd	+ 646,000	
	Total returnees		– 661,000
Maximum missing			125,000

It is generally the case that camp populations are normally exaggerated by an average of 10 percent and much more when controlled by militants. If this is the case, then even these figures may be inflated by at least 80,000 and possibly as much as 200,000. Assuming the lower figure, this would make the genuine Rwandan Hutu refugee population in Zaire just over 700,000. Of these, 15,000 were forcefully repatriated by the Zairian army in August 1996. An additional 646,000 repatriated spontaneously in November. Assuming that only genuine refugees repatriated – 670,000 of them – this left 30,000, rather than 125,000 missing refugees.

The Canadian[31] and American military estimated the camp population to be only 900,000 (not 966,000). Based on that figure, an additional 60,000 rather than 125,000 fled or were forced to flee with the genocidists. Some of these were probably family members of the militants. Others were killed.[32] Sixty thousand would likely be a maximum figure for missing refugees.

There was a second, related problem – one of classification – that directly affected the issue of facts. Refugee warriors,[33] as distinct from genuine refugees (as indicated above), numbered about 180,000 if families of the militants were included. The camps had been controlled by ex-FAR and interahamwe militia, which had been largely responsible for the genocide. Thus, armed warriors, who, under international law, are not genuine refugees – and many of whom were likely criminals guilty of genocide, people who had launched military excursions into Rwanda, killed civilians, and instigated conflict between local Hutus and the Bamyamulenge – were included under the designation "refugee" as people needing humanitarian assistance. The international community, which provided the aid to the refugee camps, had been impotent with regard to separating the innocent refugees from their militant controllers in order to facilitate repatriation. They even failed to ensure that excess humanitarian aid was not purloined by the ex-FAR and sold on the black market.

But this was not the view conveyed by many, if not most, of the highly respected international human rights bodies. They conveyed an image of helpless deprived refugees fleeing westward, when many were, in fact, genocidal killers and militants.

> The Commission estimates that based on various reports and testimonies of allegations approximately 200,000 refugees on Zairean soil, the majority of whom are ethnic Hutus, have lost their lives or disappeared in an arbitrary manner,[34] as a result of a deliberate strategy of gradual extermination of a portion of the Rwandan population. To this end, procedures were adopted, in a premeditated, constant, and persistent manner that strongly ressemble [sic!] acts of genocide.[35]

As Amnesty International had concluded earlier in the opening page of its report of 3 December 1997, *Democratic Republic of Congo: Deadly Alliances in Congo Forests,* "many of the more than 1,000,000 refugees from Rwanda and several hundred thousand from Burundi were being deliberately and arbitrarily killed in large numbers by forces of the main armed opposition group, the *Alliance des forces démocratiques pour la libération du Congo* (AFDL), Alliance of the Democratic Forces for the Liberation of Congo."[36] The confusion over basic facts such as numbers, and the categories for communicating those facts, had somehow turned the tables so that the killers suddenly became the victims of genocide.[37] This position just happened to dovetail with the propaganda strategy of the ex-FAR.

The political issues were directly related to the above ethical issues. A military mission led by Canada was planned. From the very beginning, the major issue was how to separate the criminals from the innocent refugees. When the rebel forces attacked and emptied the camps, the mission to separate genuine refugees from militants was accomplished by rebel forces. The case of the missing refugees became a phantom issue, and there was neither a significant protection issue nor a humanitarian issue left to address. Doubt about the military mission was widespread in the media. See, for example, the *Vancouver Sun* front page of 19 November 1996, the *Globe and Mail* front page of 18 November 1996, or the *Toronto Star* front page of 18 November 1996. The next day the same papers ran front-page headlines announcing that the mission would proceed. By 21 November 1996, the *Winnipeg Free Press* (B1) and the *Montreal Gazette* (B1) were pronouncing the Canadian plan in disarray, no doubt due to Chrétien's statement the day before that Canada might give aid rather than troops.[38]

This issue of numbers became a critical factor in the debate over continuing the military mission after the 646,000 refugees had returned home in November 1996, following the 15,000 that had been forced to return three months earlier. Some UN and NGO spokespersons insisted that the mission continue because 400,000 refugees were still missing and dying in the jungles of Zaire. For example, the UN Secretary-General himself said that, "as of 18 November 1996, approximately 600,000 and close to 150,000 Burundian refugees remain in Zaire."[39] The news reports had already reported that 500,000 refugees had been repatriated.[40] UNHCR spokesperson Melita Sunjik issued a statement on 22 November 1996 indicating that 700,000 refugees, who had been located in satellite photos, remained in eastern Zaire.[41] The January UN Secretary-General's Report tried to introduce some correction. It stated that the number of returnees had been underestimated because 646,000 refugees had been referred to as "several hundred thousand." At the same time, the missing were reduced from hundreds of thousands to tens of thousands in a diplomatic balancing act that insisted that this "does not mean that the refugee problem has been solved. At a minimum, several tens of thousands remain unaccounted for in Zaire, their whereabouts undiscovered and their living conditions unknown. It is clear, however, that every effort should continue to be made to locate them and provide them with food, shelter, and medicines to meet their humanitarian needs."[42] Hundreds of thousands had become tens of thousands, consistent with the belief of many that the only people really left in Zaire from Rwanda were the *génocidaires,* their families, and their captive Hutu carriers. The rest were phantom refugees.

The military eventually told a different story. According to Canadian reports, the total number of refugees moving away from the border with Rwanda remained at about 200,000 when 640,000 refugees had already returned. The Canadian report further concluded that humanitarian access to those refugees was available and that their mission had been accomplished, especially given the erosion in support in the region for the deployment of the Multinational Neutral Force (MNF). This confirmed MNF commander general Maurice Baril's assessment on 3 December 1996 that the MNF mission had largely been accomplished and that the mandate should come to an end. More significantly, Baril noted that "some HRAs persist in their attempt to paint a continued humanitarian crisis in the making and deny the factual information made available to them at the local level."[43]

The debate over numbers had an important impact on the question of what would be done following the spontaneous return of refugees to Rwanda – a debate that should have and could have been resolved but, instead, led to a great deal of animosity between peacekeepers and NGOs.[44] Who was to blame for the confusion around numbers? The UNHCR had originally used inflated figures, but these were later corrected. Most NGOs, on the other hand, fixed on the highest possible figures and fed them to the media, which disseminated them to the public. The NGOs also accused the American military of a cover-up and the Canadian forces of being lap dogs of the Americans.

But all NGOs cannot be tarred with the same brush. An MNF assessment report of 10 December 1996 states:

> If one begins with the figure of 1.1 million and takes account of possible over-estimates of up to 20% based on generous food distribution and over-registration, it is possible that the real number of refugees in eastern Zaire at the beginning of Nov 96 was closer to 900,000. Some 640,000 are known to have returned to Rwanda in the past few weeks. If the figure of 200,000 is accepted as being a reasonable estimate of those who may not want to return then we would be able to account for 90% of the original estimate of the total refugee population.[45]

The failure to resolve this basic debate made it much more difficult to arrive at a policy for the "missing" refugees and directly affected the credibility of the United Nations and the UNHCR. It also affected the perception of who should be held responsible for moral crimes against humanity.

Coherence

Confusion over numbers and categories was not the only source of disagreement in determining how to respond to the crisis. Originally, two strategies for a peacekeeping force had been proposed. The first entailed directly addressing the issue of the militants who controlled the camps. There were two purposes for dealing with the issue of refugee warriors:

1 They controlled and used genuine refugees for military, political, and economic purposes in the pursuit of the conflict with the new government in Rwanda. This could have been stopped and the refugees freed to make their own decisions.
2 The militants could have been prevented from attacking Tutsi (Banyamulenge) in Zaire (as they had in the Masisi district) and from launching military excursions into Rwanda. Not one but two wars could have been ended by dealing with the instigators of the war.

There were other possible goals, such as bringing the *génocidaires* to justice, but they were not considered. The second strategy entailed providing protection for humanitarian relief supplies for the refugee camps and for the refugees who had fled the camps.

Numerous parties had been promoting the first strategy, including the UNHCR and the head of USAID.[46] The summit of regional leaders held in Nairobi on 5 November 1966 recommended the first strategy. However, the UN adopted the second strategy for the Canadian-led mission.

Would an international intervention to disarm the ex-FAR militants and interahamwe have forestalled the attack by the rebels against the camps? If successful, would it have prevented the alleged disappearance of tens of thousands of refugees? Alternatively, was it more prudent to leave the "freeing" of the camps to the rebels, with the consequent return of the bulk of the refugees? Leaving the camps to the rebels was clearly not the intent of those advocating the restriction of humanitarian intervention to the protection of relief corridors for refugees supplies.

The international community was in total disarray over the humanitarian use of coercive forces. Eight types of actors were concerned with the refugees:

1 refugee organizations claiming to represent the refugees (in this case, such agencies were inseparable from the control of the ex-FAR and the interahamwe)
2 the various ethnic groups involved – the Congolese Tutsi or Banyumulenge, the Katangans, the Kasai, and so on
3 various rebel groups in Uganda, Sudan, Angola, and so on who could forge alliances to obtain military training, arms, bases, and actions

that could undermine the governments they were intent on overthrowing
4 humanitarian agencies delivering aid, food, and health care to the refugees
5 international agencies with a prime concern with refugees (UNHCR) and the political situation (the UN itself and the OAU)
6 local states, particularly the states in which the refugees were located (Zaire) and the state from which the refugees fled (Rwanda and Burundi) but including Uganda, Tanzania, Kenya, Angola, and (given the regional implications of the crisis) Sudan, Ethiopia, and Eritrea as well
7 overseas states with a concern for the refugees and/or the impending crisis in Zaire – the US, France, the EU, as well as countries such as Canada that were apparently more concerned with the humanitarian issues than with the geo-political aspects of the crisis
8 military security services, mercenaries, local military and gendarmes, including forces of the Zairian army employed by the UNHCR for security purposes.

These agents had different priorities, values, modes of operation, and constituencies to which they were accountable. Refugee organizations represent the refugees but may not be accountable to them, particularly when militant political factions control the refugee camps. In the case of Zaire, the militants were opposed to repatriation and certainly to any intervention in which they were the targets. Humanitarian agencies are concerned with the welfare rather than with the political interests of the refugees; these organizations need to sustain themselves and raise the funds necessary to help the latter. On the issue of intervention, the NGOs were divided. A few supported the need to separate the militants from the genuine refugees. Others, while eventually conceding that military intervention was necessary to protect the lives of refugees, opposed the use of the military for anything but the security of humanitarian aid. International agencies, such as UNHCR, answer to their benefactors as well as to their humanitarian mandates. This restricts their activities to established modes and objectives (such as "voluntary" return) and limits their ability to provide security, while they insist that their prime function is protection for the refugees. In this case, UNHCR took an active and leading position in requesting security forces (1) to separate the militants from the rest of the refugees and (2) to protect the refugees and the aid workers.

The intervention option was restricted to providing support for a purely humanitarian mission. Within this context, the Canadian initiative was given support on condition that the mission had a restricted humanitarian mandate. This alienated the regional states in Africa that had not been consulted. Though not predicted, it was predictable that these states, Rwanda in particular, would not cooperate with such an intervention.[47]

What becomes clear is that our values are skewed. Our volunteers go to these countries ostensibly to serve others, and our peacekeepers go, at some risk to themselves, to mitigate conflicts in which they have little self-interest. But our actual priorities are protecting a state's reputation, protecting our own soldiers, protecting international humanitarian workers, and, last, protecting the local population. The reality of this triage in security comes directly into conflict with the governing foreign policy rhetoric. There is little recognition that this no-risk, self-interested policy is a product of the Cold War and is counterproductive. This allows policy makers to operate in a fantasy world that disregards local concerns, interests, and, especially, goals. Without local cooperation, security services were in no position to fulfil even a very restricted humanitarian mandate.

Fortunately, the spontaneous return of over 600,000 refugees to Rwanda allowed the military mission to declare victory without actually even being deployed on the ground. The decision to deploy the troops was the catalyst that advanced the rebel timetable for attacking the camps.

Nevertheless, innocent women and children were effectively abandoned, even if they were the wives and children of *génocidaires,* and up to 60,000 genuine refugees were forced to flee with them. We still do not know how many of them died and how they met their deaths, although there are too many substantiated rumours not to suspect that thousands were killed. The abandonment of these people must be attributed, in good part, to the failure of the international community to adopt a coherent and effective policy for dealing with the refugee crisis.

Within and among these groups there were many debates on how to cooperate and create coherent action.[48] But the inability to effect such coherence had drastic effects on the security and welfare of the refugees, as in the Kibeho massacre,[49] and affected decisions regarding how to effect repatriation, the timing of return, the modes and pace of return, the destinations for returnees, and so on. In reading the debates, one cannot help concluding that each agency's position in the policy debate, as well as factual and categorical debates, depended as much, if not more, on the culture that agency represented as it did on objective data. Peacekeepers from leading states and many international agencies took one side in the debate while many NGOs and virtually all human rights organizations took the other.[50]

Control, Repatriation, and Peace

Most refugee returns are spontaneous,[51] preceding or immediately following the signing of an accord.[52] The key decision makers in refugee repatriation are often not the international brokers or the parties to the conflict.

The refugees themselves are the key decision makers – provided they are able to make decisions free from coercion. Peace agreements rarely provide for this, or for the calculus refugees must make regarding relative risks, or for the suddenness of refugee movements. In some cases, refugees are forced to return to their home countries or other countries following a war,[53] with no provision or international assistance.[54] In such cases, refugees are one result of the "peace."

The initial repatriation of Tutsi refugees in 1994 was the result of war and the victory of the RPF (Rwanda Patriotic Front) rather than a peace agreement. The flight of the Hutu into Zaire in 1994 was different from the original 1959-64 flight of the Tutsi in at least three respects.

1 The massive exodus of the Hutu in 1994 followed the breach of a peace agreement, the Arusha Accords, by the extremist Hutus, who were eventually defeated; flight followed that defeat. Between 1959 and 1964, flight also followed the defeat of the ruling Tutsis, but no peace accord was breached.
2 The Tutsi refugees between 1959 and 1964[55] were not repatriated and satisfactorily integrated; as often happens, they metamorphosed into refugee warriors and perpetuated a cycle of violence. However, in Zaire, from 1994 to 1996, the refugee warriors were warriors first and only became refugees when the defeated army and militias fled across the Rwandese border.
3 Between 1959 and 1964, the international community ignored the Tutsi exodus. Between 1994 and 1996, the international community did not respond effectively to the genocide; however, when the genocide was virtually over and the perpetrators, along with hundreds of other innocents, fled Rwanda, the humanitarian intervention of the international community was swift and relatively effective.[56]

Nevertheless, the eventual repatriation of the Hutu from Zaire conformed to the dominant norm – it followed a military defeat (that of the militant extremist Hutu by the rebels in Zaire) – and was unanticipated, sudden, and spontaneous. The most unique feature, however, of the Rwandese refugee plight in Zaire was that the attacks on the camps were the catalyst for the spontaneous return of over 600,000 refugees from Zaire to Rwanda. Nevertheless, there were still at least 180,000 to 240,000 extremists, their families, and genuine refugees who fled westward. The fate of the remaining refugees remained a problem, but one that the dissipated effort at humanitarian intervention was unable to tackle. Furthermore, this group would pose a continuing security problem both for Zaire and for Rwanda.

Whether dealing with security in the camps, refugee repatriation, arms flows into the area, or the development of military armies among the refugees, the international community ends up looking like a paper tiger, with very little control over the direction or pace of events.

Fundamental Ethical Clashes and Moral Consistency

Underpinning the cultural clashes and incoherence, and overlaying the apparent impotence of the international community, are fundamental differences over values and their ranking. Should refugees have the right to move anywhere or are they virtual prisoners within their welfare camps? This right to movement is also a right not to be forcefully returned, though sometimes refugees are induced, pressured, or even forced to stay as refugees. If not-so-gentle means of persuasion are adopted to effect a return – for example, cutting down food rations to induce movement, presumably within a context where militants might have been preventing a free choice – then the refugees have not really been free to stay or return. All this assumes that the state to which the refugees are destined to return is genuinely interested in taking them back. Thus, both the right to return *and* not to return clash with the need to find a permanent solution for the refugees.[57]

Added to that conflict is the principle of the state as the primary agent responsible for protecting citizens or strangers on its territory. In the interest of accelerating refugee return and preventing camps from breeding a new wave of refugee warriors, governments sometimes adopt an active policy on refugee return, as did Tanzania following the massive return of Hutu refugees from Zaire to Rwanda. An inverse situation is prevalent in Israel[58] and the Republika Srbska, where state sovereignty and a commitment to the primary national group may stand in the way of refugee return and an acknowledgment of refugee rights of return. In Macedonia, the right of a small country to protect itself from an overwhelming influx of refugees who could claim a right of asylum resulted in another dimension of the conflict. Fortunately, this one was overcome through the principle of burden sharing, and many of the refugees were relocated from Macedonia. How do you rank the state's legitimate interest in security against international laws and conventions that are based on universal moral benchmarks like human rights and the rights of individuals to live in a state that provides protection?

Physical threats to the lives of the refugees and even humanitarian workers has led some humanitarian agencies to put physical security higher on their priority list and to adopt more "realist"-oriented policies, including the use of peacekeepers to guard their own organizations as well as the refugees. Some of these organizations have even actively advocated humanitarian intervention through the use of coercive force.

Protection is, thus, the primary issue – protection from whom, by whom, against what threat, and to what end.[59] The issue of protection applies to the period of flight, when refugees live in camps, and when they return. Protection extends to local inhabitants as well as to refugees.[60] The rights of refugees is not the only problem. There is also the duty to disarm refugee warriors. Furthermore, the problem of human rights protection is greatly complicated by refugee flows.[61] Kumar argues that a human rights field operation (HRFOR – Human Rights Field Operation in Rwanda) should be incorporated into a regional approach that would focus on: (1) disarming refugee warriors, (2) separating those who are suspected of having committed violations of international humanitarian law from those who are not so suspected, (3) providing an environment conducive to repatriation for refugees who want to return, and (4) policing borders to deter violent incursions.[62] UNHCR adds to that list a formal invitation on the part of the new government to repatriate; the establishment of international tribunals to end the impunity of those who commit crimes against humanity; and the establishment of staging areas, transit camps, and relief centres in order to ensure the proper management of the repatriation process.[63]

The above suggests that the problem is not the competing interest of states, or the conflict between state interests and individual human or refugee rights, or the failure of existing international regimes to be effective, or even the failure to observe international laws (let alone very lofty international norms). The competing ethical grounds seem to be the problem, but they are not. They appear to be the problem only if ethics is presumed to consist of the implementation of abstract principles. Such a conception demands that we have a moral framework that can encompass the variations between different ethical theories. But there is no overarching principle that can encompass the differences between those who espouse conflicting fundamental premises for determining international policy. Classical realists believe that the prime determinants of international affairs are self-interest and power. Liberal international regime realists agree but believe that international agreements, treaties, and institutions can mitigate these interest and power conflicts. Grotians hold international law to be the final arbiter of international affairs. Moralists believe that international action should be rooted primarily in a concern for such moral principles as human rights.

If coherence can only be established by using an overarching ethical theory capable of resolving these differences, then we lack the necessary foundation for constructing effective actions. Humanitarian interventions are simply products and compromises for competing perspectives. Efforts to develop a coherent approach to dealing with international humanitarian situations, and in particular to mitigating disasters, flounder in the absence of a solid ethical base. We have division rather than a consistent foundation for determining behaviour.

However, the most unethical position of all is to allow ourselves to be frozen into inaction or into repeating ineffective actions; instead, we should take the position that these competing elements – self-interest and power, international regimes, international laws, and international moral principles – all play a role. We require a judgment that takes into account both competing principles and the context within which they occur.

Context Related to Domains or Levels of Decision Making

How do we then deal with the issue that different countries see situations differently? These various states remain the prime decision makers in international affairs, whatever the degree of erosion in sovereign national power effected by globalization. What will work in Pretoria very much depends on what other crises are rampaging throughout the world and what the media decides to cover. Is the conflict in a place with enormous potential wealth (e.g., the Congo/Zaire) or is it in a strategic centre?

Context alone makes it impossible to deduce what can and should be done from abstract moral principles. Context includes not only the region in crisis, but also the countries proposing to intervene. And there is a temporal context as well. What can and should be done in a world with a globalized economy and globalized communications is very different from what could have and should have been done when distances were long and regions remote. Furthermore, a past crisis can cast a long shadow over a current one. What happened in Somalia cast a shadow over the decisions that were made with regard to Rwanda. The failures in Rwanda made the international community eager to act, yet decision makers were unable to overcome the long shadows of Vietnam, of Afghanistan, and of the Cold War in general. Frozen into impotence, the Zaire crisis was allowed to develop without any intervention. Indeed, one of the most important contextual factors is the unwillingness of interveners to act unless there is a crisis.

This simply means that ethical judgments require a sophisticated analysis of the *full* context – one that takes various temporal as well as geographical factors into account when attempting to make decisions involving ethical norms. Ethics is a matter of making informed decisions about competing norms. It is crucial that one not refuse to make those decisions, or that one not make foolish or ineffective decisions, because of the complexity of the factors involved.

In the case of Canada, Canadians must recognize both the strengths and weaknesses that they bring to the international arena and to complex emergencies. Along with the Scandinavians, Canada generally brings an international and humanitarian focus to world issues. In doing so, it pays too little attention to competing interests and powers and begins to resemble an NGO. International initiatives seem to be propelled by moral considerations, without sufficient attention being paid to practicalities and the realities of competing interests. This does not mean that Canada should reduce its internationalism. Quite the reverse. It means that Canada should become more effective in context analysis and in making the difficult judgments necessary to taking competing moral perspectives into account.

Meta-Ethical Principles for Ethical Judgments

The above analysis does not mean that, because there are no overarching ethical norms from which decisions can be deduced, there are no ethical guidelines to help one make such decisions.[64] My own proposal is based on five meta-ethical *complementary second-order norms,* which I call the Five Cs. They are: correspondence, coherence, control, consistency, and context. The first correspondence principle requires that ethical determinations have a base in reality and correspond to facts. That makes the numbers of missing refugees in Zaire at the end of 1996 a critical factor, for there is an enormous difference between what should be done if 20,000 are missing versus what should be done if 600,000 are missing. I can provide numerous instances of such discrepancies in humanitarian accounting, all of which affect ethical decisions and judgments. As another example, OXFAM, following the Israeli invasion of Lebanon in 1982, published full-page ads declaring that 600,000 were made homeless by the war. This was done in order to raise money to assist the victims. The Israelis published a figure of 19,000. The first figure was based on a misinterpretation of a Red Cross cable that stated that 600,000 people were *affected* by the invasion. The Israeli figure was too low, as there was a calculation error of 10,000 and some of the areas where the homeless took refuge had been missed. Thus, even though the count had been prepared by a reputable Israeli scholar, the real figure of the homeless in south Lebanon (excluding Beirut, which had not yet been attacked) was slightly more than double the Israeli figure; namely 40,000. The latter figure was provided by the Centre for Refugee Studies at York University following an audit of all counts and was used by all sides in the conflict.[65] Of course, number counts are only the most basic of facts, and there are numerous other factual issues. However, the determination of factual issues is crucial in making ethical judgments.

The second meta-ethical principle is coherence. The general argument is that incoherence in international action contributes to, rather than mitigates, harm. Therefore, it is incumbent upon all parties to make their best efforts to arrive at a coherent policy when attacking the issue. Just as in an operating room, so in international interventions: you cannot have each of the parties pursuing different goals and following different procedures.

One must also recognize that striving for correspondence and working for coherence are often at odds with one another. However, much incoherence is based on discrepancies about facts, and these can be resolved by a number of basic techniques, such as the use of independent auditors.

Setting up institutional mechanisms to sort out factual issues is a crucial precondition, but not a sufficient condition, for developing coherent policies among divergent actors.

The third principle is control. The operation must lead to enhanced predictability in outcomes even if initial efforts are based on relatively low effectiveness. Using a medical analogy, heart transplant operations may initially contribute little to the decline in mortality rates from heart disease; however, if repeating the process yields improved outcomes each time, then following and developing the procedure is worthwhile. Thus, different forms of intervention in complex emergencies must be evaluated repeatedly, not just in one instance, in order to monitor effectiveness in predicting and controlling outcomes. At the same time, it is important to recognize how relatively little control outside countries have in any actual situation. Furthermore, interveners do not even control their own ethical agendas; rather, major powers seem to adhere to a realist agenda while middle powers are prone to base actions to some degree on moral principles. Yet, if they are to be effective, then ethical principles must be consistent among cooperating states.

Consistency is the fourth principle, and seems to be in direct contrast to those principles based on control and predictability, for the predictability encourages innovation and experimentation in order to achieve increased control. Consistency reinforces conservative practices and argues that old patterns should be continued unless they can be shown to be ineffective and counterproductive. Thus, when, in 1994, the UN Human Rights Commission began visiting prisoners charged with genocide in Rwanda and used untried methods to assess prisoners' rights, this led to the Rwandan government's decision to cancel all international visitation privileges. The International Red Cross was appropriately furious at the amateur bungling of the Human Rights Commission, whose processes, which took no account of the lessons the former had learned in over a century of working within such circumstances, ended up leading to the temporary cancellation of their own access. This does not mean that all past practices must be preserved; it only means that new practices must be treated as experimental, carried out within a context of experimentation, and incorporated only when it can be established that they are more effective and humanitarian than other practices. In all cases, judgments must be made, and some second-order guidelines to ensure that such judgments are made in a reasonable manner.

Finally, there is the principle of context; that is, no judgment can be derived from a single principle. All ethical judgments are the result of reconciling competing principles within the context of a particular situation. The most important implication of this is that ethical actions cannot be derived from single principles, whether those principles be human rights,

rights to refugee repatriation or protection, or whatever; rather, competing ethical principles are weighed against one another within a context of second-order procedural norms – norms that I suggest be based on the Five Cs described above.

Acknowledgment
Two different drafts of this paper were originally presented. The first was at the Canadian Defence and Security Workshop, Centre for International and Security Studies, York University, in the fall of 1997. The second was at the Congress of the Social Sciences and Humanities, Canadian Society for the Study of Practical Ethics, 30 May to 1 June 1998 at the University of Ottawa. I am grateful for the comments received at these two venues for they contributed to this very different final version.

Notes

1 Howard Adelman with David Cox, "Overseas Refugee Policy," in *Immigration and Refugee Policy: Australia and Canada Compared,* 2 vols., ed. Howard Adelman, Lois Foster, Allan Borowski, and Meyer Burstein (Melbourne: University of Melbourne Press, 1994), 255-82; Howard Adelman, "The Right of Repatriation – Canadian Refugee Policy: The Case of Rwanda," *International Migration Review,* Special issue, *Ethics, Migration, and Global Stewardship* 30 (Spring 1996): 289-309.

2 Complex emergencies are sometimes defined in terms of the complexity of the crisis because ethnic conflicts; refugees; and economic, political, and military factors are all present. Complex emergencies are also defined in terms of the complexity of the response; many actors are involved – local states and larger powers, international agencies, and NGOs. The latter may include humanitarian as well as human rights and development aid organizations. Furthermore, the various actors are involved in many ways – diplomatically, through providing economic aid, through volunteering as observers and as peacekeepers, and so on. This case is complex in all of the above senses, and the crisis was complex. All the various classes of outside actor were involved, and all were involved in a variety of ways. See Thomas G. Weiss and Cindy Collins, *Humanitarian Challenges and Intervention: World Politics and the Dilemmas of Help* (Boulder, CO: Westview Press, 1996).

3 From a human security perspective, violent conflict is approached in terms of preventive diplomacy and other initiatives focused on people-centered conflict resolution and peacebuilding activities. Intervention to protect populations at risk is viewed as part of the spectrum of these initiatives, albeit an extreme one.

4 Canada hosted an International Conference on War Affected Children in Winnipeg in September of 2000 attended by Foreign Ministers from many countries.

5 Foreign Minister Lloyd Axworthy, at the Conference on The Global Compact and UN Institutions in Tokyo, Japan (14 July 2000), stated, "Canada has also made the issue of humanitarian intervention a priority ... Deciding what intervention is warranted poses serious questions. Under what auspices? By what criteria? Recognizing what standards? Using what tools?" Canada went on to sponsor an international commission to look into the ethical norms that ought to govern humanitarian interventions.

6 For purposes of brevity, I have omitted an overview of ethical approaches in international relations. For an overview of the different theoretical traditions of international ethics, see Terry Nardin and David R. Mapel, *Traditions of International Ethics* (Cambridge: Cambridge University Press, 1992).

7 Raimo Väyrynen, "Introduction: How Much Force in Humanitarian Intervention?" in *The Ethics and Politics of Humanitarian Intervention,* ed. Stanley Hoffman (Notre Dame: University of Notre Dame Press, 1996).

8 For a more detailed argument for this choice, see Howard Adelman, Dr. Abbas H. Gnamo, and Dr. Shally B. Gachuruzi, *A Framework for Conflict Resolution: Peacebuilding and National Reconciliation in the Great Lakes Region of Africa* (Zaire, Rwanda and Burundi) (Toronto: YCISS, York University Press, 1997).

9 This was also true of the study of the Rwanda intervention. See Howard Adelman, "The Ethics of Intervention: Rwanda," in *Local Sovereignty and International Responsibility,* ed. Michael Keren and Christian Tomuschat (Berlin: Humboldt University Press, 1997).

10 Estimates vary from 500,000 to 800,000 or even 1,000,000 Tutsi, aside from the moderate Hutu who were killed. Some recent figures have settled on the low end of that range. For example, Alan J. Kuperman ("Rwanda in Retrospect," *Foreign Affairs* 79, 1 [January/February 2000]: 101) argues that only 500,000 were killed. Alison des Forges (*Leave None to Tell the Story: Genocide in Rwanda* [New York: Human Rights Watch, 1999], 15) has downsized her earlier estimates to 507,000.

11 UNHCR, *The State of the World's Refugees: In Search of Solutions* (Oxford: Oxford University Press, 1995), 32.

12 Howard Adelman, "Early Warning and Humanitarian Intervention: Zaire – March to December 1996" (London: FEWER, 1998).

13 In Zaire, militants of the same ethnic group as the genuine refugees controlled the camps from within and helped prevent repatriation; but refugee repatriation was upheld as the prime goal for solving the refugee situation. See Tim Allen and Hubert Morsink, eds., *When Refugees Go Home: African Experiences* (Geneva: UNRISD, 1994).

14 The preamble to the 1969 Convention on the Refugee Problems in Africa affirms that the signatories are "determined to discourage" refugees from using their status for subversive activities (paras. 4 and 5). Article 3 deals in its entirety with "Prohibition of Subversive Activities," prohibiting refugees from engaging in subversive activities against any member state of the OAU (3.1). The article requires that the host states undertake to "prohibit refugees residing in their respective territories from attacking any State Member ... by use of arms, through the press, or by radio." (3.2). To further ensure that these conditions are met, Article 2(6) advises that, "for reasons of security," refugees shall settle "at a reasonable distance from the frontier of their country of origin." These provisions are unique to regional African instruments of international refugee law. More generally, the Charter of the Organization of African Unity expresses "unreserved condemnation" for subversive activities on the part of neighbouring states or any other state (Article 3.5). The African Charter on Human and People's Rights states unambiguously that, "territories [of signatory states] shall not be used as bases for subversive or terrorist activities" against another party (Article 23[2]b).

15 This concern with benefitting the other side was heightened by the general suspicion of the international community. After all, the same international community had failed to stop or even mitigate the genocide, and it had failed to do anything about the extremists who controlled the camps. Since the rebels and, more important, their backers in Rwanda and Uganda had no reason to trust the international community to act with dispatch and effectiveness, there was little incentive for the local states to cooperate with the humanitarian intervention force. They concluded that their own position would be made worse and even jeopardized by the international initiative.

16 Signatories to the 1948 Genocide Convention have the legal right and the moral obligation, under international law, to investigate and to take measures to halt genocide and punish the perpetrators.

17 Intervention in Rwanda appeared at first to involve some risk, although that risk turned out to be virtually nil. This low risk had been signalled by the non-resistance to the French Operation Turquoise, but perhaps this was only because the French never provided a significant threat to the militants and did not venture into the countryside to prevent the killings there. In fact, many interpreted the French intervention as a cover to allow the militants to escape. See Gerard Prunier, *The Rwanda Crisis: History of a Genocide* (New York: Columbia University Press, 1995). In refugee camps, soldiers provided the infrastructure support for relief and protection for the aid workers who were at very little risk. Thus, a humanitarian intervention restricted to a humanitarian mission seemed without risk. Alternatively, any action against the well equipped and apparently well trained ex-FAR and the interahamwe seemed to be very risky. On the one hand, this proved to be a gross overestimation, given the lack of real resistance the armed Hutu extremists offered to the rebels; on the other hand, there was a gross underestimation of the fire-power in the

hands of the militants, given the array of arms and the number of soldiers under the control of the militants.

18 PDD 25 was a US presidential directive promulgated in May 1994 at the beginning of the genocide in Rwanda and in the aftermath of the Somalia fiasco. Its purpose was to severely restrict the use of American military forces in humanitarian interventions.

19 Peter J. Schraeder, *United States Foreign Policy Toward Africa: Incrementalism, Crisis and Change* (Cambridge: Cambridge University Press, 1994); Michael Mandelbaum, "The Reluctance to Intervene," *Foreign Affairs* 95 (Summer 1994): 3-18.

20 Greg Philo compiled the number of refugees reported as returning and as missing on British broadcasts between the 15 and 19 November 1996. See Greg Philo, "The Zaire Rebellion and the British Media: An Analysis of the Reporting of the Zaire crisis in November 1996 and 1997," Glasgow Media Group, Background Paper to the Dispatches from Disaster Zones Conference, London, 28 May 1998. The numbers of returnees in twenty-three different reports were reasonably consistent in spite of some significant variations, generally using a figure of 400,000 to 500,000. However, the numbers said to be missing were all over the map, varying from 100,000 to 800,000:
"Still Hundreds of Thousands Missing," ITN *Channel Four News,* 15 November 1996;
"700,000 People at Least Missing (Aid Worker)," ITN *News at Ten,* 15 November 1996;
"Another 800,000 Out There (UN)," BBC2 *Newsnight,* 15 November 1996;
"100,000 Starving Refugees Fled," *The Mirror,* 16 November 1996;
"400,000," ITN 2045, 16 November 1996;
"About 180,000 Have Fled in the Opposite Direction," BBC1 2125, 17 November, 1996;
"Another 500,000 to Come," *The Mirror,* 19 November 1996.

21 Lord Eric Avebury, Vice-chair, Parliamentary Human Rights Group, House of Lords, letter to the editor, *Genocide Forum* 4, 7 (February 1998): 3, argued that 281,000 refugees were missing. Henry Huttenbach, the editor of the same newsletter in which Lord Avebury's note appeared, argued that, "unless it can be *proven otherwise* that less than the 50% of the 685,000 refugees actually came back to Rwanda, it is safe to add at least another 340,000 to the 281,000 still unaccounted for making a total of 625,000 'lost' Hutus." "The original claim published in *TGF* was that 670,000 Hutu refugees may have been killed or forced to die of exposure" (*Genocide Forum* 4, 7 [February 1998], 3). This deformed use of mathematical reasoning was presumably intended to establish some sort of moral equivalence between the crisis that struck the Hutu refugees in Zaire and the genocide in Rwanda.

22 US Committee for Refugees, "How Many Refugees Are in Eastern Zaire? Why Estimates Vary Widely," press release, 26 November 1996. The NGO community claimed that the US, for its own political purposes, had deliberately understated the figures. Nick Stockton of OXFAM, UK, labelled the press release as part of "Operation Restore Silence" (Press release, OXFAM, February 1997), and claimed that there was a concerted effort to "airbrush" the allegedly missing refugees out of international consciousness.

23 See Study 3 of the Rwanda Evaluation, *Humanitarian Aid and Its Effects* (Copenhagen: DANIDA, 1996), 106. See also clause 17 of the UNHCR response to the evaluation (EC/46/SC/CRP.28), 4.

24 Most Hutu refugees were concentrated in Eastern Zaire. After 100,000 to 200,000 spontaneously repatriated within the first two months of their arrival in Zaire before the ex-FAR and interahamwe established full control over the camps, there were an estimated 850,000 refugees in Goma, 332,000 in Bukavu, and 62,000 in Uvira. The official refugee population in Zaire was reported to be 1,194,000 after taking into account the approximately 50,000 that died in the cholera outbreak in Goma. One hundred and forty thousand of these were Hutus from Burundi. Therefore, there were said to be 1,044,000 Rwandese Hutu refugees in Zaire. Even these figures were said to be exaggerated because the militants in the camps prevented a proper census. It is generally believed that these figures were exaggerated by at least 10 percent (more likely 15 percent).

25 Even President Pasteur Bizimungu of Rwanda, in September 1996, referred to 1.1 million Rwandan refugees in Zaire (Christian Jennings, Reuters, 10 September 1996) and failed to distinguish between genuine refugees and armed militants.

26 Of the 140,000 Burundians in the total, 103,000 were repatriated and 20,000 remained in

the DRC. Either 17,000 went missing or the original number of 140,000 had been exaggerated by about 12 percent.

27 This figure was about 55,000 higher than that indicated in the conclusions of Study 3 of the Rwanda Evaluation (*Humanitarian Aid and Its Effects* [Copenhagen: DANIDA, 1996], 106), which determined that there were 170,000 in Ngara and 740,000 in Goma, for a total of 910,000. These figures might be able to be reconciled since an estimated 50,000 individuals died in Goma in 1994 as a result of cholera. Furthermore, tens of thousands of refugees repatriated to Rwanda before the militants gained full control of the camps and prevented further repatriations.

28 The militants and their families constituted the bulk of the refugee population who fled west and relocated in Tingi Tingi, near Kisingani, after the refugee camps on the border of Rwanda were destroyed by the ADFL attack.

29 There were two or three divisions – 18,000 to 40,000 men under arms. The notion that there were three divisions in the ex-FAR in Zaire is based on a number of sources. However, other documents (Project Liberation Rwanda) indicate that there were only two divisions, for a total number of almost 18,000. Furthermore, *Restructuration des Forces Armées Rwandaises,* a document signed by Major General Augustin Bizimungu (commander of the FAR) and stamped top secret lists the order of command, clearly indicates that there were only two divisions. I am grateful to Massimo Alberitzi of the Italian newspaper, *Corriere Della Sera,* from whom I indirectly obtained many of the documents on the military capacity and armaments of the ex-FAR and interahamwe.

30 Degni-Ségui, "Report to the Secretary-General on Zaire" (New York: United Nations, 1994), 16.

31 Earlier, Canadians were totally confused about the refugee figures. Once, the Canadian Department of Defence estimated that there were about 200,000+ refugees fleeing west (these were most likely the militants and their families). At the same time, on 19 November 1996, the Canadian foreign minister was telling the House of Commons, with complete confidence, that there were 500,000 refugees still in Zaire. The very same day the government interdepartmental task force wrote a memo stating: "The refugee situation in eastern Zaire remains unclear. Reports provided by the international relief agencies on the ground, as well as discussions conducted by Canadian officials and allied countries, are often conflicting. The fact of the matter is that we do not know exactly the number, the location or the needs of the refugees and displaced persons in that country."

32 Both American and Canadian estimates claim an original total camp population of only 900,000 after the original 100,000 to 200,000 spontaneous repatriation. If 15,000 were forced across the border in August of 1996, if 640,000 Rwandan refugees spontaneously returned in November, if 140,000 of the original group of refugees were from Burundi, if approximately 180,000 refugee warriors and their families fled eastward, then this figure may be too low. In any case, no significant number of missing refugees existed when the camps were evacuated.

33 Astri Suhrke coined the phrase "refugee warriors" in the now classic volume by Aristide Zolberg, Astri Suhrke and Sergio Aguayo, *Escape from Violence: Conflict and the Refugee Crisis in the Developing World,* (Oxford: Oxford University Press, 1989). Strictly speaking, the phrase "refugee warrior" is a misnomer. By international and OAU law, a refugee cannot resort to violence. See Gören Melander, "The Concept of the Term 'Refugee,'" in *Refugees in the Age of Total War,* ed. Anna Bramwell (London: Unwin Hyman, 1986), 7-14; Louis Henkin et al., *Right v. Might: International Law and the Use of Force* (New York: Council on Foreign Relations, 1991); Guy Goodwin-Gill, *The Refugee in International Law,* 2nd ed. (Oxford: Clarendon Paperbacks, 1996); and Jean-Yves Carlier, Dick Vanheule, Klaus Jullmann, and Carlos Peña Galiano, eds., *Who Is a Refugee? A Comparative Case Law Study* (The Hague: Kluwer Law International, 1997). According to the OAU law, refugees are not permitted to exercise their "right of return" through armed force. More generally, the Charter of the OAU expresses "unreserved condemnation" for subversive activities on the part of neighbouring states or any other state (Article 3[5]). The African Charter for Human and People's Rights also states unequivocally that territories of signatory states shall not be used as bases for subversive or terrorist activities against another party (Article 23, 2:b). In law, a person may either be a refugee or a warrior, but he or she cannot be

both. Although the phrase "refugee warrior" is used, refugee warriors are not, in fact or in law, refugees. Therefore, the number of refugees versus warriors in the refugee camps in Zaire needs to be sorted out because the numbers in each group will be critical to understanding how the situation in Zaire developed.

34 If the numbers of refugees that were killed had been reasonably documented, then those figures could be used as another source to estimate the original number of refugees in Zaire. Unfortunately, this has not been the case. The ICHRDD and ASADHO report of June 1998, which was written on the basis of a synthesis of all other documents and reports, has no reliable basis using its own numbers. Thus, although 15,000 refugees who survived and went on to Tingi Tingi after fleeing Walikali are estimated as having died (presumably because no one knew what happened to them), because there were no eyewitnesses to the killings, I did not include them in my figures.

35 The International Centre for Human Rights and Democratic Development (ICHRDD), and L'Association Africaine pour la Défense des Droits de l'Homme en République Démocratique du Congo, *International Non-Governmental Commission of Inquiry into the Massive Violations of Human Rights Committed in the Democratic Republic of Congo (Formerly Zaïre), 1996-1997,* Montreal, June 1998. This was not the only report to cite such numbers. MSF, in its 16 May 1997 report, estimated that 190,000 persons had disappeared. MSF accused the ADFL of a "deliberate strategy aiming at the elimination of all remaining Rwandese refugees, including women and children (16 May 1997). Further, the ICHRDD report, while being dogmatic in its summary, waffles considerably in its content. For example, page 5 refers to "tens or hundreds of thousands" as having lost their lives. This means the range of the death toll was between 20,000 and 400,000 – quite a range.

36 Amnesty International, *Democratic Republic of Congo: Deadly Alliances in Congo Forests,* London, 3 December 1997, 1.

37 My focus, however, is not on whether genocide was intended or committed. Furthermore, based on reports, I find it entirely credible that there occured large-scale murder, torture, rape, illegal detention, and so on. What I find unclear is how these became blown up to a figure of 200,000 when there is not even the least effort to reconcile counts or to consider contrary evidence and interpretations offered by reputable parties. My only conclusion is that this figure was a product of the misleading figure of 1.2 million refugees assumed to be in Zaire as well as the failure to track where the "refugees" who had fled into the interior had gone.

38 Canadians would soon conclude that they had been misled by the figures of the humanitarian agencies. Canadian military analysts did not get their figures from the US but, rather, by directly downloading US and UK reconnaissance data and undertaking their own analysis. What were their conclusions? The presentation to the MNF Eastern Zaire Group Meeting of 13 December 1996 in Uganda reported that the fighting had sent "approximately 200,000 refugees into the mountains to the west. The group initially camped in the area of Numbi where I observed them from the air on 21 Nov 96 ... By 28 Nov a large number of these refugees had detached themselves from the main group and gathered in Minova on the western edge of lake Kivu. Approximately 30,000 refugees would return to Rwanda in the following two days. The remaining refugees in the Numbi area continued to move west from Numbi to the Lowa Valley." The report continued, stating definitively that the rebels did not come into contact with the refugees who split into smaller groups and fled into the forest, where reconnaissance aircraft were only able to track 20 percent of them. The rest had "disappeared." The report also concluded that "there were no signs of force used to persuade the refugees to move west."

39 UN Secretary-General's Report to the Security Council on the Implementation of Resolution 1078 (1996), 20 November 1996, para. 35.

40 See, for example, the *Montreal Gazette,* 18 November 1996. If the UN secretary-general were correct, and since he had already discounted the Burundian refugees, there would would have been 1.1 million Rwandan refugees in Zaire alone before the 1996 war started. However, in the same report, paragraph 25 refers to only 400,000 returnees. The inconsistency in the secretary-general's use of figures is evident in paragraph 24a, where he states: "While hundreds of thousands of refugees have started to return to Rwanda, an approximately equal number are still scattered in eastern Zaire without access to help from the

international community." In diplomatic mathematics, 600,000 remaining and 400,000 repatriated become approximately equal.

41 K, Channel 4, 1900-1950, 21 November 1996: "The UNHCR has used satellite technology and reconnaissance planes to locate up to 700,000 Rwandan refugees, missing in Eastern Zaire. The Rwandan government had claimed that most of the refugees had returned home. But the UNHCR says finding the missing people shows that international help is still needed." See Greg Philo, ed., "The Zaire Rebellion and the British Media: An Analysis of the Reporting of the Zaire Crisis in November 1996 and 1997 by the Glasgow Media Group," background paper to the Dispatches from Disaster Zones Conference, London, 28 May 1998, 17. In Philo's "Background Paper" (19), he cites the following: "The UN officials warn, there are a third of a million Rwandans still displaced in Zaire, trapped in a civil war and being abused by all sides." See ITN 2200-2230, 29 April 1997.

42 Report of the Secretary-General of the United Nations, clause 10, p. 5, 1 January 1997, "The Implementation of Resolution 1080." This report concerned the launching of the MNF, led by Canadians, into Zaire.

43 Memorandum, General Maurice Baril, 3 December 1996.

44 Reducing the debate to its simplest form, and one upon which most would agree, it resolved around two different calculations. If one starts with 1.2 million refugees and then deducts the Burundian refugees, the *génocidaires* and their families, and the number of returnees, then there would still be 150,000 to 315,000 missing refugees. This would be consistent with the MSF 16 May 1997 report that said that there were 340,000 Hutu *refugees* (emphasis mine) dispersed in the Zairian forests.

1,200,000	
- 140,000	Burundians
- 100,000 to 260,000	*génocidaires*
- 646,000	returnees
314,000 to 154,000	missing refugees, including refugee warriors

45 Australian MNF Assessment Report, "Refugees in Zaire," 10 December 1996.

46 Brian Atwood made precisely such a proposal at the Rwanda Roundtable in Geneva in June 1994.

47 In the visit on 5 November 1996 of Ambassador Raymond Chretien with Paul Kagame, vice-president of Rwanda, Kagame made it clear that he would take direct action to deal with the ex-FAR in Zaire if the international community failed to act.

48 Roger Winter, "Ending Exile: Promoting Successful Reintegration of African Refugees and Displaced People," in *African Refugees: Development Aid and Repatriation,* ed. Howard Adelman and John Sorenson (Boulder, CO: Westview Press, 1994), 159-71.

49 Howard Adelman, "The Failure to Prevent Genocide: The Case of Rwanda," in *Mediterranean Social Sciences Review,* ed. Anthony Spiteri (Valletta, Malta: Foundation for International Studies, 1997d).

50 Antonio Donini, "Beyond Neutrality: On the Compatibility of Military Intervention and Humanitarian Assistance," *Fletcher Forum of World Affairs* 19, 2 (Summer/Fall 1995): 31-45.

51 Joshua O. Akol, "Southern Sudanese Refugees: Their Repatriation and Resettlement after the Addis Ababa Agreement," in *Refugees: A Third World Dilemma,* ed. John Rogge (Totawa, NJ: Rowman and Littlefield, 1987), 143-57; Tom Kuhlman, "Organized versus Spontaneous Settlement of Refugees in Africa," in *African Refugees,* ed. Adelman and Sorenson,17-142; Roger Winter, "Ending Exile: Promoting Successful Reintegration of African Refugees and Displaced People," in ibid., 168.

52 This was certainly the case after the Arusha Accords were signed on 4 August 1993. While great detailed plans had been made to return the internally displaced to their homes, particularly by the United Nations Development Program (UNDP), systematically and carefully, within three weeks of the signing, before UNDP could even launch its operation, over 700,000 refugees simply got up and walked home.

53 This was the case with the Palestinians from Kuwait who went to Jordan following the Gulf War. See Howard Adelman, "Humanitarian and Conflict-Oriented Early Warning: An Historical Background Sketch," in *Early Warning and Conflict Prevention: Limitations and Opportunities,* ed. Alfred van Staden and Klaas van Walgraven (The Hague: Clingendael 1997b), chap. 2.

54 Anthony H. Richmond, *Global Apartheid: Refugees, Racism, and the New World Order* (Toronto: Oxford University Press, 1994), 215.

55 Aristide R. Zolberg, Astri Suhrke, and Sergio Aguayo, *Escape from Violence: Conflict and the Refugee Crisis in the Developing World* (New York: Oxford University Press, 1989); Edward Khiddu-Makubuya, "Voluntary Repatriation by Force: The Case of Rwandan Refugees in Uganda," in *African Refugees,* ed. Adelman and Sorenson, 143-58; UNHCR, *The State of the World's Refugees: In Search of Solutions* (Oxford: Oxford University Press, 1995).

56 That intervention was not a sign of moral virtue but, rather, of failure. It signified the decision to provide humanitarian assistance to refugees where Western aid workers were involved and where there was massive media coverage. In contrast, no timely and effective decision was made to protect hundreds of thousands of lives from genocide in Rwanda or the subsequent ethnic cleansing in Masisi.

57 See Elizabeth Ferris, *Beyond Borders: Refugees, Migrants and Human Rights* (Geneva: World Council of Churches, 1993); D. Forsythe and K. Pease, "Human Rights, Humanitarian Intervention and World Politics" *Human Rights Quarterly* 15, 2 (1993): 290-314; Adam Roberts, "Humanitarian War: Military Intervention and Human Rights," *International Affairs* 69 (July 1993): 429-49; Adam Roberts, "Human Rights and the Refugee Dilemma," in *Brown Journal of World Affairs* 1, 2 (1994 – Special Edition); Roberta Cohen, *Refugees and Human Rights* (Washington: Refugee Policy Group, 1995); James C. Hathaway and John A. Dent, *Refugee Rights: Report on a Comparative Survey* (Toronto: York Lanes Press, 1995); Peter M. Manikas and Krishna Kumar, "Protecting Human Rights in Rwanda," in *Rebuilding Societies after Civil War: Critical Roles for International Assistance,* ed. Krishna Kumar (Boulder, CO: Lynne Rienner, 1997), 63-83.

58 Adelman and Sorenson, *African Refugees;* and Howard Adelman, "Palestine Refugees, the Right of Return and the Peace Process," in *Economics of Peace in the Middle East,* ed. Bashir Al Khadra (Yarmouk: Yarmouk University Press, 1996).

59 Peter H. Koehn, "Refugee Settlement and Repatriation in Africa: Development Prospects and Constraints," in Adelman and Sorenson, *African Refugees,* 97-116.

60 For example, in October 1997 within Rwanda thirty-seven Tutsi were killed by Hutu extremists. The Tutsi were in a transit camp where they were waiting to be resettled from their former houses into new plots and houses.

61 Krishna Kumar, ed., *Rebuilding Societies After Civil War: Critical Roles for International Assistance* (Boulder, CO: Lynne Rienner, 1997), 63.

62 Ibid., 77-78.

63 United Nations High Commission for Refugees, *The State of the World's Refugees: In Search of Solutions* (London/New York: Oxford University Press, 1995), 44.

64 Part of the root of the problem is an insistence that goes back to the Greeks: Ethics must be principled. Ethics concerns claims derived from ethical first principles – principles that are akin to those found in geometry. This is erroneous *and unethical.* Ethics is fundamentally judgmental; that is, it concerns weighing competing ethical norms within the context of a given situation in order to come to a reasoned judgment.

65 Howard Adelman, *Homeless Refugees and Displaced Persons in Southern Lebanon Resulting from the Israeli Invasion of Lebanon* (Toronto: Centre for Refugee Studies, York University Press, 1982).

11
Promoting Democracy in Haiti: Assessing the Practical and Ethical Implications

Tom Keating

> Between those who said we could do nothing and those who said we could do it all there has to lie a position where the ethics of commitment meets the ethics of responsibility, where the commitments we make to strangers in danger can be backed up by believable achievable strategies of rescue. If we cannot find such a *via media,* policy and public opinion are both likely to lurch between the Scylla of hubristic over-commitment and the Charibdis of cynical disengagement.
>
> – Michael Ignatieff, "The Seductiveness of Moral Disgust"

In an essay assessing the moral dimensions of humanitarian interventions, Michael Ignatieff refers to Joseph Conrad's *Heart of Darkness* to illustrate the tendency of some societies to assume they have both the wisdom and the power to create just conditions in other societies.[1] The history of such imperial ambitions is littered with examples of "good intentions" gone wrong. Taking up the "White man's burden" has never been particularly appealing to Canadian foreign policy makers, at least until recently. This sort of thing has always been more popular with Canada's former colonial masters and its neighbours to the south. Promoting democracy abroad has been an established tradition in American foreign policy for a good part of the past century. Some of their most elaborate interventions and occupations of foreign lands have been undertaken with these noble objectives as guiding principles. Canadians, on the other hand, have been more reticent about, if not deeply suspicious of, such adventures. That is not to say that Canadians have completely avoided the missionary spirit. They tended, however, to leave this to those missionaries inspired by matters of the spirit. Times and circumstances have changed. In the post-Cold War environment Canadians in and out of public office have been infected with the crusading spirit and have decided that promoting democracy and related noble causes such as human security is indeed a worthwhile activity deserving of official support and public resources.

This chapter focuses on one specific case, that of Haiti, and examines the practical and ethical issues raised by the Canadian government's experiences in promoting democracy in Haiti between 1991 and 1999. A review of Canada's involvement in the restoration and reconstruction of democratic institutions and practices in Haiti addresses a number of the themes discussed in this collection. First, it reflects the relationship between values, or ethics, and practice in Canada's approach to the new agenda of security issues. It also illustrates how this agenda has changed with the end of the Cold War as Canada moved to the forefront in articulating a more interventionist role for governments and international institutions in the domestic affairs of other states. Finally, it critically examines the values that Canada has pursued in Haiti, its ability to support these values, and the relationship between capacity and ethics in this area of Canadian security policy. The conclusions, while on balance pessimistic about the alleged benefits of external efforts to create democratic practices, nonetheless acknowledge the strong sense of obligation, not to mention the ethical and political pressures, that have encouraged such efforts.

Enshrining Good Governance

For more than ten years successive Canadian governments have systematically and explicitly reformulated security policy, moving from its traditional emphasis on interstate conflict conducted chiefly through formal arrangements with the United States and its NATO allies to a more fluid and diffuse involvement in intrastate conflict primarily under the auspices of the UN. The security of states has given way to the security of individuals, and the Canadian response – whether animated by principles of good governance, peacebuilding, or human security – has deliberately challenged traditional norms of international politics. Former prime minister Brian Mulroney expressed his concern with the constraints that the principles of state sovereignty and non-intervention imposed on attempts to respond to humanitarian disasters such as the one then developing in the former Yugoslavia: "Some Security Council members have opposed intervention in Yugoslavia where many innocent people have been dying, on the grounds of national sovereignty. Quite frankly, such invocations of the principle of national sovereignty are as out of date and as offensive to me as the police declining to stop family violence simply because a man's home is supposed to be his castle."[2] These sentiments were echoed frequently in statements by his foreign minister Barbara McDougall: "The new doctrines of humanitarian intervention and peacemaking are global in scope. The whole concept of national sovereignty is being rethought as we move into the post-statist world."[3] This marked a significant shift in Canadian foreign policy, which moved away from an acceptance of the principle of non-intervention and the constraints imposed by state sovereignty, and towards support for more direct and intrusive forms of intervention in foreign states for humanitarian purposes. While Canadian officials did not go as far as did some of their French counterparts in asserting an obligation of humanitarian intervention, they were certainly among the most vocal supporters of a right to such intervention in response to humanitarian crises.

In an effort to incorporate such concerns into the framework of Canadian foreign policy, in a mid-term 1990 policy document the government adopted "good governance" as one of its foreign policy priorities. The good governance policy contained at least three explicit objectives and an implicit, but sometimes acknowledged, fourth. The explicit objectives were: respect for human rights, democratic government, and sound public administration. The implicit one was respect for free markets.[4]

The government set about implementing the good governance policy in a variety of foreign policy arenas, including: development assistance programs, support for and contributions to more interventionist peacekeeping operations, and in proposals for reforming multilateral associations in which it held membership. The government also established the International Centre for Human Rights and Democratic Development (ICHRDD) to facilitate more extensive involvement by non-governmental organizations (NGOs) in implementing the good governance initiative. In the early 1990s, the government sought support for the good governance policy in multilateral associations, including the Organization of American States (OAS); the Commonwealth, la Francophonie, and the Conference on Security and Cooperation in Europe (CSCE). The good governance policy survived the 1993 federal election and was reaffirmed with a more explicit link between values and security in the Liberal government's foreign policy document *Canada in the World*. "Application of our values – respect for democracy, the rule of law, human rights and the environment – will be critical to the struggle for international security in the face of new threats to stability. Their adoption internationally will also be essential to ensuring that they are viable in our country."[5] Good governance was recast as a central element of the Liberal government's initiatives in the areas of peacebuilding and human security.

The decision to give a higher priority to these objectives in Canadian foreign policy, while a departure from past practice in Canada, was consistent with developments in other countries, including, among others, middle powers such as the Netherlands and Norway. It also resulted from important changes brought about by the end of the Cold War. The end of the Cold War was both a source and a reflection of a broader trend towards democratization and other pressures for political change in many parts of the world. At times, these pressures degenerated into violent civil conflict. These conflicts created much hardship for civilians and were one reason for the increased attention on human security. The Cold War's end also provided an opportunity for Western governments to assert themselves unencumbered by competitors. In this vein national governments and the international institutions they controlled began to attach "political conditionality" to their relations with non-Western states. Gillies defines "political conditionality" as "legitimate intervention by aid donors in the domestic affairs of borrowing countries in order to alter the political environment in ways that will sustain human as well as economic development."[6] Whether recipients and donors could agree on the meaning of legitimate intervention has been a relevant but untested premise as the practice has increased during the 1990s.

Making the Hemisphere Safe for Democracy

The adoption and promotion of good governance reflected a significant shift in the Canadian government's view of state sovereignty and nonintervention. Policy makers, however, continued to see international institutions as important vehicles for the articulation and legitimation of these initiatives. One of the more important and effective vehicles used by the government was the OAS. Throughout the 1980s domestic groups and parliamentarians pressured the Canadian government to place a greater emphasis on peaceful change and human rights in Canada's foreign policy towards Central and Latin America.[7] Yet the government's decision to join the OAS late in 1989 was criticized on the grounds that the government would be subjected to excessive American pressure and unable to exercise an independent influence within the organization or the region. In less than two years, however, the Canadians went one step further and became more American than the Americans in leading the rallying cry for democracy and free markets in the hemisphere.[8] One of the government's first initiatives in the OAS was to gain unanimous approval for the establishment of a Unit for the Promotion of Democracy (UPD) at the OAS General Assembly in June 1990. "The role of the UPD was envisioned broadly to promote and reinforce democratic institutions in the hemisphere, to help in the monitoring of elections, and to give practical training to men and women at both the grass-roots and official level."[9] In addition to its diplomatic efforts, the Canadian government provided funding for the UPD, and the former Canadian ambassador in the region, John Graham, was appointed as the unit's first director. The UPD, with a rather modest mandate of election monitoring and related work to strengthen democratic institutions, would be only the beginning of the organization's acceptance of a more intrusive set of regimes to promote democracy. An even more impressive set of measures emerged the following year, when Canadian diplomacy was instrumental in securing the support of member governments for the Santiago Commitment.

On the occasion of the twenty-first general assembly of the OAS in Santiago in June 1991, the Canadian delegation was at the forefront of a proposal that became known as the Santiago Commitment to Democracy and the Renewal of the International System. This ambitious-sounding declaration committed member governments "to adopt efficacious, timely, and expeditious procedures to ensure the promotion and defence of representative democracy."[10] The specific measures included an immediate response to the overthrow of democratically elected governments and assistance programs in order to preserve and strengthen democratic practices. The successful adoption of the Santiago Commitment reflected well on Canadian diplomatic skills. It also created a more permissive environment for intervention in a region that traditionally had been opposed to such measures – and for good reason. The region's troubled and turbulent historical experiences with American intervention, often under the guise of liberal democratic principles, raised concerns among some member governments. Hurrell, for one, has noted that, "while democratic values are widely shared throughout the Americas, the dangers of abuse of hegemonic power have led, and will continue to lead, Latin American states to try to limit the scope for 'democratic interventions.'"[11] Canadian officials were, however, able to gain the support of other governments in the region, especially those from the Southern cone, who were interested in solidifying the democratic reforms that had so recently been won. With this coalition, Canada won over the support of others.

As part of the Santiago Commitment member governments declared "their firm political commitment to the promotion and protection of human rights and representative democracy, as indispensable conditions for the stability, peace and development of the region."[12] The identification of democracy as an "indispensable condition" for the region not only reflected the extent to which the political conditions in the region had evolved, but it also infused the OAS with a substantive purpose well beyond that for which it was originally established: "In the past, the OAS generally refrained from sitting in judgment on the internal politics of member countries."[13] When Venezuela ratified this commitment, however, the OAS Charter was amended to include these democratic criteria. While one may question the strength of the commitment, its mere inclusion in the charter is of considerable significance, for it identifies a particular form of government as a prerequisite for membership and status within the organization.[14] The Canadian government's support for the entrenchment of a particular form of government as a criterion for participation in a multilateral institution was markedly different from the more inclusive view of participation that had guided policy makers in the past. Membership was now to be a matter of establishing one's credentials. Canada and the organization did not have to wait long for the first test of the new commitment as democratic practices were challenged in the hemisphere's most impoverished nation, Haiti.

Haiti: Waiting for Democracy

A detailed account of the Canadian response to the 1991 coup d'état in Haiti will not be presented here;[15] instead, the following discussion reviews some of the major developments in Canadian policy, especially those actions that involved the OAS and the UN. The response of these institutions to the democratic crisis in Haiti was driven by a mix of state and institutional interests. The Canadian government, however, repeatedly emphasized the need for these institutions to take the lead. In part, this was necessary in order to legitimize the international response to the crisis and the substantive values of liberal democracy that were being promoted through this response. It was also viewed as a way of confirming the relevance of these institutions in supporting and implementing Canada's good governance policy. The government also looked at the Haitian crisis as an opportunity to promote the OAS. While there was a general consensus among the members of the OAS that the regional institution should take the lead in trying to effect change in Haiti, there were differences over how and why this should be done. There were also clear institutional limits to the organization's ability to bring about a resolution of the conflict. The OAS lacked both the mandate and the resources to effect change through either sanctions or force. In their place, the organization was limited to collective diplomatic pressure and neighbourly censure, neither of which proved sufficient in convincing the military to yield power.

The crisis in Haiti was not unprecedented and did not mark a major departure from past practice in that traumatized country. It did, however, occur at a time when the OAS and its member governments could not ignore it. The event that precipitated the response was the violent removal of Haiti's first democratically elected president, Jean-Bertrand Aristide, on 30 September 1991 by a military coup led by General Raoul Cedras. Aristide's election in December 1990 appeared to end the chaotic transition from the Duvalier regimes that had oppressed Haitians for more than a generation. The transition was far from over, however, as a military coup sent Aristide fleeing into exile.

The Canadian government's reaction was immediate and unequivocal. Prime Minister Mulroney condemned the coup and implied that it should be overturned with force, if necessary. The idea of using force to support democratically elected regimes was a radical departure from past Canadian practice and reflected the extent to which attitudes had changed within the Canadian government towards the principles of non-intervention and state sovereignty. It also demonstrated a new approach to security. Ethical priorities were shifting, and matters of good governance were now being privileged by political leaders such as Mulroney and his foreign minister Barbara MacDougall. The prime minister also sought and received the support of other governments in the region, including the Americans, in opposing the coup. The issue was immediately taken to the OAS. The institution's response to the power struggle in Haiti was governed by the Santiago Commitment to Democracy and the related Resolution 1080 on representative democracy, adopted less than two months earlier. The OAS Permanent Council, with the widespread support of the membership, held an emergency meeting on 30 September 1991. The council convoked a meeting of foreign ministers, which, in rapid succession, condemned the coup, demanded the reinstallation of President Aristide, and moved to isolate the military junta and impose sanctions on Haiti. One observer described this as "undoubtedly the strongest resolution the OAS had adopted against any government."[16] Over the next thirteen months, influenced by both practical and political considerations, the institution's measures to pressure the Haitian regime failed.

On the practical side, the OAS lacked the capacity to enforce its sanctions policy: "The lack of authority on the part of the OAS to compel its members to participate in a trade embargo was one factor in a situation of significant noncompliance with the embargo against Haiti. Equally important is the absence of any authority to require states outside the OAS to join in the embargo."[17] It was also unable to undertake more extensive or intrusive measures as it had no history of peacekeeping or peace enforcement. The political reticence to move in this direction stemmed from a concern that the OAS might become too interventionist in its practices. Once the response to the crisis in Haiti required more coercive measures and a military presence, the OAS backed away from direct involvement. There were strong political inhibitions against extending the institution's mandate into such areas, given the region's historical experiences with US-led interventions. Thus, despite the Santiago Commitment's call for removing nondemocratic governments, there appeared to be little support for applying the coercive measures that would be necessary in the event that diplomatic efforts failed.

In response to the lack of success and limited options, the OAS turned to the UN. The Ad Hoc Meeting of Ministers of Foreign Affairs in December 1992 decided "to mandate the Secretary General of the Organization of American States to go to the extreme within the framework of the Charter to seek a peaceful resolution of the Haitian crisis, and, in conjunction with the Secretary-General of the United Nations, to explore the possibility and advisability of bringing the Haitian situation to the attention of the United Nations Security Council."[18] As Tacsan has noted, the request for support from the UN came at a time when the organization "realized that dialogue could not yield resignation by Cedras and that the type of measures prescribed in Chapter VII of the UN Charter were made necessary." Moreover, he writes that, "by recognizing Aristide as the legitimate president and decreeing an economic, financial, commercial and arms embargo on Haiti, the OAS *permitted* the UN's involvement in what otherwise would be treated as a purely domestic matter"[19] (emphasis added).

The request for UN involvement was widely supported by member governments. This support was particularly important in identifying the strong consensus in the region that something should be done and in confirming that this was not simply a case where the US was defining its own interests as those of the region. This made it easier for governments such as Canada's to press the UN Security Council to take action. By moving the issue to the UN, the Canadian government gained wider support for its objectives and moved the process to a venue in which Canada was more comfortable as well as one which, they assumed, had a greater capacity to intervene should this become necessary. The UN was important in legitimizing this new ethic of intervention and attempting to distinguish the Haiti operation from past interventions by the US. At the same time, by passing the issue to the UN, other governments, such as Mexico and Brazil, could ensure that the OAS did not undertake a military operation or establish any precedents that would encourage future interventions. The UN Security Council's decision to intervene in Haiti also marked an unprecedented commitment on the part of that organization to support democracy and suggested a broadening of its views of permissible interventions: "Arguably, not only was the right to democratic governance confirmed, but, for the first time in history, the existence of this right, rather than geopolitical ambition, provided the main rationale for military intervention, overriding claims of 'sovereignty' and 'domestic jurisdiction.'"[20] The decision illustrated the willingness of the UN Security Council to abandon the principle of non-intervention and implicitly accept the argument that sovereignty was not an inherent right of all states but, rather, one that could be denied to those that did not adhere to certain values and practices. It was a view that was supported by policy makers in Ottawa.

The involvement of the UN did not lead to any dramatic change on the ground. The most notable area of interaction between the two institutions was in the monitoring of human rights violations under the auspices of the OAS/UN International Civilian Mission in Haiti (MICIVIH), which, in February 1993, replaced a comparable OAS mission. The inclusion of UN personnel drawn from Canada and other countries with more extensive experience in human rights monitoring, and the separation of the military peacekeeping and police training activities (managed by the UN) from the monitoring and election supervising activities (managed jointly or by the OAS), was considered by some observers to be a more effective check on the Haitian authorities. The attempt to coordinate the allotment of responsibilities between the OAS and the UN did not, however, prevent a breakdown in the operation.

The crisis dragged on into 1993 before an agreement was brokered between Aristide and General Cedras that would see the former return to Haiti and to power by 30 October 1993. The Governor's Island agreement also guaranteed the military amnesty. The apparent breakthrough soon degenerated into a breakdown. The thirtieth of October passed with the military still firmly in control and Aristide still in exile. The embarrassing and politically significant retreat of the USS *Harlan County* from the harbour of Port-au-Prince in October 1993 sent a message to the Haitian military that neither the UN nor its member governments were willing to use force to restore democracy. Both had been scarred by events in Somalia and were unwilling to assume new risks.

Under these conditions "a hostile demonstration of armed thugs" was the only deterrent needed to prevent an intervention. Within a matter of hours of this retreat, the Canadian prime minister, Kim Campbell, in the midst of an election campaign, withdrew a contingent of Canadian police monitors operating under the UN mandate. The MICIVIH then evacuated its human rights observers. Such actions, while taken to demonstrate the frustration of outside governments with the junta and to protect foreign observers operating in Haiti, posed a more serious risk to those Haitians who were unable to leave and who had come to rely on the protection and support that they had received from the combined UN/OAS mission.

The withdrawal of these observation missions raised concerns about the sustainability of outside commitments to the democratic process in Haiti. It demonstrated a great reluctance to employ even limited amounts of force, and it called into question the credibility of demands for Aristide's return to power. It also indicated a shift on the part of the Canadian government away from former prime minister Mulroney's threat to use force. The Haitian military had effectively secured its position for another year, rid the country of foreign observers, and ensured that, when Aristide was returned to power, he would have precious little time left in his mandate to accomplish anything of significance. Throughout this period it appears that national differences among the "friends of Haiti" were manipulated by the Haitian military to hold onto power and to defer and diminish the effects of outside intervention. The military displayed a willingness to work with conservative elements in the US who, in addition to their concern with furthering American economic interests in the region, were suspicious of both Aristide and the UN. As a result they were willing to seek some sort of accommodation with Cedras and were in no hurry to see Aristide return to power. As discussed below, democracy meant different things to the parties involved. The Canadians, in contrast, were more critical of the regime, more supportive of Aristide, and continued to press for an unconditional guarantee of his return to power.[21] They were, however, unwilling to commit the use of military force to ensure that this would happen and, instead, relied on economic sanctions as the primary tool of persuasion. These divisions over objectives and means (also apparent in such areas as Rwanda [see Adelman, Chapter 10, this volume]) illustrate one of the common problems in multilateral interventions.

The final sequence of events that brought Aristide back to power (the threat of American intervention and the last minute agreement secured by ex-president Jimmy Carter) reveal not the strengthening commitment to good governance in the Clinton administration but, rather, the pressure of other factors – refugees, the Black Congressional caucus, and Clinton's concern for his foreign policy image. They also demonstrate the Canadian government's continued resistance to military intervention, even as it supported the American "right" to do so. In explaining the Canadian position, newly elected prime minister Chrétien said: "We want to maintain the role of Canada as a peacekeeper so when the intervention is over we are in a better position to play a useful role."[22] In refusing to participate in the initial American intervention in September 1994, the Chrétien government indicated its willingness to participate in peacekeeping and peacebuilding exercises under the auspices of the UN. The UN operation, which was established in 1995 and has been sustained in part because of Canada's willingness to absorb the financial costs of its own contribution, completed its two-and-one-half-year mandate in December 1997. It was subsequently replaced by a more limited operation, to which Canada also contributed funds and personnel, that concentrated on what had been identified as the critical task of training the country's police force. The UN operation in Haiti experienced an ongoing set of problems, including uncertain commitments because of the persistent opposition of China (as a result of Haiti's recognition of Taiwan) and strong domestic opposition in the US to anything related to the UN. These had repercussions in areas such as financing, mandate, and personnel questions. Finally, and most important, there have been differences in opinion over the direction that democratic development should take in the country. Outside pressures finally secured the return of Aristide to power, but it was a power that was severely circumscribed. The price was a commitment on Aristide's part to refrain from political activities after his term ended as well as the acceptance of an International Monetary Fund (IMF) plan that undermined Aristide's more radical economic reforms. This solution led Richard Falk to ask: "What kind of democracy is taking place if the program and orientation of the elected leader is being scrapped as a condition for the support of his return?"[23]

Following the return of Aristide to power on 15 October 1994, a presidential election was held in 1995 that resulted in the selection of a new President, René Préval, a candidate more amenable to American views of democracy. Aristide, whose return to power had been delayed until 1994, was, as a result of constitutional limitations, prevented from running in the election. He ended up serving a little more than one year of his five-year term. Since that time Aristide had taken on the role of government critic and had been instrumental in forcing a virtual halt to government operations. As another presidential election approached in 2000, his role became more ambiguous. By spring 2000, the international community had substantially reduced its involvement in Haiti. Conditions in Haiti, however, remained perilous:

> Haiti had no jobs to give its sons and daughters. The government had proved incapable of either reforming or privatizing its corrupt monopolies, foreign investors had stayed away, foreign aid was frozen in escrow. Lavalas had divided like an amoeba. Each cell at the other's throat. The bureaucracy was paralyzed with incompetence, elected officials were strangling on their own greed, and parliamentary elections had been dishonest. Electricity and water were still a lottery you would never win; roads remained impassable, and people were starving. The narcotraffickers were back in business, crime was ubiquitous, the elite families had hired private armies, and an epidemic of assassinations had been orchestrated by – depending on who was raking through the evidence – Aristide, the oligarchic families on the mountaintop, or the CIA. The president was a sullen drunk, and the ex-president, toasted by Anthony Lake at his wedding, had become a husband, a father, a family man who lived in a big house with a swimming pool, separated from the people by the high walls of silence.[24]

All of this had been accomplished under the watchful eye of the UN and the OAS and its contributing member governments, especially the United States and Canada. The situation in Haiti speaks to the problems of Haiti, but it also speaks to the problems of promoting democracy and the profound limitations that confront outsiders who try to bring their own solutions to such complex situations. The full history of the operation to restore Haitian democracy remains to be written. Despite some limited successes, from the vantage point of Canada's good governance and peacebuilding policies, the Haitian experience raises more questions than answers about the ethical and practical grounds for promoting democracy abroad.

In Whose Interests?

The promotion of good governance and human security has become a growth industry. But its growth is most noteworthy within Western governments and the institutions they control. Interventions in the name of democracy, human rights, and human security have been undertaken by these governments against some of the weakest and poorest states in the world. The sovereignty of these states, it is argued, must yield to the higher value of human rights and human security. Authoritarian regimes and practices must be replaced with democratic procedures and institutions. Much of the rationale for such interventions is presented with reference to the values that govern our own liberal democratic societies and the ethical principles enshrined in human rights declarations. Yet human rights and procedural democracy are not the only values being promulgated through these interventions. Without questioning the sincerity of the ethical claims of governments, institutions, and NGOs, it is noteworthy that these interventions are also accompanied by other values and interests. It is, for example, common to find economic conditionalities that privilege free markets accompanying demands for democratic institutions and processes. This was certainly the case in Haiti. According to one report: "Haiti was forced to accept an IMF regimen that required slashing tariffs, laying off state employees and selling the most profitable state-run industries to foreign corporations as the price of Aristide's return and $1.8 billion (US) in loans and grants. Prices for basic commodities like food and fuel have soared, localized famines have occurred and the country's debt has ballooned more than 60 percent since 1994."[25] Just as many of Haiti's poorest were the victims of the economic sanctions imposed against the regime between 1991 and 1994, so too have they been hit hardest by the economic reforms that were instituted in 1994. The value of human security promoted through democratic reforms has been compromised by economic conditionalities that value markets over the state and that often serve to exacerbate gross disparities in wealth.

Outside interventions are also never completely free from material interests. Once again, this is not to deny or to denigrate the presence or significance of ethical principles in such interventions; rather, it is to argue that the unavoidable presence of other material interests interferes with, and may ultimately override, the more humanitarian principles and objectives that inspire interventions. The importance and influence of these competing interests are readily apparent in Haiti, where the economic and political interests of Canada and the United States, alongside the institutional interests of the OAS and the UN, contaminated the more principled motivations and sullied the intervention. It is quite clear that the Americans were as much concerned about refugees washing ashore and drug dealers as they were about the democratic rights of Haitians. The Canadian government, while no doubt genuinely concerned about the plight of Haitians, was also concerned about these and other considerations. As one Liberal MP said: "If we don't continue to help Haiti, we will increasingly have immigrants coming from that country who, because of the great social and economic disparities between their country and ours, will be difficult to integrate into Canada."[26] Canada also had its own economic interests at risk, if not specifically in Haiti, then in the region.[27] The government's support for intervention was also a response to concerns emanating from the Haitian community in Montreal and the perceived need to address these "francophone" interests in the government's foreign policy. The significance of this is aptly illustrated in the comments made by the Canadian ambassador to Haiti, Gilles Bernier, to the House of Commons Standing Committee on Foreign Affairs and International Trade in December 1997. Finally, the government's response was influenced by its ongoing concern with the credibility of its own good governance policy, especially within the context of the initiatives it had undertaken in the OAS in the early 1990s.

It has been argued that, by multilateralizing the decision-making process, one is likely to make the decision more legitimate and less infected by the particular interests of member governments. Walzer has noted this tendency to turn to multilateral associations to secure support for interventions: "Behind this preference is an argument something like Rousseau's argument for the general will: in the course of a democratic decision procedure, Rousseau claimed the particular interests of the different parties will cancel each other out, leaving a general interest untainted by particularity."[28] This was certainly part of the motivation behind the Canadian government's proposal for moving the Haitian issue to the UN. It did not, however, eliminate the political considerations that influence UN decisions, considerations that became more significant as intervention turned from the removal of the generals to democratic development. Unlike its more traditional peacekeeping operations, refurbishing and/or constructing the institutions of government and civil society are much more politically sensitive undertakings for the UN and the OAS. While successive Canadian governments have encouraged such a role, it is questionable whether international institutions are any better suited than national governments for advancing ethical principles. The Haitian experience demonstrates that the institutions are not easily distinguished from the policies of foreign governments and that they tend to be viewed with a similar degree of scepticism.

As intervening governments and institutions attempt to impose particular solutions, they also generate considerable resentment. In Haiti, for example, the effort to establish a secure environment rested, in part, on dismantling the Haitian army and developing an indigenous civilian police force. Problems were compounded by the differing interests of the two principal peacebuilders – the United States and Canada. Effective solutions become more problematic when different national participants in a multinational enterprise do not share the same objectives. As Adelman points out (Chapter 10, this volume), the competing and conflicting objectives and practices of the different agents involved in "humanitarian" operations confound effectiveness, not to mention efficiency. They also fundamentally distort the ethical basis for the intervention.

Canadian officials had pressed the Americans to disarm the Haitian military as part of the original occupation of the country in October 1994, but the Americans refused. The decision not to disarm the country's former army officers or members of the paramilitary descendants of the Tontons Macoutes – FRAPH (Front révolutionnaire pour l'avancement et le progrès en Haiti) – created a considerable amount of insecurity. The newly created 6,000-member Haitian National Police (HNP) force, which the RCMP has been involved in training, has not resolved the problem. Similar differences arose between the Americans and the Canadians in their approach to the HNP force. According to RCMP sergeant Malcolm MacKinnon, the RCMP sought "to train civil police officers, while Americans are training a military style force."[29] The HNP have been unable to eliminate the abuses of the past. According to a report made in spring 1997: "Human rights violations are rampant and include executions, torture and intimidation by the very police the Mounties are supposed to be training."[30] The UN missions in Haiti have been unable to avoid being affected by these practices as the interests of their contributing governments colour all aspects of the operation. In an analysis of UN involvement in Haiti and the degree of opposition within the organization, Morris has identified a number of these problems: "Irrespective of the existence of Security Council authorization, intervention in circumstances such as these does little to allay the fears of less powerful members of the international community that talk of a new international order and an agenda promoting human and political rights is little more than a sham."[31]

Whither Civil Society?

One of the primary objectives in Canada's promotion of good governance and in its human security initiatives has been to empower civil society in these countries to play a more constructive role in the process of democratization. Not surprisingly, however, Canadians' approach to good governance has been strongly conditioned by our liberal democratic values. It is difficult to avoid transferring one's own values and experiences to other settings, but they may not be the best solution: "To cling to the notion of traditional parliamentary democracy as one's political ideal and to succumb to the illusion that only this 'tried and true' form is capable of guaranteeing human beings enduring dignity and an independent role in society would, in my opinion, be at the very least shortsighted."[32] Similar influences guided UN missions in Haiti as much of the work of the interveners was designed to support institutions of policing, justice, public administration, and electoral democracy. Drawing from her review of the UN's missions in Haiti, Zanotti concludes that "the primary focus of the international operation on institutional reforms as opposed to civil society's participation and social and economic development may help to explain some shortfalls of the process promoted by the international community, and the disillusion of the Haitians with 'democratization.'"[33] As an American reporter noted in 1999, "Haitians will participate in elections only if they feel their vote counts, and recent Haitian history has done little to reinforce that notion. No amount of foreign aid, no quantity of foreign troops or international observers will bring people to the polls if they don't have concrete examples of what can be accomplished by competent, honest leaders working for the benefit of the country."[34] Thus despite nearly a decade of foreign intervention very little has changed for many Haitians. Perhaps for this reason, Haitians developed a considerable animosity towards the intervention, as is reflected in numerous demonstrations and strikes. The Haitian legislature, despite UN lobbying, even passed a law banning foreign troops from the country.[35]

There is the related possibility that, whether through action or inaction, outside intervention may impede the development of indigenous social movements. Michael-Rolph Truillot has argued that the first American intervention in Haiti, between 1915 and 1934, "left the country with two poisoned gifts: a weaker civil society and a solidified state apparatus."[36] As Zanotti has argued, many aspects of the current intervention seem likely to replicate this condition. And this is so despite the fact that Canada, for one, has emphasized programs designed to support civil society initiatives. Much of the emphasis to date, however, has been on politics, law, and administration. Yet, as Trouillot has written: "The deepest roots of Haiti's problems are not in the country's politics. Institutional reform will not erase them ... The moral turpitude of the elites is real, but its roots are in the socio-economic organization of the country. The deepest roots of Haiti's political problems lie in social inequality and economic maldistribution."[37] Many of these issues have not been addressed in this intervention. Once again many elements of civil society have been excluded and left to fend for themselves as the apparatus of the state is reconstructed. The nature of the intervention, dominated as it is by international and national civil servants and by military and police forces, makes it difficult for the voices of local actors to be heard or to have much influence over the course of events.

Staying the Course and Paying the Price

While outside governments and organizations are willing to assume responsibility for resolving the problems of others, they often lack the ability to sustain their commitment for the time needed to bring about effective change. A number of factors contribute to this problem. Changes in government and governmental personnel and budgetary considerations are most important and influence the size and sustainability of the commitment. During Canada's decade-long involvement in Haiti, there have been three prime ministers, each of whom took a different view of that country. Prime Minister Mulroney adopted the most assertive approach to intervention, whereas his successors, Kim Campbell and Jean Chrétien, took a more cautious approach. Each of them retained some level of commitment, but the focus has shifted from more forceful measures to peacekeeping, to police training, and now to long-term and indirect support through development assistance programs. On the financial side, democratic development has not been cheap. The Canadian government has spent in excess of $400 million dollars on Haiti over the past decade, and the US has spent more than $2 billion. While such figures are not, in themselves, excessive, they do begin to indicate the ongoing costs involved in this process. When considered in light of the ongoing problems confronting Haiti, and the fact that much more remains to be done in the critically important area of poverty elimination, the lack of adequate financial resources becomes an important limitation – one that must be taken into account.

The ability of international organizations to persist in their commitment to democratic development is compounded by the need to maintain the continued support of their member governments, many of whom get tired of paying the bills or want to move on to other causes. The result is too often a series of short-term mandates with uncertain prospects for renewal, along with a series of uncoordinated missions. The Haitian case provides an illustration of these unfortunate practices as five different UN operations (including one joint operation with the OAS), most working on six-to twelve-month commitments and experiencing unpaid contributions, have sought to guarantee human rights and to construct effective institutions of justice and government. These are hardly the types of commitment that are going to instill confidence in local populations. Julian Harston has noted that "the frequent rotation of nearly two-thirds of the civilian police element, in accordance with the regulations of some contributing countries had a negative impact on training and continuity; and second, the short renewals of the mandate of UNSMIH (UN Support Mission in Haiti) created uncertainty within the HNP and the Mission."[38] It is difficult to rely on support when it is not certain that it will be there when you need it most. When outsiders go home, the locals often suffer the consequences. As the head of the UN mission was reported to have said as he left the country in December 1997: "Democracy has not been able to deliver the goods – and that's a dangerous situation."[39] Or, as Henri, the hotel proprietor, was quoted as saying of his fellow Haitians: "They know the white is coming and he is leaving. All they have to do is wait."[40] Haiti, like many of the countries subjected to these exercises, has experienced occupation in the past, and the long-term results have not been encouraging.

Conclusion

As the experience in Haiti demonstrates, finding a balance between the ethics of responsibility and the ethics of commitment exposes a dilemma that is inherent in efforts to promote democratic development. If Canadians want to get into the business of, in the words of Teddy Roosevelt, "[protecting] countries from the consequences of their own misdeeds," then we had best be prepared to stay the course while accepting the limitations of our actions. Yet these very limitations make it exceedingly difficult to justify and sustain our involvement. When the situation on the ground fails to respond to outside interventions, we will and must critically examine the role of outsiders and their ability to contribute to a solution. We should start by recognizing that sustainable democratic development rooted in local capacities and practices cannot be established when outsiders adopt competing and conflicting approaches that threaten to impede, if not to stifle, local alternatives. Consensus, coordination, capabilities, and conviction are all essential prerequisites to carrying out an effective ethically informed intervention. The record is not promising. Canadians must also recognize that, despite their ethical motivations, material interests – their own and others – will infect the intervention and influence both the practice and the outcome. Whether the inevitable interference of these interests is enough to make interventions counterproductive can only be assessed on a case-by-case basis. Yet to turn our back provides a decidedly unsatisfactory answer. When confronted with media images of violence and chaos in foreign countries, our values, not to mention other more material interests, are challenged and we are uncomfortable in adopting the cynical response of turning our backs on the sufferings of others. It is a response that is increasingly unacceptable to governments and their public. Yet, in adopting an "ethic of responsibility," we assume that we have a solution and the capacity and commitment to effectively implement it. As international organizations and national governments back away from Haiti, leaving the country with a very uncertain future, a thorough reflection on both assumptions seems a necessary prerequisite before championing a crusade for democracy.

Acknowledgment

Research for this chapter has been supported by a grant from the Social Sciences and Humanities Research Council of Canada (Grant No. 410 971628). The author would like to thank Francis Kofi Abiew, Aaron Maltais, and Patience Akpan for their assistance in the research for this chapter.

Notes

1 Michael Ignatieff, "The Seductiveness of Moral Disgust," *Social Research* 62 (Spring 1995): 84.
2 Canada, Office of the Prime Minister, *Notes for an Address on the Occasion of the Centennial Anniversary Convocation,* Stanford University, 29 September 1991.

3 Barbara McDougall, "Canada and Russia – Managing Change," Department of External Affairs and International Trade, *Statement No. 93/6,* 4 February 1993.
4 An illustration of aspects of the policy can be found in *Promoting Respect for Human Rights, Sustaining Democratic Development and Fostering Good Governance through the Development Assistance Programme* (Ottawa: Canadian International Development Agency, 1992).
5 Government of Canada, *Canada in the World* (Ottawa: Government of Canada, 1995), 11.
6 David Gillies, *Between Principle and Practice: Human Rights in North-South Relations* (Montreal and Kingston: McGill-Queen's University Press, 1996), 22.
7 See, for example, the final report of the 1982 Parliamentary Committee on Canada's relations in the region. Canada, House of Commons, Standing Committee on External Affairs and National Defence, *Canada's Relations with Latin America and the Caribbean* (Ottawa: Queen's Printer, 1982).
8 For a discussion of Canadian policy in the OAS see, among others, Jean Daudelin, "The Politics of Oligarchy: 'Democracy' and Canada's Recent Conversion to Latin America," in *Democracy and Foreign Policy,* ed. Maxwell Cameron and Maureen Appel Molot (Ottawa: Carleton University Press, 1995), 145-62; Edgar J. Dosman, "Canada and Latin America: The New Look," *International Journal* 47 (1992): 529-54; Tom Farer, *Collectively Defending Democracy in a World of Sovereign States: The Western Hemisphere's Prospect* (Montreal: International Centre for Human Rights and Democratic Development, 1993).
9 David MacKenzie, "Canada in the Organization of American States: The First Five Years," *Behind the Headlines* 52, 1 (1994): 5.
10 For a more detailed discussion of these measures and their implications, see Farer, *Collectively Defending Democracy.*
11 Andrew Hurrell, "Latin America in the New World Order: A Regional Bloc of the Americas?" *International Affairs* 68 (1992): 135.
12 The Santiago Commitment to Democracy and the Renewal of the Inter-American System, Twenty-First Regular Session, General Assembly, Organization of American States, 3 June 1991, AG/DOC. 2734/91.
13 Thomas W. Lippman, "OAS Charter Shuns Coup-Based States," *Manchester Guardian Weekly,* 5 October 1997, 16.
14 In a telling comment, Venezuelan foreign minister Miguel Angel Burelli Rivas was quoted as saying: "There is a revolution in the Americas. We have achieved political democracy. Now we must make certain it reaches the minds and souls of our people." This was not a grassroots revolution. Cited in Ibid.
15 A good account of Canadian policy can be found in Peter McKenna, "Canada and the Haitian Crisis," *Journal of Canadian Studies* 32 (1997): 77-98.
16 Domingo E. Alcevedo, "The Haitian Crisis and the OAS Response," in *Enforcing Restraint: Collective Intervention in Internal Conflicts,* ed. Lori Fisler Damrosch (New York: Council on Foreign Relations, 1995), 132.
17 Ibid., 136.
18 OAS Resolution 4/92, cited in Joaquin Tascan, "Searching for OAS/UN Task-Sharing Opportunities in Central America and Haiti," in *Beyond UN Subcontracting,* ed. Thomas G. Weiss (New York: St. Martin's, 1998), 91-114.
19 Ibid., 103.
20 Richard Falk, "The Haiti Intervention: A Dangerous World Order Precedent for the United Nations," *Harvard International Law Journal* 36, 2 (1995): 44.
21 A good discussion of these events can be found in Ian Martin, "Haiti: Mangled Multilateralism," *Foreign Policy* 95 (1994): 72-89. See also Richard L. Millett, "Panama and Haiti," in *U.S. And Russian Policy Making with Respect to the Use of Force,* ed. Jeremy R. Azrael and Emil A. Payin (Santa Monica, CA: Rand Corporation, 1996). Available at <http://www.rand.org/publications/CF/CF129/CF-129.chapter9.html/>.
22 Quoted in *Toronto Sun,* 14 August 1994.
23 Falk, "Haiti Intervention," 353.
24 Bob Shacochis, *The Immaculate Invasion* (New York: Viking, 1999), 393.
25 Dan Coughlin, "Haitian Lament: Killing Me Softly," *Nation,* 1 March 1999, 20.
26 Raymonde Folco, Liberal Member of Parlaiment from Laval West to the House of Commons

Standing Committee on Foreign Affairs and International Trade, 11 December 1997. <www.parl.gc.ca/InfoComDoc/36/1/FAIT/Meetings/Minutes/FAITMN21-E.htm>.

27 See, for example, the comments in "RIP: The Great Canadian Refugee Rescue Mission," *Financial Post,* 14-16 December 1996, 57.

28 Michael Walzer, "The Politics of Rescue," *Dissent* 42 (Winter 1995): 39.

29 Ibid.

30 Linda Diebel, "Haiti: Canada's Mission Impossible," *Ottawa Citizen,* 23 February 1997, D8. See also Amnesty International, *Haiti: Still Crying Out for Justice,* Amnesty International Report, July 1998. Available at <www.web.amnesty.org/ai.nsf/index/AMR360021998>.

31 Justin Morris, "Force and Democracy: UN/US Intervention in Haiti," *International Peacekeeping* 2, 3 (1995): 406.

32 Václav Havel, "The Power of the Powerless," in *Open Letters: Selected Writings 1965-1990* (New York: Vintage Books, 1992), 209.

33 Laura Zanotti, "Bringing about Democracy through Oeacekeeping: The United Nation's Definition of Its Task in Haiti," paper prepared for presentation at the 1999 Annual Meeting of the Academic Council of the United Nations System, United Nations, New York, 16-18 June 1999, 17.

34 Kathie Klarreich, "Time for Haitians to Fix Haiti," *Christian Science Monitor,* 29 December 1999, 9.

35 See accounts in Coughlin, "Haitian Lament"; and Linda Diebel, "Tough Times in a Haitian Slum," *Toronto Star,* 26 September 1999.

36 Cited in Noam Chomsky, "Democracy Enhancement, Part II: The Case of Haiti," *Z Magazine,* July-August 1994.

37 Michel Rolph Trouillot, cited in Zanotti, "Bringing about Democracy," 17.

38 Julian Harston, "The Civilian Police Element in United Nations Peacekeeping: The Case of Haiti," in *Adapting the United Nations to a Post Modern Era: Lessons Learned,* ed. W. Andy Knight (Basingstoke, Hampshire, UK: Macmillan Press, 2001).

39 Andrew Phillips, "Canada's Troops Head Home," *Maclean's,* 8 December 1997, 46.

40 Cited in Shacochis, *Immaculate Invasion,* 292.

Part 6
The Ethics of Energy and Natural Resource Security: Fishing and Nuclear Policy

12
The Ethics of CANDU Exports

Duane Bratt

This volume addresses two essential, but interrelated, themes. The first is the relationship/linkage between ethics and security in Canadian foreign policy. Some of the other authors in this book (i.e., Nef and Penz) assess this relationship in an abstract, philosophical fashion. This chapter, on the other hand, examines a specific issue area: the export of the Canadian Deuterium Uranium (CANDU) nuclear reactor. This case study approach is useful because, at its very essence, foreign policy decision making is the act of choosing between competing objectives. These objectives are the values of a society. Since states have a multitude of interests and values – some tangible, others intangible – it is analytically useful to divide them into categories. This chapter divides Canada's foreign policy objectives into four broad categories: (1) economics (increases in Canada's gross domestic product, employment, standard of living, etc.); (2) politics (Canada's ties with other countries); (3) security (the protection of Canada's territorial borders, ensuring global peace and security); and (4) ethics. The second theme of this chapter involves an examination of human security as a Canadian foreign policy objective. This chapter contributes to the discussion of human security by focusing on its policy-making dimension, which will be assessed from both a historical and contemporary perspective.

Ethical considerations are the hardest of Canada's foreign policy objectives to determine. Ethics can be divided into two large groupings: normative and descriptive. Normative ethics is naturally derived and supported through philosophical justifications, while descriptive ethics is positivist and is supported by identifying those values that are actually held. This chapter makes use of descriptive ethics in examining two phenomena – sales to human rights violators and the environmental consequences of nuclear power – that have been prominent in the debate over Canada's export of nuclear reactors.[1] These issues can be ascertained by examining governmental policy statements, critiques from the anti-nuclear movement, and the academic literature. The formulation of ethics, then, is based solely on the case that is being studied. This means that the ethical considerations pertaining to nuclear technology may very well be different from those pertaining to the issues of development assistance or the creation of an international criminal court. Descriptive ethics – even those broadly similar – will vary across cases (as may be seen by comparing this chapter with Peter Stoett's chapter on the Turbot war [Chapter 13, this volume]).

This chapter seeks to answer the question: What has been, and what will be, the role of ethical considerations – as opposed to security, economic, or political considerations – with regard to CANDU exports? I have chosen to focus on nuclear exports because the CANDU has been an important component of Canada's foreign policy. This can be illustrated in a variety of ways. The building and maintenance of nuclear reactors constitutes a large-scale industrial project between, at a minimum, two countries. It costs billions of dollars and employs tens of thousands of people over a multi-year timeline. There is also substantial governmental involvement in the nuclear trade at both the supplier and the recipient end. With the exception of the US firms of Westinghouse and General Electric (GE), most nuclear suppliers, like Atomic Energy of Canada Limited (AECL) (which designs and oversees the construction of the CANDU), are government-owned. In addition, and even when the firms are privately owned, politicians and bureaucrats try to help secure reactor exports. In the Canadian case, prime ministers from Louis St. Laurent to Jean Chrétien, with ample support from bureaucrats in the Department of Foreign Affairs and International Trade (DFAIT) and Natural Resources Canada (NRCan), have tried, with varying degrees of success, to flog CANDUs.[2]

In addition to the above characteristics, which the international nuclear trade shares with all multinational industrial megaprojects (like dams or airports), the export of nuclear technology and materials also presents a series of unique challenges. First, successive governments have considered the CANDU to be "Canada's last and/or best chance for developing and maintaining a high-technology-based and internationally competitive and respected industry."[3] The prestige of nuclear power has meant that the CANDU has assumed an important place, one that extends beyond simple monetary value, in Canada's international trade. It also helps to explain why successive senior Canadian politicians have been so willing to expend so much political capital in trying to sell CANDUs abroad. For example, Jean Chrétien, both as prime minister and as former energy minister, "was a great booster of nuclear enterprise both at home and abroad."[4] Second, there is an inevitable connection between nuclear power and nuclear weapons. This has meant that there is considerable overlap between, on the one hand, Canada's efforts at creating and maintaining an international nuclear non-proliferation regime, and, on the other, its concurrent efforts at exporting the CANDU. It is because of this security risk that there are numerous international institutions and treaties, like the International Atomic Energy Agency (IAEA) and the Nuclear Non-Proliferation Treaty (NPT), with responsibility for the nuclear trade. Finally, the potential of an environmental catastrophe is an unfortunate by-product of nuclear power.

This chapter is divided into five parts. Parts 1 and 2 describe the economic and political arguments that have been used to justify the foreign sales of CANDUs. Parts 3 and 4 identify the competing security and ethical issues surrounding CANDU exports. The experience of previous CANDU sales (see Table 12.1) will be used to illustrate each of these foreign policy objectives. In general, economic and political arguments have facilitated CANDU exports, and security and ethical issues have constrained them; however, there have been several instances in the past when the opposite occurred. Part 5 assesses how the clash between economics, politics, security, and ethical considerations may be resolved in future CANDU exports.

Economics

Canada achieves enormous economic benefits from CANDU exports. These benefits include: an immediate increase in balance of trade; the continued employment of over 30,000 Canadians; an increased capacity to break into new markets with a high value-added manufactured product; the subsidization of the domestic nuclear market due to economies of scale; and technological spin-offs from nuclear research.[5]

Table 12.1

Canada's nuclear reactor exports

Country	Ordered	On-line
India (CIRUS – research reactor)	1956	1960
India (RAPP I)	1963	1973
Pakistan (KANUPP)	1965	1972
India (RAPP II)	1966	1981
Taiwan (TRR – research reactor)	1969	1971
Argentina (Embalse)	1973	1984
South Korea (Wolsung I)	1973	1983
Romania (Cernavoda I)	1978	1996
Romania (Cernavoda II)	1982	Under construction
South Korea (Wolsung II)	1990	1997
South Korea (Wolsung III)	1992	1998
South Korea (Wolsung IV)	1992	1999
China (Qinshan I)	1996	Under construction
China (Qinshan II)	1996	Under construction

Stark consequences would arise if Canada failed to obtain sufficient CANDU exports. Initially, Canada would move back down the nuclear learning curve. If this sales drought continued, then the result would be the collapse of the Canadian nuclear industry. This would likely result in higher energy costs, a less self-sufficient energy supply, a massive "brain-drain" of nuclear engineers and scientists, and the psychological blow of losing another high-tech industry.

The combination of the significant economic benefits that accompany nuclear reactor exports and the huge costs of insufficient exports has resulted in intense competition among the world's nuclear supplier states (Canada, France, Germany, and the United States). Canada is especially vulnerable to competition because it is unique among suppliers in that its nuclear technology is based on heavy rather than on light water. Also heightening this competition is the fact that the available market for nuclear reactors is quite small. This is because most developing countries do not possess the necessary technological infrastructure to justify their acquisition of nuclear power, and no country with an indigenous nuclear industry will import reactors. This means that the nuclear market is largely limited to newly industrialized countries (i.e., Argentina, South Korea, Indonesia, Egypt, Turkey, etc.).

The history of CANDU exports shows that Ottawa's decision-making process was guided by the presumed economic benefits of the sale of nuclear technology.[6] However, there has been growing criticism that there are, in fact, little economic benefits to Canada's nuclear program. In fact, it becomes obvious that the entire Canadian nuclear industry has been heavily subsidized. There are several ways that CANDU exports benefit from government subsidies. First, the federal government has supported the research and development efforts of AECL. From 1952 to 1997, the federal government provided AECL with over $4.3 billion in research and development (R&D) subsidies.[7] Second, it has provided grants and loans that have been used to help finance specific CANDU exports (see Table 12.2). With regard to some loans pertaining to CANDU exports, like the $1.5 billion loan to secure the sale to China, the Export Development Corporation (EDC) must place the loan on its "Canada Account."[8] The Canada Account, which is carried on the Department of Foreign Affairs and International Trade's (DFAIT's) books, is used by the EDC when the loan is extremely large and/or when there is an extreme risk to the project. In addition, as Peter Berg has noted, "Canadian taxpayers have also supported prototype and commercial reactors, heavy water plants, the high costs of regulating the industry, and the exemption of provincial utilities from federal income taxation."[9] Finally, Martin and Argue have asserted that the full extent to which the Canadian nuclear industry has been subsidized can only be

Table 12.2

Federal financing of nuclear reactor exports (in $ million)

Country	Grants	Loans (CIDA/EDC)
India (CIRUS)	9.5	0
India (RAPP I-II)	0	33.5
Pakistan (KANUPP)	0	47.2
Taiwan (TRR)	0	0
Argentina (Embalse)	0	200
South Korea (Wolsung I)	0	560
Romania (Cernavoda I-II)	0	2178.3
South Korea (Wolsung II-IV)	0	0
China (Qinshan I-II)	0	1500

Source: The figures for India and Pakistan were compiled from data in Canada, Department of Energy, Mines and Resources, *Nuclear Policy Review: Background Papers* (Ottawa: EMR, 1981), 314. For Argentina, South Korea, and Romania the data are from Export Development Corporation, *Annual Reports* (1974-79). Additional information on Romania was acquired from Canada, *News Release No. 199,* 17 September 1991. For China, the data are from Canada, Natural Resources Canada, *Speech* 96/116, 26 November 1996.

assessed by calculating its opportunity costs, which they have determined to be at least $73 billion since 1952.[10]

One controversial aspect of the use of Canadian subsidies to secure CANDU exports has been the incidence of bribery. There was a great scandal in the mid-1970s over AECL's use of sales agents. For example, an AECL sales agent named Shaul Eisinberg paid over $20 million worth of bribes to high-level nuclear officials in order to help secure CANDU sales in South Korea and Argentina.[11] Unfortunately, corruption in CANDU exports did not end in the 1970s. In 1994, a bribery scandal involving the Korean Electric Power Corporation and AECL's Korean agency, Samchang Corporation, resulted in the incarceration of several senior officials from both companies.[12]

Politics

Foreign sales of CANDUs have been concluded as much for political reasons as for economic ones. The first of these foreign policy goals involved assisting the economic and political development of Third World states. Canada believed that the peaceful benefits of nuclear power should be at the disposal of all states. Former prime minister Pierre Trudeau asserted that "it would be unconscionable under any circumstances to deny to the developing countries ... the advantages of the nuclear age."[13] "The basic argument," as articulated by J.G. Hadwen, a former senior official with external affairs, "was that Canada, during the war period, had developed considerable expertise in the generation of electricity by nuclear processes.

We believed that Canadian technology was the most efficient of the nuclear technologies available. We thought of it as the safest of alternatives and as the one best suited to peaceful generation of electricity."[14] Canada's commonwealth partners in India and Pakistan would be the primary recipients of Canadian nuclear assistance.

The second major foreign policy goal was anti-communism. Throughout the Cold War, a central pillar of Canadian foreign policy was preventing the spread of communism. Canada implemented this policy in many well known ways: joining Western defence alliances like NATO and NORAD, fighting the Korean War, and generally maintaining only limited relations with either the Soviet bloc or communist China. With regard to the international nuclear trade, for two main reasons Canada did not wish to see countries going to the Soviet Union to supply their nuclear needs: (1) a reactor sale meant a long-term partnership between supplier and recipient, and Canada did not want to see stronger economic relations emerge between the USSR and other states, especially vulnerable Third World countries; and (2) given the potential military application of nuclear power, there was the fear that reactor exports would be the first step in a military alliance between the USSR and the recipient state.

Canada's interest in containing communism during the Cold War could be seen through its efforts on the Indian subcontinent. In the case of India, Canadian officials rationalized that it woud be better if India acquired "nuclear expertise and facilities through cooperation with countries like Canada than as a result of assistance from the Soviet Union."[15] Nuclear exports to Pakistan were also encouraged because it was a firm member of the Western alliance and played a strategic role in the containment of communism in Asia. There were two other instances of Cold War politics that had a role in Canada's nuclear reactor export program. The first was the decision to terminate all nuclear cooperation with Taiwan following the diplomatic recognition of the People's Republic of China (PRC) and the second was the use of CANDU sales to Romania in 1978 as a way of reducing East-West tensions, and, paradoxically, of encouraging Romania's emergence as an independent communist country.[16]

Security

A prominent feature of Canada's multilateral efforts in international security is in the area of arms control. Ottawa's leadership in securing the signing of an anti-personnel landmines treaty (see Andrew Latham, Chapter 9, this volume) is only the most recent example. Given Canada's stated commitment to arms control, it is no surprise that Ottawa has a significant interest in ensuring that its CANDU exports are not used to develop nuclear weapons. For this reason, Ottawa's nuclear policy is designed (1) to promote the evolution of a more effective and comprehensive international non-proliferation regime and (2) to ensure that Canada's nuclear exports do not contribute to nuclear proliferation.[17]

The major means by which proliferation can be prevented, or at least slowed down, is through the application of stringent nuclear safeguards. Safeguards are "the regulations and restraints that a nuclear supplier country imposes on its exports of nuclear materials and equipment."[18] In particular, nuclear safeguards "have the potential to slow the progress of a country determined to develop a nuclear weapon capability, and this delay may provide sufficient time for security issues to be adequately addressed, for a change of leadership to occur, for a negotiated end to the programme to be reached or for the decision to be reversed for some other reason."[19]

Prior to 1974, Canada's economic and political arguments heavily outweighed any security considerations that it may have had over nuclear proliferation. For example, the only safeguard on Canada's first export – the CIRUS research reactor, which was sent to India in 1956 – was a simple clause stating that the reactor was for "peaceful purposes only." Subsequent nuclear reactor exports during this period contained more stringent safeguards, but significant gaps still existed. In particular, the refusal of India and Pakistan to sign the non-proliferation treaty (NPT) meant that, throughout its entire nuclear program, the safeguards contained in the treaty were not applied uniformly. Canada's lack of concern with nuclear proliferation would come back to haunt it when, in 1974, India, utilizing Canadian nuclear technology and fuel, exploded a nuclear device. This event deeply traumatized Ottawa and led to two years of significantly strengthening its nuclear safeguards policy. This process culminated in 1976, when Canada announced that, henceforth, reactor sales would be restricted to states that had ratified the NPT or that would accept safeguards on their entire nuclear programs.[20] In implementing this policy, Canada unilaterally terminated nuclear assistance to India and Pakistan, renegotiated nuclear safeguards agreements with South Korea and Argentina, and suspended uranium shipments to Japan and the European Community. The fact that Canada suffered a definite commercial price for its new stand on nuclear proliferation illustrates the impact that the Indian nuclear explosion had on its security concerns about nuclear proliferation.[21]

In addition to the application of full-scope nuclear safeguards, Ottawa needs to take into account the implication of sales within the context of regional conflicts. Because nuclear reactors will always possess the technological capability of enabling a state to develop nuclear weapons, the Canadian government is concerned about allowing reactors into geographic areas that are unstable. The Canadian government's 1982 *Nuclear Policy Review* acknowledged the importance of this factor: "Apart from specific safeguards requirements, Canada makes political and economic assessments of potential reactor customers and discourages sales to countries which may be subject to domestic or external instabilities or security threats."[22] Unfortunately, the history of CANDU exports reveals that each recipient of Canadian nuclear technology has been in the midst of a regional conflict: India versus Pakistan, Taiwan versus China, Argentina versus Brazil, and South Korea versus North Korea.

Ethical Considerations

Human Rights

The issue of human rights has been raised by many of the authors in this volume: In Chapter 2 Jorge Nef asserts that security can only be created through adherence to a human rights framework; in Chapter 7 W. Andy Knight looks at Canada's efforts to establish a permanent international criminal court; and in Chapter 5 Heather Smith argues that economic trade issues hinder the promotion of international standards of human rights. In this section I examine the general issue of the apparent incompatibility between human rights and trade that Smith describes, but I concentrate specifically on CANDU exports.

What are the problems with exporting nuclear reactors to human rights violators? A CANDU transaction requires a long-term relationship. Does Canada want close economic and political ties with states that abuse their own people? Moreover, regimes that have very poor human rights records also tend to be quite unstable. Politically unstable nations often seek quick, and radical, change in the components and character of their regimes, usually through coups d'état but sometimes through revolution. Political instability means that, in a long-term relationship such as that entailed by a nuclear reactor transaction, it is almost impossible to maintain continuity of political responsibility and accountability. Canada's principal tool for preventing nuclear proliferation has been its safeguards agreements, which require a certain level of trustworthiness between the parties to any transaction. Can a regime that violates its own domestic social contract by subjecting its citizens to human rights atrocities be trusted to adhere to its international responsibilities? Finally, by helping a human rights violator, through the provision of greater energy resources produced by nuclear reactors, Ottawa may be providing the regime with increased means of state repression. In other words, Canada may actually be increasing the scale and scope of human rights abuses by exporting CANDUs to the offending state.

In examining past CANDU exports, it is apparent that the role of human rights concerns was negligible. Almost every regime that has purchased a CANDU was, at the time, a military dictatorship with a poor human rights record: Pakistan, Taiwan, South Korea, Argentina, Romania, and China. Canada may have been willing to censure these countries in international fora, but it would not refrain from selling them CANDUs. In fact, the Romanians even used forced labour to build its CANDUs.[23] A typical example of Canada's policy of exporting CANDUs to human rights abusers is its 1996 sale to China. China is a well known human rights abuser, with its most infamous atrocity occurring in June 1989 with the Tiananmen Square massacre. China's human rights record has led to calls for Canada to cut all economic ties to that country, never mind providing it with nuclear materials. However, Canada's current position is that international trade, as exemplified by CANDU exports, can be used as a mechanism to improve China's human rights record. The Canadian secretary of state (Asia-Pacific), Raymond Chan, noted in a speech that "trade is also a powerful tool. It encourages co-operation, and co-operation leads to understanding and appreciation, with which we can better manage concerns such as human rights development."[24] A more convincing – if, to many Canadians, unacceptable – explanation of why Canada was willing to export CANDUs to a major human rights violator involves Canada's interest in using the CANDU to gain access to the huge Chinese market. In fact, the signing of a nuclear cooperation agreement with China, and the subsequent sale of two CANDUs in 1996, was a major objective of the 1994 "Team Canada" trade summit to Beijing.

In only one case – the negotiations to sell the Atucha 2 reactor to Argentina in 1979 – has the issue of human rights been an important consideration. Following its 1976 coup, the Argentine military junta cracked down on left wing groups, using such methods as arrests, torture, killings, and, perhaps most insidious of all, "disappearances." For the first time there was, on the basis of human rights, significant domestic opposition to Canada's nuclear export policy. A lobby group – No CANDU for Argentina – was formed, which advertised the fact that "Canada is selling a potential weapon of mass destruction to a regime that represses, tortures, and murders its own citizens."[25] As a result of this domestic opposition, Ottawa decided that, while it needed to obtain the contract for Atucha 2 because of economic necessity, it would put conditions on the sale, even if this meant jeopardizing the sale by upsetting Argentina.[26] One of those conditions was supplied by External Affairs Minister Flora MacDonald, who was personally appalled by Argentina's atrocious human rights records, when she publicly singled out Argentina as a human rights abuser in her first UN address.[27] MacDonald's intervention, which occurred days before Buenos Aires planned on announcing the winning bid for Atucha 2, contributed to AECL losing the contract despite having the least expensive bid. Nevertheless, the Argentine case is the exception that proves the rule: the human rights record of recipient states has not deterred CANDU exports.

Environment

Environmental protection has only recently come to the surface as an issue in Canadian foreign policy. A common dilemma for all governments, including Canada's, is what to do when protection of the environment has an adverse effect on economic growth. For example, Peter Stoett, in examining the 1995 Turbot dispute (Chapter 13, this volume), looks at how global environmental policy can be obtained within the context of economic self-interest and resource scarcity caused by environmental degradation. In this section I assess the extent to which Canada's export of CANDUs has been constrained by the potential environmental consequences of nuclear power.

In a 1975 speech to the Canadian Nuclear Association, Prime Minister Pierre Trudeau reminded the industry that it had an obligation to provide "safe sources of energy" and to "preserve the environment." This must be done through all of the stages of nuclear power "exploration, mining, processing, fabrication, design, and sales."[28] Presumably, this commitment to domestic nuclear safety and environmental protection should have an important influence on Canada's export policies.

The safety of the reactors poses the biggest environmental threat. The most common potential reactor accident involves a loss of coolant, but the more serious safety issue involves the potential for a core meltdown. The most infamous core meltdown occurred at Chernobyl, Ukraine, in 1986, when hundreds were immediately killed and thousands will likely die as a result of cancer, the contamination of the food chain, an increase in all types of infectious diseases, and increased radiation levels. Equally dangerous potential environmental concerns include: (1) the extent to which the public is exposed to the tritium radiation that is emitted from CANDUs, (2) the safe disposal of vast amounts of radioactive nuclear waste (which has a half-life of several hundred years), and (3) the decommissioning of old nuclear reactors.

Environmental concerns have, on the whole, been largely non-existent when decisions on CANDU exports have been made. This was best illustrated when Ottawa waived the requirements for an environmental impact study for the CANDUs being built in China.[29] International Trade Minister Art Eggleton maintained that "the act was never intended to apply to the Export Development Corporation's commercial financing operations in foreign countries."[30] However, a more likely reason, as revealed in briefing notes prepared for Cabinet by DFAIT, was the belief that requiring environmental assessments would put Canada at a great disadvantage with regard to other nuclear suppliers.[31]

In addition to constraining CANDU exports, however, environmental considerations sometimes facilitate them. For example, in 1991, Canada decided to renew nuclear assistance to Romania by providing a $315 million

Export Development Corporation (EDC) loan. This decision was justified, in part, by Canada's fear that, if it left the reactors half-built, then Romania might attempt to finish them on its own, and do so in a substandard manner, thereby creating environmental risks. Romanian nuclear engineers at Cernavoda have since remarked that, in the years just prior to the 1989 revolution, "a lot of work was performed without being checked in an appropriate way."[32] By continuing with the project, Canada could help ensure that Cernavoda reactors remained safe. Indeed, once the renewed commitment was made, "the Canadian technical advisory team on-site strictly supervised completion of repair work to piping wielding: which had previously been done by the Romanians, evidence of the safety advantages stemming from Canada's continuing cooperation."[33]

The Future of CANDU Exports

What effect will ethical considerations like human rights and environmental protection have on future CANDU exports? The historical record has shown that ethical considerations have been quite marginal when matched up against Canada's economic and political interests. Only security concerns via the threat of nuclear proliferation have had sufficient weight to restrict CANDU exports. This section assesses the impact that three recent events may have on the future of CANDU exports: (1) the 1997 decision of the largest domestic CANDU customer, Ontario Hydro, to temporarily shut down seven of its nineteen reactors, (2) the nuclear tests conducted by India and Pakistan in May and June 1998, and (3) AECL's unsuccessful effort to sell two CANDUs to Turkey in the late 1990s.

It is tentatively argued that the historically constraining factors pertaining to CANDU exports (i.e., nuclear non-proliferation and ethical considerations) may soon outweigh facilitating factors (i.e., economic benefits and political interests). However, this will not be due so much to the increasing importance of ethical considerations in Canadian foreign policy as it will be to the corresponding weakening of Canada's economic and political interests in securing nuclear sales. With the end of the Cold War, the containment of communism has ceased to constitute a political rationale for continuing nuclear exports. This has also meant that ethical issues, like human rights, which may have been submerged during the Cold War, are now being allowed to surface. In addition, there has been an increasing discrediting of the belief that nuclear exports are economically beneficial to Canada.

In the realm of security, the impact of nuclear proliferation on CANDU exports had reached its peak in the period immediately following India's 1974 nuclear test. However, in May and June 1998, the issue regained its primacy as India exploded five nuclear devices and Pakistan replied with six of its own. These tests, which were widely condemned by the international community, represented a major blow to the non-proliferation regime[34] and led to fears of a nuclear arms race in South Asia between China-India-Pakistan.[35] Canada immediately applied sanctions against India and Pakistan, which included recalling its high commissioners and discontinuing non-humanitarian development assistance.[36]

Canada was quick to claim that it had not, in any way, played a role in these most recent tests. Ottawa argued that it had terminated nuclear assistance with India and Pakistan following India's 1974 nuclear test. In addition, the plutonium that fuelled the 1998 tests, unlike in 1974, came from indigenous reactors. As Prime Minister Chrétien argued, "that was 25 years ago. Since then technological evolution has been such that the technology of 1974 is completely *passé*. They have their own scientists, and the old technology doesn't mean anything now."[37] Nevertheless, there is some evidence that "Canada bears special responsibility for the current nuclear escalation between India and Pakistan by beginning the nuclear programme of both countries."[38] Canada's nuclear exports in the 1950s and 1960s established the facilities for the development of an indigenous nuclear capability in India and Pakistan. Moreover, the first generation of Indian and Pakistani nuclear scientists, the backbone of any nuclear program, were also trained in Canada.

Canada appeared to be downgrading its nuclear sanctions against India and Pakistan by inviting them to join the CANDU Owners Group (COG) in 1988.[39] The decision to include India and Pakistan in COG's information exchange program came about due to Canada's concern about the safety of the CANDUs that it had exported to them in the 1960s. After building the reactors, and then withdrawing all nuclear cooperation, Canada feared that another Chernobyl was now brewing on the Indian subcontinent. This is a good rationale for reinstating some form of dialogue on nuclear matters. The problem, as Canadian officials have admitted, is that, in addition to addressing environmental concerns, Canada may also have been improving India's and Pakistan's nuclear programs because "you cannot clearly delineate between operational efficiency and safety with a nuclear reactor."[40] This "backdoor" cooperation even led to Indian nuclear scientists touring Canadian nuclear plants and Canadian experts visiting Indian reactors (including those that were free of IAEA safeguards).[41] The shock value of the 1998 nuclear tests did not approach that of the 1974 test, but its impact on CANDU exports should not be underestimated. If the purpose of the unofficial visits of Canadian and Indian nuclear scientists was, in the words of P.K. Iyengar (former chairman of India's Atomic Energy Commission), "to rebuild ties," then that has surely ended.[42] In fact, Canadian sanctions against India and Pakistan have been some of the toughest in scope and duration.[43] This can be traced, just as it could in 1974, to Canadian guilt over its role in the testing. In addition, it can be expected, just as it could in 1974, that there will be a period of heightened concern about the potential link between nuclear exports and nuclear weapons proliferation.

The issue of whether or not non-proliferation concerns have renewed their importance can be tested by examining the unsuccessful attempt to sell Turkey two CANDUs. Despite the July 2000 decision by Ankara not to continue with its plans to purchase nuclear power plants, this case, for two reasons, is still worth examining: (1) because Canada was still willing to sell the reactors to Turkey, and it was only due to the latter's financial problems that Ankara decided to cancel the proposed project; and (2) because this episode provides a very recent example of the interplay between ethics and security, which remains at the heart of Canada's CANDU export program. Notwithstanding Turkey's ratification of the NPT, fears remain that it may be a potential proliferation threat. Over the last thirty years, Turkey has made serious efforts to acquire a substantial civilian nuclear power program, but it has been consistently rebuffed because of fears concerning its plans for weapons production. In the late 1980s, AECL officials acknowledged that Turkey had withdrawn its bid for a nuclear reactor contract because of "pressure from Western countries," which feared that "Turkey may build a nuclear bomb based on CANDU technology."[44] There has also been concern over the re-transfer of nuclear materials and technology to third parties. For example, following Pakistan's nuclear tests in June 1998, reports circulated that Islamabad would assist Ankara in developing nuclear weapons. Pakistani prime minister Nawaz Sharif has gone on record as offering to "work together on nuclear weapons" with Turkey.[45] In addition, because of its regional conflict with Greece, symbolized in the dispute over Cyprus, Turkey may indeed possess a security incentive to acquire nuclear weapons.

There is little indication that human rights will play a greater role in CANDU exports in the future than they have in the past. Turkey, for instance, has been a frequent target of human rights activists. Amnesty International has condemned Turkey for its "gross violations" of human rights and has pointed out that "torture of political and criminal detainees in police stations was routine and systematic."[46] The European Union has also cited Turkey's human rights record as one of the reasons for its continued exclusion from that entity.[47] In addition, while Turkey may be considered a formal democracy, its armed forces have frequently intervened in the political process, with successful military coups occurring in 1960, 1971, and 1980.[48] Evidence that the Turkish military continues to play an important role in domestic politics was revealed when, in spring 1997, it forced the resignation of Prime Minister Necmettin Erbakan because it believed that he was trying to de-secularize Turkey.[49] A particular target of Turkey's oppression are its minority Kurds. The Kurdish Workers' Party

(PKK) is the largest, and most militant, political organization of Kurds inside of Turkey. The PKK has demanded either an independent Kurdish state or, at a minimum, the establishment of an autonomous region inside Turkey. In response to this secessionist movement, the Turkish government outlawed the PKK through its Anti-Terror Law. Although intended for the PKK, this law has also been used "to prosecute and imprison innocent Kurds."[50] The Turkish government also, in 1995 and 1997, launched major military attacks – involving tens of thousands of troops backed by tanks, heavy artillery, and fighter jets – on PKK bases across the border in northern Iraq. Despite the 1999 capture of Kurdish rebel leader Abdullah Ocalan, relations between the Turkish government and the Kurds has not improved.[51]

If it appears that human rights may remain marginal, the opposite is true of environmental protection. This is primarily due to Ontario Hydro's decision to temporarily shut down seven of its nineteen reactors. This decision was based on an internal report that stated that the safety standard that existed in Ontario's nuclear plants was only "minimally acceptable," the lowest grade that could be given to a reactor before revoking a utility's nuclear licence.[52] The nuclear plants were portrayed as being operated by poorly trained workers with a blatant disregard for safety. Numerous instances were documented of unqualified radiation safety technicians, unauthorized ad hoc modifications to the CANDU design, unsafe storage of dangerous chemicals, and alcohol and drugs in the workplace.[53]

Potential foreign customers may now have doubts about the CANDU's safety and reliability. AECL's competitors will also undoubtedly attempt to capitalize on Ontario Hydro's decision to shut down one-third of its reactors, telling potential customers that "Canadians are shutting down their own CANDUs because they are unsafe. Why should you buy one from them?" Ontario Hydro, as Gordon Edwards, the president of the Canadian Coalition for Nuclear Responsibility, points out, is "best-placed in the world to understand and maintain the CANDU and they can barely do it. How do we expect these other countries to be able to run these plants safely?"[54] AECL recognizes that Ontario Hydro's announcement will significantly compromise its ability to secure future exports. In a notable understatement, Gary Kugler, AECL vice-president of commercial operations, said: "It's certainly not great advertising for us."[55]

The decision to continue with the proposed CANDU export to Turkey showed that Canada was still not dissuaded by environmental factors. This is because Turkey, according to Karl Buckthought, president of Earthquake Forecasts Inc., is "one of the most earthquake-prone areas on the face of the earth."[56] The devastating earthquake of 17 August 1999 – which killed more than 17,000 – brought the fear of earthquakes into the open. Nevertheless, Ottawa continued with its efforts to sell the CANDU. Prime Minister

Chrétien minimized the earthquake risk, saying that "Turkey is a very big country,"[57] and Canada planned, in a repeat of its decision in the Chinese sale, to exempt Turkey's purchase of CANDUs from Canada's environmental assessment rules.[58] It is true that Akkuyu Bay is over 500 kilometres from the site of the last earthquake, but it is only 25 kilometres from another major fault line that runs through southern Turkey. It is for this reason that earthquake experts like Buckthought believe that "it's very irresponsible to build a nuclear reactor in Turkey."[59]

The Turkish case also shows that Ottawa was still willing to subsidize CANDU exports. For example, the Cabinet had approved a $1.5 billion EDC loan to help finance the two proposed CANDUs for Turkey.[60] This EDC loan, as was the case with the Chinese project, would have come from its Canada Account. Moreover, Canadian taxpayers could have been on the hook for the entire loan if the Turkish state-owned electrical utility TEAS had defaulted because Ankara would not offer a hard sovereign guarantee of payment. In fact, at the time of the Turkish decision to cancel the project, AECL and Westinghouse (another bidder on the project) were both giving serious consideration to beginning the project without a sovereign guarantee of payment.[61] There were several realistic scenarios that could have seen TEAS default on its loan. First, a substantial downturn in Turkey's economy might have made it difficult for TEAS to make its loan payments. Canadian Cabinet documents reveal that there was serious concern expressed over "several structural problems that could ultimately affect [Turkey's] creditworthiness over the long term."[62] Second, construction delays, which are not unusual when building CANDUs, might have caused TEAS to unilaterally renegotiate its repayment schedule. Third, the reactor could have been damaged beyond financially viable repair via an earthquake or through PKK sabotage.[63]

The extent of government subsidies for the Turkish sale, looked at from another angle, might be seen as a last ditch attempt to save a desperate Canadian nuclear industry. AECL's high level of government subsidies are already slowly declining. In 1998-99, the federal government's contribution to AECL's research and development (R&D) was only $100 million, down from $174 million in 1996-97.[64] An independent review of AECL by Nesbitt Burns in 1995 had stated that it would need to sell ten reactors in ten years to remain viable with only $100 million worth of government subsidies each year. Added pressure for a sale was provided in June 2000, when AECL lost an Australian contract for a research reactor.[65] Now that AECL has failed to win the Turkish contract it seems highly unlikely that it will be able to hit the "ten in ten" requirement. Moreover, acquiring additional government assistance will be very difficult now that Ontario Hydro, its biggest domestic customer, has apparently lost faith in the technology. It is doubtful that AECL will be able to maintain a high level of nuclear

R&D without vast government support. This will erode its innovation ability in nuclear technology and will make it that much harder for AECL to compete with other nuclear suppliers. In short, the combination of a lessening of annual multi-million-dollar subsidies from Ottawa and the loss of its largest domestic market may eventually mean the end of an independent nuclear industry in Canada.

The nuclear industry continues to proclaim the economic benefits of CANDU exports. For example, AECL had estimated that selling a CANDU to Turkey would have resulted in the creation of 125,000 person-years worth of work in Canada.[66] However, the growing evidence suggests that the economic benefits of CANDU exports have been exaggerated. One of the major selling points, as presented by AECL and its patrons in Ottawa, has been the safety and reliability of the CANDU. Former energy minister Anne McLellan used to brag that "the CANDU 6 reactor is acknowledged to be among the safest and best performing designs in the world."[67] Unfortunately, as the CANDU has aged its efficiency rating has greatly decreased and has fallen behind those of other reactor designs.[68]

There has also been growing scepticism over the view that Canada has economically benefited from CANDU exports. For example, in 1987, George Lermer wrote a monograph for the Economic Council of Canada in which he argued that, although each CANDU sale had lost money, Canada had still received a modest benefit from its investment in the CANDU.[69] However, as a result of the steadily decreasing efficiency rate of the CANDU and the future costs of decommissioning old reactors, Lermer, less than a decade later, dramatically reversed his position and argued that "the federal expenditure on CANDU has been a financial disaster."[70]

Conclusion

Throughout much of this book it has been argued that Canada's security interests and ethical considerations operate at cross-purposes. Several authors have tried to rectify this by suggesting that there should be a synthesis of security and ethics. This has been done by broadening the concepts (i.e., moving from traditional security to human security). However, in this case study, there has been no need for this type of reconceptualization. This is because security and ethics have worked in tandem to constrain the export of CANDUs. For example, critics of the effort to sell Turkey a CANDU argued that it would have risked the proliferation of nuclear weapons (security), assisted an undemocratic regime that violates the human rights of its Kurdish population (ethics), and might have led to an environmental catastrophe by building a nuclear reactor in a major earthquake zone. In the case of CANDU exports the fault line is not between security and ethics but, rather, between security/ethics and economics/politics. Moreover, the combination of the end of the Cold War and a decrease in Canada's commitment to help less-developed countries (see Pratt, Chapter 4, this volume) has resulted in the disappearance of Canada's traditional political objectives in exporting CANDUs. Thus, the division is now solely between economics and security/ethics.

This chapter has made two additional arguments. First, it argues that, historically, ethical considerations have played only a limited role in CANDU exports. Only security concerns due to the threat of nuclear proliferation have been successful in halting efforts to sell the CANDU, and even this only started to occur following the 1974 Indian nuclear explosion. Second, it argues that the historic trend of Canada's economic interests outweighing its security/ethical considerations will likely be reversed. Although, as the discussion on the failed attempt to export CANDUs to Turkey demonstrated, the human rights record of recipient states will likely continue to be a non-factor in Ottawa's decision-making process, other ethical issues have become more influential. For example, Ottawa would have been very hard pressed to go ahead with its proposed CANDU sale after the massive earthquakes that hit Turkey in 1999. The environmental consequences, particularly in light of Ontario Hydro's closing of its own reactors, would be too risky. In addition, the nuclear tests by India and Pakistan have, once again, raised the spectre of nuclear proliferation. Finally, it has become evident that the economic arguments put forward by AECL and its supporters in government, which have historically swayed the decision to export CANDUs, will now be scrutinized more heavily (if they have not already been largely discredited). This collapse in the economic benefits of nuclear power will be the most important reason for the expected rise in ethical considerations as constraints on CANDU exports.

Notes

1 There are many additional ethical considerations surrounding CANDU exports that could be addressed. For example, there is a large ethical dimension to the role that nuclear energy plays in the socio-economic development of recipient countries. Nevertheless, due to space limitations, this chapter must restrict itself to an examination of the two most influential ethical considerations.

2 DFAIT and NRCan were previously known, respectively, as the Department of External Affairs (DEA) and the Department of Energy, Mines, and Resources (EMR). In addition, prior to its amalgamation with DFAIT, officials in the Department of International Trade and Commerce (ITC) used to help sell CANDUs.

3 G. Bruce Doern, "The Politics of the Canadian Nuclear Industry," in *Canadian Nuclear Policies,* ed. Bruce Doern and Robert Morrison (Montreal: The Institute for Research on Public Policy, 1980), 47.

4 "Chrétien Government Pro-nuclear," *Nucleonics Week,* 11 November 1993, 15.

5 The most recent study outlining the economic benefits of nuclear exports is Ernst and Young, *The Economic Effects of the Canadian Nuclear Industry* (Toronto: Ernst and Young, 1993).

6 Duane Bratt, "CANDU or CANDON'T: Competing Values behind Canada's Nuclear Sales," *Nonproliferation Review* 5, 2 (1998): 1-16.

7 AECL, *Annual Reports,* 1951-52 to 1996-97.

8 David H. Martin, *Exporting Disaster: The Cost of Selling CANDU Reactors* (Ottawa: Campaign for Nuclear Phaseout, 1996), 6.

9 Peter Berg, *Nuclear Power Production: The Financial Costs* (Ottawa: Library of Parliament, 1993), 10.

10 David Martin and David Argue, *Nuclear Sunset: The Economic Costs of the Canadian Nuclear Industry* (Ottawa: Campaign for Nuclear Phaseout, 1996), table 1.

11 For more information on the sales agent scandal, see Ron Finch, *Exporting Danger: A History of the Canadian Nuclear Energy Export Programme* (Montreal: Black Rose Books, 1986), 54, 58-61.

12 Martin, *Exporting Disaster,* 35-36.

13 Canada, Prime Minister Pierre Trudeau, "Canada's Obligations as a Nuclear Power," *Statements and Speeches* 75, 22 (17 June 1975): 3.

14 J.G. Hadwen, "A Foreign Service Officer and Canada's Nuclear Policies," in *Special Trust and Confidence: Envoy Essays in Canadian Diplomacy,* ed. David Reece (Ottawa: Carleton University Press, 1996), 160.

15 Iris Lonergan, "Canada and India: The Negotiations for the Supply of the NRX, 1955-56," *Bout de papier* 8, 2 (Spring 1991): 15.

16 Duane Bratt, "Is Business Booming? Canada's Nuclear Reactor Export Policy," *International Journal* 51, 3 (1996): 495-96.

17 Canada, Department of Energy, Mines and Resources, *Nuclear Industry Review: Problems and Prospects 1981-2000* (Ottawa: EMR, 1982), 29.

18 William Epstein, *The Last Chance: Nuclear Proliferation and Arms Control* (New York: The Free Press, 1976), 147.

19 Richard Kokoski, *Technology and the Proliferation of Nuclear Weapons* (Stockholm: SIPRI, 1995), 6.

20 Canada, Parliament, House of Commons, *Debates,* 22 December 1976, 2255.

21 Bratt, "Is Business Booming?" 494, 497.

22 Canada, Department of Energy, Mines and Resources, *Nuclear Policy Review: Background Papers* (Ottawa: EMR, 1981), 275.

23 Dave Todd, "Forced Labour Used in Romanian CANDU," *Toronto Star,* 30 December 1989, A1, A20.

24 Canada, DFAIT, Notes for an Address by the Honourable Raymond Chan, Canadian Secretary of State (Asia-Pacific), to the Society of Democratic Movement, Vancouver, 28 May 1995.

25 Bob Carty, "No CANDU for Argentina," *New Internationalist* 6 (March 1978): 27.

26 For more information on the Atucha 2 episode, see: Warner Troyer, *200 Days: Joe Clark in Power* (Toronto: Personal Library Publishers, 1980), 112-21.

27 Canada, Secretary of State for External Affairs Flora MacDonald, "An Examination of Conscience at the United Nations," *Statements and Speeches,* 25 September 1979.

28 Trudeau, "Canada's Obligations," 6.

29 Jeff Sallot, "Ottawa Skips Reactor Advice: Liberals Ignore Recommendations in Studies before Selling Nuclear Plants to China," *Globe and Mail,* 11 August 1997, A4.

30 Canada, Parliament, House of Commons, *Debates,* 8 November 1996, 6314.

31 Sallot, "Ottawa Skips Reactor Advice," A4.

32 Jennifer Wells, "Going Critical," *Report on Business Magazine* (June 1995): 46.

33 Atomic Energy of Canada Limited, *Annual Report 1990-91,* 11.

34 See the special issue of *Nonproliferation Review* 5, 3 (1998).

35 See John Stackhouse and Rod Mickleburgh, "Indian Bomb Raises Fears of Cold War," *Globe and Mail,* 13 May 1998, A1, A8; and John Stackhouse, "Pakistan Goes Nuclear," *Globe and Mail,* 29 May 1998, A1, A8.

36 Canada, DFAIT, Notes for a Statement by the Honourable Lloyd Axworthy, Minister of Foreign Affairs, to the Standing Committee on Foreign Affairs and International Trade, "India's Nuclear Testing: Implications for Nuclear Disarmament and the Nuclear Nonproliferation Regime." Ottawa, 26 May 1998; and Canada, DFAIT, *Press Release No. 136,* 28 May 1998.

37 John Saunders, "Canada Steers Clear of India," *Globe and Mail,* 14 May 1998, A8.
38 Nomi Morris, "Is Canada to Blame?" *Maclean's,* 8 June 1998, 41.
39 Martin, *Exporting Disaster,* 52-56.
40 Ibid., 55.
41 John Stackhouse, "How the Nuclear Ban Bent for India," *Globe and Mail,* 15 June 1998, A1, A9.
42 Ibid.
43 John Stackhouse, "Canadian Businesses Protest Tough Stand on India, Pakistan," *Globe and Mail,* 23 November 1998, A10.
44 Mustafa Kibaroglu, "Turkey's Quest for Peaceful Nuclear Power," *Nonproliferation Review* 4, 3 (Spring-Summer 1997): 36.
45 Allan Thompson, "Reactor Sales Come Under Fire," *Toronto Star,* 9 July 1998, A25. Rumours have also been circulating through the Turkish press that members of the government – most prominently the country's minister of transportation, Enis Oksuz – were endorsing Turkey's right to build nuclear weapons. See Shawn McCarthy, "Bid to Sell CANDU Reactor to Turkey Raises Proliferation Fears," *Globe and Mail,* 14 April 2000, A2.
46 Amnesty International, *The 1995 Report on Human Rights around the World* (London: Amnesty International Publications, 1995), 291.
47 Heinz Kramer, "Turkey and the European Union: A Multi-Dimensional Relationship with Hazy Perspective," in *Turkey Between East and West: New Challenges for a Rising Regional Power,* ed. Vojtech Mastny and R. Craig Nation (Boulder, CO: Westview Press, 1996), 216-22.
48 Clement H. Dodd, "Developments in Turkish Democracy," in Mastny and Nation, *Turkey Between East and West,* 131-40.
49 Freedom House, *Freedom in the World 1998-99: Turkey.* Available at <http://freedomhouse.org/survey99/country/turkey.html>.
50 Amnesty International, *1995 Report,* 294.
51 Amnesty International, *Annual Report 2000: Turkey,* 2. Available at <www.amnesty.org>.
52 Ontario Hydro, "Report to Management IIPA/SSFI Evaluation Findings and Recommendations," *News Release,* 13 August 1997.
53 Paul Waldie and Chad Skelton, "Documents Itemize How Nuclear Plants Earned Low Rating," *Globe and Mail,* 15 August 1997, A4.
54 Shawn McCarthy, "Hydro Fallout May Hit Candus: Reactor Sales Could Suffer," *Globe and Mail,* 14 August 1997, A4.
55 Tom Spears, "Candu Believes Ontario's Woes Will Hurt Sales," *Calgary Herald,* 21 August 1997, A7.
56 Thompson, "Reactor Sales Come Under Fire," A25. For more information on the earthquake risk at Akkuyu Bay, see: David H. Martin, *Nuclear Threat in the Eastern Mediterranean: The Case Against Turkey's Akkuyu Nuclear Plant* (Oxbridge, ON: Nuclear Awareness Project, 2000), 55-63.
57 Anne McIlroy, "PM Defends Selling Reactors after Quakes," *Globe and Mail,* 18 November 1999, A1.
58 MacCarthy, "Cabinet Approves Loan," A6.
59 Jessica Aldred and Christina Frangou, "Quake Prompts Call for Canada to Withdraw Nuclear Sale Bid," *Calgary Herald,* 27 August 1999, A13.
60 MacCarthy, "Cabinet Approves Loan," A6.
61 Shawn McCarthy, "AECL Seeks More Public Funding to Extend Bid for Selling CANDU to Turkey," *Globe and Mail,* 22 July 2000, B3.
62 Shawn McCarthy, "Candu Loan Rejected as Risky Was for Less Than One Approved Later," *Globe and Mail,* 10 December 1998, A5.
63 David H. Martin, *The CANDU Syndrome: Canada's Bid to Export Nuclear Reactors to Turkey* (Ottawa: Campaign for Nuclear Phaseout, 1997), 19.
64 Canada, Parliament, House of Commons, *Debates,* 15 April 1996, 1310.
65 Janet McFarland, "With No CANDU Sales in Sight, AECL Should Justify Its Existence," *Globe and Mail,* 27 July 2000, B10.
66 McCarthy, "Cabinet Approves Loan," A6.
67 Canada, NRCan, *Speech* 96, 116, 26 November 1996

68 Bratt, "CANDU or CANDON'T," 13-14. See also International Atomic Energy Agency, *Reactors Connected to the Grid,* 31 December 1996. Available at <www.iaea.org/programmes/ne/nenp/npes/index.htm>.

69 George Lermer, *Atomic Energy of Canada Limited: The Crown Corporation as Strategist in an Entrepreneurial, Global-Scale Industry* (Ottawa: Economic Council of Canada, 1987).

70 George Lermer, "The Dismal Economics of CANDU," *Policy Options* (April 1996): 16-20. Also agreeing with this position are Martin and Argue, *Nuclear Sunset;* and Berg, *Nuclear Power Production.*

13
Fishing for Norms: Foreign Policy and the Turbot Dispute of 1995

Peter J. Stoett

> Everything becomes uncertain if we withdraw from law.
>
> – Hugo Grotius, *De Jure Belli ac Pacis* [1625][1]

> When the law is violated, and a new situation is brought about by the triumph not necessarily of justice but of force, international law accepts this new situation as legitimate, and concurs in the means whereby it has been brought about.
>
> – Hedley Bull, *The Anarchical Society* [2]

In the post-Cold War era we witness the development of new security concerns within a normative context bereft of the simplistic ethical dichotomy afforded by superpower rivalry. As many of the chapters in this volume make quite clear, Canadian security is no longer about physical protection from the incursions of other states; rather, it is about protecting the livelihood and values of Canada, and this naturally leads us to concerns with the environment, immigration, trade, and other non-military matters. Still, Canadian connections with the global community are stronger than ever, and Canada plays a role advocating the universal acceptance of international law; that is, of accepting the necessity of a common set of rules, reflective of specific values, in order to lessen the damage insecurity can inflict on human beings and the environment. However, there are times when this adherence to international law becomes severely tested and when states such as Canada may find it in their best interests to actually break, rather than follow, international legal norms.

Governments have an obligation to develop long-term polices designed to maximize environmental security.[3] From a *neoliberalist*[4] or *normative globalist*[5] perspective this is self-evident; *realists,* meanwhile, would agree that even the most blatant self-interest of states necessitates some sort of policy response to global environmental threats and contemporary mutual vulnerability. Where there appears to be a convergence of state policy priorities over time, reflected in trends in international law, analysts identify norms (for different treatments of "norms" in international law, see Black,

Chapter 8, this volume; and Knight, Chapter 7, this volume). The nexus between ethics and security is quite apparent in the area of environmental foreign policy, and it has implications for an evolving set of international legal parameters.

In the Canadian case, recent aggressive fisheries policy has contradicted international legal orthodoxy in the name of conservation of fish stocks. This provides a case study that demonstrates the disaster-induced evolution of the foreign policy of a coastal state with peripheral regions highly dependent on resource extraction. It suggests there are cases in which governments are willing to go beyond the norms established by customary and positive international law. The broader question is whether such an act, which involves both innovation and violation, contradicts emergent conservation norms within the international context. If so, will it, in turn, contribute towards the evolution of future trends in norm setting, such as the rising acceptance of the precautionary principle as well as thoughts on equality, both spatial and temporal? This exploratory chapter begins with a brief discussion of the turbot case study, then goes on to look at emerging norms in international law and conservation ethics. It concludes with a brief discussion of the need to strive for progressive domestic problem solving before venturing into the less controllable area of global environmental policy.

The Turbot Dispute

Fisheries disputes have been around for a long time; and the international management of this common resource has received a great deal of diplomatic, and analytic, attention.[6] Economists have found fisheries disputes to be classic collective goods problems.[7] The disputes are exacerbated, and often precipitated, by two interrelated crises within the fishing industry: overinvestment in fisheries, often encouraged by government subsidies; and overfishing. The latter has two main components: growth overfishing and recruitment overfishing. The first occurs when smaller fish are taken by fishers due to the depletion of larger, more valuable fish. Net size is a pertinent factor in avoiding growth overfishing, as Brian Tobin would point out (in as public a method as possible) during the heated dispute with the Spanish. Recruitment overfishing refers to a reduction in total population size, since the breeding population is reduced by overfishing. Significantly, this can be avoided "only with more stringent measures limiting fishing effort by imposing catch quotas, limiting gear to less efficient forms, limiting the number of boats and fishers involved, or allocating exclusive rights to fish particular areas."[8] In other words, technical solutions simply won't do the job: we need political ones.

Historically, whaling, sealing, and large-scale fisheries operations have often followed a typical boom-bust economic cycle. Originally, the depletion of fish stocks was not seen as a major problem, since the fisheries were not overcrowding each other; as Peterson writes, "depletion of stocks in a particular area was not taken as a cause for alarm, but as a signal to start shifting effort somewhere else."[9] This changes dramatically in the contemporary era, when the global fishing industry becomes overcrowded itself, and when the introduction of the 200-nautical-mile exclusive economic zone (EEZ) gives coastal states the right to administer previously open waters. Leaving aside, temporarily, the threats posed by habitat alteration and direct land- and sea-based pollution, it would seem safe to conclude that almost "all important stocks of bottom-dwelling fish species are either fully exploited or over-fished"[10] and that the potential of aquaculture to replace ocean fishing has proven controversial to say the least. Management strategies based on maximum sustainable yield are based on imperfect information, and the management effort is further complicated when it involves multilateral coordination. Flags of convenience fly on the open seas, making concrete action to impose quota restrictions even more difficult.

Some fisheries disputes have become the stuff of legend; more important, they have contributed to major changes in international law. In the 1970s Iceland proved aggressive, moving to a fifty-nautical-mile and then a 200-nautical-mile fishing zone, provoking the so-called "cod wars" with the United Kingdom and Germany. Iceland was successful, even in the International Court of Justice; but a similar transformation of the Law of the Sea, which would eventually legitimate the 200 EEZ, was under way at the time.[11] Canada's Arctic waters initiative, under which Canada imposed a 100-nautical-mile Arctic waters pollution prevention zone on the world (and, in particular, on the United States, in response to the passages of the US oil tanker *Manhattan* through the Northwest Passage)[12] was also superseded by events pertaining to the establishment of the Law of the Sea and what McDorman refers to as the "200-n. mile zone tidal wave of the mid-1970s."[13]

For Canada many fishing disputes, on both the east and west coasts, have involved the United States. This is hardly surprising, given the proximity and appetite of Canada's superpower neighbour to the south. What may be more surprising, perhaps, is the usual aggressiveness with which Canada pursues its claims on these matters, whether it be overfishing off the coast of Maine, or claiming jurisdiction over straddling stocks of crustaceans, or the imposition of obstacles to salmon fishing in the west. For example, Canada was quite aggressive with its transit licence measure in 1994, under which American salmon vessels from Washington and Oregon heading to and from Alaska were required to purchase a licence. This was certainly an aggressive measure in the eyes of the Americans involved, but it hardly contravened international law. At the time, then vice-president Al Gore intervened, promising to renegotiate a new Pacific Salmon treaty and refrain from overfishing, and Canada then withdrew the transit licence measure. Canada would also seize American vessels fishing for sedentary species of scallops; this was consistent with the United Nations Conference on the Law of the Sea (UNCLOS) and the 1958 Geneva Convention on the Continental Shelf. Though the US and Canada entered a short dispute over whether the Icelandic scallops in question were in fact sedentary species, the US eventually accepted this categorization.[14] Of a much more serious nature is the dispute over the Pacific Salmon Treaty of 1985, which has been roundly condemned as inadequate for managing the shared resource of west coast salmon.

An in-depth analysis of the turbot conflict is not intended here,[15] but a short overview of the context is in order. Since Turbot (or Greenland Halibut) has appeared in recent years beyond the 200-nautical-mile limit on the Flemish Cap and the nose and tail of the Grand Banks, Spanish and Portuguese fishers have engaged in progressively intensive fishing efforts. The average Spanish turbot catch in the early 1990s was approximately 50,000 tons per year. Newfoundlanders, in contrast, took around 3,000 tons in 1994. However, with the cod moratorium forcing Canadian fishers to look elsewhere, there arose a large demand for turbot in that year. The quota determined by the Northwest Atlantic Fisheries Organization (NAFO)[16] was a mere 3,400 tons for the European Union (EU) – namely, the Spanish and the Portuguese – and 16,300 tons for Canada. The EU objected to NAFO quotas, and, consistent with the rules of NAFO, established its own quota, which was much higher than that suggested by NAFO. The Spanish made little effort to hide the fact that they were grossly overfishing off the Grand Banks, but this was, in fact, legal activity. For the Canadian government this came as little surprise; foreign overfishing has long been a hot political issue.[17]

On 9 March 1995, the Canadian Coast Guard fired over the bow of the Spanish trawler *Estai* and seized the vessel for overfishing turbot; its crew members were held, temporarily, on Canadian soil. The Spanish government sent vessels to protect the remainder of its fleet; but on 20 March Canadian officials cut the nets of another Spanish trawler. Canada had imposed a unilateral moratorium, concerned with the depletion of turbot stocks, and eventually seized the trawler, claiming it was not only violating the quota rules but was using illegal fish nets in the process. Since the vessel was on the high seas Canada was, in effect, breaking international law, even if it was in an action directed against a state with a less-than-perfect reputation for foreign fishing practices.

Canada's seizure of the Spanish trawler led to international tension because Canada's international legal jurisdiction stops after the 200-nautical-mile limit imposed by the EEZ provision of the Law of the Sea. Before 1977, Canada had a twelve-mile limit; it was expanded that year and non-Canadian trawlers, at one point the largest consumers of cod, withdrew. However, foreign vessels, often associated with European nations but flying the flags of Central American countries, continued to take cod and other fish immediately beyond the limit on the Grand Banks. Thus, the fishery dilemma quickly became a foreign policy problem. Spain argued freedom of the high seas had been broken; Canada argued it was necessary, given the greater concern of conserving fish stocks. Spain sent military vessels to escort its remaining ships, but no further violence ensued; instead, an agreement was hammered out with the EU, which had (perhaps surprisingly) steadfastly supported Spain throughout the episode, and an eventual agreement negotiated through the United Nations would, in the retrospective way international law enables, roughly justify Canada's initial unilateralism.

Understandably, the frustration had been mounting in already economically depressed areas along Canada's east coast, especially Newfoundland, where the local unemployment rate was as high as 20 percent following the imposition of the cod moratorium. This can lead to some rather unique explanations for the ecological shadow created by past policies. For example, calls have rung out for a massive increase in the hunting of harp seals (mammals of such audacious disposition that they not only reproduce but eat as well). This upset the animal rights movement, which has considerable influence over consumer habits in the European marketplace and which placed great emphasis on stopping the whiteskin seal harvest in the 1970s. (The ecosystemic links between rises in seal population and cod depletion are tenuous at best.) Though many would attribute the cod crisis to other factors, such as domestic overfishing, weather patterns, and even voracious seals, foreign overfishing became the popular rallying point for both Ottawa and Newfoundlanders. One major player, fishers union leader Richard Cashin, suggested fishers take direct action to protect "their" area. The anger was reflected in a Letter to the Editor published in the *Globe and Mail:* "The world's greatest fishery is on the verge of extinction ... [what] remains of the stock is being exterminated by foreign ships ... diplomacy has clearly failed ... Canada's pathetic appeasement of the exterminators just makes us a laughingstock ... It's about time we used our armed forces where we need them, in the Grand Banks rather than Somalia."[18]

The federal government had repeatedly declared a willingness to block non-NAFO members from sending trawlers into the Grand Banks off Newfoundland. Eventually, Canada passed legislation that would make it legal (within the domestic context, if not the international) to physically stop ships from fishing near the 200-mile EEZ. Canadian fisheries minister Brian Tobin, who made this announcement during a meeting with EC fisheries commissioner Vannis Paleokrassas, told reporters: "It's an act of conservation; nobody could call it an act of war. We're out to declare enough is enough when it comes to the desecration of cod stocks by nations that operate outside of any civilized norms"[!].[19] The 1994 Amendment of the Canadian Coastal Fisheries Protection Act unilaterally extended Canadian jurisdiction to deal with pirate vessels fishing in adjacent international water.[20]

The *Estai* was also accused of using undersized nets (which take underage fish), of keeping a false hold to conceal illegal catches, and of misreporting its activity (in a theatrical display, Canada towed the seized nets up the Hudson River to UN Headquarters). Canada, a firm supporter of international law, had clearly gone beyond the latter's limitations; the government was eager to legitimate this in the eyes of the world.

According to McDorman (1995), there were several reasons for the emergence of Canada's "get tough" strategy on international fishing disputes. The collapse of the fish stocks themselves, in eastern coastal regions in particular but also in the case of west coast salmon, is obviously a major factor, for without this scarcity there would be no need for aggressive policies in the first place. Bilateral negotiations with the US on salmon were proving quite fruitless, and the Spanish, as well as other fishers using flags of convenience, were not deterred by earlier Canadian rhetoric. A "newly-elected Federal government was in Ottawa with a fresh outlook, a new team of Ministers, and a clear desire to be seen as proactive rather than reactive on international fisheries issues. The latter was particularly true of the minister of fisheries and oceans, Brian Tobin, and it was his department which took the lead in the aggressive actions."[21] Indeed, the actions of an intumescent fisheries minister (who later became premier of Newfoundland and is now federal minister of industry) in themselves will make for exciting reading when his biography is written. Ultimately, however, one can suggest that Canada did not emerge a clear victor in this confrontation, even though that was certainly the spin at home.

After an agreement that went into effect on 1 January 1996, the total allowable catch was dropped to 20,000 tons (from 27,000); Canada was to take 15 percent of it (3,000 tons), and the EU 55 percent (11,000 tons). This represented an absolute loss of 45 percent for Canada, hardly a victory in the quantitative sense. On the other hand, stricter observation procedures[22] have been implemented, reducing the chances of improper overfishing techniques being employed in the area, and the incident added pressure to the diplomatic agenda of the evolving law of the sea, which at this time was struggling to add the answer to the question of how to manage straddling stocks to the international oceans regime.

Canada had sought a species-based approach to fisheries conservation at the earliest negotiations on the Law of the Sea Convention (LOSC) in the 1970s, which would have permitted coastal states to manage adjacent stocks; however, the less contentious 200-mile EEZ was accepted instead.

This left the management of some stocks to multilateral organizations such as NAFO or, worse, to the freedom of the high seas. Retrospectively, and in the international sense, the Canadian effort to make straddling stocks a serious part of the LOSC started too late. It began in earnest only in 1980, with a campaign to negotiate an addition to Article 63 dealing with cooperation between two or more coastal states with regard to conserving fish stocks occurring in both (or all) their EEZs. The US and the EC wanted to keep Article 63 at the level of simple cooperation,[23] without any serious implications for management procedure. A separate treaty process was eventually implemented instead, culminating in the August 1995 Rio-inspired Conference on Straddling and Highly Migratory Fish Stocks, which enhances verification provisions and gives coastal states more authority to place inspectors on other ships within zones of arrangement. It calls for greater sharing of data on stocks; it includes a voluntary call for aid from rich to poor states to facilitate its implementation; and it clearly accepts the precautionary principle (described below). However, in order to board and detain non-compliant vessels outside the 200-mile EEZ, coastal states would still need the permission of the vessel state's (i.e., the flag state's) government.

We see, then, that fisheries disputes raise the twin variables we mentioned earlier: (1) fairly high-profile environmental crises and (2) the interface between governments and international law in order to implement a global environmental policy, often custom-made for the issue at hand. Did Canada overreact to the Spanish turbot take? Did it act largely in self-interest? If so, then is this such a bad thing if it encouraged conservation and even helped move us towards a tighter, if hardly failproof, multilateral regime for managing straddling stocks?

International Legal Norms

International environmental law is "soft law"; it is evolving into a complex network of agreements, treaties, and the outputs of multilateral regulatory bodies. The evolution of international fisheries law in recent decades has, in effect, been the story of the expansion of coastal state jurisdiction. The idea of coastal states managing straddling stocks is not a new one. The Declaration of Santiago on the Maritime Zone – a declaration signed on 18 August 1952 and pertaining to Chile, Ecuador, and Peru – stated the duty of each government to prevent overexploitation, even outside of its direct jurisdiction. This was simply a claim to extend limited national jurisdiction, not territory. In the end, UNCLOS negotiations did not incorporate the straddling stocks issue into its final agreement (see below), and the 200-mile EEZ became the standard conception of the extent of a state's jurisdictional rights.

This is slowly beginning to change, partly, one might argue, as the result of recent, and illegal, Canadian actions in the turbot dispute. By boarding a ship on the high seas Canada ran up against one of the oldest international legal norms in existence. In terms of reciprocity, then, Canada perhaps played a dangerous game, since by breaking international convention it becomes hard pressed to simultaneously argue for the expansion and solidification of the latter, even though that has been, at least rhetorically, a staple Canadian foreign policy initiative in the post-Second World War era. The principle here is a fairly self-evident one: a state should stick to the international legal norms it has signed onto, even if the results of the related legal process are not favourable to it.[24] Ted McDorman argues that "Canada's apparent willingness to disregard the international law of the sea and the accepted procedures of NAFO creates a legitimacy problem for Canada in seeking to have other countries comply with international law and improved NAFO regulations."[25]

One might view Canada's aggressive action as another instalment in the saga of ocean enclosure, or what Ken Booth calls "creeping jurisdiction" – a "mixture of nationalism, economic ambition, environmental concern and a legalistic keeping-up-with-the-Joneses."[26] Almost one-third of the oceans are currently under some sort of national administration. However, it is not apparent that we are on a trend towards a 200-mile territorial sea. And the freedom of the high seas as a concept still survives today. We will return to the question of whether or not Canada's violation of that principle was justified or whether it does, indeed, render hollow future Canadian exhortations with regard to this issue. The important point here is that decision makers operate within a milieu that, from the external environment, includes a tradition of international legal norms, most commonly referred to as "customary law."

Customary law stresses the validity of repeated modes of interaction over time. This means that, in what is known as the positivist sense, actual customs that occur over time can be said to constitute some form of law-like behaviour, while natural or divine law (said to have come from the heavens) is rejected. Obviously, there is an important psychological element to customary law, in the sense that it requires "a conviction felt by states that a certain form of conduct is *permitted* by international law."[27] For example, in the so-called *Fisheries Case* in the International Court of Justice (ICJ) (*United Kingdom* v. *Norway,* 1949-51), the United Kingdom complained that Norway had reserved an exclusive fishing zone for its nationals within a four-mile zone that had been drawn according to several fixed points along the coastline instead of according to the configuration of the actual coastline itself. The court found that Norway had been using this method for decades without any objections from other states and that, therefore, it was permissible under customary international law. The scope of international environmental law and policy is growing, and this growth sets a precedent that, short of establishing a tangible normative context (if such a thing is possible), does reproduce parameters of acceptable behaviour. International law is best perceived as a dynamic process and not as a static end point; or, to adopt the language of postmodernists (without adopting the assumptions that perspective raises), what we need is a framework approach rather than a comprehensive approach. A comprehensive approach, according to a distinction made by Brent Hendricks, claims a

> groundedness or "presence" in which the law silences its political rumblings and achieves a transcendent and controlling position over the real world problem it was designed to control. Not only is the thinking static, it pursues stasis as its ultimate goal.
>
> In contrast, the framework approach considers the political problem as an ongoing one ... leaving us with only the constant play of politics leading ultimately and only to a self-referential conversation about what needs to be done.[28]

Going beyond strict legal convention, international institutions do help us define acceptable behaviour, though this is not an inherently progressive function. Regulatory regimes may be negative, serving to redefine certain types of behaviour as illegitimate and then proscribe them. These have been specifically referred to as *global prohibition regimes:* they are guided by norms that "strictly circumscribe the conditions under which states can participate in and authorize these activities and proscribe all involvement by nonstate actors."[29] Slavery is often used as an example of an international activity that came to be viewed as inhumane by key actors in the global system (of course, there are other explanations for the demise of slavery, and it continues today in several areas). The global moratorium against commercial whaling may be viewed as a similar normative transition, though this is a rather Western and simplistic perspective.[30] Overfishing on the high seas, however, has by and large escaped the imposition of a strong global prohibition regime; Canadian officials buttressed the raw national interest orientation of Canadian actions during the turbot dispute with the larger claim that they were, in essence, contributing to the creation of a new one.

At the same time, regulatory regimes have a corresponding positive function – to legitimize behaviour. This could include, for example, behaviour that is arguably hazardous to environmental health, such as the spread of nuclear power, which is one of the stated goals of the International Atomic Energy Agency (see Duane Bratt, Chapter 12, this volume). The tendency to equate regime formation with a progressive evolution in world affairs overlooks the dual nature of institutions and organizations, which have both promotional and regulatory roles. NAFO may be better, with its current regulations and surveillance methods, but it still facilitates the extraction of fish. Finally, mainstream regime analysis is often criticized for overlooking the contemporary role of non-governmental actors, despite the fact that the rise of such actors helped promote thinking about interdependence. It is still a government-oriented approach to fisheries regulation.

The Equality Principle

There are several dimensions to the equality of environmental security. Many environmentalists argue that we should abandon the old, enlightenment view of nature as something without intrinsic worth. But, simply put, it is difficult to galvanize public attention to the plight of turbot (relatively unattractive bottom feeders) without having the Spanish villains in the play. In a recently published essay Paul Wapner suggests that ethical standards can only be formed in relation to human-human relations and interaction.[31] It may constitute epistemic violence against nature to reduce it to utility, to resources, but it is obviously a prevalent perspective at this point in time. In the 1958 Convention on Fishing and Conservation of the Living Resources of the High Seas (559 UNTS 285), Article 2 states that the expression "conservation of the resources of the high seas" means "the aggregate of the measures rendering possible the optimum sustainable yield from those resources so as to secure a maximum supply of food and other marine products. Conservation programmes should be formulated with a view to securing in the first place a supply of food for human consumption." Despite the attractiveness of arguments that all species must be treated as perfectly equal,[32] this normative stance has not changed.

As for inter-human equality, however, we have another kettle of fish. We might argue, with Paul Wapner, that environmental problems have disproportionate effects on the people who suffer their consequences. Spatial equality suggests that governments should attempt to enact policies and legislation designed to at least minimize this difference in effect. The workers displaced by the cod moratorium, for example, need government assistance, be it to retrain them for other work or to support them temporarily (or, more pessimistically, for a very long time). Wapner uses the concept of environmental displacement, which is "about exploiting one's shadow ecology. It involves discounting the lives of those who live in areas that supply natural resources or find themselves on the receiving end of the industrial waste-stream."[33]

The principle of equality would, at the very least, suggest that, in order to deal with what has been less than perfect fisheries management over the years, we should not displace blame and make others suffer – including Spanish fishers, who, after all, are simply doing their jobs. As a general rule, when a policy is to be applied to the granting of aid, loan granting, military involvement in foreign lands, or any other significant foreign policy activity, there should be an explicit attempt to identify who will be most affected by its environmental impact. There should also be a commitment to reduce this impact when it affects those with few resources. This would obviously preclude the assumption that all trade is good trade; it would also demand that Canada take an earnest approach (albeit one that is ultimately shaped by self-interest) to compensating those injured by a policy's ecological shadow.

We should note at the outset that the debate over the turbot affair was, according to specialist Ted McDorman, "primarily about the *sharing* of the reduced NAFO quota, the unfairness of the allocations given the EU and the legality of Canada's unilateral enforcement of the quota. The need for conservation and a reduced total quota was *not* in question."[34] So we can see that it was, in fact, the Spanish that cried foul in this case because of perceptions of inequality in the distribution of the quota. However, the attendant formula for ethical standards (simply put, governments should avoid causing such displacement) is less easily applied in a concrete case such as the turbot dispute because Spanish fishers have become dependent upon the resource as well. Some sort of Canada-Spain joint program to adjust these working populations would be unlikely, given the other distinctions between the two countries (although this is a remote possibility).

Just as important as the foregoing, environmental ethicists urge us to think about *intergenerational* equality: what effect will current resource extraction patterns have on the livelihood and quality of life of those yet unborn? Ignoring this question is an act of greed, a manifestation of the advanced stages of chronic collective myopia. At the very least, one could argue that we are obligated to future generations to avoid driving today's species into extinction. Indeed, the imperative of intergenerational ethics was even accepted in the Rio Declaration, which emerged from the UN Conference on Environment and Development (UNCED). In an academic vein, Edith Brown Weiss has most extensively articulated the concept of equality. She distinguishes between three principles of equality that relate to future generations: (1) the conservation of options; (2) the conservation of quality, which requires "the development of predictive indices of environmental quality, the establishment of baseline measurements, and an integrated monitoring network"; and (3) the conservation of access, in the intergenerational sense.[35] All of this points directly to the importance of accepting another principle as a guiding light in long-term policy formation: precaution.

The Precautionary Principle

As Weiss intones, we need to develop some manner of measuring whether or not the principle of equity of environmental quality is being compromised, and this necessitates some knowledge of where trends are taking us.

This, in turn, relies heavily on the common acceptance of scientific methods, for example, those found within relevant "epistemic communities." It also implies that we err on the side of caution if consensus cannot be attained, either in order to achieve greater knowledge about possible consequences or in order to try to deal with significant cultural differences of perception (messy as this may be). The thrust of the precautionary principle, then, is that the environment should be protected from the unknown.

At the rhetorical level, there is a growing acceptance of the value of this principle. In 1992 alone, it was endorsed in the consensual-based Rio Declaration (Principle 15), Agenda 21 (chap. 17, para. 17.2), the UN Framework on Climate Change, and the Convention on Biological Diversity. It was also endorsed by the Montreal Protocol on Substances that Deplete the Ozone Layer (1990), adopted by the North Sea and Baltic regions at the May 1990 Bergen Conference on Sustainable Development, and was accepted at the November 1990 Second World Climate Conference. Multilateral fisheries arrangements are also beginning to accept the principle.

The Revised Management Procedure of the International Whaling Commission (IWC), if it is ever permitted to function through the lifting of a global moratorium on commercial whaling (which currently dominates the commission's actions and internal debates), emphasizes the need to err on the side of caution when estimating whale stocks and maximum sustainable yield. S.M. Garcia believes that the UN Resolution on large-scale pelagic driftnet fishing in the high seas (res. 44/125, December 1989) is an expression of the precautionary principle, and it was also recognized at the International Conference on Responsible Fishing at Cancun, Mexico, in May 1992. More specifically, the recently negotiated straddling stocks treaty explicitly deals with the "precautionary approach," in that Article 6 is dedicated to its implementation.

We should not be convinced by these exhortations that the precautionary principle is a current international norm. In fact, it is at best a slowly emergent one; however, it has common sense on its side. There will always be reason for contention regarding the degree to which states should adhere to such a principle; and the global warming debate is certainly bringing out the implications of this contention. But one can argue that precaution is necessary in order to avoid violating both extant international legal norms and the equality concerns described above.

Ultimately, the best we can hope for is that governments will take seriously the argument that uncertain science "cannot be taken as a reason for inaction ... It is irresponsible to focus on 'worst-case' results in order to justify major policy changes, but it is equally irresponsible to focus on 'best-case' results in order to justify a complacent 'wait-and-see' posture."[36] In retrospect, it appears that Canada, no doubt out of self-interest and for largely internal political purposes, advanced the international acceptance of the precautionary principle with its aggressive pursuit of Spanish fishers. And it did so in a unilateral fashion, breaking the Canadian proclivity towards multilateral foreign policy initiatives.

Unilateral Enforcement/Innovation

In 1990, after Namibia had finally won its independence from South African domination, one of the first things the government did was declare its coastal boundary in order to move Spanish fishing ships out of its waters.[37] Such unilateral moves make solid sense when decision makers perceive clearly environmentally destructive behaviour. It is difficult to argue that contemporary governments can do anything they want to without external coordination. Yet sovereignty continues as an institution; one need only look at the homage paid to the principle of non-intervention in the Rio Declaration and other major international environmental agreements in order to see this.

In the turbot case it is quite evident that Canada acted unilaterally in its own national interest. This has, of course, come under critical evaluation: "Whatever the risk to its bilateral relations with Spain or with Europe, whatever the consequences to international law, Canada turned to gunboat diplomacy ... Here was the national interest at its crudest."[38] But a historical overview suggests that, far from an anomaly, the Canadian response to the turbot dispute was an extension of earlier policy. During the Canada-Spain confrontation, Liberal MP Edward McWhinney was quoted as saying that "almost all of the law of the sea starts with unilateral action."[39]

Most of the significant changes in Canada's international fisheries policy have, in fact, been unilateral actions. In 1964 Canada moved from a three- to a twelve-mile fisheries limit; in 1971 it established exclusive Canadian fishing zones by drawing "closing lines" in the Gulf of St. Lawrence and Bay of Fundy in the east, and across Queen Charlotte Sand, Dixon Entrance, and Hecate Strait in the west. The Arctic protection legislation was likewise unilateral in character. The historical record suggests that recourse to unilateralism is often effective. Though Canada once claimed it would not unilaterally declare an economic zone but would "work for Law of the Sea approval of such a concept,"[40] it went ahead and did so.

No doubt, one can explain Canada's insistence on curtailing Spanish overfishing as part of what Cooper calls the politics of external deflection. Many domestic forces had "considerable incentive to try to externalize the crisis: by placing the blame for the situation in the fisheries on 'foreigners,' the onus of responsibility in terms of causation could be redirected outside of Canada."[41] At the same time, however, the government was adamant in using the case as a unilateral demonstration to the rest of the world of the seriousness of the issue. Breaking with international legal convention was justified by the primacy of the equality and precautionary principles discussed above, and the only way to reinforce this was through a unilateral initiative because no strong multilateral mechanism exists to punish transgressors of extant legal arrangements. There are also bound to be cases where the prevalent norms shaping multilateral decision making are at fundamental odds with the prevalent decision-making circle in Ottawa, as was the case with Canada's withdrawal from the IWC in 1982.[42]

Unilateralism gets rather bad press in an age in which the multilateral effort is seen as the norm. Of course, some of this is related to the unilateral acts of hostility that preceded the Second World War and, arguably, the recent war in the Persian Gulf region. Yet, while one might question the ethical standing of unilateral actions if they are solely designed to reinforce an unjust power structure at home, and/or to deflect attention from other issue-areas among the general population, there is nothing inherently bothersome about unilateral action designed to reinforce the principles discussed above. The link between unilateralism and nationalism continues to be of concern to students of ethics. Of course, conventional wisdom suggests that Canadians are far too sophisticated to become infatuated with anything like a nationalistic concern for adjacent fish stocks. In the long run, the west coast salmon dispute may in fact generate more pro-Canadian (or, more specifically, anti-American) sentiment.

However, it is fairly safe to assume that, in the North and South, resource protection maintenance will be one of the more visible military operations of large states in the future. Cooper argues the turbot episode "endorsed the need for conducting an altered sort of intellectual conversation (and, by implication, an altered policy-making process) on security issues. The crossover of this type of environmental issue into the official security concerns, however, also confirmed the essential incompatibility between the two agendas."[43] Policies are made based on electoral currents and the pull of deeper power structures, and there is inherent tension within most decision-making efforts. This takes place whether or not a government is considering unilateral action, and the present effort to redefine security will also be shaped by such forces.

Conclusion: Responsibility and Progress

We've seen that there are many dimensions to environmental security and that fisheries disputes reveal many aspects of them. There are several concerns stressed here regarding our thinking about ethical policy making: it is necessary for governments to seriously consider the impact of their policies as they pertain to international law, contemporary and intergenerational equality, and the precautionary principle. When it comes to implementing policies, there are three mechanisms that will be most tempting: unilateral action, collective environmental security (or strong multilateralism), and policy coordination (or deep multilateralism). Furthermore, we need to have a crisis before issues become front-burner material on the security agenda. This gives rise to the idea of the great catalytic push that can shove us into reworked paradigms regarding human-nature relations. Steve Rayner believes that, if the threat of climate change "did not exist we would have had to invent it, or something very much like it, to respond to the challenge of global governance at the end of the twentieth century."[44]

However, while we wait for the great paradigm shift to approach and reproach us, governments must make immediately consequential foreign policy decisions. And, regardless of the approach ultimately employed, an old line of thought suggests that it is most important to keep one's own house in order before venturing out to fix those of others. Fisheries polices are as good an indication as any of this priority. Salmon runs along the BC coast are dependent on habitat survival, often down to minute details; this presents very difficult management problems, especially for anadromous species shared by different countries of origin. Yet if forestry practices denude the rivers, then all will be lost. Likewise, on the east coast, Fisheries and Oceans (currently undergoing what, one hopes, will be a clean and deep review of its policy-making procedures) will have to deal with the ecological shadow of years of systemic overfishing that have caused such problems for both Canadian and non-Canadian (yes, even Spanish) fishers.

Ultimately, governments will make foreign policy decisions that reflect the nexus between structural power and the electoral currents of the day. When ethical questions become brightly illuminated by the tension created within this nexus, we will see much agonizing in Ottawa and much persuasive, or even "moralsuasive," rationalization of policy choices. When the tension is not so direct, however – as will often be the case with regard to environmental security issues – policies will continue to be made to fit the concerns of the day, with little regard for long-run consequences. The turbot case and the salmon case both demonstrate this tendency towards short-term thinking; the principles of equality discussed above strongly suggest that we must avoid a situation in which a government's ethical obligations are understood primarily as the protection of its electoral future, vocal industrial interests, and only then, if they are vocal enough, local fishers. The need for habitat preservation, vividly obvious in the west coast case, is quietly overlooked as it would throw so many additional stakeholders into the debate. But can this be avoided in the long run? Incorporating the principles of equality and precaution into continued multilateral frameworks can help move us away from short-term thinking, but the implementation of this shift is another matter, and aggressive unilateral actions may well be necessary.

As for the central question with which this chapter began, it is indeed responsible for a government to break with international convention, in the name of both self-interest and conservation, if policy makers expect it to result not in general chaos but, rather, in an advancement of international legal norms consistent with extending the principles of equality and precaution. This is, typically, how international law advances: it is broken. As E.H. Carr wrote several decades ago, in politics "the belief that certain facts are unalterable or certain trends irresistible commonly reflects a lack of desire or lack of interest to change or resist them."[45] Policy makers must keep this in mind as the era of globalization presents new and complex challenges to both environmental security and human security.

Acknowledgment
The author thanks the Social Sciences and Humanities Research Council of Canada for funding.

Notes

1 Hugo Grotius, *De Jure Belli ac Pacis* [1625], as reprinted in Francis Coker, ed., *Readings in Political Philosophy* (New York: Macmillan, 1994).
2 Hedley Bull, *The Anarchical Society* (New York: Columbia University Press, 1977), 92.
3 G. Dabelko and D. Dabelko, "Environmental Security: Issues of Conflict and Redefinitions" *Environment and Security* 1 (1996): 23-49.
4 Charles Kegley, ed., *Controversies in International Relations Theory: Realism and the Neoliberal Challenge* (New York: St. Martin's Press, 1995).
5 Mel Gurtov, *Global Politics in the Human Interest* (Boulder, CO: Lynne Rienner, 1988).
6 See especially M.J. Peterson, "International Fisheries Management," in *Institutions for the Earth: Sources of Effective Environmental Protection,* ed. P. Haas, R. Keohane, and M. Levy (Cambridge: MIT Press, 1993), 249-308.
7 See H.S. Gordon, "The Economic Theory of a Common Property Resource: The Fishery," *Journal of Political Economy* 62 (1954): 124-42; and Milner Schaefer, "Biological and Economic Aspects of the Management of Marine Fisheries," *Transactions of the American Fisheries Society* 88 (1959): 100-4.
8 Peterson, "International Fisheries Management," 257.
9 Ibid., 258.
10 United Nations, *Global Outlook 2000: An Economic, Social, and Environmental Perspective* (New York: United Nations Publications, 1990), 93.
11 See Hannes Jonsson, *Friends in Conflict: The Anglo-Icelandic Cod Wars and the Law of the Sea* (London: C. Hurst and Co., 1982).
12 This was certainly ahead of international law. See Alan Gotlieb and Charles Dalfen, "National Jurisdiction and International Responsibility: New Canadian Approaches to International Law," *American Journal of International Law* 67 (1973): 246-47. More generally, see John Kirton and D. Munton, "Protecting the Canadian Arctic: The *Manhattan* Voyages 1969-1970," in *Canadian Foreign Policy: Selected Cases,* ed. J. Kirton and D. Munton (Scarborough: Prentice-Hall, 1992), 205-26.
13 Ted McDorman, "Canada's Aggressive Fisheries Actions: Will They Improve the Climate for International Agreements?" *Canadian Foreign Policy* 2, 3 (Winter 1994-95): 5-28.
14 Article 77 of the UNCLOS gives coastal states the right to manage straddling stocks of so-called "creepy crawlies."
15 See Andrew Cooper, *Canadian Foreign Policy: Old Habits and New Directions* (Scarborough: Prentice Hall Allyn and Bacon, 1997), 142-72; L.C. Missios and C. Plourde, "The Canada-European Union Turbot Wars: A Brief Game of Theoretic Analysis," *Canadian Public Policy* 22, 2 (1996): 144-150
16 NAFO was established by the *Convention on Future Multilateral Cooperation in the Northwest Atlantic Fisheries,* which was signed in Ottawa on 24 October 1978. Its headquarters are in Dartmouth, Nova Scotia. Current members of NAFO include Bulgaria, Canada, Cuba,

Denmark (for the Faeroe Islands and Greenland), the EU, Estonia, France, Iceland, Norway, Japan, Korea, Latvia, Lithuania, Poland, Romania, Spain, Russia, the United Kingdom, and the United States.

17 We should note that there is certainly nothing new about Spanish fishing off the east coast. The Spanish Basques were fishing off the coast of Newfoundland as early as 1530, though they called it Terranova. By the 1580s, French Basque ships were returning from the area loaded with cod and, eventually, whale oil.

18 This letter is from R. Johnstone, Newfoundland, and was published in the *Globe and Mail* on 27 January 1994 (A24). Somewhat ironically, Somalia faces a similar problem. Fishing boats from the EC and Pacific Asia have been harvesting the lobster and tuna grounds off the Somalian coast, and that destitute nation, without a coast guard, has been unable to deter them. See "Somali Clans Threaten Foreign Fishing Boats," *Globe and Mail,* 3 February 1994, A9.

19 P. Koring, "Canada to Block Fish 'Pirates,'" *Globe and Mail,* 12 January 1994, A1 and A2.

20 This was meant especially to deal with flag-of-convenience countries, which were listed as follows: Belize, Cayman Islands, Honduras, Panama, Saint-Vincent and the Grenadines, and Sierra Leone. There is certainly nothing new about the flags of convenience problem. Furthermore, the flags are not just used to facilitate overfishing. For example, we might recall that the United States put American flags on Kuwaiti oil tankers in the Persian Gulf during the Iran-Iraq war in the 1980s. See Martin Glassner, *Neptune's Domain: A Political Geography of the Sea* (Boston: Unwin Hyman, 1990), 88. But the issue remains most visible in fisheries disputes, though a recent FAO agreement may deter future problems.

21 Ted McDorman, "Canada's Aggressive Fisheries Actions," 5-28.

22 This was, indeed, part of what Cooper calls a "quid pro quo [that] appeared in two components of the formula eventually agreed: the first was the provision for having neutral observers on any and all fishing vessels fishing the 'nose' and 'tail' of the Grand Banks; the second created an additional enforcement regime through satellite tracking and home-port inspections under the scrutiny of independent monitors" (*Canadian Foreign Policy,* 166). See also C. Farnsworth, "North Atlantic Fishing Pact Could Become World Model," *New York Times,* 17 April 1995.

23 See Clyde Sanger, *Ordering the Oceans: The Making of the Law of the Sea* (Toronto: University of Toronto Press, 1987).

24 For example, Canada was not pleased with the arbitral decision of the Canada-France Arbitral Tribunal, 17 July 1986, concerning filleting in the Gulf of St. Lawrence. France claimed that, because of the French possessions of St. Pierre and Miquelon off the Canadian coast, Canadian regulations did not apply. The tribunal found that a Canadian regulation prohibiting the use of freezer trawlers was not a fishing regulation and was, therefore, not permitted by the agreement.

25 Ted McDorman, "Canada's Aggressive Fisheries Actions," 28.

26 Ken Booth, *Law, Force and Diplomacy at Sea* (London: George Allen and Unwin, 1985), 38.

27 M. Akehurst, *A Modern Introduction to International Law,* 3rd ed. (London: George Allen and Unwin, 1977), 35.

28 Brent Hendricks, "Postmodern Possibility and the Convention on Biological Diversity," *Environmental Law Journal* 5, 1 (1996): 14-15.

29 E. Nadelmann, "Global Prohibition Regimes: The Evolution of Norms in International Society," *International Organization* 44, 4 (1990): 481.

30 See Peter Stoett, *The International Politics of Whaling* (Vancouver: University of British Columbia Press, 1997).

31 Paul Wapner, "Environmental Ethics and Global Governance: Engaging the International Liberal Tradition," *Global Governance* 3 (1997): 213-31.

32 See Arne Naess, *Ecology, Community and Lifestyle: Outline of An Ecosophy,* trans. D. Rothenberg (Cambridge: Cambridge University Press, 1989); Paul Taylor, *Respect for Nature: A Theory of Environmental Ethics* (Princeton: Princeton University Press, 1986); and Bill Devall and George Sessions, *Deep Ecology* (Salt Lake City: G.M. Smith, 1985).

33 Wapner, "Environmental Ethics," 218.

34 Ted McDorman, "Canada's Aggressive Fisheries Actions," 5-28

35 Edith Brown Weiss, *Environmental Change and International Law* (Tokyo: United Nations University Press, 1993), 342.
36 J.P. MacNeill, Wiinsemius, and T. Yakushiji, *Beyond Interdependence: The Meshing of the World's Economy and the Earth's Ecology* (New York: Oxford University Press, 1991) 17.
37 W. Caragata, "Gunboat Diplomacy," *Maclean's,* 20 March 1995, 11.
38 Andrew Cohen, "Canada in the World: The Return of the National Interest," *Behind the Headlines* 52, 4 (1995): 11. Quoted in Andrew Cooper, *Canadian Foreign Policy,* 142.
39 J. Sallot, "Agreement Could Be Sunk in 90's Dispute," *Globe and Mail,* 9 March 1995, A4.
40 J. Sullivan, *Pacific Basin Enterprise and Changing Law of the Sea* (Toronto: D.C. Heath, 1977), 41.
41 Andrew Cooper, *Canadian Foreign Policy,* 145.
42 See Stoett, *The International Politics of Whaling.*
43 Cooper, *Canadian Foreign Policy,* 145.
44 Steve Rayner, "Governance and the Global Commons," in *Global Governance: Ethics and Economics of the World Order,* ed. M. Desai and P. Redfean (London: Pinter, 1995), 60.
45 Edward Hallett Carr, *The Twenty Years' Crisis, 1919-1939: An Introduction to the Study of International Relations* (London: Macmillan, 1942) 113.

Part 7
Conclusions

14
Towards Human Security?

Rosalind Irwin

This collection brings together a wide range of perspectives on issues of ethics and security facing Canadians in the context of the turbulent global environment of the twenty-first century. Collectively, they have addressed three sets of themes: (1) the meaning of "ethics" and "security"; (2) the question of historical continuity and change (more specifically, the impact of the post-Cold War context); and (3) the implications of these shifts for Canadian foreign policy. The concept of "human security" ties these questions together by prompting engagement with the conceptual relationship between ethical and security concerns, focusing attention on historical shifts in both global order and the paradigms used to analyze global politics, and provoking considerations of the "practical politics" involved in Canadian foreign policy decision making. The ways in which contributors have approached these questions collectively form a pattern of analysis that works to link the abstract analytical and philosophical questions of "ethics" to the critical and challenging questions of decision-making practice in Canadian foreign policy.

As suggested by recent government statements and by several contributors, human security *in principle* represents a shift from the Cold War focus on national security to a more complex and *distinctive* notion of security that more fully incorporates "ethical" considerations. The claim to "distinctiveness" is important, both conceptually and historically, in that it suggests that recent leadership initiatives in Canadian foreign policy represent an *ethical* position as opposed to one grounded in *realpolitik*. Human security is also important in the context of theories of international relations and foreign policy since it raises the questions: Do ethical considerations actually *determine* decision making in the international realm? If so, to what extent? These questions have formed an important underlying theme for the contributions to this volume.

The claim of distinctiveness, particularly from American policy, and from past principles and practices, enhances the legitimacy of policies both at home and abroad and, therefore, provides an important political lever. Critics such as Heather Smith and David Black are sceptical about the degree of this distinctiveness and independence, and they point out that this claim to distinctiveness can contribute to the construction, even to the mythologizing, of Canada's international role. Others, such as Andy Knight, argue that Canada has played, and should continue to play, a constructive and unique leadership role, especially while working in concert with other "like-minded" states. While few contributors doubt that historical changes have been significant in bringing about a new context within which to reconsider security and, perhaps, an enhanced role for ethical considerations, they disagree over whether or not Canadian foreign policy has effectively responded to these new opportunities and challenges. Thus they ascribe differing importance to the potential of the concept of human security to offer radical and "distinctive" alternatives.

Contributors have sought to develop the conceptual implications of human security through an exploration of a variety of academic theories and ethical traditions. Peter Penz explores the tensions among various ethical approaches, counterposing a cosmopolitan ethic – the basis of human security approaches – to the various traditions of state-based ethics. Cranford Pratt and Heather Smith critically evaluate the relevance of human security, at least in the form that Lloyd Axworthy sought to introduce it into Canadian foreign policy discourse, to development assistance and human rights policies. Others, for example Peter Stoett and Andy Knight, focus on traditions of international law, examining changes in the sources of ethics in the codified and customary legal principles and practices of both states and individuals. Terisa Turner and her co-authors draw upon feminist theories of political economy, while Jorge Nef uses the interdisciplinary approaches exemplified by world system theories and core-periphery analysis. Others, such as David Black, Andy Knight, and Andrew Latham, use theories of international norms and global culture to understand the ethics/security nexus. This broad survey therefore links up with ongoing debates among theorists and practitioners concerning the changing nature of the relationship between ethics and security and how it pertains to decision making. More particularly, as a group, the chapters provoke an image of an uncertain world order, in which, as Jorge Nef suggests, there is a need to "develop analytical frameworks to understand this seemingly random, turbulent, and chaotic period." Although they may disagree about the nature or trajectory of change, and its implications for Canada and Canadian foreign policy, contributors agree that the increasing pace and scope of changes brought on by globalization and the growth of interdependence make an exploration of innovative theories, concepts, and approaches more compelling.

Some contributors draw attention to the need for an ethical analysis, which, as Latham argues, develops an understanding of "the sources of the ethical norms, standards, or imperatives that sometimes shape foreign and security policy." For example, in Chapter 3 Penz traces the normative and ethical basis of human security in the tradition of cosmopolitanism, a theme that is taken up by both Smith and Pratt. In Chapter 2 Nef examines the historical basis for a human security agenda in an era of mutual vulnerability, while in Chapter 13 Stoett looks to changing international legal norms and customs. In addition to looking at the *sources* of ethical codes, some have chosen to focus on the *processes* of choosing amongst competing norms – a theme developed by Black, Knight, and Adelman. Adelman argues, for example, that "we do not choose between an amoral realism and an abstract principled idealism. We really choose amongst competing norms in light of the perceived circumstances and the anticipated consequences of each alternative." Thus, whether using traditions of ethical analysis, genealogical or structural investigations of history, or inquiries into the sources of international legal norms, the chapters seek to analyze the complex balance between "agency" and "structure" that shapes foreign policy decision making and through which the imperatives of ethics and security are addressed.

Contributors also direct attention, using comparative or historical analysis, to the need for sensitivity towards contexts. Several contributors agree that, regardless of the specific issue being considered, a more sophisticated and nuanced appreciation for normative contexts should be integrated into both scholarly and policy analyses. Some of the contextual considerations dealt with in this volume include, for example: the shadow cast by past experiences on present circumstances (see Adelman and Black); the complexities of international and global normative constructs and rules (see Stoett and Latham); and the gender relations that shape the contexts within which foreign policy issues are treated (see Turner et al.). These approaches tend to prompt a broader reflection on the *consequences* and effects of decisions and actions, emphasizing that such consequentialist considerations are, or should be, an integral part of decision making.

Others choose to directly confront what Pratt refers to as "the practical significance of any discussion of what are the most essential components of an ethical foreign policy." Black summarizes the views of several contributors by stating that "the popular perception that Canada can and should use its influence to serve the cause of global justice has been honoured as much in the breach as in the practice." Addressing these issues implies a critical approach that focuses on the gap between normative aspirations and decision-making practices. As demonstrated by the works of Smith and Pratt, this approach can also shed light on other important tensions that affect Canada's global relations: for example, those between economic and ethical considerations (discussed by Duane Bratt in his chapter on Canadian nuclear policy) and between official government ideology and Canadian civil society values.

Emerging from these issues is one that particularly engaged contributors: the question of the changing role of economic considerations in Canadian foreign policy. Bratt's historical examination of the export of CANDU reactors suggests that, although often at odds, economic, political, security, and ethical considerations have sometimes worked in tandem. Some, for example Pratt and Smith, argue that traditional economic concerns have been increasingly integrated into a discourse on strategic national security – one that is at odds with ethical concerns. In terms of a human security agenda, critics suggest, this has translated into two problems. The first problem is that there has been an overall neglect of the *economic* dimension of human security, which Turner et al. have interpreted as "universal access to goods necessary to life, as opposed to privatization and exclusion of most people from these life goods." The focus, rather, has been on individual violence or state violations of political and civil rights.

The second problem is that orthodox economic security has now become equivalent to the strategic national security agenda of the past, undermining efforts to more fully realize the transformative potential of the concept of economic human security within an era of growing disparities between North and South. Tom Keating notes, for example: "The value of human security promoted through democratic reforms has been compromised by economic conditionalities that value markets over the state and that often serve to exacerbate gross disparities in wealth."

As pointed out in the introduction, the human security agenda has incorporated a wide range of priorities, from food security to human rights. Some have suggested that a continuing distinction in policy between economic and ethical considerations will likely persist and serve ultimately to undermine the potential of the human security agenda to exact changes (Smith; Keating; Pratt). Some have adopted a comprehensive methodology (Nef; Penz) to explore ways of incorporating these considerations more fully into policy and, thus, more fully realizing the potential of human security to radically alter policy priorities. At the very minimum, these debates suggest that the meaning and significance of human security as a historical, ethical, and policy concept is, and will likely continue to be, highly contested.

Another related and important set of questions surrounds selectivity and scope in foreign policy decision making. In principle and in practice, "niche diplomacy" and selectivity with regard to defining the human security agenda have had both promises and pitfalls, as summarized by Knight and Smith. While an overemphasis on selectivity can lead to an undermining of credibility and consistency on issues of importance to Canadians, as Smith argues in the case of human rights, some focused initiatives (such as the International Criminal Court campaign) appear to have successfully integrated ethical considerations and to have contributed to the construction of important global norms. Contributors to this volume, therefore, disagree over whether Canadian foreign policy will be, or should be, more selective or more expansive in scope. This is an issue that will likely become even more crucial as economic, social, and environmental globalization intensifies.

Another set of issues surrounds the tensions between crisis decision making and long-term assistance and commitment. Contributors to this volume argue that "the CNN effect"[1] played an important role in shaping Canada's assertive response to, for example, Spanish overfishing in the Grand Banks (Stoett) and the calls for intervention in Zaire (Adelman). One implication of "crisis" decision making, is that ad hoc policies may do little to change the underlying political, social, or economic problems which produce the conditions for disasters, thereby making their recurrence that much more likely. On the other hand, longer-term substantive commitments to global norms often seem to be difficult to coordinate in the absence of international consensus. At any rate, one conclusion which can be drawn from the contributions represented in this volume, is that while it is of course important to debate the immediate issues, it is also imperative to incorporate consideration of the larger patterns of global forces and their implications for long-term decision making.

Another set of questions is related to this and involves the contrast between "means" and "ends" in pursuing human security. The question of humanitarian intervention brings these dilemmas sharply into view. While working closely with allies and the United Nations may provide an important platform from which smaller powers, such as Canada, can contribute to a "new internationalism based on multilateralism and the international rule of law,"[2] former foreign affairs minister Lloyd Axworthy was forced to admit that an "enforcement dimension" to human security is necessary.[3] The new security agenda is clearly more at home with banning destructive and cruel landmines and small arms, creating an international criminal court, or ending the use of child soldiers than it is with peace enforcement.[4] In this regard, several important tensions are illuminated in this volume. An important question involves the ethics of unilateral versus multilateral action. While Stoett suggests that unilateral action, traditionally thought to be ethically questionable, can reinforce important global principles, Keating's study of the Haiti case and Adelman's study of Zaire suggest that even the more "legitimate" forms of intervention that take place under the banner of multilateralism can be fraught with ethical dilemmas.

Another issue that engaged contributors in this regard was the concept of "soft power" and its place in achieving foreign policy goals. Noting, as

Knight argues, that a strict dichotomy between "hard" and "soft" power can be problematic, several contributors drew upon the more nuanced concept of norms and normative constructs found in the international relations literature.[5] An important question here was the role of Canadian foreign policy in normative change. Knight's optimistic view of Canada as a "norm entrepreneur" is balanced against Black's more cautious approach which is echoed by Latham, who argues that global normative change poses important limitations on, and challenges to, Canadian foreign policy.

All of the contributors, in striving to address these diverse questions surrounding ethics and security in Canadian foreign policy, share a commitment to linking abstract theoretical questions with practical policy concerns. In the process, they challenge the reader to consider the fundamental purposes of the study of international relations and foreign policy, emphasizing that questions of purpose serve to frame ethical questions and dilemmas in particular ways, shaping the kinds of issues and problems that become the focus of attention. In the future, as Canada's involvement in world affairs continues to deepen, Canadians will expect and demand that Canadian foreign policy meet *both* ethical standards *and* the challenges of new security issues. Clearly, as global interdependence deepens and uncertainty increases, the necessity to think critically and clearly about the linkages between ethics and security in Canadian foreign policy will persist well into the future.

Notes

1 For more on the role of the news media in foreign policy, see Brian Buckley, *The News Media and Foreign Policy: An Exploration* (Halifax: Centre for Foreign Policy Studies, 1998); Frank P. Harvey and Ann L. Griffiths, eds., *Foreign and Security Policy in the Information Age* (Halifax: Centre for Foreign Policy Studies, 1999).

2 *Foreign Policy Themes and Priorities: 1991-92, Update* (Ottawa: Policy Planning Staff, External Affairs and International Trade Canada, December 1991).

3 For more, see Lloyd Axworthy, "Canada's UN Agenda to Strengthen Human Security" *Canadian Speeches* 12, 9 (January-February 1999): 15-22.

4 Quoted in Bruce Wallace, "Bombs and Rhetoric" *Maclean's,* 7 June 1999, 40.

5 For more, see, Audie Klotz, *Norms in International Relations: The Struggle against Apartheid* (Ithaca, NY: Cornell University Press, 1995); or Ethan A. Nadelmann, "Global Prohibition Regimes: The Evolution of Norms in International Society" *International Organization* 44 (Autumn 1990): 479-526.

Questions for Discussion

Introduction: Linking Ethics and Security in Canadian Foreign Policy

Has security been redefined in the post-Cold War era? In what ways?

What is meant by "ethics"?

How are "security" and "ethics" linked? How should they be linked?

What have been the changes (or lack thereof) in the ethics/security nexus given the transition from a Cold War to a post-Cold War era?

What is the importance or relevance of the "new" concept of "human security" given this historical transition?

Does the concept of human security represent a departure from traditional security concerns?

Is neo-realism still relevant in the study of foreign and security policy?

Have globalization and interdependence provided more or less scope for "ethical" decision making?

To what ethical codes do decision makers refer when making foreign policy decisions?

From what level of analysis should ethics be approached in the study of foreign policy?

Is human security a realistic goal in the twenty-first century?

What role might Canadians play in achieving human security globally?

Part 2: Ethics and Security: Conceptual and Analytical Issues within a Changing Global Context

How might a global situation of mutual vulnerability affect Canada in the next few years?

With which security issues should Canadians be most concerned?

Which threats represent the greatest challenges for human security in the twenty-first century?

What mechanisms of governance are most appropriate within the context of mutual vulnerability?

How might Canadian foreign policy be reformed to better meet the challenges of global criminality?

How might Canadian foreign policy be reformed to better address global conflicts?

Is there a tension between neoliberal economic programs and democratic governance? How might this be addressed?

What are cosmopolitan ethics? How do these differ from state-based ethics?

How might governance institutions be reformed to better address global problems and to promote human rights?

What are the major similarities and differences among the various traditions of ethics?

Does the concept of human security eliminate the tension between ethical and national security concerns?

Part 3: Ethics and Canadian Policies towards Human Rights and Development Assistance

What kinds of ethics are appropriate to governing development assistance?

Do Canadians have obligations to protect human rights beyond their borders?

Is the concept of the national interest compatible with an ethical approach to foreign policy decision making?

What should be the purpose of development assistance policies?

Are Canadian development assistance policies guided by a "moral vision"?

Have cosmopolitan ethics had a significant impact on Canadian foreign policy?

How might CIDA reform its aid programs to better meet the needs of the poorest?

Which is more important in Canadian human rights policies: ethics or economics?

Have Canadian policies towards China and East Timor undermined or enhanced human security in those countries?

What is "niche diplomacy"? How does it differ from a human security approach to foreign policy?

How might Canadian foreign policy be reformed to better support a "right to sustenance"?

In what ways does a gendered class analysis contribute to an understanding of global relations of power?

What lessons can be drawn from the experiences of women farmers in Kenya regarding the post-Cold War world order?

What lessons can be drawn for Canadian foreign policy as a result of the efforts of women farmers in Kenya?

How specifically do gender relations shape the context of foreign policy decision making?

How might a gendered class analysis illuminate aspects of the study of foreign policy neglected by other approaches?

What is the relationship between food security and peace?

In what ways are structural adjustment programs predicated on gender and class hierarchies?

What features makes international development assistance policy particularly important in Canadian foreign policy?

Part 4: International Humanitarian Law and Norms

What is "soft power"?

Is the distinction between "soft power" and "hard power" a useful one?

What is the relationship between international "norms" and "law"?

How might international legal norms best be made enforceable?

In what ways does the establishment of an international criminal court represent a strengthening of the rule of law internationally?

Are war crimes, genocide, and crimes against humanity currently dealt with adequately under international law?

What features make issues of war crimes, genocide, and crimes against humanity particularly important aspects of Canadian foreign policy?

Has Canada been successful in the role of a "norm entrepreneur"?

What lessons can be drawn from the history of Canadian efforts to condemn human rights violations in Nigeria?

Was Canadian human rights policy towards Nigeria successful?

Why was Canadian human rights policy towards Nigeria in the 1990s seemingly less successful than were similar past policies towards South Africa?

Why have anti-personnel landmines become a focus of foreign policy in the post-Cold War world order?

What is meant by a "standard of civilization"?

What is a "global cultural script"?

Have the "laws of war" succeeded in making warfare more "ethical"?

Have the laws of war managed to reduce suffering in warfare? If not, why not?

Are ethics in Canadian foreign policy primarily derived from domestic or global levels?

Part 5: Humanitarian Intervention and Democratization

Does humanitarian intervention contribute to a more secure world?

Are "good governance" policies interventionist?

How best might decision makers balance the "ethics of commitment" with the "ethics of responsibility"?

What features make humanitarian intervention a particularly important issue in Canadian foreign policy?

Why are issues of humanitarian intervention particularly important in the post-Cold War world order?

Have Canadian foreign policy efforts in Haiti been successful?

What lessons can be drawn from Canadian operations in Haiti?

Should democracy be a norm enshrined within such governance institutions as the OAS?

Is multilateral intervention more ethical than unilateral intervention?

Should democratization be externally enforced?

What are the limitations of enforcing democratization?

Can ethical and material interests ever be separated in democratization policy?

How might conflicting norms best be reconciled among parties to humanitarian interventions?

What norms are most appropriate to governing humanitarian intervention?

What were the lessons learned by decision makers in the case of Zaire?

What lessons can be drawn from the case of Zaire for Canadian foreign policy?

Is the use of force appropriate in a humanitarian emergency?

How important is the "CNN effect" in foreign policy decision making?

Can a "no- or low-risk" approach to peacekeeping operations be defended on ethical grounds?

Part 6: The Ethics of Energy and Natural Resource Security: Fishing and Nuclear Policy

Which is more important in Canadian nuclear export policy: ethics or economics?

What political considerations have played an important role in decisions surrounding CANDU exports?

What security considerations have played an important role in decisions surrounding CANDU exports?

What features make nuclear export policy particularly important in Canadian foreign policy?

How effective are nuclear safeguards agreements in regulating nuclear power exports abroad?

Has there been a change in Canada's nuclear export policy since 1956? Since 1974? Why or why not?

Should nuclear technologies be exported to countries involved in regional conflicts?

Should nuclear technologies be exported to countries with poor human rights records?

Should nuclear technologies be exported to countries with poor environmental records?

Do governments have an obligation to preserve long-term environmental security?

Under what conditions is it appropriate for governments to go beyond the norms established in international law?

What explains the Canadian government's aggressive stance in fishing disputes, particularly with the United States?

Was Canada's violation of the principle of freedom of the high seas justified in the case of the turbot dispute?

What is "customary international law"?

Was Canadian policy in the turbot dispute primarily motivated by national interest or by conservation concerns?

What is the precautionary principle?

Did Canadian foreign policy during the Turbot dispute support the global environmental principles of equality and the precautionary principle?

Does environmental security conflict with national security?

How might Canadian foreign policy on the environment be reformed to better reflect the need for long-term thinking?

Part 7: Towards Human Security?

What features of an increasingly turbulent world order provoke consideration of innovative thinking on ethics and security issues?

Should "ethics" be approached narrowly or broadly within Canadian foreign policy and security policy?

How and within what domains or levels should ethical issues be determined in foreign policy?

Who are/should be the "subjects" of security?

What kinds of "values" do Canadians represent and how effectively are these ethical values represented in Canadian foreign policy?

Does Canadian foreign policy represent a more ethical humane internationalism than that espoused by realpolitik?

Have orthodox economic security concerns become equivalent to Cold War national security concerns?

Should Canadian foreign policy be selective or expansive in scope?

Suggested Readings

Introduction: Linking Ethics and Security in Canadian Foreign Policy

Booth, Ken. "Security and Emancipation." *Review of International Studies* 17, 4 (1991): 313-26.

Heinbecker, Paul. "Human Security." *Behind the Headlines* 56, 2 (December 1998-March 1999): 4-9.

Krause, Keith, and Michael Williams, eds., *Critical Security Studies: Concepts and Cases.* Minneapolis: University of Minnesota Press, 1997.

Mathews, Jessica Tuchman. "Redefining Security." *Foreign Affairs* 68, 2 (Spring 1989): 162-77.

Owens, Heather, and Barbara Arneil. "The Human Security Paradigm Shift: A New Lens on Canadian Foreign Policy?" Report of the University of British Columbia Symposium on Human Security, *Canadian Foreign Policy* 7, 1 (Fall 1999): 1-12.

Rosenau, J. *Turbulence in World Politics: A Theory of Change and Continuity.* Princeton: Princeton University Press, 1990.

United Nations Development Program. *Human Development Report, 1994.* Oxford University Press, 1994.

Part 2: Conceptual and Analytical Issues within a Changing Global Context

Beitz, Charles R., Marshall Cohen, Thomas A. Scanlon, and John A. Simmons, eds. *International Ethics.* Princeton: Princeton University Press, 1985.

Bull, Hedley. *The Anarchical Society: A Study of Order in World Politics.* New York: Columbia University Press, 1977.

Chomsky, Noam, and Edward Herman. *The Political Economy of Human Rights.* Montreal: Black Rose, 1979.

Cox, Robert W., with Timothy J. Sinclair. *Approaches to World Order.* Cambridge: Cambridge University Press, 1996.

Fukuyama, Francis, *The End of History and the Last Man.* New York: Avon, 1992.

Head, Ivan. *On a Hinge of History: The Mutual Vulnerability of South and North.* Toronto: University of Toronto Press, 1991.

Huntington, Samuel. "The Clash of Civilizations?" *Foreign Affairs* 72, 3 (1993): 22-49.

Nef, Jorge. *Human Security and Mutual Vulnerability: An Exploration into the Global Political Economy of Development and Underdevelopment.* Ottawa: International Development Research Centre, 1999.

Schmid, J., and P. Crelisten. *Western Responses to Terrorism.* London: Frank Cass, 1993.

Singer, Peter. *Practical Ethics.* Cambridge, UK: Cambridge University Press, 1979/93.

Smith, David M. *Geography and Social Justice.* Oxford, UK: Blackwell, 1994.

Sterba, James P. ed. *Justice: Alternative Political Perspectives.* Belmont, CA: Wadsworth Publishing, 1980/92.

Wellington, A., A. Greenbaum, and W. Cragg, eds. *Canadian Issues in Environmental Ethics.* Peterborough: Broadview Press, 1997.

Part 3: Ethics and Canadian Policies towards Human Rights and Development Assistance

Booth, Ken. "Human Wrongs and International Relations." *International Affairs* 71, 1 (1995): 103-26.

Cohen, Andrew. "Canada in the World: The Return of the National Interest." *Behind the Headlines* 52, 4 (1995).

Cooper, Andrew F. "In Search of Niches: Saying 'Yes' and Saying 'No' in Canada's International Relations." *Canadian Foreign Policy* 3, 3 (1995): 1-13.

Hoffmann, Stanley. *Duties beyond Borders: On the Limits and Possibilities of Ethical International Politics*. Syracuse: Syracuse University Press, 1981.

Lumsdaine, David Halloran. *Moral Vision in International Politics: The Foreign Aid Regime.* Princeton: Princeton University Press, 1993.

Mahoney, Kathleen E. "Human Rights and Canada's Foreign Policy." *International Journal* 47, 3 (Summer 1992): 555-94.

Matthews, Robert O., and Cranford Pratt, eds. *Human Rights in Canadian Foreign Policy.* Montreal and Kingston: McGill-Queen's University Press, 1988.

Morrison, David. *Aid and Ebb Tide: A History of CIDA and Canadian Development Assistance.* Waterloo: Wilfred Laurier University Press, 1998.

Neufeld, Mark. "Hegemony and Foreign Policy Analysis: The Case of Canada as a Middle Power." *Studies in Political Economy* 48 (1995): 7-29.

Noel, Alain, and Jean Philippe Therien. "Welfare Institutions and Foreign Aid: Domestic Foundations of Canadian Foreign Policy." *Canadian Journal of Political Science* 27 (September 1994): 529-58.

Nossal, Kim Richard. "Pinchpenny Diplomacy: The Decline of 'Good International Citizenship' in Canadian Foreign Policy." *International Journal* 54, 1 (Winter 1998-99): 88-105.

Potter, Evan H. "Niche Diplomacy as Canadian Foreign Policy." *International Journal* 52, 1 (Winter 1996-97): 25-38.

Pratt, Cranford. "Dominant Class Theory and Canadian Foreign Policy: The Case of Counter-Consensus." *International Journal* 39, 1 (Winter 1983-84): 122-26.

Pratt, Cranford, ed. *Internationalism Under Strain: The North-South Policies of Canada, the Netherlands, Norway and Sweden*. Toronto: University of Toronto Press, 1989.

–. *Canadian International Development Assistance Policies: An Appraisal.* Montreal and Kingston: McGill-Queen's University Press, 1994/96.

Riddell, Roger C. *Foreign Aid Reconsidered.* Baltimore/London: Johns Hopkins University Press/James Currey, 1987.

Rudner, Martin. "Canada in the World: Development Assistance in Canada's New Foreign Policy Framework." *Canadian Journal of Development Studies* 172 (1996): 193-220.

Smith, Heather A. "Caution Warranted: Niche Diplomacy Assessed." *Canadian Foreign Policy* 6, 3 (Spring 1999): 57-72.

Stairs, Denis. "Canada and the Security Problem: Implications as the Millennium Turns." *International Journal* 54, 3 (Summer 1999): 386-403.

Part 4: International Humanitarian Law and Norms

Bassiouni, Cherif M. "An Appraisal of the Growth and Developing Trends in International Criminal Law." *Revue Internationale de Droit Penal* 45 (1974): 420-33.

Benedetti, Fanny, and John Washburn. "Drafting the International Criminal Court Treaty: Two Years to Rome and an Afterword on the Rome Diplomatic Conference." *Global Governance* 5 (1999): 1-37.

Cameron, Maxwell A., Robert J. Lawson, and Brian W. Tomlin, eds. *To Walk without Fear: The Global Movement to Ban Landmines*. Toronto: Oxford University Press, 1998.

Clapham, Christopher. *Africa and the International System.* Cambridge: Cambridge University Press, 1996.

Cooper, Andrew F., and Geoffrey Hayes, eds. *Canada and Mission-Oriented Diplomacy.* Toronto: Irwin, 2000.

Croll, Mike. *The History of Landmines*. London: Leo Cooper, 1998.

Dunne, Tim, and Nicholas J. Wheeler. *Human Rights in Global Politics*. Cambridge: Cambridge University Press, 1999.
Freeman, Linda. *The Ambiguous Champion: Canada and South Africa in the Trudeau and Mulroney Years*. Toronto: University of Toronto Press, 1997.
Gillies, David. *Between Principle and Practice: Human Rights in North-South Relations*. Montreal: McGill-Queen's University Press, 1996.
Gordon, N., and B. Wood. "Canada and the Reshaping of the United Nations." *International Journal* 47 (1992): 479-503.
Hampson, Fen Osler, and Dean F. Oliver. "Pulpit Diplomacy: A Critical Assessment of the Axworthy Doctrine." *International Journal* 53, 3 (1998): 379-406.
International Committee of the Red Cross. "Anti-Personnel Landmines: Friend or Foe? A Study of the Military Use and Effectiveness of Anti-Personnel Mines." Available at <www.icrc.org/icrcnews/48da.htm> (28 March 1996).
Jochnick, Chris, and Roger Normand. "The Legitimation of Violence: A Critical Analysis of the Gulf War." *Harvard International Law Review* 35, 1 (Spring 1994): 387-416.
Klotz, Audie. *Norms in International Relations: The Struggle against Apartheid*. Ithaca, NY: Cornell University Press, 1995.
Mayall, James. "Democratizing the Commonwealth." *International Affairs* 74, 2 (1998): 379-92.
Mustapha, Abdul Raufu. "The Nigerian Transition: Third Time Lucky or More of the Same?" *Review of African Political Economy* 26, 80 (June 1999): 277-93.
Price, Richard. "Reversing the Gunsights: Transnational Civil Society Targets Landmines." *International Organization* 52, 3 (Summer 1998): 613-44.
Risse, Thomas, Stephen C. Ropp, and Kathryn Sikkink, eds. *The Power of Human Rights: International Norms and Domestic Change*. Cambridge: Cambridge University Press, 1999.
Rosenbaum, Alan S. *Prosecuting War Criminals*. Colorado: Westview Press, 1993.
Stanton, John. "Canada and War Crimes: Judgement at Tokyo." *International Journal* 55, 3 (Summer 2000): 376-400.
Thakur, Ramesh, and William Malley. "The Ottawa Convention on Landmines: A Landmark Humanitarian Treaty in Arms Control?" *Global Governance: A Review of Multilateralism and International Organizations* 5, 3 (July-September 1999): 273-302.

Part 5: Humanitarian Intervention and Democratization

Adelman, Howard, Lois Foster, Allan Borowski, and Meyer Burstein, eds. *Immigration and Refugee Policy: Australia and Canada Compared*. Melbourne: University of Melbourne Press, 1994.
Bramwell, Anna, ed. *Refugees in the Age of Total War*. London: Unwin Hyman, 1986.
Cameron, Maxwell, and Maureen Appel Molot, eds. *Canada Among Nations 1995: Democracy and Foreign Policy*. Ottawa: Carleton University Press, 1995.
Farer, Tom. *Collectively Defending Democracy in a World of Sovereign States: The Western Hemisphere's Prospect*. Montreal: International Centre for Human Rights and Democratic Development, 1993.
Falk, Richard. "The Haiti Intervention: A Dangerous World Order Precedent for the United Nations." *Harvard International Law Journal* 36, 2 (1995): 341-58.
Forsythe, D., and K. Pease. "Human Rights, Humanitarian Intervention and World Politics." *Human Rights Quarterly* 15, 2 (1993): 290-314.
Havel, Václav. "The Power of the Powerless." *Open Letters: Selected Writings, 1965-1990*. NY: Vintage Books, 1992.
Henkin, Louis et al. *Right v. Might: International Law and the Use of Force*. New York: Council on Foreign Relations, 1991.
Hoffman, Stanley, ed. *The Ethics and Politics of Humanitarian Intervention*. Notre Dame: University of Notre Dame Press, 1996.
Mandelbaum, Michael. "The Reluctance to Intervene." *Foreign Affairs* 95 (Summer 1994): 3-18.
McKenna, Peter. "Canada and the Haitian Crisis." *Journal of Canadian Studies* 32 (1997): 77-98.

Nardin, Terry, and David R. Mapel. *Traditions of International Ethics*. Cambridge: Cambridge University Press, 1992.
Roberts, Adam. "Humanitarian War: Military Intervention and Human Rights." *International Affairs* 69 (July 1993): 429-49.
Shacochis, Bob. *The Immaculate Invasion*. New York: Viking, 1999.
Weiss, Thomas G., and Cindy Collins. *Humanitarian Challenges and Intervention: World Politics and the Dilemmas of Help*. Boulder, CO: Westview Press, 1996.

Part 6: The Ethics of Energy and Natural Resource Security

Bothwell, Robert. *Nucleus: The History of Atomic Energy of Canada Limited*. University of Toronto Press: Toronto 1988.
Doern, Bruce, and Robert W. Morrison, eds. *Canadian Nuclear Policies*. Montreal: The Institute for Research on Public Policy, 1980.
Ernst and Young. *The Economic Effects of the Canadian Nuclear Industry*. Toronto: Ernst and Young, 1993.
Finch, Ron. *Exporting Danger: A History of the Canadian Nuclear Energy Export Programme*. Montreal: Black Rose Books, 1985.
Glassner, Martin. *Neptune's Domain: A Political Geography of the Sea*. Boston: Unwin Hyman, 1990.
Hurst, D.G. et al. *Canada Enters the Nuclear Age: A Technical History of Atomic Energy of Canada Limited as Seen from Its Research Laboratories*. Published for Atomic Energy Canada Ltd. Montreal and Kingston: McGill-Queen's University Press, 1997.
Kokoski, Richard. *Technology and the Proliferation of Nuclear Weapons*. Stockholm: SIPRI, 1995.
Martin, David, and David Argue. *Nuclear Sunset: The Economic Costs of the Canadian Nuclear Industry*. Ottawa: Campaign for Nuclear Phaseout, 1996.
Martin, David H. *Exporting Disaster: The Cost of Selling CANDU Reactors*. Ottawa: Campaign for Nuclear Phaseout, 1996.
McDorman, Ted. "Canada's Aggressive Fisheries Actions: Will They Improve the Climate for International Agreements?" *Canadian Foreign Policy* 2, 3 (Winter 1994-95): 5-28.
Morrison, Robert W. and Wonder, Edward F., *Canada's Nuclear Export Policy*. Ottawa: The Norman Paterson School of International Affairs, 1978.
Myers, Lynne C. *Nuclear Power Systems: Their Safety*. Ottawa: Library of Parliament, 1991.
Nadelmann, Ethan A. "Global Prohibition Regimes: The Evolution of Norms in International Society." *International Organization* 44 (Autumn 1990): 479-526.
Rayner, Steve. "Governance and the Global Commons." In *Global Governance: Ethics and Economics of the World Order*, ed. M. Desai and P. Redfean. London: Pinter, 1995.
Sanger, Clyde. *Ordering the Oceans: The Making of the Law of the Sea*. Toronto: University of Toronto Press, 1987.
Stoett, Peter J. "Human Rights, Environmental Security and Foreign Policy." *Policy Options* 15, 5 (June 1994): 9-12.
Wapner, Paul. "Environmental Ethics and Global Governance: Engaging the International Liberal Tradition." *Global Governance* 3 (1997): 213-31.
Weiss, Edith Brown. *Environmental Change and International Law*. Tokyo: United Nations University Press, 1993.

Further Reading on Canadian Foreign Policy

Cooper, Andrew F. *Canadian Foreign Policy: Old Habits and New Directions*. Scarborough: Prentice Hall Allyn and Bacon Canada, 1997.
Cooper, Andrew F., and Geoffrey Hayes, eds. *Worthwhile Initiatives? Canadian Mission-Oriented Diplomacy*. Toronto: Irwin, 2000.
Cooper, Andrew Fenton, Richard A. Higgott, and Kim Richard Nossal. *Relocating Middle Powers: Australia and Canada in a Changing World Order*. Vancouver: UBC Press, 1993.
Dewitt, David B. and David Leyton-Brown, eds. *Canada's International Security Policy*. Scarborough: Prentice-Hall Canada, 1995.
Keating, Tom, *Canada and World Order: The Multilateralist Tradition in Canadian Foreign Policy*. 2nd ed. Toronto: Oxford University Press, 2001.

Madar, Daniel, *Canadian International Relations*. Scarborough: Prentice Hall Allyn and Bacon Canada, 2000.

Molot, Maureen Appel, and Fen Osler Hampson, eds. *Canada among Nations 2000: Vanishing Borders*. Toronto: Oxford University Press, 2000.

Nossal, Kim Richard. *The Politics of Canadian Foreign Policy*. Scarborough: Prentice-Hall Canada, 1997.

Tucker, Michael J., Raymond B. Blake, and P.E. Bryden, eds. *Canada and the New World Order*. Toronto: Irwin, 2000.

Contributors

Howard Adelman is professor of philosophy at York University. He has written extensively on the Middle East, humanitarian intervention, membership rights, ethics, refugee policy, and refugee resettlement. His two most recent co-edited books are: *Immigration and Refugee Policy: Australia and Canada Compared* (University of Melbourne Press and University of Toronto Press, 1994); and *African Refugees* (Westview Press, 1994). He recently published, with Astri Suhrke, a major study entitled: *Early Warning and Conflict Management: the Genocide in Rwanda,* study 2 of *International Response to Conflict and Genocide: Lessons from the Rwanda Experience* (Steering Committee of the Joint Evaluation of Emergency Assistance to Rwanda, 1996).

David Black is associate professor of political science and chair of international development studies at Dalhousie University. He is the co-author (with John Nauright) of *Rugby and the South African Nation: Sport, Cultures, Politics and Power in the Old and New South Africas* (Manchester University Press, 1998) and co-editor (with Larry Swatuk) of *Bridging the Rift: The New South Africa in Africa* (Boulder, CO: Westview Press, 1997). His current research interests and most recent publications focus on human rights in Canadian and South African foreign policies; and Canada in North-South relations.

Duane Bratt teaches political science in the Department of Policy Studies at Mount Royal College and the University of Calgary. He has written several pieces on Canada's nuclear policy, and these have been published in both Canada and abroad. He is finishing a book on this topic entitled *The Politics of CANDU Exports.* Current research interests include the international security/development dimensions of AIDS.

Rosalind Irwin teaches political science at York University and is a research associate at York's Centre for International and Security Studies. She is a graduate of York University, Simon Fraser University, and Okanagan University College. Her most recent publication is "Posing Global Environmental Problems from Conservation to Sustainable Development," in *The International Political Economy of the Environment: Critical Perspectives,* ed. Dimitris Stevis and Valerie

J. Assetto (Boulder, CO: Lynne Rienner, 2001). Her current interests include: global and Canadian environmental policy, multilateralism, peace studies, and ethics in Canadian foreign policy.

Tom Keating is a professor in the Political Science Department at the University of Alberta. He has published in the areas of international relations theory, Canadian foreign policy, Canadian defence policy, and humanitarian intervention. Among his published works are *Canada, NATO, and the Bomb* (Hurtig, 1988); and (co-authored with Larry Pratt) *Canada and World Order* (Rev. ed. Oxford University Press, 2001). He is currently conducting research on Canada's foreign policy efforts to promote democracy abroad.

W. Andy Knight is professor of international relations in the Political Science Department at the University of Alberta. He is the author of *A Changing United Nations: Multilateral Evolution and the Quest for Global Governance* (MacMillan/Palgrave, 2000) and editor of *Adapting the United Nations to a Post-Modern Era: Lessons Learned* (MacMillan/Palgrave, 2001). Professor Knight serves as co-editor of the journal *Global Governance: A Review of Multilateralism and International Organizations* and is former vice-chair of the Academic Council on the United Nations System (ACUNS).

Andrew Latham is assistant professor of political science at Macalester College in St. Paul, Minnesota. He was previously non-proliferation, arms control and disarmament research associate with the Canadian Department of Foreign Affairs and International Trade at the York Centre for International and Security Studies. He was also a member of the Canadian delegation to the group of governmental experts that was to prepare the review conference of the Convention on Conventional Weapons, Geneva, Switzerland, May 1994 and January 1995. Dr. Latham is currently working on a book entitled *Global Cultural Change and the Transnational Campaign to Ban Landmines.*

Jorge Nef is professor of rural extension studies at the University of Guelph and director of the School of Government, Public Administration and Political Science, at the University of Chile. His numerous publications deal with development, food security, terrorism, ethics and technology, comparative public administration and public policy, authoritarian regimes, social theory, international relations, and Latin American politics. His most recent research has focused on issues of corruption, administrative reform, neoliberalism, governability, conflict resolution, and human security within the context of global and inter-American relations. His most recent publication is *Human Security and Mutual Vulnerability* (IDRC, 1999).

Peter Penz is director of the Centre for Refugee Studies at York University, Toronto, and associate professor in environmental studies. His recent writings have been on forced migration and asylum, humanitarian military intervention, development ethics, development-induced displacement, global justice and the environment, the colonization of tribal lands in Asia. He has recently co-edited *Global Justice, Global Democracy* (Fernwood Press, 1997); and *Political Ecology: Global and Local* (Routledge, 1998).

Cranford Pratt is emeritus professor in the Department of Political Science at the University of Toronto. Professor Pratt's most recent publications include "Competing Rationales for Canadian Development Assistance: Reducing Global Poverty, Enhancing Canadian Prosperity and Security or Advancing Global Human Security," *International Journal* 54, 2 (1999). He is also the author of *Canadian International Development Assistance Policies: An Appraisal* (McGill-Queen's University Press, 1996).

Heather Smith is assistant professor in the International Studies Programme, University of Northern British Columbia. She received her PhD in political studies from Queen's University. Her doctoral dissertation is entitled "Canadian and British Climate Change Policies and the Impact of the Climate Change Epistemic Community." She has published on Canadian foreign policy theory and the 1994 foreign policy review, and she has pieces forthcoming on the subject of Canadian climate change policy. Current research areas include: Canadian climate change policy, feminist deconstructions of the guiding philosophies of Canadian foreign policy, and critiques of niche diplomacy.

Peter Stoett is assistant professor in the Department of Political Studies at Concordia University. His research interests include the politics of global environmental problems and human rights issues. His books include *The International Politics of Whaling* (UBC Press, 1997); *Human and Global Security: An Exploration of Terms* (University of Toronto Press, 2000); and, with Eric Laferrière, *International Relations Theory and Ecological Thought: Toward a Synthesis* (Routledge, 1999).

Terisa E. Turner teaches political science, sociology, and anthropology at the University of Guelph. She has lived and worked in Africa and the Caribbean for many years, where she has worked on energy issues and on social movements. Between 1971 and 1991 she co-directed the International Oil Working Group's program to stop shipments of oil to apartheid South Africa. Currently she is researching the involvement of women in the Mau Mau war of independence in 1950s Kenya. She continues to be involved in the international solidarity movement in support of the struggle for democracy in Nigeria. Her co-author, Leigh S. Brownhill, is pursuing her PhD. Wahu M. Kaara is a Kenyan historian, teacher, and organizer.

Index